The Gallup Poll

Public Opinion 2001

Other Gallup Poll Publications Available from Scholarly Resources

The Gallup Poll Cumulative Index: Public Opinion, 1935–1997
(1999). ISBN 0-8420-2587-1

The Gallup Poll: Public Opinion Annual Series

2000 (ISBN-0-8420-5000-0)	*1987* (ISBN-0-8420-2292-9)
1999 (ISBN 0-8420-2699-1)	*1986* (ISBN-0-8420-2274-0)
1998 (ISBN 0-8420-2698-3)	*1985* (ISBN-0-8420-2249-X)
1997 (ISBN-0-8420-2597-9)	*1984* (ISBN-0-8420-2234-1)
1996 (ISBN-0-8420-2596-0)	*1983* (ISBN-0-8420-2220-1)
1995 (ISBN-0-8420-2595-2)	*1982* (ISBN-0-8420-2214-7)
1994 (ISBN-0-8420-2560-X)	*1981* (ISBN-0-8420-2200-7)
1993 (ISBN-0-8420-2483-2)	*1980* (ISBN-0-8420-2181-7)
1992 (ISBN-0-8420-2463-8)	*1979* (ISBN-0-8420-2170-1)
1991 (ISBN-0-8420-2397-6)	*1978* (ISBN-0-8420-2159-0)
1990 (ISBN-0-8420-2368-2)	*1972–77* (ISBN-0-8420-2129-9, 2 vols.)
1989 (ISBN-0-8420-2344-5)	*1935–71* (ISBN-0-394-47270-5, 3 vols.)
1988 (ISBN-0-8420-2330-5)	

International Polls

The International Gallup Polls: Public Opinion, 1979
ISBN-0-8420-2180-9 (1981)

The International Gallup Polls: Public Opinion, 1978
ISBN-0-8420-2162-0 (1980)

The Gallup International Public Opinion Polls:
France, 1939, 1944–1975
2 volumes ISBN-0-394-40998-1 (1976)

The Gallup International Public Opinion Polls:
Great Britain, 1937–1975
2 volumes ISBN 0-394-40992-2 (1976)

The Gallup Poll

Public Opinion 2001

George Gallup, Jr.

SR Scholarly Resources Inc.
Wilmington, Delaware

ACKNOWLEDGMENTS

The Gallup Poll is the result of the efforts of a number of talented and dedicated individuals. At The Gallup Organization, I wish to express my gratitude to James Clifton, chairman and CEO; George Gallup, Jr.; and The Gallup Poll staff, including Frank Newport, editor-in-chief; David Moore and Lydia Saad, senior editors; Jeffrey M. Jones, managing editor; Joseph Carroll, operations manager; Darren Carlson, content manager for Gallup.com; Maura Strausberg, data librarian; Mark Gillespie, senior broadcast producer; Beverly Passerella, special assistant to Alec Gallup; and Dianna Gibbs, proofreader and fact checker. Special recognition goes to Judith Keneman, assistant to the editor-in-chief, who was in charge of assembling and editing the manuscript; and to R. J. Belford, who assisted in its review. Professor Fred L. Israel, City University of New York, also deserves special credit for his pioneering efforts in working on the first 26 volumes of this series. At Scholarly Resources, I would like to thank Daniel C. Helmstadter, president and publisher; James L. Preston, production manager; Carolyn J. Travers, managing editor; and Ann M. Aydelotte for their assistance. At Type Shoppe II Productions Ltd., my appreciation goes to Lydia A. Wagner and Penelope Hollingsworth for their editing, proofreading, typesetting, and design expertise. Finally, I wish to thank Elizabeth McCarthy for preparing the index.

Alec M. Gallup

⊗ The paper used in this publication meets the minimum requirements of the American National Standard for permanence of paper for printed library materials, Z39.48, 1984.

Scholarly Resources Inc.
104 Greenhill Avenue
Wilmington, DE 19805-1897
www.scholarly.com

Library of Congress Catalog Card Number: 79-56557
International Standard Serial Number: 0195-962X
International Standard Book Number: 0-8420-5001-9

CONTENTS

INTRODUCTION

The Gallup Poll: Public Opinion 2000 contains the findings of the more than 300 daily Gallup Poll reports released to the American public by CNN, *USA Today*, and the Chicago Tribune Newspaper Syndicate during the year 2000. The latest volume reveals the attitudes and opinions of individuals and key groups within the American population concerning national and international issues and events of the year. Included is a detailed presentation and analysis of the daily vote-for-president tracking data in the 2000 presidential election contest, one of the closest in the nation's history

The 2000 volume is the most recent addition to the 26-volume Gallup collection, *Public Opinion, 1935–2000*, the largest compilation of public opinion findings ever published and one of the largest reference works produced on any subject. The Gallup collection documents the attitudes and opinions of Americans (and where appropriate, citizens of other countries) on national and international issues and events from Franklin D. Roosevelt's second term to the present.

Shown in detail are results of the more than 60,000 questions that the Gallup Poll—the world's oldest and most respected public opinion poll—has asked of the public over the last seven decades. Results of the survey questions appear in the nearly 10,000 Gallup Poll reports, reproduced in the 26 volumes. These reports, the first of which was released on October 20, 1935, have been provided to client media on a continuous, two-to-five times per week basis since that time. The contents of the collection are referenced in detail in the *Gallup Poll Cumulative Index* published by Scholarly Resources in 1999.

The 26-volume collection documents public opinion from 1935 to the present in the following five separate and distinct areas:

1. *Recording the Public's Response to Major News Events*. Gallup has recorded the public's attitudes and opinions in response to every major news event of the last seven decades. Examples include Adolf Hitler's invasion of the Soviet Union, the bombing of Pearl Harbor, the dropping of the atomic bomb on Hiroshima, the assassination of President John F. Kennedy, the moon landing, the taking of U.S. hostages in Iran, the World Trade Center bombing, the O. J. Simpson trial verdict, and the Elían González custody dispute.

2. *Measuring the Strength of Support for the President, Political Candidates, and Political Parties*. For over sixty years, Gallup has measured, on a continuous basis, the strength of support for the president, for the congressional opposition, and for various political

candidates and parties in national elections. This is the role most closely associated with Gallup in the public's mind.

3. *Tracking the Public's Attitudes Concerning Enduring Societal Issues.* Since 1935, Gallup has tracked the public's attitudes and opinions concerning a wide range of enduring societal issues, including such narrowly defined issues as abortion and capital punishment as well as broader, multifaceted ones such as crime, the environment, and education. Most of Gallup's long-term subjective social indicators, which are designed to measure social, political, and economic attitudinal trends, are found in this category.

4. *Revealing American Lifestyle Trends.* Another ongoing Gallup polling activity has been to document American lifestyles, including periodic measurements of participation in a wide range of leisure activities and other pursuits. Additional examples include frequent series describing the public's tastes and favorites in various areas, and their knowledge level as revealed by national "quizzes" in geography, history, science, politics, and the like.

5. *Gauging and Charting the Public's Mood.* From its earliest days the Gallup Poll has sought to determine, on an ongoing basis, Americans' satisfaction or dissatisfaction with the direction in which the nation appeared to be headed and with the way they thought that their personal lives were progressing. This process also has involved regular assessments of the people's mood regarding the state of the nation's economy as well as the status of their personal finances, their jobs, and other aspects of their lives.

Two of the most frequently asked questions concerning the Gallup Poll are: Who pays for or provides financial support to the Poll? And who determines which topics are covered by the Poll or, more specifically, who decides which questions are asked on Gallup surveys? Since its founding in 1935 the Gallup Poll has been underwritten by the nation's daily newspapers, which pay for the column on a syndicated or shared cost basis. In recent years, funding also has come from CNN and the national daily newspaper *USA Today.* Subscribers to the Poll include Republican, Democratic, and independent newspapers that represent every shade of the ideological spectrum.

Suggestions for poll questions come from Gallup's media subscribers, from other print and broadcast media, and from institutions as well as from individuals, including members of Congress and other public officials, university professors, and foundation executives. In addition, the public themselves are regularly questioned about the problems and issues facing the nation as they perceive them. Their answers establish priorities and provide an up-to-the-minute list of topic areas to explore through the Poll.

The Gallup Poll, as it is known today, began life on October 20, 1935, as a nationally syndicated newspaper feature titled "America Speaks—The National Weekly Column of Public Opinion." For brevity's sake, the media quickly came to refer to the column as The Gallup Poll, after its founder and editor-in-chief, Dr. George H. Gallup. Although Dr. Gallup had experimented during the 1934 congressional and 1932 presidential election campaigns to develop more accurate techniques for measuring public opinion, including scientific sampling, the first Gallup survey results to appear in print were those reported in the initial October 20, 1935, column. (The Roper Poll also began operations in 1935, coinciding closely with the founding of the Gallup Poll, when Elmo Roper began conducting a quarterly public opinion column for *Fortune* magazine.)

Although the new scientific opinion polls enjoyed almost immediate popular success, their initial efforts were met with skepticism from many quarters. Critics questioned, for example, how it was possible to determine the opinions of the entire American populace based on only 1,000 interviews or less, or how one knew whether people were telling the truth. The credibility of the polls as well as their commercial viability was enhanced significantly, however, when Gallup correctly predicted that Roosevelt would win the 1936 presidential election in a landslide, directly contradicting the forecast of the Literary Digest Poll, the poll of record at that time. The Digest Poll, which was not based on scientific sampling procedures, claimed that FDR's Republican challenger, Alfred M. Landon, would easily win the election.

Over the subsequent six decades the scientifically based opinion polls have gained a level of acceptance to where they are used today to investigate virtually every aspect of human experience in most nations of the world. To a large extent, this acceptance is due to the record of accuracy achieved by the polls in pre-election surveys. For example, in the sixteen presidential elections since 1936, the deviation between Gallup's final pre-election survey figures and the actual election results is 2.2%; and, since 1960, only 1.5%. Correspondingly, in the fifteen midterm congressional elections measured since 1936, the deviation between Gallup's final pre-election survey figures and the actual election results is 1.5%. These tests of candidate strength or "trial heats," which were introduced by Gallup in the 1930s (along with the presidential "approval" ratings), demonstrate that scientific survey techniques can accurately quantify public sentiment.

A. M. G.

THE SAMPLE

Although most Gallup Poll findings are based on telephone interviews, a significant proportion is based on interviews conducted in person in the home. The majority of the findings reported in Gallup Poll surveys is based on samples consisting of a minimum of 1,000 interviews. The total number, however, may exceed 1,000, or even 1,500, interviews, where the survey specifications call for reporting the responses of low-incidence population groups such as young public-school parents or Hispanics.

Design of the Sample for Telephone Surveys

The findings from the telephone surveys are based on Gallup's standard national telephone samples, consisting of unclustered directory-assisted, random-digit telephone samples utilizing a proportionate, stratified sampling design. The random-digit aspect of the sample is used to avoid "listing" bias. Numerous studies have shown that households with unlisted telephone numbers are different from listed households. "Unlistedness" is due to household mobility or to customer requests to prevent publication of the telephone number. To avoid this source of bias, a random-digit procedure designed to provide representation of both listed and unlisted (including not-yet-listed) numbers is used.

Telephone numbers for the continental United States are stratified into four regions of the country and, within each region, further arranged into three size-of-community strata. The sample of telephone numbers produced by the described method is representative of all telephone households within the continental United States.

Only working banks of telephone numbers are selected. Eliminating nonworking banks from the sample increases the likelihood that any sampled telephone number will be associated with a residence.

Within each contacted household, an interview is sought with the youngest man 18 years of age or older who is at home. If no man is home, an interview is sought with the oldest woman at home. This method of respondent selection within households produces an age distribution by sex that closely approximates the age distribution by sex of the total population.

Up to three calls are made to each selected telephone number to complete an interview. The time of day and the day of the week for callbacks are varied to maximize the chances of finding a respondent at home. All interviews are conducted on weekends or weekday evenings in order to contact potential respondents among the working population.

The final sample is weighted so that the distribution of the sample matches current estimates derived from the U.S. Census Bureau's Current Population Survey (CPS) for the adult population living in telephone households in the continental United States.

Design of the Sample for Personal Surveys

The design of the sample for personal (face-to-face) surveys is that of a replicated area probability sample down to the block level in the case of urban areas and to segments of townships in the case of rural areas.

After stratifying the nation geographically and by size of community according to information derived from the most recent census, over 350 different sampling locations are selected on a mathematically random basis from within cities, towns, and counties that, in turn, have been selected on a mathematically random basis.

The interviewers are given no leeway in selecting the areas in which they are to conduct their interviews. Each interviewer is given a map on which a specific starting point is marked and is instructed to contact households according to a predetermined travel pattern. At each occupied dwelling unit, the interviewer selects respondents by following a systematic procedure that is repeated until the assigned number of interviews has been completed.

Weighting Procedures

After the survey data have been collected and processed, each respondent is assigned a weight so that the demographic characteristics of the total weighted sample of respondents match the latest estimates of the demographic characteristics of the adult population available from the U.S. Census Bureau. Telephone surveys are weighted to match the characteristics of the adult population living in households with access to a telephone. The weighting of personal interview data includes a factor to improve the representation of the kind of people who are less likely to be found at home.

The procedures described above are designed to produce samples approximating the adult civilian population (18 and older) living in private households (that is, excluding those in prisons, hospitals, hotels, religious and educational institutions, and those living on reservations or military bases)—and in the case of telephone surveys, households with access to a telephone. Survey percentages may be applied to census estimates of the size of these populations to project percentages into numbers of people. The manner in which the sample is drawn also produces a sample that approximates the distribution of private households in the United States. Therefore, survey results also can be projected to numbers of households.

Sampling Tolerances

In interpreting survey results, it should be borne in mind that all sample surveys are subject to sampling error—that is, the extent to which the results may differ from what would be obtained if the whole population surveyed had been interviewed. The size of such sampling errors depends largely on the number of interviews.

The following tables may be used in estimating the sampling error of any percentage. The computed allowances have taken into account the effect of the sample design upon sampling error. They may be interpreted as indicating the range (plus or minus the figure shown) within which the results of repeated samplings in the same time period could be expected to vary, 95 percent of the time, assuming the same sampling procedure, the same interviewers, and the same questionnaire.

Table A shows how much allowance should be made for the sampling error of a percentage. Let us say a reported percentage is 33 for a group that includes 1,000 respondents. First, we go to the row headed "Percentages near 30" and then go across to the column headed "1,000." The number here is 4, which means that the 33 percent obtained in the sample is subject to a sampling error of plus or minus 4 points. Another way of saying it is that very probably (95 chances out of 100) the average of repeated samplings would be somewhere between 29 and 37, with the most likely figure being the 33 obtained.

In comparing survey results in two samples, such as for men and women, the question arises as to how large must a difference between them be before one can be reasonably sure that it reflects a real difference. In Tables B and C, the number of points that must be allowed for in such comparisons is indicated. Table B is for percentages near 20 or 80, and Table C is for percentages near 50. For percentages in between, the error to be allowed for is between those shown in the two tables.

Here is an example of how the tables would be used: Let us say that 50 percent of men respond a certain way and 40 percent of women also respond that way, for a difference of 10 percentage points between them. Can we say with any assurance that the 10-point difference reflects a real difference between men and women on the question? The sample contains approximately 600 men and 600 women.

TABLE A
Recommended Allowance for Sampling Error of a Percentage

	In Percentage Points (at 95 in 100 confidence level)* Sample Size					
	1,000	750	600	400	200	100
Percentages near 10	2	3	3	4	5	7
Percentages near 20	3	4	4	5	7	9
Percentages near 30	4	4	4	6	8	10
Percentages near 40	4	4	5	6	8	11
Percentages near 50	4	4	5	6	8	11
Percentages near 60	4	4	5	6	8	11
Percentages near 70	4	4	4	6	8	10
Percentages near 80	3	4	4	5	7	9
Percentages near 90	2	3	3	4	5	7

*The chances are 95 in 100 that the sampling error is not larger than the figures shown.

TABLE B
Recommended Allowance for Sampling Error of the Difference

	In Percentage Points (at 95 in 100 confidence level)* Percentages near 20 or percentages near 80			
	750	600	400	200
Size of sample				
750	5			
600	5	6		
400	6	6	7	
200	8	8	8	10

*The chances are 95 in 100 that the sampling error is not larger than the figures shown.

TABLE C
Recommended Allowance for Sampling Error of the Difference

	In Percentage Points (at 95 in 100 confidence level)* Percentages near 50			
	750	600	400	200
Size of sample				
750	6			
600	7	7		
400	7	8	8	
200	10	10	10	12

*The chances are 95 in 100 that the sampling error is not larger than the figures shown.

Since the percentages are near 50, we consult Table C, and since the two samples are about 600 persons each, we look for the number in the column headed "600" that is also in the row designated "600." We find the number 7 here. This means that the allowance for error should be 7 points, and that in concluding that the percentage among men is somewhere between 3 and 17 points higher than the percentage among women, we should be wrong only about 5 percent of the time. In other words, we can conclude with considerable confidence that a difference exists in the direction observed and that it amounts to at least 3 percentage points.

If, in another case, men's responses amount to 22 percent and women's 24 percent, we consult Table B because these percentages are near 20. We look for the number in the column headed "600" that is also in the row designated "600" and see that the number is 6. Obviously, then, the 2-point difference is inconclusive.

GALLUP POLL ACCURACY RECORD

Presidential Elections

	Candidates	Final Gallup Survey	Election Result	Gallup Deviation
2000	Gore	46.0	48.4	−2.4
	Bush	48.0	47.9	+0.1
	Nader	4.0	2.7	+1.3
	Buchanan	1.0	0.4	+0.6
	Other	1.0	0.6	+0.4
1996	Clinton	52.0	49.2	+2.8
	Dole	41.0	40.9	+0.1
	Perot	7.0	8.5	−1.5
1992	Clinton	49.0	43.0	+6.0
	Bush	37.0	37.5	−0.5
	Perot	14.0	18.9	−4.9
1988	Bush	56.0	53.4	+2.6
	Dukakis	44.0	45.7	−1.7
1984	Reagan	59.0	58.8	+0.2
	Mondale	41.0	40.6	+0.4
1980	Reagan	47.0	50.8	−3.8
	Carter	44.0	41.0	+3.0
	Anderson	8.0	6.6	+1.4
	Other	1.0	1.6	−0.6
1976	Carter	48.0	50.1	−2.1
	Ford	49.0	48.0	+1.0
	McCarthy	2.0	0.9	+1.1
	Other	1.0	0.9	+0.1
1972	Nixon	62.0	60.7	+1.3
	McGovern	38.0	37.6	+0.4
1968	Nixon	43.0	43.4	−0.4
	Humphrey	42.0	42.7	−0.7
	Wallace	15.0	13.5	+1.5

1964	Johnson	64.0	61.3	+2.7
	Goldwater	36.0	38.6	−2.6
1960	Kennedy	51.0	49.9	+1.1
	Nixon	49.0	49.8	−0.8
1956	Eisenhower	59.5	57.6	+1.9
	Stevenson	40.5	42.1	−1.6
1952	Eisenhower	51.0	55.1	−4.1
	Stevenson	49.0	44.4	+4.6
1948	Truman	44.5	49.6	−5.1
	Dewey	49.5	45.1	+4.4
	Wallace	4.0	2.4	+1.6
	Other	2.0	3.0	−1.0
1944	Roosevelt	51.5	53.6	−2.1
	Dewey	48.5	46.0	+2.5
1940	Roosevelt	52.0	54.7	−2.7
	Willkie	48.0	44.8	+3.2
1936	Roosevelt	55.7	60.8	−5.1
	Landon	44.3	36.5	+7.8

Trend in Deviation
(For Each Candidate)

Elections	Average Error
1936–1948	3.6%
1952–1964	2.4%
1968–2000	1.5%
1936–2000 (Overall)	2.1%

CHRONOLOGY

This chronology is provided to enable the reader to relate poll results to specific events, or series of events, that may have influenced public opinion.

2000

December 16	President-elect Bush selects General Colin Powell to be his secretary of state.
December 23	President Clinton proposes a broad Middle East peace agreement.
December 28	The U.S. Census Bureau reports the 2000 census count at 281,421,906 people as of April 1. This figure shows a 13.2% increase in the nation's population since the 1990 census.

2001

January 3	The 107th Congress, the most closely divided since the 1950s, convenes amid appeals for bipartisanship.
January 17	California's Governor Gray Davis declares a state of emergency after a power shortage forces the state's electricity grid operator to order rolling blackouts.
January 20	George Walker Bush is sworn in as the forty-third President of the United States.
January 23	President Bush introduces a plan to overhaul the nation's education system by tying public schools' funding to students' standardized test scores.
February 1	President Bush's most controversial Cabinet nominee, former Senator John Ashcroft, is confirmed as Attorney General.
March 27	The United States announces its intention to withdraw from the Kyoto Protocol, a treaty that calls for a reduction of greenhouse gas emissions in industrialized nations.

April 1	A Chinese fighter jet and a U.S. surveillance aircraft collide over the South China Sea. The Beijing government detains the American crew members after they make an emergency landing on a Chinese island. The crew are released on April 12.
April 8	Tiger Woods wins the Masters Tournament in Augusta, Georgia, to become the first golfer to capture four consecutive major titles.
May 17	The United States faces its gravest energy shortage since the 1970s, according to President Bush.
June 7	President Bush signs a ten-year $1.35 trillion tax-cut bill, the most extensive tax relief legislation in more than two decades.
July 12	Campaign finance reform legislation is defeated for one more year when a bill that had passed in the Senate is tabled in the House.
August 9	President Bush agrees to permit federal funding for limited stem-cell research.
August 20	The Chandra Levy case becomes national news. Levy, a twenty-three-year-old government intern in Washington, DC, disappeared on April 30. On August 23, Rep. Gary Condit (D–CA) admits to having a "very close" relationship with her.
September 11	Nineteen hijackers commandeer four commercial jetliners, crashing two of them into the twin towers of the World Trade Center in New York City and another into the Pentagon outside Washington, DC. The fourth airliner goes down in a Pennsylvania field after its crew and passengers struggle with the hijackers. More than 5,000 people are killed as the two towers collapse. Multimillionaire Saudi exile and reputed terrorist mastermind Osama bin Laden emerges as the chief architect of the attacks, which President Bush calls "acts of war." Within days, as Americans unite to mourn, Bush rallies a broad international coalition against bin Laden and his Afghanistan-based al-Qaeda terrorist network.
September 20	In an address to Congress, President Bush demands that Afghanistan's ruling Taliban militia, which had granted bin Laden refuge, surrender him and his followers.
September 21	The Taliban rejects the ultimatum.
October 7	The United States and Great Britain launch sustained air strikes in Afghanistan against al-Qaeda and Taliban targets. The Northern Alliance, a coalition of anti-Taliban Afghan militias, joins the operation on the ground.

October 15	The offices of Senate Majority Leader Tom Daschle and NBC News anchor Tom Brokaw receive letters laced with deadly anthrax bacteria. Four anthrax-tainted letters come to light in a spate of mailings that kill five people.
October 26	President Bush signs an antiterrorism bill that expands the power of law enforcement and intelligence agencies to investigate suspected terrorists.
November 2	The Justice Department and Microsoft Corporation reach a settlement in their long-running antitrust dispute.
November 12	The crash of an American Airlines jet in New York City kills everyone on board.
November 13	The Northern Alliance captures Kabul, the capital of the Taliban forces.
	President Bush authorizes the use of military tribunals to try foreign nationals accused of complicity in terrorist attacks on the United States.
November 19	President Bush signs a bill to place airline security screening under federal control.
November 28	The Bush administration projects a deficit for the federal budget in 2002, the first since 1997.
December 2	Enron Corporation, the world's leading energy trader, files for bankruptcy in the largest-ever case in U.S. history. This action virtually wipes out Enron employees' retirement savings. The reputation of accounting firm Arthur Andersen will soon be tarnished by its dealings with Enron.
December 5	Delegates from Afghanistan's four main political factions agree to install a thirty-member multiethnic interim cabinet empowered to rule for six months.
December 7	Taliban forces withdraw from Afghanistan's Kandahar region, their political and military stronghold, thus effectively ending the Taliban's five-year rule.
December 11	The Federal Reserve lowers interest rates for the eleventh time in 2001, which brings them to the lowest level in forty years as the central bank seeks to counter a recession that began in March.
December 13	President Bush announces that the United States will withdraw from the 1972 Antiballistic Missile Treaty with Russia.

GALLUP REGIONS

EAST
New England
Maine
New Hampshire
Vermont
Massachusetts
Rhode Island
Connecticut

Mid-Atlantic
New York
New Jersey
Pennsylvania
Maryland
Delaware
West Virginia
District of Columbia

MIDWEST
East Central
Ohio
Michigan
Indiana
Illinois

West Central
Wisconsin
Minnesota
Iowa
Missouri
North Dakota
South Dakota
Nebraska
Kansas

SOUTH
Southeast
Virginia
North Carolina
South Carolina
Georgia
Florida
Kentucky
Tennessee
Alabama
Mississippi

Southwest
Arkansas
Louisiana
Oklahoma
Texas

WEST
Mountain
Montana
Arizona
Colorado
Idaho
Wyoming
Utah
Nevada
New Mexico

Pacific
California
Oregon
Washington
Hawaii
Alaska

JANUARY 3
HILLARY RODHAM CLINTON

Interview Dates: 11/13—15/00
CNN/*USA Today*/Gallup Poll
Survey #GO 132170

We'd like to get your overall opinion of one of the people in the news. Please say if you have a favorable or unfavorable opinion of this person, or if you have never heard of her:

Hillary Rodham Clinton?

	Favor-able	Unfavor-able	No opinion
2000 Nov 13–15	56%	39%	5%
2000 Oct 25–28	52	43	5
2000 Aug 4–5	45	50	5
2000 Feb 4–6	55	39	6
1999 Dec 9–12	48	48	4
1999 Sep 23–26	56	40	4
1999 Aug 3–4	56	41	3
1999 Jul 22–25	62	35	3
1999 Jun 25–27	56	42	2
1999 Mar 5–7	65	31	4
1999 Feb 19–21	65	30	5
1999 Feb 4–8	66	31	3
1998 Dec 28–29	67	29	4
1998 Oct 9–12	63	33	4
1998 Sep 14–15	61	33	6
1998 Aug 21–23	61	33	6
1998 Aug 20	60	30	10
1998 Aug 18	64	29	7
1998 Aug 10–12	60	36	4
1998 Aug 7–8	60	35	5
1998 Feb 13–15	60	36	4
1998 Jan 30–Feb 1	64	34	2
1998 Jan 28	61	34	5
1998 Jan 24–25	61	33	6
1998 Jan 23–24	60	35	5
1997 Dec 18–21	56	38	6
1997 Oct 27–29	61	34	5
1997 Jun 26–29	51	42	7
1997 Feb 24–26	51	42	7
1997 Jan 31–Feb 2	55	39	6
1997 Jan 10–13	56	37	7
1996 Oct 26–29*	49	43	8
1996 Aug 28–29**	51	41	8
1996 Aug 16–18**	47	48	5
1996 Aug 5–7**	48	45	7
1996 Jun 18–19	46	47	6
1996 Mar 15–17	47	48	5
1996 Jan 12–15	43	51	6
1995 Jul 7–9	50	44	6
1995 Mar 17–19	49	44	7
1995 Jan 16–18	50	44	6
1994 Nov 28–29	50	44	6
1994 Sep 6–7	48	47	5
1994 Jul 15–17	48	46	6
1994 Apr 22–24	56	40	4
1994 Mar 25–27	52	42	6
1994 Mar 7–8	55	40	5
1994 Jan 15–17	57	36	7
1993 Nov 2–4	58	34	8
1993 Sep 24–26	62	27	11
1993 Aug 8–10	57	33	10

*Likely voters
**Registered voters

Do you approve or disapprove of the way Hillary Rodham Clinton is handling her job as First Lady?

	Approve	Dis-approve	No opinion
2000 Nov 13–15	66%	30%	4%
2000 Feb 4–6	65	30	5
1999 Nov 18–21	66	30	4
1999 May 23–24	71	23	6
1999 Feb 19–21	80	17	3
1997 Oct 27–29	62	31	7
1997 Jan 10–13	62	34	4
1995 Jan 16–18	54	40	6
1994 Apr 22–24	56	37	7
1994 Mar 7–8	58	39	3
1993 Jan 29–31	67	16	17

Analysis: Hillary Clinton leaves the White House to embark on a new career as a U.S. senator with generally positive evaluations. Two-thirds of the public currently approve of the job Hillary Clinton is doing as First Lady and 56% have a favorable opinion of her, according to a Gallup Poll conducted November 13–15. These numbers are similar to those recorded at the beginning of Bill Clinton's first term as president. Although she is leaving on good terms with the American people, Hillary Clinton has had a volatile relationship with the public over the past eight years, with job approval ratings ranging from 54% to 80% and favorability scores ranging from 43% to 67%.

Hillary Clinton's highest favorablility ratings from the public came shortly after the House of Representatives impeached her husband in December 1998, when 67% of the public said they had a "favorable" opinion of the First Lady. She received her lowest rating (43%) in January 1996 in the midst of the Whitewater controversy.

Just seven months after Bill Clinton took office, a majority of Americans had favorable opinions of both him and the First Lady: 53% and 57%, respectively. Over the course of the next year, however, both Hillary Clinton and President Bill Clinton lost favor in the public eye. By September 1994, shortly before the Republicans won majority control of the U.S. House of Representatives, Hillary Clinton's favorability rating had dropped 9 percentage points to 48% and the president's rating had dropped by 5 points to 47%. The public's disenchantment with the Clintons may have been tied to the high-profile Whitewater investigation into their personal investments.

Until the fall of 1997, Hillary Clinton's favorability rating hovered at or under 50% while Bill Clinton's ratings improved, then fluctuated, between 51% and 62% from mid-1995 to early 1997. The president's successful reelection in 1996 may have boosted the public's positive perception of him whereas the First Lady continued to be mired in the Whitewater investigation.

By September 1998, in the wake of the Monica Lewinsky scandal, the public had soured somewhat on Bill Clinton: his favorability rating dropped by about 10 percentage points and generally ranged in the low 50s. However, the public developed a relatively positive assessment of the First Lady during the Lewinsky matter, perhaps out of sympathy. Americans maintained that opinion throughout the subsequent impeachment of her husband and her campaign for the U.S. Senate. Currently, 56% hold a favorable opinion of Hillary Clinton as she prepares to enter elected office.

As Hillary Clinton campaigned for the New York Senate seat, reporters and observers remarked on the strong support she received from women in the Empire State. Indeed, a gender gap in public opinion has characterized her entire eight years in the White House, with women holding her in much higher regard than men. One of the lowest overall favorability ratings (47%) the First Lady ever received was in March 1996, but a majority of women (54%) still expressed a high opinion of her compared to only 39% of men. Although there are big gender differences in each reading of Hillary's favorability ratings, the opinions of men and women have moved in tandem from year to year.

In the first year of the Clinton administration, young adults (those between the ages of 18 and 29) were the least likely to hold a favorable opinion of Hillary Clinton, and the oldest people (those over the age of 65) were the most likely to say they had a favorable opinion of the First Lady. Over time, younger Americans have come to view her much more positively whereas older Americans see her less positively. In early 1996, for the first time, more young people said they had a favorable opinion of Hillary Clinton than did any other age group, and that pattern has persisted until today. In the latest Gallup Poll, 63% of the youngest Americans have a favorable opinion of the First Lady, compared to 53% of those in the oldest age group.

Over the past eight years, the Clintons' approval ratings have generally moved together, either positively or negatively, but Hillary Clinton has consistently received marks higher than those of her husband. She received her lowest approval rating (54%) in January 1995, shortly after the Republicans won control of Congress, and her highest rating (80%) was in February 1999, during Bill Clinton's impeachment trial. Since then, public approval of Hillary Clinton as First Lady has been fairly high, and currently stands at a healthy 66% on the eve of her new career as a U.S. senator.

JANUARY 3
U.S. SUPREME COURT

Interview Dates: 12/15-17/00
CNN/*USA Today*/Gallup Poll
Survey #GO 132179

I am going to read you a list of institutions in American society. Please tell me how much confidence you, yourself, have in each one—a great deal, quite a lot, some, or very little:

The military?

Great deal; quite a lot 72%
Some; very little 26
None; no opinion 2

The U.S. Supreme Court?

Great deal; quite a lot 49%
Some; very little 48
None; no opinion 3

Congress?

Great deal; quite a lot 31%
Some; very little 66
None; no opinion 3

The presidency?

Great deal; quite a lot 49%
Some; very little 48
None; no opinion 3

Television news?

Great deal; quite a lot 31%
Some; very little 66
None; no opinion 3

Confidence in Supreme Court

	Great deal; quite a lot
2000 Dec	49%
2000 Jun	47
1999 Jun	49
1998 Jun	50
1997 Jul	50
1996 May	45
1995 Apr	44
1994 Mar	42
1993 Mar	44
1991 Oct	39
1991 Mar	48
1990	47
1989	46
1988	56
1987	52
1986	54
1985	56
1984	51
1983	42
1981	46
1979	45
1977	46
1975	49
1973	44

Analysis: One of the lasting lessons of the controversy surrounding the winner of the 2000 presidential election is how much a person's partisanship affects his or her political views. Throughout the controversy, Republicans and Democrats held opposing views on the vast majority of issues involved in the saga to determine the nation's next president. An interesting example of these differential perceptions based on personal party identification comes from an examination of changes in Americans' opinions of the U.S. Supreme Court between June and December of this year.

A comparison of two surveys, one taken on December 15–17 and the other conducted on June 22–25, indicates that Americans overall showed little change in their confidence in the U.S. Supreme Court following its controversial ruling in *Bush v. Gore*. The Gallup Poll conducted December 15–17 showed that 49% of Americans either had "a great deal" or "quite a lot" of confidence in the U.S. Supreme Court, which changed little from the 47% of similar levels of confidence registered during the June 22–25 poll.

But this surface stability masked significant change in the way Republicans and Democrats view the Supreme Court. Those who identify as Democrats showed a slight drop in confidence in the Supreme Court between June and December, from 44% with "a great deal" or "quite a lot" of confidence during June, to 40% during December. Independents also showed a very slight loss of faith in the Supreme Court, from 48% to 45%. Republicans, however, showed a large increase in confidence, from 48% during June to 67% during the days following the Supreme Court's decision in *Bush v. Gore*. In short, views of the nation's highest court became more politicized—at least in the short term—during the time period in which the court made the highly controversial decision that gave George W. Bush the presidency.

JANUARY 4
WOMEN IN POLITICAL OFFICE

Interview Dates: 12/2–4/00
Gallup Poll News Service
Survey #GO 132084

Do you think this country would be governed better or governed worse if more women were in political office?

	Better	Worse	No differ-ence; (vol.) no opinion
2000 Dec 2–4	57%	17%	26%
1999 Feb 4–8	57	14	29
1984 Jul 27–30	28	15	57
1975 Aug 15–18	33	18	49
Men			
2000 Dec 2–4	50	20	30
1999 Feb 4–8	51	14	35
1984 Jul 27–30	24	15	61
1975 Aug 15–18	29	17	54
Women			
2000 Dec 2–4	64	14	22
1999 Feb 4–8	62	14	24
1984 Jul 27–30	32	14	54
1975 Aug 15–18	36	20	44

Between now and the 2000 political conventions, there will be discussions about the qualifications of presidential candidates—their education, age, religion, race, and so on. If your party nominated a generally well-qualified person for president who happened to be a woman, would you vote for that person?

	Yes	No	No opinion
1999 Feb 19–21	92%	7%	1%
1987 Jul 10–13	82	12	6
1984 Jul 27–30	78	17	5
1983 Apr 29–May 2	80	16	4
1978 Jul 21–24	76	19	5
1975 Aug 15–18	73	23	4
1971 Jul 15–18	66	29	5
1969 Mar 12–17	53	40	7
1967 Apr 19–24	57	39	4
1963 Aug 15–20	55	41	4
1959 Dec 10–15	57	39	4
1958 Sep 10–15	54	41	5
1955 Feb 10–15	52	44	4
1949 Sep 25–30	48	48	4
1945 Nov 23–28	33	55	12
1937 Jan 27–Feb 1	33	64	3

Analysis: According to the December 2–4 Gallup Poll, 64% of women think that America would be in better hands if more women were in politics; half of men also feel this way. Only a minority of both men and women say that the country would be governed worse with more women at the helm: 20% of men say so and 14% of women agree. Men are slightly more likely than women not to see a difference between the governing skills of the genders: 25% of men say that electing more women would not make a difference compared to 14% of women.

The results of the 2000 election were historic in many ways, one of which is the gender composition of the new Congress. The 107th Congress now includes more women than ever before: thirteen senators (including Hillary Rodham Clinton) and fifty-nine representatives. According to a recent Gallup Poll, the public welcomes such political gains by women. A majority of Americans (57%) say that this country would be governed better if there were more women in political office. A minority (17%) thinks governing would be worse and a fifth of Americans (20%) do not think having more women in office would make a difference. These sentiments have changed significantly over the past 16 years, most of the change stemming from a decline in the belief that electing more women would not affect the quality of government. In 1984, just 28% thought increasing the number of women in politics would be beneficial, and 46% said that they did not think electing more women would make a difference in the quality of government.

Younger Americans, both men and women, are more likely than those who are older to perceive that government would benefit from adding more women. Fifty-five percent of men between the ages of 18 and 49 say that this country would be governed better if there were more women in political office, compared to 40% of men over the age of 49. Seventy percent of women between the ages of 18 and 49 see benefits from electing more women, compared to 57% of women over the age of 49. There also are interesting differences on this topic by the political and ideological orientation of Americans: 73% of liberals say that more women in politics would be good for the country compared to 45% of conservatives. Seventy percent of Democrats say that more women in politics would be beneficial, compared to 48% of Republicans.

Citizens around the world share the view that government would benefit from increasing the number of women in office. In 1995, Gallup asked people in twenty-two different countries whether government would improve by augmenting the number of women in government. Across all of these countries, more people agreed that their government would function better rather than worse if it added more women to the ranks. Americans come in at the higher "more women would be better" end of the spectrum. In the 1995 survey, 57% said electing more women would result in better government (little difference from Americans' responses in the most recent survey), compared to 50% of Canadians, 44% of Japanese, 39% of Mexicans, and 30% of Spanish citizens. In no country surveyed did the majority of citizens think they would be worse off with more women in political office. Rather, in some cases, a plurality of respondents said they did not think adding more women would make a difference in the quality of government.

Although neither the Republican nor the Democratic Party has ever nominated a woman for president, the American public overwhelmingly claims that the gender of a presidential candidate would make no difference. Ninety-two percent of Americans say they would vote for a woman if their party nominated one for the highest office. Men and women share this sentiment: 91% of men and 93% of women say they would vote for a female candidate. Not surprisingly, public opinion on this question has changed considerably over the past century: only 33% of Americans said they would vote for a woman for president back in 1937 when Gallup first asked this question.

Despite the public's willingness to vote for a woman for president, a significant portion of the public (42%) think that a man would make a better president than a woman. Thirty-one percent of those interviewed in a Gallup Poll conducted in March 1999 say, everything else being equal, a woman would make the better president, while 22% do not think the gender of the president would affect his or her performance. Women are much more likely than men to say that a woman would make a better president than a man (39% versus 22%).

JANUARY 5
ELECTORAL COLLEGE

Interview Dates: 12/15-17/00
CNN/*USA Today*/Gallup Poll
Survey #GO 132179

Thinking for a moment about the way in which the president is elected in this country, which would you prefer—to amend the U.S. Constitution so the candidate who receives the most total votes nationwide wins the election, or to keep the current system in which the candidate who wins the most votes in the Electoral College wins the election?

	Amend Constitution	Keep current system	Both; neither; (vol.) no opinion
2000 Dec 15–17 . . . . .59%		37%	4%
2000 Nov 11–12 61		35	4
Republicans 41		56	3
Independents 57		38	5
Democrats 75		22	3
Bush voters in 2004 . . .40		57	3
Gore voters in 2004 . . .75		22	3

Analysis: Both chambers of the U.S. Congress will meet in joint session on Saturday, January 6, in order to carry out Congress's ceremonial task of reading the electoral votes cast by each state, and officially certifying Texas Governor George W. Bush as the next president. In so doing, the House of Representatives and the Senate are following the requirements of Article II of the Constitution which lays out the procedures by which each state appoints a number of electors who, in turn, meet in their respective states and vote for president and vice president. The Constitution goes on to state: "The president of the Senate shall, in the presence of the Senate and House of Representatives, open all the certificates, and the votes shall then be counted. The person having the greatest number of votes shall be the president, if such number be a majority of the whole number of electors appointed."

This process, which has been carried out in the election of U.S. presidents for over 200 years, says nothing about the popular vote of U.S. citizens, thereby leaving the president and vice president as the only elected federal officials not chosen directly by the vote of the people.

The system has generated intense scrutiny this year, only the third time in history that the

winner of the Electoral College (and, therefore, the winner of the presidency) was not the popular vote winner. Just as Rutherford Hayes and Benjamin Harrison won the presidency while losing the popular vote in 1876 and 1888, respectively, George W. Bush will be taking office this year having lost the popular vote to Al Gore by more than 500,000 votes.

There is little question that the American public would prefer to dismantle the Electoral College system and go to a direct popular vote for the presidency. In Gallup Polls that stretch back over 50 years, a majority have continually expressed support for the notion of an official amendment to the U.S. Constitution that would allow for direct election of the president.

Support for changing the Constitution this year, although still clearly in the majority, may be down somewhat from previous decades because of an apparent reluctance on the part of Republicans to support the change that would have given the presidency this year to Al Gore instead of to George W. Bush. There is a 34-percentage-point difference in the level of support for the change between Republicans and Democrats, suggesting that many respondents may have been thinking about how the system would have worked to their candidate's benefit or detriment this year. Support for eliminating the Electoral College also is higher among younger Americans. Sixty-six percent of those age 18 to 29 and 63% of those age 30 to 49 say the system should be amended, compared to only 51% of those 50 years of age and older.

The significant—and predictable—variations by party in interest in amending the Constitution suggest that Americans generally understand how the system works. In fact, in a November 13–15 Gallup Poll, only about 28% of those interviewed said they didn't understand the Electoral College system well, while 72% said they understood how it works at least "somewhat well."

But despite the fact that about six out of ten Americans support the idea, the real-world chances for the success of such an amendment may not be all that robust, given the high barriers to constitutional change set up by the framers of the U.S. Constitution in Article V. Two-thirds of the members of both houses of Congress would have to approve such an amendment, and then three-quarters of the legislatures of the 50 states would have to ratify it in order to change the system to direct election of a president by popular vote.

JANUARY 9
BUSH ADMINISTRATION TRANSITION

Interview Dates: 1/5–7/01
CNN/*USA Today*/Gallup Poll
Survey #GO 132545

Do you approve or disapprove of the way George W. Bush is handling his presidential transition?

Approve 65%
Disapprove 26
No opinion 9

Apart from whether you approve or disapprove of the way George W. Bush is handling his transition to the presidency, what do you think of Bush as a person—would you say you approve or disapprove of him?

Approve 60%
Disapprove 33
No opinion 7

How would you rate the appointments President-elect George W. Bush has made so far to Cabinet-level positions—would you say his choices have been outstanding, above average, average, below average, or poor?

Outstanding; above average 38%
Average 43
Below average; poor; no opinion 19

Do you think George W. Bush's choices for Cabinet-level positions have been too liberal, too conservative, or about right?

Too liberal 9%
Too conservative .20

About right 61
No opinion 10

Who do you think will be making more of the important decisions in the next administration—George W. Bush or Dick Cheney? *

Bush 55%
Cheney 30
Both; neither (vol.) 9
No opinion 6

*Based on part sample

As you may know, George W. Bush has said he will delegate authority in his administration to his Cabinet secretaries and other high-level administrators. Do you think he will go too far in delegating authority, or do you think he will delegate about the right amount of authority? *

Go too far 27%
Right amount 62
Too little (vol.) 2
No opinion 9

*Based on part sample

Do you consider yourself to be a supporter of George W. Bush, or not?

Yes 51%
No 46
No opinion 1

Do you think the country would be better off if the Republicans controlled Congress, or if the Democrats controlled Congress?

	Republicans	Democrats	Neither; same; (vol.) no opinion
2001 Jan 5–7	39%	41%	20%
1999 Jul 16–18	37	42	21
1999 Jun 25–27	41	41	18
1999 May 23–24	36	37	27
1998 Dec 15–16	30	41	29

1998 Sep 23–24 35	41	24
1997 Aug 22–25 37	40	23
1997 Jul 25–27 37	39	24
1997 Jun 26–29 34	40	26
1996 Oct 26–29* 39	42	19
1995 Dec 15–18 41	41	18
1995 Mar 27–29 45	33	22

*Likely voters

Analysis: Despite some potentially controversial appointments, a Gallup Poll shows that the public has a generally positive image about President-elect George W. Bush as he prepares to take office later this month. While just half the public believes he was the real winner in the presidential contest, and just half consider themselves supporters of the officially elected president, most Americans approve of the way he is handling the transition and give him generally high marks for the quality of the appointments he has made. The reaction to the Bush transition is similar to that measured by a Gallup Poll in late December 1992 concerning the transition efforts of then President-elect Bill Clinton.

According to the poll conducted January 5–7, 65% approve of Bush's transition efforts, similar to the 67% received by Clinton in a December 1992 poll. Also, 38% say Bush's appointments have been either outstanding or above average, while 43% say average, and 13% say below average or poor. In December 1992, a similar pattern was found for Clinton's appointments: 32% said they were either outstanding or above average, 43% average, and 9% below average or poor.

One issue in the Bush transition that did not arise when Clinton was preparing to assume office is how much the new president himself would be involved in making decisions. There was little doubt that Clinton himself would be the principal decision-maker in his administration. But George W. Bush has signaled that he will pursue a different management style that emphasizes more delegation of power, as reflected in the substantial role that Vice President-elect Dick Cheney has assumed in the presidential transition effort. The current poll shows that about three in ten believe Cheney will be making more of the important decisions in the Bush administration

than the president himself, although a majority (55%) disagree. Similarly, 27% say Bush will go too far in delegating authority to subordinates, but 62% have confidence the president-elect will delegate just the right amount of authority.

The poll shows that the political division reflected in the election results continues to be reflected in the public's views of the president and Congress. Just about one-half (51%) say they consider themselves supporters of Bush while 48% say they are not. And 41% say that it would be better for the country if the Democrats controlled Congress, while 39% say it would be better if the Republicans did. Party identification also remains about evenly split: 47% identify as Republicans or lean in that direction, and 46% identify with or lean toward the Democratic Party.

JANUARY 10
BUSH ADMINISTRATION

Interview Dates: 1/5–7/01
CNN/*USA Today*/Gallup Poll
Survey #GO 132545

How important is it that the Bush administration does each of the following—is it a top priority, high priority, low priority, or not a priority at all?

	Top priority	High priority*
Improve education 50%		44%
Keep America prosperous 43		48
Ensure long-term strength of Social Security 46		43
Help senior citizens pay for prescription drugs 42		46
Keep federal budget balanced . . .40		48
Ensure long-term strength of Medicare 40		48
Improve health-care system 43		44
Provide military security for the country 39		46
Improve conditions for minorities and the poor 30		50
Reduce use of illegal drugs 36		42
Improve quality of the environment 30		48

Improve race relations 28   47
Cut federal income taxes 26   39
Improve way political
  campaigns are financed 25   35

*"Low," "not a priority," "no opinion" are omitted.

Top Priority Summary (by ideology)

	Conservative	Moderate	Liberal
Improve education	45%	52%	56%
Keep America prosperous	45	43	40
Ensure long-term strength of Social Security	42	48	48
Help senior citizens pay for prescription drugs	39	43	47
Keep the federal budget balanced	42	41	36
Ensure long-term strength of Medicare	37	41	41
Improve health-care system	37	45	55
Provide military security for the country	48	38	26
Improve conditions for minorities and the poor	27	30	35
Reduce use of illegal drugs	40	36	30
Improve quality of the environment	25	32	38
Improve race relations	27	27	31
Cut federal income taxes	31	24	21
Improve way political campaigns are financed	20	26	36

Analysis: The transition to the Bush presidency continues, and in addition to the focus on who will serve in the new administration, there is continuing concern about what the new administration will do. The latest Gallup Poll asked Americans to rate the priority of a series of fourteen items to which the Bush presidency could turn its attention, with the following results.

As was the case during the presidential campaign, "improve education" is at the top of the list of priorities for the new Bush administration, with 50% listing it as a "top priority" and another 44% rating it a "high priority." Americans also want President-elect Bush to address issues of concern to senior citizens to "ensure the long-term strength of Social Security" (listed as top priority by 46% and high priority by 43%), and to "help senior citizens pay for prescription drugs" (listed as top priority by 42% and high priority by 46%). During the campaign, Bush outlined plans to deal with all three issues, but will be working with a sharply divided Congress in hopes of passing new legislation for each one.

Americans also believe that Bush should work to "keep America prosperous," cited as a top priority by 43%. Other issues that many feel deserve quick attention, but at slightly lower levels of urgency, are to keep the federal budget balanced, improve the health-care system, and ensure the long-term strength of Medicare. Women, more so than men, want Bush to improve health care: 50% view it as a top priority (second only to education at 52%) and 41% as a high priority. Liberals also believe that Bush should emphasize health care: 55% rate it a top priority (second to education at 56%).

Congressional Republicans and President-elect Bush have made no secret of their desire for tax cuts. However, Americans do not view this as an urgent priority. Only 26% say cutting federal income taxes is a "top priority" while 39% view it is a high priority. Of the fourteen issues polled, only "improve the way political campaigns are financed" finished lower than tax cuts. Generally speaking, all subgroups view tax cuts as among the lowest priorities, and only 31% of Republicans believe it is a top priority.

There are few differences in priority by subgroup as most tend to put the priorities in roughly the same order, with education at the top. Ideology presents the one notable exception: conservatives (48%) rank providing military security for the country as the top priority ahead of education (45%). Additionally, liberals are much more likely to see improving the way campaigns are financed as a top priority (36%) than are conservatives (20%) or moderates (26%).

JANUARY 10
MEN PREFERRED AS BOSSES

Interview Dates: 12/2–4/00
Gallup Poll News Service
Survey #GO 132084

If you were taking a new job and had your choice of a boss, would you prefer to work for a man or for a woman?

	Prefer man	Prefer woman	No difference (vol.)*
2000 Dec 2–4	48%	22%	28%
1999 Aug 24–26	38	16	45
1995 Sep 14–17	46	20	33
1993 Aug 23–25	39	22	36
1994 Jun 25–28	35	16	47
1989 Dec 18–21	48	14	34
1982 Jun 25–28	46	12	38
1975	62	7	29
1953	66	5	25
Men			
2000 Dec 2–4	45	19	35
1999 Aug 24–26	35	12	52
1995 Sep 14–17	37	17	44
1993 Aug 23–25	33	16	49
1982 Jun 25–28	40	9	46
1975	63	4	32
1953	75	2	21
Women			
2000 Dec 2–4	50	26	22
1999 Aug 24–26	42	22	35
1995 Sep 14–17	54	22	24
1993 Aug 23–25	44	29	24
1982 Jun 25–28	52	15	30
1975	60	10	27
1953	57	8	29

*"No opinion" is omitted.

Analysis: According to a Gallup Poll conducted December 2–4, 48% would prefer to work for a man rather than for a woman, while 22% would choose a female boss and 28% do not care one way or the other. The public has preferred male bosses for more than fifty years, although the margin in favor of men over women is lower now than it was a few decades ago. In 1953, the first time Gallup asked this question, 66% preferred to work for a man while only 5% preferred a woman. In 1975, almost a quarter of a century later, opinion had not changed much, as Americans still preferred a male to a female boss by a 62%-to-7% margin. But by 1982, preference for a male boss had declined and preference for a female boss began a slow climb. Today, although there is still a minority who would prefer to work for a woman, the percentage is more than four times higher than it was in 1953 when just 5% voiced a preference for a female boss.

According to the current poll, one-half of all adult women in the United States say they would prefer to work for a man compared to 45% of men. About a quarter of women (26%) would rather work for a woman compared to 19% of men. Men are more likely than women to say the gender of their boss does not matter: 35% compared to 22%.

These findings show somewhat of a change in the pattern recorded over the past twenty years. In 1982, 1993, 1995, and 1999, men were more likely to say that the gender of their boss did not matter to them than they would prefer to have a male boss. According to the most recent survey, however, a plurality of men now say they would prefer to work for a man, and just one-third (35%) do not have a preference. This represents the strongest male bias since 1975 when 63% said they would prefer to work for a man. On the other hand, although just 19% would rather have a female boss, this is the largest percentage that have ever voiced that preference.

Although more women say they prefer a male to a female boss, this is not true among young women who show a slight preference for a female boss. Overall, 39% of women age 18 to 29 would choose to work for a woman while just 35% prefer a man. By comparison, women 30 and older prefer a male to a female boss by a 53%-to-23% margin.

Young men do not differ much from older men on this question. Forty-four percent age 18 to 29 would choose a male boss compared to 45% age 30 and older.

The public's bias in favor of male bosses is not uniquely American. International Gallup Poll data show that the preference for male bosses is strong across many different countries. In 1995, Gallup asked this question in twenty-two different countries and found that people all over the globe had a bias for male bosses. In six countries—Canada, China, Iceland, Panama, Spain, and Britain—a plurality said the sex of their boss did not matter to them, but of those who did have a preference, more said they would prefer to work for a man if given the choice. In fourteen countries (including the United States), at least a plurality, if not a majority, would choose to work for a man. In no country did a plurality say they would rather work for a woman.

JANUARY 12
PRESIDENT CLINTON

Interview Dates: 1/5–7/01
CNN/*USA Today*/Gallup Poll
Survey #GO 132545

Do you approve or disapprove of the way Bill Clinton is handling his job as president?

	Approve	Dis-approve	No opinion
2001 Jan 5–7 . . . . .65%		31%	4%
2000 Dec 15–17 66		32	2
2000 Dec 2–4 60		35	5
2000 Nov 13–15 63		33	4
2000 Oct 25–28 57		38	5
2000 Oct 6–9 58		37	5
2000 Sep 11–13 60		34	6

Apart from whether you approve or disapprove of the way Bill Clinton is handling his job as president, what do you think of Clinton as a person—would you say you approve or disapprove of him?

	Approve	Dis-approve	No opinion
2001 Jan 5–7 . . . . .41%		54%	5%
2000 Apr 28–30 29		63	8
2000 Mar 10–12 35		59	6
2000 Feb 25–27 32		63	5
2000 Jan 17–19 36		59	5
2000 Jan 7–10 31		64	5
1999 Oct 8–10 35		62	3

Thinking about the Clinton presidency, how do you think President Clinton will go down in history—as an outstanding president, above average, average, below average, or poor?

	Outstanding; above average	Average	Below average; poor*
2001 Jan 5–7 . . . . .47%		30%	22%
2000 Feb 14–15 37		34	28
1999 Feb 8–9 40		27	31
1998 Jan 24–25 31		37	30
1998 Jan 23–24 30		41	28
1997 Jan 31–Feb 2 . . .36		47	16

"No opinion" is omitted

Do you generally think Bill Clinton is honest and trustworthy?

	Yes	No	No opinion
2001 Jan 5–7 . . . . .39%		58%	3%
1999 Feb 12–13 35		62	3
1998 May 8–10 44		51	5
1997 Dec 18–21 46		48	6
1997 Oct 27–29 51		45	4
1997 Sep 25–28 51		44	5
1997 Sep 6–7 53		42	5
1996 Oct 12–13* 47		48	5
1996 Oct 11–12* 48		46	6

*Likely voters

Do you consider yourself to be a supporter of Bill Clinton, or not?

Yes 47%
No 52
No opinion 1

In your view, will Bill Clinton mostly be re-membered as president for his accomplish-ments, or for his involvement in personal scandal?

	Accomplish-ments	Scandal	Other; no opinion
2001 Jan 5–7	.28%	68%	4%
2000 Aug 11–12	.22	73	5
1998 Aug 21–23	.23	71	6

Which comes closer to your view of Bill Clinton as he prepares to leave the White House—I'm glad he is leaving, or I'll miss him when he is gone? *

Glad he is leaving .51%
Miss him when gone 45
No opinion 4

*Based on part sample

Which comes closer to your view of Bill Clinton as he prepares to leave the White House—Bill Clinton has something worth-while to contribute and should remain active in public life, or Bill Clinton should get out of public life completely? *

Remain in public life 55%
Get out of public life 43
No opinion 2

*Based on part sample

As you may know, the independent counsel in the Monica Lewinsky case is assembling a grand jury to decide whether or not to charge Bill Clinton with a crime once he leaves office. Do you think Bill Clinton should or should not be charged in a court of law with a crime for these matters after he leaves office?

	Should	Should not	No opinion
2001 Jan 5–7	.30%	67%	3%
2000 Aug 18–19	.41	54	5
2000 May 23–24	.38	56	6

| 1999 Dec 9–12 . . . . . | .35 | 62 | 3 |
| 1999 Feb 12–13 . . . . . | .39 | 58 | 3 |

If the independent counsel does indict Bill Clinton, do you think President George W. Bush should or should not pardon Clinton?

Should 52%
Should not 42
No opinion 6

Analysis: President William Jefferson Clinton will leave office next week with the highest aver-age job approval that any president of the past half century has received over his last three months in office, but with low public ratings of his personal character, and with mixed feelings about his record of accomplishments and what he should do in the future. According to the latest Gallup Poll, Americans are generally pleased with Clinton's performance in office but critical of the president's personal behavior. This is a conflicted view of Clinton that emerged during the Monica Lewinsky scandal and ensuing im-peachment trial, and that has remained with the public ever since. The poll shows that 65% cur-rently approve of the way he is handling his job as president, which is slightly above the average he has received over the past three months. In fact, Clinton's average approval for his last quar-ter in office is almost 61%, the highest final quar-ter rating any president has received in the past half century. On the other hand, just 41% approve of Clinton "as a person," and only 39% consider him "honest and trustworthy."

The public appears equally conflicted in its expectations of Clinton's place in history. By a substantial margin (68% to 28%), Americans ex-pect Clinton to be remembered more for his in-volvement in personal scandal than for his accomplishments. But at the same time, they ex-pect by a two-to-one margin (47% to 22%) that Clinton will go down in history as an above aver-age or outstanding president rather than a below average or poor one. Another 30% expect history to view him as average.

The poll also shows a public that is about evenly divided over Clinton's political future. By a 6-point margin (51% to 45%), respondents are glad he is leaving office. However, by a 12-point margin (55% to 43%), they also say Clinton should remain active in public life rather than get out completely.

Despite the public's generally sour view of Clinton's personal behavior and involvement in the Lewinsky scandal, most people do not want Clinton to be charged with a crime once he leaves office. About two-thirds (67%) say he should not be charged while 30% say he should. The public has consistently opposed charging Clinton with a crime since the question was first asked in February 1999, but the current margin of opposition is the largest found by Gallup in the five times it has been asked. If a grand jury does indict Clinton after he leaves office, 52% say President George W. Bush should pardon Clinton while 42% disagree.

Clinton began his first term of office with the highest job disapproval rating of any president in the past six decades, when a few days after he took office, a Gallup Poll showed 58% of Americans approved, but 20% disapproved of his performance. The 58% approval actually compared favorably with the first approval ratings received by Presidents Ronald Reagan and George Bush, each of whom received a 51% rating. The lowest initial job disapproval rating apart from Clinton's was recorded for Reagan at 13%, while all other presidents measured had an initial disapproval rating of 8% or lower.

President Clinton's highest ratings came during the Lewinsky scandal which coincided with the first strong evidence that the federal budget would actually produce a surplus. Still, the only time that Clinton received a rating above 70% was immediately after the House of Representatives impeached him and sent the charges to the Senate for trial. After Senate acquittal, Clinton's ratings remained in the high 60s for a couple of months, then fell back into a narrow range of high 50s to low 60s for the rest of his second term.

Clinton's average approval for his entire presidency is just over 55%, virtually identical to that of Lyndon Johnson. John F. Kennedy (70%), Dwight Eisenhower (65%) and George Bush (61%) all had higher averages, while Ronald Reagan

(53%), Richard Nixon (49%), Gerald Ford (47%), Jimmy Carter (46%) and Harry Truman (45%) ended their presidencies with lower averages.

JANUARY 16
PRESIDENTIAL ELECTION
CONTROVERSY

Interview Dates: 1/10–14/01
Gallup Poll News Service
Survey #GO 132067

Do you approve or disapprove of the way the Supreme Court is handling its job?

	Approve	Disapprove	No opinion
2001 Jan 10–14	59%	34%	7%
2000 Aug 29–Sep 5	62	29	9
Republicans			
2001 Jan 10–14	80	15	5
2000 Aug 29–Sep 5	60	35	5
Independents			
2001 Jan 10–14	54	38	8
2000 Aug 29–Sep 5	57	34	9
Democrats			
2001 Jan 10–14	42	50	8
2000 Aug 29–Sep 5	70	18	12

Do you approve or disapprove of the way Congress is handling its job?

	Approve	Disapprove	No opinion
2001 Jan 10–14	50%	40%	10%
2000 Dec 2–4	56	34	10
2000 Oct 6–9	49	42	9
2000 Aug 29–Sep 5	48	42	10
2000 May 18–21	39	52	9
2000 Jan 7–10	51	42	7

Analysis: A majority of Americans (59%) currently approve of the way the Supreme Court is handling its job, but the public is sharply divided along party lines when evaluating the nation's highest court, a pattern markedly different from several months ago. Although the 59% approval rating is down only 3 points from August when

62% approved, the composition of those approving has changed significantly, suggesting that the Supreme Court's role in ending the controversial Florida recount may have had a major impact on the public's attitudes toward the Court. According to a new Gallup Poll conducted January 10–14, Republicans now overwhelmingly approve of the job the Supreme Court is doing (80%) compared to just 42% of Democrats. In the August poll, a majority of both Republicans and Democrats approved, with Democrats being slightly more positive. At that time, 60% of Republicans and 70% of Democrats approved of the way the Court was handling its job. Judicial involvement in the presidential election apparently has had less of an impact on independents, 54% of whom approve of the Court today, little changed from the 57% who approved in August.

Gallup has recorded Bill Clinton's approval rating 253 times since he took office eight years ago. According to the latest poll—representing the last time Gallup will take this measure on Clinton while he is in office—66% approve of the way Bill Clinton is handling his job as president and 29% disapprove. As is now the case for the Supreme Court, this presidential evaluation is highly partisan (as it has been throughout Clinton's presidency); 93% of Democrats approve of Clinton and just 39% of Republicans approve. Fifty-five percent of Republicans disapprove compared to 48% of Democrats.

Fifty percent currently approve of the way Congress is handling its job, while 40% disapprove and 10% have no opinion. Congress has suffered a very slight setback in the public's eye over the past six weeks: in early December, 56% approved of Congress. Approval of the legislative branch of government is less partisan than that of the executive and judicial branches. Fifty-five percent of Republicans approve of the job Congress is doing, compared to 48% of Democrats. Thirty-seven percent of Republicans disapprove, as do 41% of Democrats.

JANUARY 17
ECONOMIC CONDITIONS/
PERSONAL FINANCES

Interview Dates: 1/10–14/01
Gallup Poll News Service
Survey #GO 132067

How would you rate economic conditions in this country today—excellent, good, only fair, or poor?

	Excellent; good	Only fair; poor	No opinion
2001 Jan 10–14	67%	33%	*
2000 Dec 2–4	63	36	1
2000 Nov 13–15	72	28	*
2000 Oct 6–9	71	28	1
2000 Aug 18–19	74	25	1
2000 Jul 25–26	74	25	1
2000 May 18–21	66	33	1
2000 Apr 3–9	60	39	1
2000 Jan 7–10	71	28	1

* Less than 1%

Right now, do you think that economic conditions in the country as a whole are getting better or getting worse?

	Getting better	Getting worse	Same (vol.); no opinion
2001 Jan 10–14	32%	56%	12%
2000 Dec 2–4	39	48	13
2000 Nov 13–15	50	38	12
2000 Oct 6–9	54	34	12
2000 Aug 18–19	60	26	14
2000 Jul 25–26	58	29	13
2000 May 18–21	52	37	11
2000 Jan 7–10	69	23	8

Next, we are interested in how people's financial situation may have changed. Would you say that you are financially better off now than you were a year ago, or are you financially worse off now?

	Better off	Worse off	Same (vol.); no opinion
2001 Jan 10–14	49%	30%	21%
2000 Oct 6–9	55	22	23
2000 May 18–21	53	26	21

Looking ahead, do you expect that at this time next year you will be financially better off than now, or worse off than now?

	Better off	Worse off	Same (vol.); no opinion
2001 Jan 10–14 . . . . . .63%	21%	16%
2000 Oct 6–9 68	11	21
2000 May 18–21 67	13	20

Are you worried or not worried that you or your spouse may lose your job in the next twelve months?

Worried 19%
Not worried 65
Doesn't apply; not employed (vol.);
no opinion 16

Are you worried or not worried about the rate of inflation and rising prices today?

Worried 70%
Not worried 29
No opinion 1

If you had a thousand dollars to spend, do you think investing it in the stock market would be a good idea or a bad idea?

	Good idea	Bad idea	No opinion
2001 Jan 10–14 . . . . . .42%	53%	5%
2000 Dec 2–4 46	49	5
2000 Oct 13–14 57	36	7
2000 Jan 7–10 67	28	5
1999 Oct 21–24 51	44	5
1999 Sep 10–14 60	33	7
1999 June 4–5 60	34	6
1999 Mar 12–14 59	35	6
1998 Sep 1 46	48	6
1998 Apr 17–19 65	28	7
1997 Oct 30 46	47	7
1997 Oct 27 53	43	4
1997 Jul 25–27 62	33	5
1994 Mar 9–10 38	46	16
1990 Feb 26	68	60

Thinking ahead to a year from now, do you think the stock market will be much higher, somewhat higher, about the same, somewhat lower, or much lower than it is today?

Much higher 5%
Somewhat higher 29
About the same 34
Somewhat lower 19
Much lower 6
No opinion 7

Analysis: As President Bill Clinton prepares to leave office, a Gallup Poll shows that Americans rate the current economy very highly, but at the same time, believe that economic conditions are getting worse rather than better. In addition, most people are worried about rising prices, and among those who are employed, almost one-fourth are concerned that either they or their spouse will lose their job in the next year. Also, for the first time in more than seven years, a majority say that it is a bad idea to invest in the stock market. Nevertheless, Americans remain generally upbeat about their own financial situation, with most expecting to be better off next year than they are now.

The poll conducted January 10–14 finds that 67% of Americans rate the economy as excellent or good, 27% as fair, and just 6% as poor. These figures are comparable to the beginning-of-the-year ratings found by Gallup for the previous three years but significantly higher than the ratings in 1997, shortly after Clinton was reelected. When Clinton first won election over George Bush in 1992, almost four times as many Americans rated the economy poor as rated it excellent or good.

Despite these high ratings of current economic conditions, Americans express a rather pessimistic view of where the economy is headed. A clear majority (56%) believe that the economy is getting worse while just 32% say it is getting better. This is the most negative projection of the economy that the public has rendered in the past four years. At the beginning of 1996, more Americans said the economy was getting worse (49%) than better (39%), but by the end of the year—before the election—sentiment had turned in the opposite direction. By a small margin in 1997, but by margins of two-to-one or better for the following three years, Americans described the economy as getting better rather than worse.

This same pattern is found in the data on whether people think it is a good or bad idea to invest in the stock market. The current results show that a majority (53%) say that if they had $1,000 to spend, it would be a bad idea to invest in the stock market, while 42% say it would be a good idea. This is the worst margin against investing in the stock market since before 1997.

While Americans tend to be generally pessimistic about the future of the economy, they are more positive about their own financial situation. By 49% to 30%, they say they are better off today financially than they were a year ago, and by 63% to 21%, they expect to be better off next year than they are today. Still, there are some warning signs. Both of these personal financial measures, although positive, are the lowest in the past several years. And among people who are employed, about one-quarter (26%) say they are worried that either they or their spouse might lose their job in the coming year, and 70% are worried about inflation and rising prices.

JANUARY 18
JOHN ASHCROFT

Interview Dates: 1/15–16/01
CNN/*USA Today*/Gallup Poll
Survey #GO 132685

We'd like to get your overall opinion about one of the people in the news. Please say if you have a favorable or unfavorable opinion of this person, or if you have never heard of him:

Attorney General nominee John Ashcroft?

Favorable 34%
Unfavorable 28
Never heard of 17
No opinion 21

Turning to the Cabinet, based on what you have read or heard, do you think the Senate should or should not confirm former Missouri Senator John Ashcroft as Attorney General, or don't you know enough to say?

Should 26%
Should not 21
Don't know enough 53

As you may know, the Senate is holding hearings on Ashcroft's nomination this week during which several issues will be discussed. If you were convinced that each of the following was true, would that make you more likely to support Ashcroft for Attorney General, less likely, or would it have no effect:

Ashcroft opposed the appointment of a judge to the federal court because of his race?

More likely 11%
Less likely 69
No effect; no opinion 20

Ashcroft opposed affirmative action?

More likely 22%
Less likely 43
No effect; no opinion 35

Ashcroft opposed abortion?

More likely 30%
Less likely 41
No effect; no opinion 29

Ashcroft had voted against several gay rights bills?

More likely 26%
Less likely 41
No effect; no opinion 33

Ashcroft opposed the appointment of a judge to the federal court because of his record on sentencing criminals?

More likely 29%
Less likely 34
No effect; no opinion 37

Suppose the president nominated someone to his Cabinet who significantly disagreed with many senators on important issues but had not done anything unethical. Would it be justified or unjustified for a senator to oppose a nominee only because of policy disagreements?

Justified 26%
Unjustified 70
No opinion 4

Analysis: As the Senate continues to hold confirmation hearings this week on President-elect George W. Bush's Cabinet appointments, one nominee in particular has been caught in a web of controversy: John Ashcroft, Bush's choice for attorney general. He has come under intense scrutiny from Democrats and liberal interest groups because of his conservative positions on abortion, affirmative action, and gay rights. Although Ashcroft is the center of attention this week inside the Washington Beltway, he has not yet become a well-known figure to the general public. According to a Gallup Poll conducted January 15–16, 38% cannot offer an opinion on Ashcroft, either because they have never heard of him (17%) or because they simply have no opinion even though they have heard of him (21%). Among those who do have an opinion of Ashcroft, attitudes tilt toward the positive. Thirty-four percent rate the former Missouri Senator favorably and 28% have an unfavorable opinion of him. Among Republicans, 61% have a favorable opinion and just 9% have an unfavorable one. Not surprisingly, Democrats are much more negative; only 13% have a favorable opinion of Ashcroft while 48% have an unfavorable one.

When Gallup asks Americans about whether Ashcroft ought to be confirmed as attorney general, a majority (53%) say they do not know enough about the former Missouri Senator to have an opinion. Among the remaining, opinion is closely split with 26% supporting his confirmation and 21% opposed. Ashcroft is a long-time member of the conservative wing of the Republican Party. However, half of the self-identified conservatives polled are unsure whether or not he ought to be

confirmed. Still, they are more supportive than liberals as 42% percent back his nomination compared to just 6% of liberals. Only 8% oppose his nomination compared to 43% of liberals.

Forty-one percent of Americans say they would be less likely to support Ashcroft if they are convinced he opposed abortion, 30% would be more likely to support him, and 27% say it would have no effect either way. Forty-three percent of Americans would be less likely to support him if they are convinced he opposed affirmative action, 22% would be more likely to support him, and 29% say it would not matter to them either way. Forty-one percent of the public would be less likely to support him if they were sure he opposed several gay rights bills, 26% would be more likely to support him, and 30% say it would have no effect either way.

Although these conservative issue positions obviously get more support from Republicans than Democrats, a notable number of Republicans say they would be less likely to support Ashcroft if they were sure he took these issue stances: 25% of Republicans would be less likely to support him if they were sure he opposed abortion, 30% would be less likely to support him if they were sure he opposed affirmative action, and 23% if they were sure he voted against gay rights legislation.

Despite the fact that many Americans would not support Ashcroft if they were sure he took these conservative positions, 70% does not think policy disagreements alone are a justifiable reason for the Senate to oppose Ashcroft's nomination. Only 26% do think such opposition would be justified.

In addition to the conservative issue positions generating such a political firestorm, some civil rights groups have claimed that Ashcroft blocked the appointment of a federal judge because he was an African American. Ashcroft and his supporters vigorously deny that assertion, claiming that he opposed judge Ronnie White because he had a "soft" record on sentencing criminals. If the public was convinced that Ashcroft opposed White on the basis of his race, it could have significant political consequences: 69% would be less likely to support him. On the other hand, if the public was persuaded that Ashcroft's opposition stemmed from the nominee's sentencing record, only 34% would be less likely to support him, 29% would be more likely, and 30% say it would not effect them either way.

JANUARY 19
PRESIDENT CLINTON/
INDEPENDENT COUNSEL AGREEMENT

Interview Dates: 1/5–7/01
CNN/*USA Today*/Gallup Poll
Survey #GO 132545

Analysis: The agreement reached between President Bill Clinton and Independent Counsel Robert Ray is generally consistent with the American public's beliefs and preferences. This agreement will allow Clinton to avoid possible indictment for his involvement in the Monica Lewinsky affair in return for his admission of making misleading statements, paying a $25,000 fine, and accepting a five-year suspension of his law license. Here is a review of public opinion relating to each of the major components of the agreement.

  • *Clinton "acknowledged a violation of one of the Arkansas-model rules of professional conduct because of testimony in my Paula Jones case deposition" and stated that "I acknowledge having knowingly violated Judge Wright's discovery orders in my deposition in that case;" "I now recognize that . . . certain of my responses to questions about Ms. Lewinsky were false."* This comes as no great shock to the public. As the Lewinsky scandal unfolded throughout 1998 and 1999, a majority consistently indicated in polling that they believed Clinton had sexual relations with Lewinsky despite his statements, and that he had not only "misled" the grand jury and the public, but also actually committed perjury. In 1998 and 1999, Clinton's honesty and trustworthiness ratings fell below the majority level, and in three separate polls conducted since May 1998, including one just completed, over

half of respondents said that Clinton was not honest and trustworthy.
  • *Clinton accepted a five-year suspension of his law license.* Disbarment in Arkansas is seemingly an appropriate action according to the public. Polls conducted in 1999 and 2000 indicated a majority were in favor of this penalty.
  • *Perhaps the most important component of the deal is the Independent Counsel's agreement to drop efforts to have Clinton indicted by a grand jury once he leaves office.* This, too, is in accord with what Americans would like to see done. Asked about a possible indictment of Clinton, a majority in five separate polls consistently said that he should not be charged in a court of law with a crime "for these matters."

It is difficult to tell at this time what impact the agreement will have, if any, on history's ultimate verdict on the Clinton presidency, but polling has consistently shown that the American public strongly believes that it is his involvement in scandals, not his accomplishments, for which Bill Clinton will be remembered.

JANUARY 19
INAUGURATION PROTESTS

Interview Dates: 1/15–16/01
CNN/*USA Today*/Gallup Poll
Survey #GO 132685

Do you see this week's inauguration more as a celebration by all Americans of democracy in action, or a political celebration by the supporters of the candidate who won the presidential election?

Celebration by all Americans 26%
Celebration by supporters 72
No opinion 2

What are your expectations for George W. Bush's inauguration speech—do you think his speech will be excellent, good, just okay, poor, or terrible?

Excellent 16%
Good 45
Just okay 30
Poor 4
Terrible 3
No opinion 2

Regardless of whether you think people have a right to protest during the presidential inaugural ceremonies, do you think it is appropriate or inappropriate for them to do so?

Appropriate 28%
Inappropriate 71
No opinion 1

Analysis: The inauguration of George W. Bush as the forty-third president of the United States may prove to be one of the most widely protested in American history. Citizens upset by the election outcome in Florida, civil rights groups, and anti-death penalty organizations are just some of the groups expected to be part of the crowd of protesters estimated to be anywhere from 25,000 to 100,000 strong. Some experts predict that by the time the event is over, it will have drawn a larger crowd of protesters than has any other inauguration except Richard Nixon's second swearing-in in 1973.

According to a Gallup Poll, most Americans think that protests at the inauguration, while legal, are inappropriate. Democrats are more likely than Republicans to see the protests as appropriate by a 35%-to-16% margin. Almost half of the nonwhite population (48%) thinks the protests are appropriate compared to 25% of whites. Also, younger people are more likely to see the protests as appropriate: 37% of 18- to 29-year-olds feel this way, compared to 29% of 30- to 49-year-olds and 24% of those age 50 and over.

More generally, the American public sees the inauguration ceremonies as a celebration by George W. Bush's supporters rather than as a celebration by all Americans of democracy in action, by a margin of 72% to 26%. Forty percent of Republicans see the inauguration as a celebration for all Americans compared to only 13% of Democrats.

The majority of Americans think that newly sworn-in President Bush will give either a "good" (45%) or "excellent" (16%) inaugural address. Another 30% expect a speech that will be "just okay." Very few (7%) expect either a "poor" or "terrible" speech. Not surprisingly, political affiliation affects expectations of Bush's performance. Thirty percent of Republicans expect to hear an excellent speech compared to 4% of Democrats. Just 2% of Republicans think the speech will be poor or terrible, while 14% of Democrats think it will be.

JANUARY 19
BUSH ADMINISTRATION TRANSITION

Interview Dates: 1/15–16/01
CNN/*USA Today*/Gallup Poll
Survey #GO 132685

Do you approve or disapprove of the way George W. Bush is handling his presidential transition?

	Approve	Disapprove	No opinion
2001 Jan 15–16	61%	25%	14%
2001 Jan 5–7	65	26	9

So far, based on what you have heard or read, do you approve or disapprove of President-elect Bush's Cabinet appointments?

Approve 59%
Disapprove 29
No opinion 12

Next, we'd like to get your overall opinion of one of the people in the news. Please say if you have a favorable or unfavorable opinion of this person, or if you have never heard of him:

George W. Bush?

	Favorable	Unfavorable	Never heard of; no opinion
2001 Jan 15–16	62%	36%	2%
2000 Dec 15–17	59	36	5

| 2000 Dec 2–4 | ......56 | 40 | 4 |
| 2000 Nov 13–15 | .....53 | 43 | 4 |

Which of the following comes closer to your view—George W. Bush will personally make the decisions in his administration that a president should make, or other people aside from George W. Bush will make the decisions in his administration that a president should make?

Bush will make decisions 45%
Other people will make decisions 52
No opinion 3

George W. Bush has frequently described himself as a "compassionate conservative." Do you think Bush will or will not govern in a way that is truly compassionate?

Will 58%
Will not 39
No opinion 3

Would you describe George W. Bush more as a uniter or a divider?

Uniter 58%
Divider 36
No opinion 6

Now, I'd like you to think about George W. Bush's ability to handle a number of things over the next four years. Please tell me whether you are very confident, somewhat confident, not too confident, or not at all confident that Bush can:

Set a good moral example?

Very confident 49%
Somewhat confident 32
Not too, not at all confident; no opinion 19

Use military force wisely?

Very confident 41%
Somewhat confident 37
Not too, not at all confident; no opinion 22

Prevent major scandals in his administration?

Very confident 39%
Somewhat confident 38
Not too, not at all confident; no opinion 23

Manage the Executive Branch effectively?

Very confident 33%
Somewhat confident 44
Not too, not at all confident; no opinion 23

Handle an international crisis?

Very confident 32%
Somewhat confident 39
Not too, not at all confident; no opinion 29

Fulfill the proper role of the United States in world affairs?

Very confident 31%
Somewhat confident 41
Not too, not at all confident; no opinion 28

Work effectively with Congress to get things done?

Very confident 27%
Somewhat confident 47
Not too, not at all confident; no opinion 26

Who do you, personally, consider to be the real winner of the presidential election— George W. Bush or Al Gore?*

Bush 57%
Gore 38
No opinion 5

*Based on part sample

Which comes closest to your view of the way George W. Bush won the election—he won fair and square, he won but only on a technicality, or he stole the election?*

Won fair and square 45%
Won on technicality 31

Stole the election 24
No opinion . . . .**

*Based on part sample
**Less than 1%

Analysis: This Saturday, the nation will inaugu-
rate George W. Bush as the forty-third president
of the United States. As he prepares to take the
oath of office, Bush is viewed positively by a majority of Americans, 62% of whom in the latest
Gallup Poll have a favorable opinion of the former Texas governor. Additionally, the public
generally approves of the way he has handled his
presidential transition (61%) and his Cabinet appointments (59%).

Once the inauguration festivities are over,
attention quickly will turn to how the new president will govern. The latest poll suggests that
Bush's promise of "compassionate conservatism"
is more than just campaign rhetoric. Additionally,
Americans expect that Bush will set a strong
moral example for the country. They are, however, less confident in Bush's ability to handle
foreign policy matters, and in how successful he
will be in working with Congress to get things
done. A slight majority are concerned that Bush
will allow other members of his administration to
make decisions that he, as president, should make
on his own.

Bush made the ideological philosophy of
compassionate conservatism a centerpiece of his
presidential campaign. This philosophy combines
typical conservative beliefs in individualism and
traditional moral values with a recognition that
government has a role to play in helping the less
fortunate in society. Many critics of Bush thought
that this slogan was largely campaign rhetoric,
but 58% believe that Bush will govern in a way
that is "truly compassionate" while 39% do not.
Perhaps not surprisingly, those who voted for
Bush in the 2000 election overwhelmingly believe that he will govern compassionately (91%)
while only about one-quarter (23%) of Al Gore's
supporters accept this view.

Another common theme of the Bush presidential campaign was his insistence that he was a
uniter who could bring people of various back-

grounds and political leanings together to accomplish common goals, as opposed to a "divider"
who would make no attempt at bringing people
together. When asked to choose which of the two
words better described Bush, 58% choose "uniter"
while 36% choose "divider." Again, there are
stark differences between Bush and Gore voters,
as 95% of Bush voters describe him as a uniter
while only 26% of Gore voters do so. Interestingly, even a majority (52%) who view the
country as more divided today than in recent
years, think of Bush as a uniter while 43% think
he is a divider. Among those who do not think the
country is more divided, 70% characterize Bush
as a uniter while only 24% term him a divider.

One of the criticisms of Bush is that he may
rely too much on others to make decisions rather
than making the decisions himself. Bush's harsh-
est critics suggest that he may be less authorita-
tive than most presidents, allowing Vice
President Dick Cheney to make many of the decisions of consequence (Bush himself has admitted
that he will rely heavily on his staff and advisors
to help with his decision-making.) The public
tilts toward the view that Bush may go too far in delegating decision-making as 52% say that other
people in the administration will make "decisions
a president should make" while 45% believe
Bush himself will be responsible for them. There
are predictable partisan differences on this matter
as a strong majority of Republicans think Bush
will make the decisions himself (72% compared
to 26% who believe others will make the decisions), and while Democrats believe others (73%)
instead of Bush (24%) will make the decisions.
Independents tend to believe that others will
make the important decisions in the Bush administration (56%) instead of the president (41%).

Few would doubt that Bush faces a tough
political environment as he enters office, having
won a close and very controversial election. In
the latest poll, 31% think Bush "won on a technicality" and 24% that he "stole the election."
Forty-five percent say he "won fair and square"
while 38% still consider Gore to be the "real winner of the election."

A near majority of respondents in a recent
poll (49%) are very confident that Bush can set a

good moral example as president. Similarly, substantial numbers expect that Bush can prevent major scandals in his administration. Americans also are largely optimistic that Bush will be able to use military force wisely.

At the other end of the spectrum, Americans are least confident in Bush's ability to work with Congress to get things done which is perhaps understandable, given the extremely close partisan divisions in both the House and Senate. The public also is somewhat less confident in Bush's abilities in the international arena, as just 31% are very confident that he can "fulfill the proper role of the United States in world affairs" and only 32% are very confident that he can "handle an international crisis."

JANUARY 23
BUSH ADMINISTRATION

Interview Dates: 1/15–16/01
CNN/*USA Today*/Gallup Poll
Survey #GO 132685

I have some questions about the Bush administration that will take office later this month. Regardless of which presidential candidate you preferred, do you think the Bush administration will or will not be able to do each of the following?

	Will	Will not*
Provide military security for the country	81%	16%
Improve education	66	32
Keep America prosperous	63	33
Increase respect for presidency	61	36
Improve respect for United States abroad	58	38
Improve moral values	55	41
Ensure long-term strength of Social Security	50	44
Keep federal budget balanced	50	46
Ensure long-term strength of Medicare	49	44
Cut federal income taxes	49	46
Improve health care system	46	49
Improve conditions for minorities and the poor	44	51
Reduce crime rate	44	50
Improve race relations	44	51
Improve quality of the environment	42	52
Heal political divisions	41	53

*"No opinion" is omitted.

Analysis: President George W. Bush begins his first week in office with relatively strong support for the direction of his policies. The public is fairly optimistic that Bush will be able to improve education and keep the country prosperous, but less convinced that he will be able to fix Social Security or improve health care.

Despite the neck-and-neck nature of the contentious presidential contest this past year, a clear majority believes that President Bush's policies will move the country in the right direction rather than the wrong direction by a 56%-to-36% margin. Additionally, Bush himself has a healthy 62% favorable rating, and a majority of Americans interviewed before his inauguration on Saturday approved of his Cabinet appointments and of the way he was handling the transition.

Nonetheless, expectations for the next four years are somewhat muted compared to eight years ago when Bill Clinton took office. Only 46% today believe the country will be better off four years from now while almost as many (42%) believe the country will be worse off. By contrast, in November 1992, 51% were optimistic that the country would be better off in four years while just 31% thought things would be worse.

These figures no doubt reflect the different economic environments in which the two presidents took office. Clinton won the presidency at a time when Americans believed the United States was in an economic recession, so perhaps it was less of a leap of faith to forecast that the country would be getting better four years hence, particularly with Bill "It's the economy, stupid" Clinton taking the helm. Bush is taking office after two years of record-high public evaluations of the economy (leaving relatively little room for improvement) and at the beginning of what appears to be growing public concern about the nation's economic outlook. Low expectations, of course, may not be bad for the Bush administration. Bush himself, in the weeks prior to his inauguration, repeatedly said that he was worried about the direction of the economy, perhaps helping to create the type of diminished economic expectations picked up in the new poll.

JANUARY 24
INCOME TAX CUTS

Interview Dates: 1/15–16/01
CNN/*USA Today*/Gallup Poll
Survey #GO 132685

Based on what you have read or heard, do you favor or oppose the federal income tax cuts that George W. Bush has proposed?

Favor 52%
Oppose 33
No opinion 15

Do you think that Bush will or will not be able to pass the federal income tax cuts that he has proposed?

Will 38%
Will not 50
No opinion 12

Analysis: At first glance, it appears that Americans are overwhelmingly in favor of tax cuts; 74% favor "a cut in federal income taxes," according to a Gallup Poll conducted in September of last year. For the past twenty-five years, in fact, over 70% have favored a generic tax cut. The highest level of support came in 1994 when 80% favored it. At the same time, when Americans are presented with the tough choice of tax cuts versus spending cuts, they become more ambivalent. When the maintenance of such high-profile programs as Social Security and Medicare are presented as alternatives to tax cuts, support for cuts drops significantly. Additionally, there are mixed opinions on the choice of targeted versus across-the-board tax cuts, and recent surveys confirm that tax cuts are not a high priority for Americans in 2001.

There is no question that the issue of tax cuts will be important this year. One of the central issues in last year's presidential campaign was a debate between George W. Bush and Al Gore about what should be done with the federal budget surplus. Bush's campaign touted a $1.3 trillion tax cut that would reduce the tax rate of all taxpayers, regardless of their income. Gore proposed a battery of smaller, more targeted cuts that would benefit individuals and families with specific needs, such as college tuition and child care expenses. Both candidates claimed they would use much of the surplus to strengthen Social Security. The scope and specifics of tax cuts were a salient campaign issue, and will be a challenge for the Bush administration because the public has an appetite for federal tax cuts but still supports specific spending measures.

Congress began debating Bush's $1.3 trillion tax cut this week. Phil Gramm (R-Texas) and Zell Miller (D-Georgia) introduced an across-the-board tax cut to the Senate on Monday. The House Republican leadership plans to follow course in the next few days. Although the public has not been asked specifically about the Gramm/Zeller bill, a Gallup Poll conducted January 5–7 showed that over one-half (52%) favor Bush's tax plan based on what they have read or heard. However, the public is generally pessimistic about the new administration's ability to actually pass the tax cut. Only 38% think Bush will be able to pass such legislation, 50% do not, and 12% have no opinion on the matter.

JANUARY 25
SOCIAL SECURITY

Interview Dates: 1/5-7/01
CNN/*USA Today*/Gallup Poll
Survey #GO 132545

George W. Bush has made a proposal that would allow people to put a portion of their Social Security payroll taxes into personal retirement accounts that would be invested in private stocks or bonds. Do you favor or oppose this proposal?

	Favor	Oppose*
2001 Jan 5-7	.60%	36%
2000 Jun 6-7	.59	31
By Age		
18 to 29 Years	.78	19
30 to 49 Years	.65	32
50 to 64 Years	.59	40
65 Years and Over	.34	56
By Income		
$75,000 and Over	.72	26
$50,000 and Over	.68	31
$30,000 to $50,000	.62	34
$20,000 to $30,000	.52	44

*"No opinion" is omitted.

Do you think Bush will or will not be able to make the changes to Social Security that he has proposed?

Will	.40%
Will not	.51
No opinion	.9

Analysis: Social Security emerged as a key issue in the 2000 presidential campaign and remains a significant concern for the majority of the public. According to a Gallup Poll conducted January 5–7, nearly nine in ten Americans (89%) believe that the long-term solvency of the Social Security system should be a top or high priority for the Bush administration to address, placing it third behind improving education with 94% and keeping America prosperous with 91%.

A majority (60%) support President Bush's proposal for securing the strength of the Social Security system, which would allow Americans to put a portion of their Social Security payroll taxes into personal retirement accounts that would be invested in stocks or bonds. Thirty-six percent oppose it while 4% have no opinion.

Public support for Bush's proposal is split based on several demographic characteristics. Younger people embrace Bush's proposal more enthusiastically than do older Americans, with 78% of those 18 to 29 years old supporting the plan compared to 34% of those 65 years and older.

Americans with higher income levels are more likely to support Bush's Social Security proposal. While a majority favor Bush's proposed changes to Social Security, less than one-half (40%) believes the administration will be able to put the proposal into practice. This may reflect the fact that politicians have always been nervous about making significant changes to the Social Security system. Additionally, President Bush is facing a sharply divided Congress that may not agree that his plan will work.

Younger people express more confidence than older Americans in Bush's ability to make his proposed changes to Social Security. Nearly three in five age 18 to 29 think he will be able to make the changes (57%) compared to only 24% of those 65 years and over. More than one-half of Republicans (54%) believe that Bush will make the changes, compared to 34% of independents and 32% of Democrats. More than twice as many Bush supporters believe he can make the changes compared to those who do not support Bush: 54% versus 25%.

JANUARY 26
SUPER BOWL

Interview Dates: 1/15–16/01
CNN/*USA Today*/Gallup Poll
Survey #GO 132685

In general, do you describe yourself as a sports fan, or not?

Yes, fan	.58%
No	.42

Which of the following major national sporting events would you most like to get a ticket to—pro football's Super Bowl, baseball's World Series, hockey's Stanley Cup finals, college basketball's men's finals, pro basketball's NBA finals, or the college football bowl game that determines the national champion?

	National adults	Fans only
Pro football's Super Bowl	.34%	40%
Baseball's World Series	.20	18
College basketball's men's finals	.11	13

Pro basketball's NBA finals 11   10
College football bowl
  game that determines the
  national champion 10   11
Hockey's Stanley Cup finals 7   7
No opinion 7   1

Which team would you like to see win this year's Super Bowl game—the Baltimore Ravens or the New York Giants?

	National adults	Pro football fans
Baltimore Ravens	.32%	37%
New York Giants	.48	52
No preference (vol.); not fan; no opinion	20	11

Regardless of whom you favor, which team do you think will win—the Baltimore Ravens or the New York Giants?

	National adults	Pro football fans
Baltimore Ravens	.26%	35%
New York Giants	.55	57
No preference; not fan; no opinion	19	8

Are you a fan of professional football, or not?

	Yes, fan	Somewhat of a fan (vol.)	No; no opinion
2001 Jan 15–16	.44%	14%	42%
2000 Aug 24–27	.42	12	46
1999 Mar 5–7	.47	9	44
1999 Jan 22–24	.51	10	39
1998 Jan 16–18	.45	11	44

Analysis: The latest Gallup Poll asked fans to choose among six major sporting events, and 40% said they would most like tickets to the Super Bowl. Baseball's World Series followed with 18% of fans choosing this event. Four other events—the men's college basketball finals, college football's national championship game, professional basketball's NBA finals, and hockey's

Stanley Cup finals—were chosen by 13% or fewer of sports fans interviewed.

The New York Giants will apparently have more fans pulling for them on Super Bowl Sunday than will the Baltimore Ravens. Fifty-two percent of pro football fans say they would like to see the Giants win the game compared to 37% who say they would like to see the Ravens win. Nine percent of fans express no preference for a team.

The January 15–16 Gallup Poll also asked pro football fans who they thought would win, regardless of which team they favor. Here, the Giants do even better. Fifty-seven percent of football fans think the Giants will win compared to 35% who predict a Ravens victory. The public (football fans or not) also picks the Giants over the Ravens, 55% to 26%. The public's track record for selecting the eventual winner is a fairly sound one. In the five previous years that Gallup has asked this question, the public has predicted the winner four times. The lone exception was the Denver Broncos' upset win over the Green Bay Packers in 1998.

JANUARY 29
MOOD OF AMERICA

Interview Dates: 1/10–14/01
Gallup Poll News Service
Survey #GO 132067

In general, are you satisfied or dissatisfied with the way things are going in the United States at this time?

	Satisfied	Dis-satisfied	No opinion
2001 Jan 10–14	.56%	41%	3%
2000 Dec 2–4	.51	46	3
2000 Nov 13–15	.58	41	1
2000 Oct 6–9	.62	36	2
2000 Aug 29–Sep 5 ...	.59	38	3
2000 Aug 18–19	.63	33	4
2000 Jul 14–16	.61	35	4
2000 Jun 22–25	.56	39	5
2000 May 18–21	.55	42	3
2000 Apr 3–9	.59	37	4
2000 Feb 25–27	.65	32	3
2000 Jan 7–10	.69	28	3

In general, are you satisfied or dissatisfied with the way things are going in your state at this time?

Satisfied 65%
Dissatisfied 33
No opinion 2

All in all, are you satisfied or dissatisfied with the way things are going in your local community?

Satisfied 76%
Dissatisfied 22
No opinion 2

Analysis: A Gallup Poll conducted January 10–14, just prior to the inauguration of George W. Bush, finds a majority of Americans still satisfied with the way things are going in the country. Fifty-six percent are satisfied with the way things are going in the United States overall while 41% are dissatisfied. Americans appear even more upbeat about public affairs when they reflect on matters closer to home. Nearly two-thirds (65%) are currently satisfied with the way things are going in the state in which they reside and three-quarters (76%) are satisfied with their local community.

The generally positive evaluations about the country, overall, can be placed in both historical and economic contexts. First, the public's satisfaction with the way things are going in the country is down compared to the twin peaks of 63% recorded in January 1998 and 71% in January 1999. However, both of these spikes were temporary; using this measure, the average satisfaction with the country since 1998 has been only 59% or 60%, not dissimilar to the 56% recorded today. The current satisfaction level is much higher than it was during most of the past two decades, so these remain very good times by comparison.

However, Americans currently express their newfound concern over the economy. While two-thirds currently believe the economy is in "excellent" or "good" shape, a majority believes the U.S. economy is getting worse rather than better for the first time since 1992. So far, this pessimism has resulted in no discernable impact on

Americans' evaluation of current economic conditions, with most believing the economy is in excellent or good shape, and two-thirds feel positively about it today, similar to the 71% recorded a year ago.

FEBRUARY 1
MARITAL STATUS

Interview Dates: 1/10–14/01
Gallup Poll News Service
Survey #GO 132067

Which of the following best describes your marital status—currently married, living together with a partner, widowed, divorced, separated, or never married?

Married 51%
Living with partner .7
Widowed 8
Divorced 11
Separated 3
Never married 20

Analysis: A January Gallup Poll offers a snapshot into the marital status of Americans today. Just about one-half of the U.S. adult population is currently married: about 20% have never been married; and the rest are either living with a partner, divorced, separated, or widowed. As Americans age, marriage becomes more and more the norm; only a very small number of older people say they have never been married. Over one-third of those living in low-income households are separated or divorced, a much higher percentage than is the case in high-income households.

Currently, 51% of the adult population—age 18 and over—say they are married, and another 7% indicate they are living together with a partner. On the flip side, 14% are either separated or divorced. Finally, 8% of Americans are widowed and another 18% claim to have never been married.

Not surprisingly, the majority of those who have never been married fall into the age 18 to 29 range. Fifty-four percent of that group say they have never been "down the aisle," a percentage that drops to 13% for age 30 to 49 and just 4% for those age 50 and over.

FEBRUARY 1
ENERGY POLICIES

Interview Dates: 1/10–14/01
Gallup Poll News Service
Survey #GO 132067

We'd like to know how you feel about the state of the nation's energy policies—are you very satisfied, somewhat satisfied, somewhat dissatisfied, or very dissatisfied?

Very satisfied 5%
Somewhat satisfied 27
Somewhat dissatisfied 28
Very dissatisfied 21
No opinion 19

Next, how important is it to you that the president and Congress deal with energy policies in the next year—is it extremely important, very important, moderately important, or not that important?

Extremely important 26%
Very important 43
Moderately important 25
Not that important 2
No opinion 4

With which one of these statements about the environment and the economy do you most agree—protection of the environment should be given priority, even at the risk of curbing economic growth; or economic growth should be given priority, even if the environment suffers to some extent?

	Protect environment	Economic growth*
2000 Apr 3–9	.67%	28%
2000 Jan 13–16	.70	23
1999 Apr 13–14	.67	28
1999 Mar 12–14	.65	30
1998 Apr 17–19	.68	24
1997 Jul 25–27	.66	27
1995 Apr 17–19	.62	32
1992 Jan 5–Mar 31	.58	26
1991 Apr	.71	20
1990 Apr	.71	19
1984 Sep	.61	28

*"Equal priority (vol.)" and "no opinion" are omitted.

Analysis: A January Gallup Poll focusing on the state of the nation finds nearly one-half of respondents holding a dim view of the government's energy policies. Only 32% are satisfied with these policies while 49% are dissatisfied, putting energy in the bottom half of twenty public policy issues rated in the January 10–14 poll. These results make George W. Bush's recent formation of a Cabinet-level task force to review the nation's energy problems look like good politics.

At the same time—despite high fuel prices and a serious energy crisis confronting the state of California—the poll finds that energy is only moderately important relative to other issues. Education, the economy, health care, crime, and taxes all outrank energy as issues Americans would like to see the president and Congress address this year. This relative lack of priority given to energy concerns also is evident from Gallup's open-ended measurement of the "most important problem" facing the country today. Only 6% cite the lack of energy sources or the price of fuel oil as the nation's most pressing problem. While this is slightly higher than the percentage who mentioned these problems one year ago (4%), it is still lower than the number who today are most concerned about declining moral values (13%), education (12%), and crime (9%).

The detailed satisfaction ratings in the new poll show that only 5% are "very satisfied" with energy policies and another 27% are "somewhat satisfied," while 28% are "somewhat dissatisfied" and 21% are "very dissatisfied." Energy ranks fourteen out of the twenty issues tested by Gallup, based on the ratio of the total percentage who are satisfied compared to the percentage who are dissatisfied. On this basis, reaction to the energy situation is at about the same level as gun policies, the Social Security and Medicare systems, the quality of public education, and the level of immigration. Americans express general dissatisfaction with the state of affairs in all of these areas. By comparison, the level of dissatisfaction is even greater when it comes to health care, campaign finance laws, and taxes. Respondents are most satisfied with the state of the economy, the status of women, the nation's military preparedness, and the role America plays in world affairs.

Bush's campaign pledge to support new oil exploration in Alaska's Arctic National Wildlife Refuge and his nomination of an interior secretary with a record of supporting such policies has set off criticism from environmental activists concerned about the protection of public lands. The struggle to balance these competing interests will not only continue to be an important one for policy makers but also for the public.

Previous Gallup surveys suggest that when economic and environmental concerns conflict, the public is most likely to tilt toward the environment. For example, a Gallup question asked a number of times since 1984 finds the public consistently inclined to say environmental protection should take priority over economic growth, most recently by a 67%-to-28% margin. Whether that sentiment holds up against future hikes at the gas pump or rolling power blackouts remains to be seen.

FEBRUARY 2
MOOD OF AMERICA

Interview Dates: 1/10–14/01
Gallup Poll News Service
Survey #GO 132067

I'm going to read some aspects of life in America today. For each one, please say whether you are very satisfied, somewhat satisfied, somewhat dissatisfied, or very dissatisfied:

The overall quality of life?

Very, somewhat satisfied 89%
Somewhat, very dissatisfied 10
No opinion 1

The opportunity for a person in this nation to get ahead by working hard?

Very, somewhat satisfied 76%
Somewhat, very dissatisfied 22
No opinion 2

Our system of government and how well it works?

Very, somewhat satisfied 68%
Somewhat, very dissatisfied 30
No opinion 2

The influence of organized religion?

Very, somewhat satisfied 64%
Somewhat, very dissatisfied 32
No opinion 4

The size and power of the federal government?

Very, somewhat satisfied 50%
Somewhat, very dissatisfied 47
No opinion 3

The size and influence of major corporations?

Very, somewhat satisfied 48%
Somewhat, very dissatisfied 48
No opinion 4

The moral and ethical climate?

Very, somewhat satisfied 36%
Somewhat, very dissatisfied 62
No opinion 2

Next, we'd like to know how you feel about the state of the nation in each of the following areas. For each one, please say whether you are very satisfied, somewhat satisfied, somewhat dissatisfied, or very dissatisfied:

The state of the nation's economy?

Very, somewhat satisfied 68%
Somewhat, very dissatisfied 27
No opinion 5

The position of women in the nation?

Very, somewhat satisfied 67%
Somewhat, very dissatisfied 31
No opinion 2

The role America plays in world affairs?

Very, somewhat satisfied 61%
Somewhat, very dissatisfied 34
No opinion 5

*The nation's military strength and prepared-
ness?*

Very, somewhat satisfied 61%
Somewhat, very dissatisfied 32
No opinion 7

The quality of the environment in the nation?

Very, somewhat satisfied 56%
Somewhat, very dissatisfied 40
No opinion 4

*The position of blacks and other racial mi-
norities in the nation?*

Very, somewhat satisfied 53%
Somewhat, very dissatisfied 40
No opinion 7

The quality of medical care in the nation?

Very, somewhat satisfied 48%
Somewhat, very dissatisfied 49
No opinion 3

*The nation's policies to reduce or control
crime?*

Very, somewhat satisfied 45%
Somewhat, very dissatisfied 52
No opinion 3

The state of race relations?

Very, somewhat satisfied 44%
Somewhat, very dissatisfied 48
No opinion 8

*The nation's policies regarding the abortion
issue?*

Very, somewhat satisfied 43%
Somewhat, very dissatisfied 47
No opinion 10

The quality of public education in the nation?

Very, somewhat satisfied 40%
Somewhat, very dissatisfied 57
No opinion 3

The nation's laws or policies on guns?

Very, somewhat satisfied 38%
Somewhat, very dissatisfied 57
No opinion 5

The Social Security and Medicare systems?

Very, somewhat satisfied 38%
Somewhat, very dissatisfied 57
No opinion 5

The acceptance of homosexuality in the nation?

Very, somewhat satisfied 35%
Somewhat, very dissatisfied 57
No opinion 8

The nation's energy policies?

Very, somewhat satisfied 32%
Somewhat, very dissatisfied 49
No opinion 19

*The level of immigration into the country
today?*

Very, somewhat satisfied 32%
Somewhat, very dissatisfied 55
No opinion 13

*The nation's efforts to deal with poverty and
homelessness?*

Very, somewhat satisfied 30%
Somewhat, very dissatisfied 66
No opinion 4

The availability of affordable health care?

Very, somewhat satisfied 29%
Somewhat, very dissatisfied 68
No opinion 3

The amount Americans pay in federal taxes?

Very, somewhat satisfied 26%
Somewhat, very dissatisfied 71
No opinion 3

The nation's campaign finance laws?

Very, somewhat satisfied 23%
Somewhat, very dissatisfied 56
No opinion 21

Analysis: A January Gallup Poll finds that 56% of all Americans are satisfied with the way things are going in the United States and 41% are not. While these figures suggest a mostly contented public, a battery of satisfaction questions asked in the poll reveals a more varied picture, with areas of substantial discontent as well as areas of great satisfaction. Americans tend to be most satisfied with the overall living conditions in the country such as the quality of life, the opportunities for people to get ahead, and the nation's economy. They also are quite satisfied with the general political position of the country such as the system of government and how well it works, the role America plays in world affairs, and the nation's military strength and preparedness.

At the other end of the spectrum, Americans are quite dissatisfied with the moral climate, the amount of taxes they have to pay, the country's efforts to deal with poverty and homelessness, and the availability of affordable health care. And in several areas, they are almost equally divided, with only slight differences between the number who are satisfied and the number who are dissatisfied with the state of race relations, the nation's policies on abortion, the quality of medical care, the size and power of the federal government, and the size and influence of major corporations.

About nine in ten are either "very" or "somewhat" satisfied with the quality of life in the coun-try, while just 10% say they are "very" or "somewhat" dissatisfied, the most positive response to any of the twenty-seven items measured in the survey. More than three-quarters also are satisfied with the opportunity for a person to get ahead by working hard, while at least six in ten are satisfied with the country's system of government, the influence of organized religion, the nation's economy, the position of women, the role America plays in world affairs, and the nation's military strength. Slight majorities also are satisfied with the quality of the environment, and with the position of blacks and other racial minorities in the country.

The highest level of dissatisfaction is found in Americans' views about the amount of taxes they pay, with 71% saying they are dissatisfied while just 26% are satisfied. In addition, about two-thirds are dissatisfied with the availability of affordable health care, and with the nation's efforts to deal with poverty and homelessness. These latter two items do not necessarily suggest, however, that Americans feel they should be paying higher taxes to address these problems. Previous Gallup Polls have shown that virtually all of the dissatisfaction Americans express about their taxes is that they pay too much, not too little.

Substantial majorities also express dissatisfaction with the moral and ethical climate in the country, campaign finance laws, the level of immigration today, the acceptance of homosexuality, the Social Security and Medicare systems, laws on guns, and the quality of public education.

A special statistical analysis of the poll results suggests that there are five separate clusters of satisfaction attitudes: living conditions, the federal government, the moral climate, social policy issues, and the positions of women and minorities in society. Among these five clusters, Americans' satisfaction with living conditions is the one that relates most strongly to the overall satisfaction with the way things are going in the country. To a lesser though still significant extent, respondents' feelings about the size and power of the federal government and about the moral climate also are related to their overall satisfaction. The level of satisfaction expressed in specific policy areas does not seem to predict overall satisfaction with the way things are going.

FEBRUARY 7
HILLARY RODHAM CLINTON/BILL CLINTON'S PRESIDENTIAL PARDONS

Interview Dates: 2/1–4/01
Gallup Poll News Service
Survey #GO 132811

We'd like to get your overall opinion of some people in the news. As I read each name, please say if you have a favorable or unfavorable opinion of this person, or if you have never heard of him or her:

Hillary Rodham Clinton?

	Favorable	Unfavorable	No opinion
2001 Feb 1–4	52%	43%	5%
2000 Nov 13–15	56	39	5
2000 Oct 25–28	52	43	5
2000 Aug 4–5	45	50	5
2000 Feb 4–6	55	39	6

Bill Clinton?

	Favorable	Unfavorable	No opinion
2001 Feb 1–4	51%	48%	1%
2000 Dec 2–4	57	41	2
2000 Nov 13–15	57	41	2
2000 Oct 25–28	54	44	2
2000 Sep 15–17*	46	48	6
2000 Aug 18–19	48	48	4
2000 Aug 4–5	42	54	4
2000 Apr 28–30	47	51	2

*Registered voters

How closely have you been following the news about the presidential pardons issued by Bill Clinton during his last week in office—very closely, somewhat closely, not too closely, or not at all?

Very closely 20%
Somewhat closely 42
Not too closely 22
Not at all 15
No opinion 1

*Based on part sample

*Overall, do you approve or disapprove of the presidential pardons issued by Bill Clinton?**

Approve 34%
Disapprove 50
No opinion 16

*Based on part sample

Analysis: The public's response to the controversial pardons issued by President Clinton during his final days in office tends to be critical, but not greatly so. According to a Gallup survey conducted February 1–4, only 34% approve of these pardons while 50% disapprove. However, a substantial number (16%) offer no opinion on the matter. This evaluation is similar to Americans' reaction to President George Bush's pardon of former Defense Secretary Caspar Weinberger in 1992 for his role in the Iran-Contra affair of which 27% approved, 54% disapproved, and 19% had no opinion. However, unlike the Weinberger pardon that drew little public notice, many today (62%) report paying fairly close attention to news of the Clinton pardons. Twenty percent have followed it "very closely" and another 42% have followed it "somewhat closely." Only 37% percent are not following the story to any degree. By contrast, only 43% paid close attention to the Weinberger pardon, including just 10% who followed it "very closely."

Among the 140 presidential pardons issued by Clinton during his final week in office, several have been strongly criticized including the one given to former fugitive Marc Rich, a commodities trader indicted in 1983 on more than fifty counts of wire fraud, racketeering, illegally trading oil with Iran, and a record-high tax-evasion scheme. Other pardons raising eyebrows include those for Whitewater figure Susan McDougal and former Congressman Mel Reynolds.

Republicans are particularly critical of Clinton's pardons. Seventy-four percent disapprove and a majority of independents (51%) disapprove as well. Democrats are neither highly critical nor highly supportive. Many simply chose to express no opinion. Fifty-one percent of Democrats say they approve of Clinton's pardons and 25% disapprove. Twenty-four percent say they are unsure.

Perhaps it is this relatively close scrutiny of Clinton's pardons that has brought about a slight decline in his image since leaving office. The percentage holding a favorable view of Bill Clinton declined from 57% in early December to 51% today. With 48% currently holding an unfavorable opinion of Clinton, up from 41% in December, the public's judgment about Clinton is now decidedly mixed.

FEBRUARY 8
ECONOMIC CONDITIONS/
PERSONAL FINANCES

Interview Dates: 2/1–4/01
Gallup Poll News Service
Survey #GO 132811

How would you rate economic conditions in this country today—excellent, good, only fair, or poor?

	2001 Feb 1–4	2001 Jan 10–14
Excellent	7%	11%
Good	44	56
Only fair	36	27
Poor	13	6
No opinion	*	*

*Less than 1%

Right now, do you think that economic conditions in the country as a whole are getting better or getting worse?

	2001 Feb 1–4	2001 Jan 10–14
Getting better	23%	32%
Getting worse	66	56
Same (vol.)	8	8
No opinion	3	4

Looking ahead, how do you think economic conditions in this country will be a year from now—excellent, good, only fair, or poor?

Excellent	6%
Good	41
Only fair	33
Poor	16
No opinion	4

Next, we are interested in how people's financial situation may have changed. Would you say that you are financially better off now than you were a year ago, or are you financially worse off now?

	2001 Feb 1–4	2001 Jan 10–14
Better off	46%	49%
Worse off	30	30
Same (vol.)	23	21
No opinion	1	*

*Less than 1%

Looking ahead, do you expect that at this time next year you will be financially better off than now, or worse off than now?

	2001 Feb 1–4	2001 Jan 10–14
Better off	61%	63%
Worse off	19	21
Same (vol.)	16	13
No opinion	4	3

How likely do you think it is that there will be a recession in the country during the next twelve months—very likely, fairly likely, not too likely, or not at all likely?

	Very, fairly likely	Not too, not at all, likely	Already in recession (vol.)**
2001 Feb 1–4	53%	42%	–
2000 Dec 2–4	45	50	–
1990 Dec	74	14	10
1990 Nov	70	20	6
1990 Oct 25	69	19	6

1990 Oct 11–14 76	19	5
1990 Oct 3–4 77	18	5
1990 Sep 27–30 78	19	3
1990 Aug 23–26 69	23	8
1990 Aug 9–12 65	28	7

*Based on part sample
**"No opinion" is omitted.

Analysis: George W. Bush has been setting the stage all week for the official presentation of his tax cut to Congress, a major promise from his presidential campaign. If it becomes law, Bush's tax cut will be the largest since Ronald Reagan's cuts of the 1980s. Proponents of the cuts argue that the sluggish economy needs a jumpstart, while critics assert that spending money on large cuts will jeopardize the federal budget surplus and risk the long-term financial health of the country. One thing is clear from the Gallup Poll conducted February 1–4: the public is increasingly likely to perceive that the economy is getting worse, not better, and a significantly smaller number are willing to rate the economy as excellent or good than was the case as recently as three weeks ago.

According to the poll, 51% rate the current economic conditions as excellent or good, down from 67% who gave the economy positive ratings just three weeks ago. Forty-nine percent currently gives the economy either an "only fair" or "poor" rating, up from 33%.

Looking ahead, the majority (66%) now think economic conditions are getting worse while just 23% think things are getting better. The increase in these negative perceptions has been steady since December. At that point, 48% said things were getting worse, up from 38% in November. By mid-January, the "getting worse" number was up to 56%. Since then, the number is up by another 10 percentage points to the current 66%. The current numbers are almost exactly the reverse of the situation one year ago when 69% thought the economy was improving and 23% thought it was worsening.

Other data from the weekend poll show that the public does not necessarily envision that the economy will be in terrible shape in the future, despite the fact that two-thirds say the economy is getting worse. When asked to predict the shape the economy will be in a year from now, respondents give a mixed forecast. Forty-seven percent predict that things will be excellent or good one year from now, and 49% think things will be fair or poor. A slight majority (53%) think there is likely to be a recession in the next year. The number of people predicting recession has risen since early December when 45% of the public thought a recession was likely in the next twelve months. But this is still well below the 74% in 1990 who felt recession was near: a prediction that proved accurate.

About six in ten think they will be better off financially this time next year than they are today, 19% think they will be worse off, and 16% do not expect their financial situation to change. The discrepancy between Americans' predictions for the economy overall and their personal financial situation may be part of a larger phenomenon in public opinion: people generally perceive the national situation in many areas such as education and health care to be in worse shape than in the local situation. Although the number who think they will be better off in the next year has fluctuated somewhat over time, there has never been an instance when more people thought they would be worse off financially instead of better off.

FEBRUARY 9
DEFENSE SPENDING

Interview Dates: 2/1–4/01
Gallup Poll News Service
Survey #GO 132811

Do you, yourself, feel that our national defense is stronger now than it needs to be, not strong enough, or about right at the present time?

	Stronger than needs to be	Not strong enough	About right*
2001 Feb 1–4 . . . . .7%		44%	48%
2000 May 18–21 6		38	55

2000 Jan 13–16 6	39	52
1999 May 7–9 7	42	48
1990 Jan 4–7 16	17	64
1984 15	36	46

*"No opinion" is omitted.

Analysis: Despite a campaign promise to increase defense spending significantly over the next several years, President George W. Bush announced recently that there would be no new spending on defense, at least for the present time. A review of recent polls shows that the president is not likely to find much of an outcry in reaction to his decision since the issue is of relatively low salience to the public, and there is no general consensus about either increasing or cutting defense expenditures.

The most recent Gallup Poll conducted February 1–4 shows that 41% of Americans say the country is spending too little on national defense and the military, 19% too much, and 38% about the right amount. These numbers are similar to those measured in a Gallup Poll last August when 40% said too little was being spent, 20% too much, and 34% about right. A review of all of these survey results suggests that no matter how the question is put to the public, less than a majority feel that defense spending needs to be increased.

A review of Gallup trends on this question over the past three decades shows that rarely has there been a majority who felt that spending was either too little or too much. For most of the time, the number who say defense spending is "about right" has varied in the 30% to 40% range, with the rest divided between a pro- and an antispending stance. In general, more people have said there was too much rather than too little spending. Two major exceptions occurred in the context of presidential elections when the two major candidates favored increased spending.

FEBRUARY 12
MIDDLE EAST CRISIS

Interview Dates: 2/1–4/01
Gallup Poll News Service
Survey #GO 132811

As far as you are concerned, should the development of a peaceful solution to the Palestinian-Israeli situation be a very important foreign policy goal of the United States, a somewhat important goal, not too important a goal, or not an important goal at all?

	Very, somewhat important	Not too important	Not at all important; no opinion
2001 Feb 1–4 . . . . . . .83%		10%	7%
2000 Jul 6–9 77		14	9
2000 Jan 25–26 78		12	10
1999 Jul 22–25 82		9	9
1993 Sep 10–112 77		11	12
1991 Mar 87		6	7

In the Middle East situation, are your sympathies more with the Israelis or more with the Palestinian Arabs?

	Israelis	Palestinian Arabs	Both; neither (vol.); no opinion
2001 Feb 1–4 . . . . . . .51%		16%	33%
2000 Jul 6–9 41		14	45
2000 Jan 25–26 43		13	44
1999 Jul 22–25 43		12	45
1998 Dec 4–6 46		13	41
1997 Aug 12–13 38		8	54
1996 Nov 21–24 38		15	47
1993 Sep 10–12 42		15	43
1991 Feb 64		7	29
1989 Aug 50		14	36
1988 May 13–15 37		15	48

Do you think there will or will not come a time when Israel and the Arab nations will be able to settle their differences and live in peace?

	Will	Will not	No opinion
2001 Feb 1–4 . . . . . . .41%		56%	3%

2000 Jan 25–26	.49	45	6
1999 Jul 22–25	.49	47	4
1998 Dec 4–6	.40	56	4
1997 Aug 12–13	.36	56	8

In the Middle East conflict, do you think the United States should take Israel's side, take the Palestinian Arabs' side, or not take either side?*

	Israel's side	Palestinian Arabs' side	Neither; no opinion
2000 Jul 6–9	16%	1%	83%
2000 Jan 25–26	15	1	84
1998 Dec 4–6	17	2	81
1998 May 8–10	15	2	83

*Based on part sample

Is your overall opinion of each of the following countries very favorable, mostly favorable, mostly unfavorable, or very unfavorable?

	Favorable*
Canada	.90%
Australia	.85
Great Britain	.85
Italy	.78
France	.77
Germany	.75
Japan	.73
Brazil	.69
Mexico	.67
Egypt	.65
Israel	.63
The Philippines	.63

*"Mostly, very unfavorable" are omitted.

Analysis: Secretary of State Colin Powell announced that he would be traveling to the Middle East later this month to meet with area leaders. Powell will assess the situation for the first time in his new role as head of the State Department. His choice of a first trip abroad closely matches the perceptions of the public that considers finding a solution to the Middle East situation an important priority for the United States. At the same time, many respondents are skeptical that a solution to the crisis there ever will be found. Americans, as they have been for years, are more sympathetic to Israel than to the Palestinian Arabs, although Israel is not as favorably perceived as are many more traditional American allies.

A recent Gallup Poll focusing on the public's attitudes about foreign affairs underscores Americans' feelings that the solution to the Israeli-Palestinian crisis should be a major priority. Over eight out of ten in the February 1–4 poll say that a peaceful solution to the situation should be either a somewhat or very important goal for the United States. Forty-three percent say it is very important—slightly higher than last year but roughly on a par with results from previous years—while another 40% say it is somewhat important.

Older people who perhaps have a better historical appreciation for the wars and disputes that have resulted over the years from the Middle East imbroglio, are more likely to say that helping solve the crisis should be an important goal of U.S. foreign policy. Among those age 50 and over, 52% assign it as "very" important compared to 37% of those age 18 to 49.

At the same time they recognize its importance, Americans remain skeptical that the situation in the Middle East ever will be resolved. Asked "Do you think there will or will not come a time when Israel and the Arab nations will be able to settle their differences and live in peace?" only 41% say yes while 56% say no. There was a little more optimism when Gallup asked this question in January 2000 and July 1999, when 49% were optimistic. The current pessimism levels are identical to those of 1997 and 1998.

Secretary of State Powell will meet with the newly elected Prime Minister of Israel, Ariel Sharon; with Yasir Arafat, the Palestinian leader; and with leaders of other countries in the region. Gallup Poll results suggest that Americans strongly feel that the U.S. should not officially take sides in the conflict, even though their sympathies lie with Israel instead of with the Palestinian Arabs. When asked directly where their sympathies lie, respondents choose the

Israelis over the Palestinian Arabs by a 51%-to-16% margin. That leaves about one-third that doesn't have an opinion, or favors either both sides or neither side. These types of responses have been roughly the same for the thirteen years that Gallup has been asking the question. The major exception came during the Persian Gulf War when sympathies for Israel shot up as the country suffered from the well-publicized Scud missile attacks launched by Iraq. Despite these leanings toward Israel, however, other Gallup Poll questions have shown that a significant majority—74% in a July 2000 poll—say the U.S. officially should remain neutral and not take either side's position in the conflict.

The recent Gallup Poll also asked Americans to indicate whether they have a favorable or an unfavorable view of a list of countries. Sixty-three percent of Americans have a favorable view of Israel while 32% have an unfavorable view. Despite these differences, Israel comes in at only the eleventh position on the list of countries evaluated. Israel is viewed not only less favorably than are other English-speaking countries and a number of European countries with traditional ties to the U.S., but also less favorably than Japan, Mexico, Brazil, or Egypt.

FEBRUARY 13
PRESIDENT BUSH

Interview Dates: 2/9–11/01
CNN/*USA Today*/Gallup Poll
Survey #GO 132976

Do you approve or disapprove of the way George W. Bush is handling his job as president?

	Approve	Dis-approve	No opinion
2001 Feb 9–11	57%	25%	18%
2001 Feb 1–4	57	25	18

Apart from whether you approve or disapprove of the way George W. Bush is handling his job as president, what do you think of Bush as a person—would you say you approve or disapprove of him?

	Approve	Dis-approve	No opinion
2001 Feb 9–11	65%	27%	8%
2001 Jan 5–7*	60	33	7

*Question wording: *Apart from whether you approve or disapprove of the way George W. Bush is handling his transition to the presidency, what do you think of Bush as a person—would you say you approve or disapprove of him?*

Thinking about the following characteristics and qualities, please say whether you think it applies or doesn't apply to George W. Bush:

Is tough enough for the job?

Applies 68%
Doesn't apply 28
No opinion 4

Is honest and trustworthy?

Applies 64%
Doesn't apply 29
No opinion 7

Is a strong and decisive leader?

Applies 61%
Doesn't apply 34
No opinion 5

Can manage the government effectively?

Applies 61%
Doesn't apply 31
No opinion 8

Shares your values?

Applies 57%
Doesn't apply 39
No opinion 4

Inspires confidence?

Applies 57%
Doesn't apply 39
No opinion 4

Cares about the needs of people like you?

Applies 56%
Doesn't apply 39
No opinion 5

Understands complex issues?

Applies 55%
Doesn't apply 38
No opinion 7

Generally agrees with you on issues you care about?

Applies 53%
Doesn't apply 43
No opinion 4

Is a person you admire?

Applies 49%
Doesn't apply 47
No opinion 4

Whom do you want to have more influence over the direction the nation takes in the next year—George W. Bush or the Republicans in Congress?

Bush 44%
Republicans in Congress 31
Both; neither (vol.) 20
No opinion 5

Whom do you want to have more influence over the direction the nation takes in the next year—George W. Bush or the Democrats in Congress?

Bush 48%
Democrats in Congress 41

Both; neither (vol.) 8
No opinion 3

Analysis: George W. Bush may have lost the popular vote for president, but he receives positive reviews—both personally and professionally—from a majority of Americans three weeks into his presidency. A Gallup Poll conducted February 9–11 finds that 57% approve of the job Bush is doing as president thus far, and 65% approve of him as a person. Bush also enjoys positive evaluations on a number of character dimensions rated in the new poll, particularly as someone who is "tough enough for the job," and "honest and trustworthy." While Bush's image ratings are similar to those of one year ago, the perception of him as "tough" has increased markedly over the past year.

Today, President Bush's overall job performance rating is identical to where it stood one week ago: 57% approve of the way he is handling the job of president, 25% disapprove, and 18% are unsure. Republicans in particular praise President Bush today, with 88% saying they approve of the way he is handling the job. But a majority of independents (54%) also approve of his performance as do close to one-third of Democrats (31%).

A separate question asked respondents for their reaction to Bush "as a person" rather than as president. Democrats are somewhat more supportive on this basis, but the plurality still disapproves. Ninety-one percent of Republicans, 63% of independents, and 40% of Democrats say they approve of Bush as a person. But perhaps a reflection of the acrimony produced by the election controversy, 49% of Democrats still disapprove of Bush, the man.

While Bush, as a new president, may face more animosity from the public than he would like, he does enjoy a generally positive personal image, largely unharmed by the election. According to a Gallup measure asking whether or not each of ten characteristics apply to the president, Bush's public image appears to be one of a "straight-talking, no-nonsense" chief executive officer. While he scores positively on softer virtues such as "cares about the needs of people like you," these do not lead the list. Two-thirds (68%) currently see Bush as "tough enough for the job," up from only 50% who felt this way about him when Gallup measured it roughly one year ago. Nearly as many (64%) see him as honest and trustworthy, while about six in ten (61%) also view him as "a strong and decisive leader" and one who "can manage the government effectively."

Slightly smaller majorities perceive Bush as someone who shares their values, inspires confidence, cares about their needs, and agrees with them on the issues they care about. And despite the criticism often leveled by his political foes, a majority also believe Bush understands complex issues. Just under a majority (49%) describe Bush as "someone they admire."

The ratings on most of these items are quite similar to those from Gallup surveys conducted in January, February, and March 2000. The only significant change is seen in the percentage that believe Bush is tough enough for the job, jumping 18 points in the past year.

FEBRUARY 14
INCOME TAX CUTS

Interview Dates: 2/9–11/01
CNN/*USA Today*/Gallup Poll
Survey #GO 132976

How important is it that the Bush administration does each of the following—is it a top priority, high priority, low priority, or not a priority at all: *

Improve education?

Top priority 49%
High priority 44

Keep America prosperous?

Top priority 43%
High priority 50

Deal with the energy problems facing the nation?

Top priority 38%
High priority 48

Keep the federal budget balanced?

Top priority 36%
High priority 50

Provide military security for the country?

Top priority 36%
High priority 46

Cut federal income taxes?

Top priority 28%
High priority 39

*"Low priority," "not a priority at all," and "no opinion" are omitted.

Based on what you have read or heard, do you favor or oppose the federal income tax cuts President Bush has proposed?

	Favor	Oppose	No opinion
2001 Feb 9–11	.56%	34%	10%
2001 Jan 5–7	.52	33	15

Do you think President Bush will or will not be able to pass the federal income tax cuts that he has proposed?

	Will	Will not	No opinion
2001 Feb 9–11	.51%	41%	8%
2001 Jan 5–7	.38	50	12

Just your best guess—if there is a cut in federal income taxes, how much, in dollars, would you expect your own taxes to be cut per year?

$1,500 or more 13%
$1,000 to $1,499 10
$500 to $999 9
$100 to $499 18
Less than $100 6

None; zero (vol.) 11
No opinion 33

Mean   **$790.61**
Median   **$400**

Looking ahead, how much of a difference would this tax cut make for you and your family—a big difference, some difference, only a little difference, or no difference at all?

Big difference 18%
Some difference 26
Only a little difference 33
No difference at all 20
No opinion 3

Consider the following statement. The government ought to cut taxes even if it means putting off some important things that need to be done. Now, would you say you have an opinion on this or not? [Asked of those who have an opinion: Do you agree that the government should do this, or do you agree the government should not do this?]

	Agree	Do not agree	It depends (vol.); no opinion
2001 Feb 9–11	.28%	33%	39%
1999 Aug 16–18	.21	59	20
1979 Jan 9–22	.62	12	26

If President Bush is able to enact his tax cut plan, do you think that Bush's tax cut would make a recession more likely or less likely, or would it have no effect?

	More likely	Less likely	No effect; no opinion
2001 Feb 9–11	.22%	35%	43%
2001 Jan 5–7	.34	29	37

If President Bush is able to enact his tax cut plan, how likely is it that each of the following would happen—very likely, somewhat likely, not too likely, or not at all likely:

It would cause a federal budget deficit?

Very likely 20%
Somewhat likely 33
Not too likely 29
Not at all likely 13
No opinion 5

It would take money away that is needed to protect Social Security?

Very likely 30%
Somewhat likely 27
Not too likely 22
Not at all likely 17
No opinion 4

It would mostly benefit the rich?

Very likely 46%
Somewhat likely 29
Not too likely 14
Not at all likely 8
No opinion 3

Analysis: A majority of Americans (56%) favor the cuts in federal income taxes proposed by President Bush, up very slightly (four points) from one month ago. But there are signs in a new poll that the public is not overwhelmed by the thought of the money such tax cuts might save them. Additionally, a majority says it is at least somewhat likely that tax cuts could result in an increased deficit or hurt Social Security, and three-quarters say that the tax cuts would mostly benefit the rich. There is no consensus about the impact of a tax cut plan on the nation's economy. The public is split on whether it will make a recession less likely, more likely, or not have much of an effect either way.

Americans usually favor tax cuts (for more than 25 years, 70% or more of respondents have told Gallup they favor a cut in federal income taxes), and Bush's current plan is no exception.

In the most recent February 9–11 Gallup Poll, 56% favor the "federal income tax cuts President Bush has proposed" while 34% are opposed. However, Gallup has consistently found that when people are forced to choose between tax cuts and spending on popular government programs such as Social Security and Medicare, they are more apt to favor spending over tax cuts. The same pattern appears in the most recent poll: only 28% believe the government ought to cut taxes "if it means putting off some important things that need to be done." Thirty-three percent disagree, saying the government ought to cut taxes anyway, and 39% have no opinion.

Although over one-half favors Bush's tax proposal, majorities also agree with some of its critics' claims. Fifty-three percent think it is likely the plan will cause a budget deficit, 57% think it is likely to take money away from Social Security, and 75% think it will mostly benefit the rich. These perceptions are clearly partisan, as would be expected; Democrats are more likely than Republicans to think Bush's plan will have dismal results.

The Democratic leaders in Congress have been trying to persuade the public that a tax plan that disproportionately benefits the rich is unacceptable. This may not be the most effective strategy, according to Gallup's data. Those who think the plan will increase the deficit or diminish the Social Security fund are more likely to oppose Bush's plan than favor it. However, those who think the plan will mostly benefit the rich are as likely to support Bush's plan as oppose it.

President Bush has argued that a tax cut plan is necessary to help prevent an economic recession. Thirty-five percent agree, but another 22% say tax cuts actually will make a recession more likely, while another 36% say that tax cuts won't have much of an effect on the probability of a recession either way. These perceptions mark a slight change from January, when 34% said that tax cuts would make a recession more likely and 29% said they would make a recession less likely.

Gallup asked respondents to estimate how much money they would save under the Bush tax plan, and the median response was about $400.00. Asked to characterize the impact of the tax savings on their lives, most think the amount they would save would not make much of a difference to them or to their families.

The survey finds that perceived monetary savings is related to whether or not people support the tax cuts: the more people think they will save, they more likely they are to support Bush's plan. This is true for both Republicans and Democrats, although most Democrats oppose the plan, regardless of the amount they think they will save.

According to a poll conducted shortly before Bush assumed office, most did not think that he would be able to successfully pass the tax cuts he championed during the campaign. Bush's loss of the popular vote, coupled with the extended post-election controversy in Florida and a narrowly divided Congress, created a less-than-perfect atmosphere to execute his agenda. According to a Gallup Poll conducted January 5–7, only 38% thought that Bush would be able to pass his tax package. Now that Bush is getting settled into the Oval Office and Alan Greenspan, Chairman of the Federal Reserve, has supported the idea of large tax cuts, more of the public has been persuaded that Bush will have some legislative success in the tax arena. Fifty-one percent now think the president will be able to pass his tax legislation, 41% do not think he will be able to, and 8% have no opinion.

FEBRUARY 14
POST-PRESIDENCY CLINTON APPROVAL

Interview Dates: 2/9–11/01
CNN/*USA Today*/Gallup Poll
Survey #GO 132976

Which comes closer to your view of Bill Clinton after leaving the White House—I'm glad he has left, or I'll miss him now that he is gone?

	Glad he left	Miss him	No opinion
2001 Feb 9–11	55%	38%	7%

*Based on part sample

Which comes closer to your view of Bill Clinton's actions in his last week in office, including the pardons he granted and the gifts he took with him—do you think Clinton's actions were worse than what most other presidents have done, or most other presidents have done similar or worse things when leaving office?

Clinton's actions worse 45%
Other presidents similar, worse 50
No opinion 5

Still thinking about Clinton's actions in his last week in office, which comes closer to your point of view about the controversy that it has caused—you agree with the people who criticize Clinton for what he did, or you think this is mainly Clinton's enemies trying to get him one more time?

Agree with criticism 49%
Clinton enemies trying to get him 47
No opinion 4

Analysis: Despite having left office nearly a month ago, Bill Clinton remains a prominent figure in the news. The media have focused on several controversial decisions Clinton made just before leaving office including renting expensive office space in Manhattan, taking several gifts that many believed were intended to stay in the White House, and pardoning fugitive Marc Rich. While the news stories have cast these actions in a decidedly negative light, the public is divided as to the seriousness of what Clinton did.

In the latest Gallup Poll conducted February 9–11, 50% say other presidents "have done similar or worse things when leaving office," while 45% think "Clinton's actions were worse." The public is equally divided as to whether the criticism of Clinton is mainly a product of his "enemies trying to get him one more time" (47%) or because they "agree with the people who criticize Clinton for what he did" (49%). More than eight

in ten (83%) who think Clinton's enemies are out to get him think his actions are comparable to other presidents' actions, while nearly eight in ten (79%) who think the criticism is fair think Clinton's actions are worse than what other presidents have done.

Older people are more likely to think that Clinton's actions are worse than previous presidents'. Fifty-three percent of those age 50 and over express this view, compared with just 36% of those age 18 to 29, and 44% between age 30 to 49. Men are slightly more likely than women to think Clinton's actions were worse by a 49%-to-42% margin. As expected, there are big differences of opinion according to partisanship.

Americans' reactions to Clinton's departure have not yet been greatly and negatively impacted by the recent controversies. When given the choice, 55% are "glad that he has left" the presidency while just 38% say they "miss him." This represents a relatively minor change compared to a poll conducted January 5–7 when 45% said they would miss him. The percentage that is now "glad that he has left" has increased in the time since that poll was conducted, but by only four percentage points.

The slight movement also conceals a rather significant change among older people. In the January poll, 47% of adults age 50 and over were glad Clinton was leaving office whereas that percentage has now increased to 63%. Overall, this movement is counterbalanced by the fact that those age 30 to 49 are now slightly more likely to say they miss Clinton than they were in January.

FEBRUARY 15
TIGER WOODS

Interview Dates: 2/9–11/01
CNN/*USA Today*/Gallup Poll
Survey #GO 132976

Are you a fan of professional golf, or not?

	Yes	No	Some-what of a fan (vol.)
2001 Feb 9–11 ......26%		69%	5%
2000 Mar 30–Apr 2 ...26		66	8

If you know that Tiger Woods is going to be playing in a golf tournament on television, does that make you more likely to watch that tournament, less likely to watch that tournament, or doesn't it matter?

	National adults	Fans only
More likely	.25%	51%
Less likely	.4	1
Doesn't matter	.71	48

Analysis: As the PGA season reaches the midpoint of its second full month of competition, almost one-third of Americans (31%) say they are a fan of professional golf. This finding remains on a par with the 34% who said the same last spring. The new Gallup Poll conducted February 9–11 also finds that golf fans are more likely to be male than female, and to have relatively high levels of household income.

Tiger Woods' success on the golf course has made him one of the most recognizable figures in sports. Last fall, Woods became involved in a somewhat controversial dispute with the PGA over marketing rights. Woods believed he was a driving force behind increased television ratings and golf's increased popularity. Woods has since rescinded some of his statements and come to an agreement with the PGA tour. Nonetheless, the viewing habits of golf fans show his claims have some merit. Among fans of professional golf, just over half (51%) are more likely to watch a golf tournament on television if they know Tiger Woods will be playing. Only 1% of fans say it makes them less likely and 48% say it doesn't matter if Woods is playing or not.

FEBRUARY 15
JOB ANXIETY

Interview Dates: 2/9–11/01
CNN/*USA Today*/Gallup Poll
Survey #GO 132976

How likely is it that your own personal financial situation will get worse in the next twelve months—it is certain to get worse, it is very likely to get worse, it is somewhat likely to get worse, it is not very likely to get worse, or there is no chance it will get worse?

Certain	.5%
Very likely	.13
Somewhat likely	.26
Not very likely	.42
No chance	.12
No opinion	.2

Do you, personally, know anyone who has lost his or her job within the last twelve months?

	Total	Employed full time
Yes, know someone	.47%	53%
No, do not know someone	.53	47

Asked of employed adults: Thinking about your pay, benefits, and the amount of work you do, how likely is it that your own job situation will get worse in the next twelve months—it is certain to get worse, it is very likely to get worse, it is somewhat likely to get worse, it is not very likely to get worse, or there is no chance it will get worse?

Certain	.3%
Very likely	.7
Somewhat likely	.19
Not very likely	.46
No chance	.25

*Based on half sample

Also asked of employed adults: If you were to lose your job, how likely is it that you would find a job just as good as the one you have now—very likely, somewhat likely, not very likely, or not at all likely?

Very likely	.35%
Somewhat likely	.29
Not very likely	.24
Not at all likely	.11
No opinion	.1

*Based on part sample

Also asked of employed adults: If you were to lose your job, how long could you go without a job before experiencing significant financial hardship—up to one week, up to one month, up to four months, up to one year, or more than one year?*

Up to one week 15%
Up to one month 31
Up to four months 30
Up to one year 13
More than one year 10
No opinion 1

*Based on part sample

Analysis: As Federal Reserve Board Chairman Alan Greenspan warns Congress that the economy still faces substantial risks, a new Gallup Poll shows that almost one-half of all Americans say their own financial situation is likely to get worse in the next year. In addition, among those who are currently employed, about three in ten expect their job situation to decline, and about one-half think that if they lost their job, they would not be able to find another one as good as the one they have now.

Key findings from the new Gallup Poll conducted February 9–11 show that 44% say their financial situation is either certain (5%), very likely (13%), or somewhat likely (26%) to get worse in the next twelve months. At the same time, 54% say that their financial situation is not very likely to get worse (42%) or that there is no chance of that happening to them (12%).

Forty-seven percent personally know someone who has lost his or her job within the last year. About three out of ten employed Americans say that the pay, benefits, and amount of work they do is at least somewhat likely to get worse in the next year. Almost two-thirds of this same group say it is likely they could find another job as good as the one they have now if they were to be laid off. One in ten says it is not at all likely. Almost one-half couldn't last much more than a month without experiencing significant financial difficulties if they were laid off. Only one out of ten could last more than a year.

The poll also shows that among those workers who expect their job situation to get worse in the next year, more than one-half (15%) say that if they do lose their jobs, they are not very likely to get another one that is as good as the one they have now. Moreover, most cannot be jobless for long without suffering significant financial hardship. About one in six (15%) couldn't last for more than a week, but among the workers who are most concerned about their jobs, almost one-quarter (24%) could not last that long.

Concerns about job security appear to be related at least in part to what workers observe among their friends. More than one-half (53%) of all full-time employed workers (47%) personally know someone who has lost a job in the past year. Among this group, more than one-third expect their own job situation to get worse in the next year compared to 23% who feel that way among the rest of the American workforce.

FEBRUARY 16
VIEW OF FOREIGN NATIONS

Interview Dates: 2/1–4/01
Gallup Poll News Service
Survey #GO 132811

Is your overall opinion of each of the following countries very favorable, mostly favorable, mostly unfavorable, or very unfavorable:*

	Very, mostly favorable	Mostly, very unfavorable**
Canada 90%		7%
Australia 85		8
Great Britain 85		9
Italy 78		12
France.....................77		17
Germany...................75		16
Japan 73		21
Brazil 69		17
Mexico 67		26
Egypt 65		23
Israel......................63		32

The Philippines 63	25
Taiwan .63	22
India 58	30
South Africa 57	33
Russia .52	42
Saudi Arabia 47	46
Vietnam 46	44
China .45	48
North Korea 31	59
Colombia 30	59
Cuba .27	68
The Palestinian Authority 22	63
Iran 12	83
Libya .11	75
Iraq 9	85

*Based on part sample
**"No opinion" is omitted.

Analysis: Which countries around the world are viewed most favorably by Americans today and which countries are most unpopular? Gallup has asked Americans to rate their perceptions of foreign countries for a number of years, and in a recent poll, public attitudes toward twenty-six different countries around the world were updated.

Although many Americans have never been out of the U.S. and very few have visited more than just a handful of foreign nations, most were able to give opinions of the countries. Only a small number of countries generated strongly positive or strongly negative feelings. Perhaps not surprisingly, countries that predominantly speak English (Canada, Australia, and Great Britain) are the most popular, and three countries with whom the U.S. has had direct negative dealings (Iraq, Iran, and Libya) receive ratings that are the most negative.

Countries that formerly were enemies of the United States (Japan, Germany, Russia, and China) now receive at least mid-range, if not positive, evaluations. There have been only a few significant changes in the ranking of countries over time, including a dramatic upswing in South Africa's favorable ratings, since 1991.

The U.S. shares borders with Canada and Mexico, and both are viewed positively, with Canada getting a higher favorable rating than any other country measured. U.S.-Mexican affairs may be on the upswing with the election of President George W. Bush, the former governor of Texas whose state borders Mexico. According to current Gallup Poll data, more than two-thirds (67%) feel favorably toward Mexico. This represents an increase of 24 percentage points since 1993 when Mexico and Canada were involved in the rancorous U.S. debate on NAFTA, the controversial free-trade agreement.

FEBRUARY 19
GREATEST U.S. PRESIDENT

Interview Dates: 2/9–11/01
CNN/*USA Today*/Gallup Poll
Survey #GO 132976

Whom do you regard as the greatest U.S. president?

	2001 Feb 9-11*	2000 Feb 14-15*	1999 Feb
Ronald Reagan 18%		11%	12%
John Kennedy 16		22	12
Abraham Lincoln 14		18	18
Bill Clinton 9		5	12
Franklin Roosevelt 6		12	9
Harry Truman 6		3	4
George Washington . . .5		5	12
Jimmy Carter 4		3	3
George Bush 3		3	5
Theodore Roosevelt . . .2		3	3
Thomas Jefferson 1		3	2
Richard Nixon 1		2	2
Dwight Eisenhower . . .1		3	2
Other (vol.) 5		3	1
None (vol.) 2		**	1
No opinion 7		4	2

*Asked of part sample
**Less than 1%

Asked of Democrats: Whom do you regard as the greatest U.S. president?

Bill Clinton 22%	
John F. Kennedy 19	

Franklin D. Roosevelt 10
Abraham Lincoln 9

*Based on part sample

*Asked of Republicans: Whom do you regard
as the greatest U.S. president?**

Ronald Reagan 31%
Abraham Lincoln 19
George Washington 8
John F. Kennedy 8

*Based on part sample

*If it were possible, whom would you rather
see as president of the United States today—
George Washington or Abraham Lincoln?**

George Washington 28%
Abraham Lincoln 62
No opinion 10

*Based on part sample

Analysis: Presidents Day gives Americans an opportunity to celebrate the February birthdays of
George Washington (America's first president)
and Abraham Lincoln, as well as all past U.S.
presidents. The Gallup Poll conducted February
9–11 asked respondents to name the one man
they consider to have been America's greatest
president. The winner was Ronald Reagan,
named by 18%. John F. Kennedy, with 16%,
follows in second. Third place belongs to
Abraham Lincoln with 14%, and the most recent
ex-president, Bill Clinton, comes in fourth with
9%. George Washington receives just 5% of all
mentions, and is seventh on the list behind
Franklin D. Roosevelt and Harry S. Truman.

Ronald Reagan moved to the top spot after
being only number four last year, and it is possible that the timing of the poll this year may have
affected the results. The poll was taken the weekend after Reagan's 90th birthday, which received
considerable media coverage. Although there is
no way to tell for sure, it is probable that the
heightened news coverage boosted his image in
the public's consciousness.

Over one-half century ago, in a February
1945 Gallup Poll, a plurality (42%) thought that
Lincoln was a greater president than Washington.
Near the end of the twentieth century, that sentiment still prevailed. In a June 1999 poll, 67%
said that Lincoln was greater than Washington
while 28% said Washington was the more re-
markable leader. Apparently, the public continues
to have a greater affinity for the man who freed
the slaves than for the one who led the American
Revolution. When Americans were asked
whether they would rather see Washington or
Lincoln as president today, 62% preferred
Lincoln and 28% chose Washington.

FEBRUARY 21
GENDER-SPECIFIC STEREOTYPES

Interview Dates: 12/2–4/00
Gallup Poll News Service
Survey #GO 132084

*I would like to ask about some specific char-
acteristics of men and women. For each one,
please tell me whether you think it is generally more true of men or more true of women:*

	More true of men*	More true of women*	Point advantage of men over women
Aggressive	68%	20%	+48
Courageous	50	27	+23
Ambitious	44	33	+11
Easygoing	45	38	+7
Intelligent	21	36	−15
Creative	15	65	−50
Patient	19	72	−53
Talkative	10	78	−68
Affectionate	5	86	−81
Emotional	3	90	−87

	"Men"	"Women"	"Equally true" (vol.)*
Men Only			
Aggressive	73%	17%	10%
Emotional	4	90	5

Talkative	11	78	11
Intelligent	28	29	40
Courageous	59	16	23
Patient	23	68	8
Creative	24	54	21
Ambitious	52	28	19
Easygoing	50	35	14
Affectionate	3	90	6
Women Only			
Aggressive	62	23	13
Emotional	2	90	7
Talkative	10	78	11
Intelligent	14	43	40
Courageous	41	37	20
Patient	15	75	9
Creative	7	75	16
Ambitious	37	37	24
Easygoing	42	40	17
Affectionate	6	81	11

*"No difference (vol.)" is omitted.

Analysis: A December Gallup Poll shows that Americans have little difficulty associating specific personality characteristics with one gender or the other, despite the existence of at least some social pressures in today's society to view men and women equally. The poll gave Americans the opportunity to associate particular characteristics with either men or women, and the results show that even today, people are likely to say that the words "emotional," "affectionate," "talkative," "patient," and "creative" describe women, while associating characteristics such as "aggressive" and "courageous" with men. Neither sex is more likely to be described by the terms "intelligent," "easygoing," and "ambitious."

One of the most interesting findings is the degree to which the public is willing or able to ascribe the characteristics to a specific gender rather than claiming that the term describes both equally. Those who volunteered that there was no difference between the genders were in the minority in all cases, and for only one adjective (intelligent) did more than one-quarter volunteer that the dimension described both genders equally. The question did not give the respondent

a specific choice that encompassed the "no difference" alternative.

Out of the ten dimensions tested, on only three (ambitious, easygoing, and intelligent) was the gap between the percentage choosing men and the percentage choosing women less than 20 points. On all others, there appeared to be a high degree of consensus that the personality trait described one of the sexes particularly well.

Women are somewhat more likely than men to say that the traits apply to their gender. In fact, they say that only one trait (aggressive) is more applicable to men than to women. Men, on the other hand, are somewhat more likely to ascribe the traits to women, believing that five of those tested are more applicable to women than to their own gender.

Intelligence is the characteristic that both men and women are most likely to say applies equally to the two genders (40%). There are significant differences, however, among those who do make a choice. Women tend to ascribe intelligence to women more than to men, while men split evenly in ascribing the trait to the two genders. In a Gallup Poll conducted in 1946, 40% said that men were more intelligent than women (compared to just 21% today), 21% said that women were more intelligent, and 36% thought the sexes were equally intelligent.

Men are much more likely than are women to think of themselves as the more courageous sex (59%) while only 16% say that women are more courageous. On the other hand, women are much more evenhanded: 41% of women say that men have more courage while 37% say that the term "courageous" applies best to women. In 1950, Gallup asked Americans whether they thought men or women were more courageous. Interestingly, 35% said men, 33% said women, and 22% said the sexes were equally courageous. It is noteworthy that fifty years later, the number of people who think men are more courageous than women has increased rather than decreased.

We observe a similar pattern with the characteristic "ambitious." A slight majority of men (52%) think that they are the more ambitious group while 28% choose women. Among women, there is a tie: 37% of women say that the term fits women and 37% of women say that the term fits men.

There are six dimensions on which a majority of both men and women agree, but the characteristic "aggressive" is the only trait that both genders agree applies more to men than women. A majority of both men and women say that women are more emotional, talkative, patient, affectionate, and creative.

Gallup last asked this series in 1995. Those findings differed only slightly from the current ones in that more people volunteered that men and women were equally courageous, creative, ambitious, easygoing, and affectionate.

FEBRUARY 23
ENERGY PRICES

Interview Dates: 2/9–11/01
CNN/*USA Today*/Gallup Poll
Survey #GO 132976

Thinking about the cost of electricity, gasoline, natural gas, oil, and other forms of energy, have recent price increases for energy caused any financial hardship for you or your household?

Yes 56%
No 44

How likely is it that the price increases for energy will cause any financial hardship for you or your household in the next twelve months—very likely, somewhat likely, not too likely, or not at all likely?

Very likely 38%
Somewhat likely 33
Not too likely 18
Not at all likely 10
No opinion 1

Analysis: A new Gallup Poll conducted February 9–11 shows 86% of Americans believe the nation's energy problems should be a priority for the Bush administration, and 56% say they and

their families have suffered financial hardships because of recent price hikes for electricity, natural gas, heating oil, and gasoline. As might be expected, those who have been hardest hit are those least able to afford price increases.

While no one knows what the next twelve months could bring, there is a growing expectation that energy prices could cause even more problems for the American people. Seven out of ten (71%) expect that higher energy prices are "very" or "somewhat" likely to cause them financial hardships in the coming year.

FEBRUARY 26
PERSIAN GULF WAR

Interview Dates: 2/19–21/01
Gallup Poll News Service
Survey #GO 133064

Thinking back to the Persian Gulf War in 1990 and 1991, all in all, do you think the situation in the Persian Gulf region was worth going to war over, or not?

	Yes	No	No opinion
2001 Feb 19–21	.63%	31%	6%
1992 Feb 6–9	.66	32	2
1992 Jan 6–9	.59	38	3

Would you favor or oppose sending American troops back to the Persian Gulf in order to remove Saddam Hussein from power in Iraq?

	Favor	Oppose	No opinion
2001 Feb 19–21	.52%	42%	6%
1993 Jun 29–30	.70	27	3
1992 Mar 30–Apr 5	.55	40	5

Analysis: According to a February 19–21 Gallup Poll, as Americans reflect on their country's participation in the Gulf War a decade ago, they believe the situation in the region at that time was worth going to war over by a two-to-one margin (63% to 31%). And by a much smaller margin

(52% to 42%), they would favor sending U.S. troops back to the Persian Gulf in order to remove Iraqi President Saddam Hussein from power.

By the end of the Persian Gulf War, there was widespread public support for U.S. participation in the war and approval of the way President George Bush was handling the situation. In fact, in the wake of the cease-fire, Bush received the highest job approval rating any president has received since Gallup began asking the question in the 1930s, with 89% of Americans indicating their approval and just 8% disapproval.

Despite the eventual popularity of the Persian Gulf War, Americans had to be coaxed into support for that effort. In response to the Iraqi invasion of Kuwait, they gave immediate support to President Bush's decision to send U.S. forces to Saudi Arabia in early August 1990 by 78% to 17%, but were about evenly divided over whether the situation there was really worth going to war over: a majority opposed the U.S. initiating military efforts to drive the Iraqis out of Kuwait.

The current results about whether it was worthwhile to fight the war show major differences between African Americans and white Americans, and between men and women. While whites say the war was worthwhile by a margin of 67% to 27%, blacks take the opposite point of view by 51% to 37%. On virtually all questions about U.S. participation in the Persian Gulf War (as with most military conflicts) asked by Gallup over the years, the views of blacks and whites reflect deep differences with blacks generally much more opposed than whites. By a two-to-one margin (61% to 33%), blacks today oppose sending U.S. troops to remove Saddam Hussein from power while whites express support by 56% to 38%. During the Persian Gulf War, similar divisions were found.

FEBRUARY 28
STATE OF THE UNION SPEECH

Survey Date: 2/27/01
CNN/*USA Today*/Gallup Poll
Survey #GO 133101

What was your overall reaction to President Bush's speech tonight—very positive, some-

what positive, somewhat negative, or very negative?

Very, somewhat positive 92%
Somewhat, very negative 7
Both; mixed (vol.); no opinion 1

Thinking just about President Bush's speaking style and delivery, what was your reaction to his speech tonight—very positive, somewhat positive, somewhat negative, or very negative?

Very, somewhat positive 93%
Somewhat, very negative 7

Thinking about the policies of President Bush and his administration, in your view, is George W. Bush leading the country in the right direction or in the wrong direction?

	Right direction	Wrong direction	No opinion
2001 Feb 27 (Post) . . .84%	12%	4%
2001 Feb 27 (Pre) 73	12	15

How confident are you in George W. Bush's ability to carry out his duties as president—very confident, somewhat confident, not too confident, or not at all confident?

	Very, somewhat confident	Not too, not at all confident	No opinion
2001 Feb 27 (Post) . . .86%	14%	0%
2001 Feb 27 (Pre) 81	17	2

Do you generally support or oppose the proposals that President Bush outlined tonight?

Support 85%
Oppose 12
No opinion 3

Thinking about taxes, do you favor or oppose the federal income tax cuts President Bush has proposed?

	Favor	Oppose	No opinion
2001 Feb 27 (Post) . . .79%	19%	2%	
2001 Feb 27 (Pre) 68	24	8	

How important a priority do you think federal income tax cuts should be for the Bush administration—a top priority, a high priority, a low priority, or not a priority at all?

	Top, high priority	Low, not at all	No opinion
2001 Feb 27 (Post) . . .83%	17%	0%	
2001 Feb 27 (Pre) 77	22	1	

Thinking about the federal income tax cuts President Bush has proposed, do you expect your taxes to go down a lot, go down a little, or not go down at all?

	Down a lot	Down a little	Not down at all*
2001 Feb 27 (Post) . . .13%	69%	15%	
2001 Feb 27 (Pre) 12	66	18	

*"No opinion" is omitted.

How confident are you that the economy is currently strong—very confident, somewhat confident, not too confident, or not at all confident?

	Very, somewhat confident	Not too, not at all confident	No opinion
2001 Feb 27 (Post) . . .73%	27%	0%	
2001 Feb 27 (Pre) 67	32	1	

Do you approve or disapprove of the proposals President Bush outlined tonight for dealing with the issue of Social Security?

Approve 82%
Disapprove 14
No opinion 4

Analysis: A Gallup Poll conducted immediately after President George W. Bush's February 27 speech shows that most viewers reacted very positively to the speech, believe that the president is leading the country in the right direction, feel confident in his abilities to carry out his duties as president, generally support the proposals he outlined, and specifically support his tax cuts. Viewers also give strong endorsement to the proposals he presented for dealing with Social Security. On the other hand, only about one-fifth indicate that the tax cuts should be a top priority for the Bush administration, and most expect that Bush's tax cut proposal would cause their taxes to go down a little instead of a lot.

The poll was conducted among 399 viewers who had been called February 25–26 and who indicated that they would be watching the speech. On Tuesday evening, more than nine in ten (92%) felt positive about Bush's speech, with 66% saying "very" positive.

Even before his speech, most gave high marks to Bush, but after the speech, the ratings were even higher. More than eight in ten (84%) said he was leading the country in the right direction, up from 73% who said that two days before the speech, and 86% felt either very or somewhat confident in his abilities to carry out his duties as president, up from 81% who said that before the speech.

The poll also shows that few indicate that the tax cuts should be a top priority for the Bush administration. Overall, 22% said it should be a top priority and another 61% a high priority. Last January, a poll of the general public showed 26% saying federal tax cuts should be a top priority and 39% a high priority, but that ranked the issue thirteenth out of the fourteen issues mentioned. One reason for the relatively low priority of the issue may be that few expect to benefit greatly from the program. Overall, 13% expected their taxes would go down a lot, while 69% said a little, and 15% said not at all.

MARCH 1
RELIGION IN PUBLIC SCHOOLS

Interview Dates: 2/9–11/01
CNN/*USA Today*/Gallup Poll
Survey #GO 132976

I'm going to read a variety of proposals concerning religion and public schools. For each one, please tell me whether you would generally favor it or oppose it:

Making public school facilities available after school hours for use by student religious groups?

	2001 Feb 9–11	1999 Jun 25–27
Favor	72%	78%
Oppose	26	21
No opinion	2	1

Allowing daily prayer to be spoken in the classroom?

	2001 Feb 9–11	1999 Jun 25–27
Favor	66%	68%
Oppose	34	70
No opinion	0	2

Allowing students to say prayers at graduation ceremonies as part of the official program?

	2001 Feb 9–11	1999 Jun 25–27
Favor	80%	77%
Oppose	20	21
No opinion	0	2

Thinking about the presence that religion currently has in public schools in this country, do you think religion has too much of a presence in public schools, about the right amount, or too little of a presence in public schools?

Too much	7%
About the right amount	28
Too little	63
No opinion	2

Analysis: Should student religious groups be allowed to hold their after-school meetings on public school grounds? The U.S. Supreme Court began hearing arguments this week in a case involving this separation of church and state question. While lower courts have issued conflicting rulings on the issue, the answer is clear for most Americans. According to a Gallup Poll conducted February 9–11, 72% favor the use of schools for this purpose while just 26% are opposed.

Not only is there widespread public support for opening school doors to religious groups, but—unlike the issue of school prayer—it is relatively noncontroversial. At least two-thirds or more of most major population subgroups find it acceptable for faith-based student groups to meet on public school grounds.

The Gallup Poll finds that Americans, overall, are generally tolerant of several possible religious activities that might be carried out on school grounds. In addition to the 72% who support making public school facilities available after hours for student religious groups, 80% believe students should be allowed to recite a spoken prayer at school graduations, and two-thirds (66%) think spoken prayer should be allowed in the classroom. Public attitudes on these issues have changed little since Gallup first asked these particular questions in 1999.

MARCH 2
DEATH PENALTY

Interview Dates: 2/19–21/01
Gallup Poll News Service
Survey #GO 133064

Are you in favor of the death penalty for a person convicted of murder?*

	For
2001 Feb 19–21	67%
2000 Aug 29–Sep 5	67
2000 Jun 23–25	66
2000 Feb 14–15	66
1999 Feb 8–9	71
1995 May 11–14	77
1994 Sep 6–7	80
1991 Jun 13–16	76
1988 Sep 25–Oct 1	79

1988 Sep 9–11 79
1986 Jan 10–13 .70
1985 Jan 11–14 .72
1985 Nov 11–18 75
1981 Jan 30–Feb 2 66
1978 Mar 3–6 62
1976 Apr 9–12 66
1972 Nov 10–13 57
1972 Mar 3–5 50
1971 Oct 29–Nov 2 49
1969 Jan 23–28 .51
1967 Jun 2–7 54
1966 May 19–24 42
1965 Jan 7–12 452
1960 Mar 2–7 53
1957 Aug 29–Sep 4 47
1956 Mar 29–Apr 3 53
1953 Nov 1–5 68

*Based on part sample

*Why do you favor the death penalty for persons convicted of murder?**

An eye for an eye; they took a life;
  fits the crime 48%
Save taxpayers money; cost associated
  with prison 20
Deterrent for potential crimes; set an
  example 10
They deserve it 6
Support; believe in death penalty 6
Depends on the type of crime they commit . . .6
They will repeat their crime; keep them
  from repeating it .6
Biblical reasons 3
Relieves prison overcrowding 2
If there's no doubt the person
  committed the crime 21
Life sentences don't always mean
  life in prison 2
Don't believe they can be rehabilitated 2
Serve justice 1
Fair punishment 1
Would help; benefit families of victims 1
Other (vol.) 3
No opinion 1

*Total adds to more than 100% due to multiple replies.

If you could choose between the following two approaches, which do you think is the better penalty for murder—the death penalty, or life imprisonment with absolutely no possibility of parole?

	Death penalty	Life imprisonment	No opinion
2001 Feb 19–21	.54%	42%	4%
2000 Aug 29–Sep 5	.49	47	4

What do you think should be the penalty for murder—the death penalty, or life imprisonment with absolutely no possibility of parole?

	Death penalty	Life imprisonment	No opinion
2001 Feb 19–21*	.57%	41%	2%
2000 Aug 29–Sep 5*	.50	47	3
2000 Feb 20–21	.52	37	11
1999 Feb 8–9*	.56	38	6
1997 Aug 12–13*	.61	29	10
1994 June 22	.50	32	18
1993 Oct 13–18	.59	29	12
1992 Mar 30–Apr 5	.50	37	13
1991 Jun 13–16	.53	35	12
1986 Jan 10–13	.55	35	10
1985 Jan 11–14	.56	34	10

*Asked of half sample

Analysis: The death penalty—long an issue in American politics—promises to return to the headlines as the scheduled execution of Oklahoma City bombing mastermind Timothy McVeigh approaches. The McVeigh case is taking on added controversy given his desire, and the desire of some families of victims, to have his execution televised. The Gallup Poll conducted February 19–21 shows that Americans' support for the death penalty has remained steady over the last year. Sixty-seven percent favor the death penalty for murder while 25% are against it. The numbers are essentially unchanged compared to three separate readings of the public's view on the death penalty from last year.

Gallup has been asking the public whether they "are in favor of the death penalty for a person convicted of murder" since 1953, and there have been a number of shifts in opinion over that time period. Support was initially high in 1953, but throughout the late 1950s and into the 1970s, Americans generally favored the death penalty but not by overwhelming margins. The percentage in favor of the death penalty ranged from 42% to 54% during that time. At one point (1966) more were against the death penalty (47%) than were for it (42%). There was much discussion about the constitutionality of the death penalty during this time, and no executions took place in the U.S. between 1968 and 1977.

When the Supreme Court finally ruled in 1976 that the death penalty in and of itself did not constitute "cruel and unusual punishment," it was restored in many states. In 1977, Gary Gilmore became the first inmate executed since its suspension in 1968. Perhaps in reaction to the Supreme Court decision, support for the death penalty began to increase in 1976 when 66% were in favor of it, the highest level of support since 1953. Support continued to increase over the next two decades, pushing past 70% in 1985 and reaching a high of 80% in 1994. Since then, support has declined, dropping to the current level of 67%. Even news of the Oklahoma City bombing, and the federal government's seeking (and obtaining) the death penalty for McVeigh in 1995, did not reverse the downward trend.

The standard Gallup trend question provides a basic view of support for the death penalty. Some critics have argued, however, that the public should be presented with alternatives to get what they consider to be a more realistic view of support for the death penalty. Therefore, Gallup also has gauged support for the death penalty by giving respondents a choice between the death penalty and life imprisonment with no possibility of parole. According to the latest poll, 54% favor the death penalty while 42% favor life imprisonment. This question has been asked several times over the years, and while the level of support for the death penalty is less compared with the standard question, more always have said they favored the death penalty to life imprisonment.

Gallup also asked supporters why they favored the death penalty. The question was asked in an open-ended format so respondents provided, in their own words, reasons why they favored the death penalty. The results show that Americans are most likely to support the death penalty because they believe it provides appropriate justice, or even vengeance, for the crime committed. A majority give a response touching on these aspects, including 48% who say the punishment "fits the crime," 6% who say "they deserve it," and 1% each who say that it is "fair punishment," "serves justice," or "benefits the families of the victims."

The data appear to show that more pragmatic reasons are much less important motivators of support for the death penalty. Twenty percent believe the death penalty "saves taxpayers money" and 10% think it is a deterrent to committing severe crimes. Despite the relatively small proportion who mentions these arguments, they are two of the primary ones cited by most death penalty proponents.

MARCH 5
CREATIONISM VS. EVOLUTION

Interview Dates: 2/19–21/01
Gallup Poll News Service
Survey #GO 133064

How informed would you say you are about the theory of evolution—do you feel that you are very informed, somewhat informed, not too informed, or not informed at all?

Very informed 34%
Somewhat informed .47
Not too informed 11
Not informed at all 6
No opinion 2

How informed would you say you are about the theory of creationism—do you feel that you are very informed, somewhat informed, not too informed, or not informed at all?

Very informed 40%
Somewhat informed .40

Not too informed 10
Not informed at all .7
No opinion 3

Would you say that you believe more in the theory of evolution or the theory of creationism to explain the theory of the origin of human beings, or are you unsure? [Those who were unsure were asked: Do you lean more toward the theory of evolution or the theory of creationism?]

Theory of evolution .28%
Lean toward evolution 5
Lean toward creationism 9
Theory of creationism 48
No opinion 10

Just your opinion—do you think that Charles Darwin's theory of evolution is a scientific theory that has been well supported by evidence, or just one of many theories and one that has not been well supported by evidence, or don't you know enough about it to say?

Supported by evidence 35%
Not supported by evidence 39
Don't know enough to say 25
No opinion 1

*Which of the following statements comes closest to your views on the origin and development of human beings—human beings have developed over millions of years from less advanced forms of life, but God guided this process; human beings have developed over millions of years from less advanced forms of life, but God had no part in this process; or God created human beings pretty much in their present form at one time within the last 10,000 years or so?**

	God guided process	God no part of process	God created present form
2001 Feb 19–21	.37%	12%	45%
1999 Aug 24–26	.40	9	47
1997 Nov 6–9	.39	10	44
1993 Jun	.35	11	47
1982	.38	9	44

*"No opinion" is omitted.

Analysis: Although most scientists subscribe to the theory of evolution as the best explanation for the origin of human beings, a recent Gallup Poll shows that the public is much more divided in its own beliefs. Americans choose "creationism" over "evolution" when asked which of these two terms better describes human origins, but slightly larger numbers choose one of two evolutionist explanations than choose a strict creationist explanation when given a choice between three specific views. At the same time, only about one-third say that Charles Darwin's theory of evolution is well supported by evidence.

These different beliefs about the origins of the human race have long been important topics of public debate. The Kansas Board of Education's recent reversal of its previous decision to omit references to many evolutionary concepts in its public school standards has focused more attention on the topic in recent weeks. While much of the debate centers on issues surrounding the separation of church and state in public school classrooms, the discussions often are premised largely on individuals' personal beliefs about Charles Darwin's theory of evolution and the biblical theory of creationism.

Gallup has asked respondents several times over the last twenty years to choose between three statements that describe the origin and development of the human race. Generally speaking, the plurality have come down on the side of a creationist approach to human origins, while slightly fewer have agreed with a statement that reflects an evolutionary process guided by God, and only a small number have agreed with an evolutionary process in which God had no part.

Most recently, in Gallup's February 19–21 poll, 45% chose "God created human beings pretty much in their present form at one time within the last 10,000 years or so," the statement that most closely describes biblical creationism. A slightly larger percentage (almost one-half), chose one of the two evolution-oriented statements: 37% selected "Human beings have developed over millions of years from less advanced forms of life, but God guided this process" and 12% chose "Human beings have developed over millions of years from less advanced forms of life, but God had no part in this process."

The public has not notably changed its opinion on this question since Gallup started asking it in 1982. After asking which of the three statements on the origin of humans they agreed with, Gallup asked respondents, by name, which of the two theories they believe in more. Given this choice, more than one-half believe in or lean toward the "theory of creationism" (57%) while far fewer believe in or lean toward the "theory of evolution" (33%), and one out of ten are unsure.

Generally, there is a good deal of consistency between responses to the two questions. The majority (two out of three) who believed more in creationism selected the statement "God created human beings pretty much in their present form at one time within the last 10,000 years or so." But interestingly, more than one-quarter of creationists selected a statement that can be seen as compatible with the scientific findings of evolutionary scholars: "Human beings have developed over millions of years from less advanced forms of life, but God guided this process." Only 1% of creationists selected the evolutionary statement saying that "God had no part in the process" while almost no creationists believe that humans developed without God's help, a not insignificant minority believes that human beings developed from lower forms of life, as evolutionary scientists suggest, but that God helped the process along.

People who choose evolution as their preferred theory are most comfortable with the idea that God guided an evolutionary process of human development. A majority (51%) selected the statement "Human beings have developed over millions of years from less advanced forms of life, but God guided this process," while 34% selected that statement with the condition that "God had no part in this process." Finally, just 10% chose the statement that God created human beings within the last 10,000 years. These findings tell us that only a very small minority of evolutionists choose a creationist explanation when confronted with the specifics of the theories. The vast majority of evolutionists are consistent and choose an evolutionary explanation, with or without God's involvement. On the other hand, over one-quarter who believe in the creationist perspective choose an evolutionary statement, albeit the one that has God's involvement. Therefore, it appears that a substantial proportion of creationists cannot be distinguished from the majority of evolutionists in the way they think about the origins and development of humankind. While 57% lean toward the label creationist, only 41% are creationists who do not support an evolutionary way of thinking about human development. The difference suggests that there is either a very broad interpretation of the term creationism—one that does not support the biblical account of the creation of the human race—or that there is misunderstanding about what the label creationism means, among at least some of the creation-leaning public. Another question included in the recent poll asked directly about the evidence supporting Charles Darwin's theory of evolution. Given a choice between three alternatives, only about one-third think that Charles Darwin's theory is "well supported by evidence," while slightly more (39%) believe that it is not well supported, and that it is "just one of many theories" on this subject. A substantial percentage (one in four) felt they didn't know enough to say.

However, not all Americans are consistent in their beliefs. Seventeen percent who say evolution is the best theory to explain human origins feel that evidence does not support the theory well in response to this specific question about Darwin's theory, while 16% indicate they don't know enough to say. Among people who prefer creationism, one out of five says the evidence supports Darwin's theory while 24% report they don't know enough to say.

Only 34% of Americans consider themselves to be "very informed" about the theory of evolution, while a slightly greater percentage (40%) consider themselves to be "very informed" about the theory of creation.

MARCH 7
DOGS VS. CATS

Interview Dates: 2/19–21/01
Gallup Poll News Service
Survey #GO 133064

Which animal do you think makes a better pet—a cat or dog?

Cat 23%
Dog 73
Neither; either (vol.); no opinion 4

Do you, or does any other member of your household, own a dog or dogs?

Yes 45%
No 55

Asked of dog owners: How many dogs do you own?

Mean   1.78
Median   1

Do you, or does any other member of your household, own a cat or cats?

Yes 34%
No 66

How many cats do you own?

Mean   2.05
Median   1

Analysis: In the perennial argument over which species of animal—canines or felines—are "man's best friend," a Gallup Poll suggests that Americans overall have given their heartfelt endorsement to the traditional favorite. By a margin of 73% to 23%, respondents say that dogs rather than cats are the "better pet." These results are similar to those found five and a half years ago when a Gallup Poll also found dogs the winner by more than a three-to-one margin (65% to 20%).

The public's widespread pro-canine sentiments are not simply a reflection of greater dog ownership, as the poll shows only a relatively slight advantage in the number of dog owners over cat owners. Overall, 45% own one or more dogs, while 34% own one or more cats. The perceptual advantage dogs have over cats comes not just from dog owners, but also from the 41% who currently own neither a cat nor a dog, as well as the 20% who own both. Those who own only dogs express the most lopsided sentiment in favor of that pet, with 93% saying dogs are better and just 6% choosing cats. But people who own both cats and dogs opt for dogs by 75% to 18%. People who don't even own a pet favor dogs by a similar margin of 72% to 24%. Only people who own cats—and cats alone—constitute a pro-cat majority, as 61% of this group choose their furry felines as the better pet. Still, more than a third of these exclusive cat owners (35%) rate dogs as better.

The poll shows that 25% own only a dog, 14% own only a cat, and 20% own both. Cat owners tend to have more cats per household than dog owners have dogs, but the number is not so great as to suggest there are actually more pet cats in this country than pet dogs. Among cat owners, the average number of cats in the household is 2.1, compared with 1.8 dogs among dog owners. However, when the total number of cats and dogs is compared across all households, Gallup results suggest that for every 100 households in the country, there are about 79 dogs and 68 cats.

MARCH 8
PRESIDENT BUSH/U.S. WORLD POSITION

Interview Dates: 2/1–4/01
Gallup Poll News Service
Survey #GO 132811

Do you approve or disapprove of the way George W. Bush is handling:

The economy?

Approve 53%
Disapprove 27
No opinion 20

Foreign affairs?

Approve 46%
Disapprove 21
No opinion 33

Do you think leaders of other countries around the world have respect for George W. Bush, or do you think they don't have much respect for him?

Respect him 49%
Do not respect him 38
No opinion 13

On the whole, would you say that you are satisfied or dissatisfied with the position of the United States in the world today?

	Satisfied	Dis-satisfied	No opinion
2001 Feb 1–4	.67%	30%	3%
2000 May 18–21	.65	33	2

How much trust and confidence do you have in our federal government in Washington when it comes to handling the following problems—a great deal, a fair amount, not very much, or none at all:

Domestic problems?

	Great deal; fair amount	Not very much; none at all	No opinion
2001 Feb 1–4	.63%	36%	1%
2000 Jul 6–9	.58	40	2
2000 May 18–21	.65	33	2

International problems?

	Great deal; fair amount	Not very much; none at all	No opinion
2001 Feb 1–4	.75%	23%	2%
2000 Jul 6–9	.72	27	1
2000 May 18–21	.53	46	1

In general, how do you think the United States rates in the eyes of the world—very favorably, somewhat favorably, somewhat unfavorably, or very unfavorably?

	Very, somewhat favorably	Somewhat, very unfavorably	No opinion
2001 Feb 1–4	.75%	24%	1%
2000 May 18–21	.73	26	1

Next, we would like you to think about the role the United States should play in trying to solve international problems. Do you think the United States. should take the leading role in world affairs, take a major role but not the leading role, take a minor role, or take no role at all in world affairs?

Leading role 16%
Major role 57
Minor role 21
No role 4
No opinion 2

Turning to the issue of foreign aid, do you think the United States is now spending too little on foreign aid, about the right amount, or too much on foreign aid?

Too little 9%
About the right amount 32
Too much 53
No opinion 6

Next, I'm going to read a list of possible foreign policy goals that the United States might have. For each one, please say whether you think it should be a very important foreign policy goal, a somewhat important goal, not too important a goal, or not an important goal at all?

	Very important
Preventing the spread of nuclear weapons	. . .82%
Securing adequate supplies of energy	79
Defending our allies' security	62

Maintaining superior military
power worldwide 59
Promoting and defending human
rights in other countries 51
Helping to improve the standard of
living of less developed nations 40
Protecting weaker nations against
foreign aggression 39
Building democracy in other countries 32

*Which of the following roles would you like
to see the United Nations play in world affairs today—should it play a leading role
where all countries are required to follow
United Nations policies, a major role where
the UN establishes policies but where individual countries still act separately when
they disagree with the UN, or should it play
a minor role with the UN serving mostly as
a forum for communication between nations
but with no policy making role?*

Leading role 19%
Major role 49
Minor role 28
Should not exist . . . .*
Other (vol.) 1
No opinion 3

*Less than 1%

Analysis: Today, Secretary of State Colin Powell
will be outlining further the Bush administration's approach to foreign policy when he testi-
fies before the Senate Foreign Relations
Committee. A recent Gallup Poll shows that 67%
of the public is satisfied with the U.S. position in
the world today while only 30% are dissatisfied.
The numbers are essentially unchanged from
May 2000, when 65% were satisfied and 33%
dissatisfied. Additionally, the vast majority
(75%) think the United States is viewed favorably in the eyes of the world.

Even though George W. Bush has little experience in the international arena, and to date, has
focused his attention on domestic issues such as
his budget and tax plan, Americans think that foreign leaders respect President Bush. According to

the poll, 49% think other world leaders respect
Bush, 38% think foreign leaders do not have
much respect for him, and 13% have no opinion.

In addition, the latest poll numbers show
that 46% approve of the way George W. Bush is
handling foreign affairs while only 21% disapprove. This poll was conducted before Bush's
most significant international action to date, the
recent air strikes against Iraq, which contributes
to the fact that one in three do not yet have an
opinion of his foreign policy expertise.

Part of Secretary Powell's new job of conducting foreign policy for the Bush administration will be to establish the U.S. level of
involvement in international affairs. Gallup's recent survey finds that Americans think the U.S.
should be a prominent player in the international
arena but not necessarily the world's leader. Only
16% thinks that the U.S. should take the leading
role in world affairs while 57% think the U.S.
should take a major role. A small minority
prefers that the U.S. should have only a minor
role (21%) or no role at all (4%) in solving international problems.

Another question for the Bush foreign policy
team to resolve is how much the U.S. should
spend on foreign aid. Traditionally, respondents
have been in favor of cutting the amount the government spends on foreign aid. In this poll, 53%
say that the U.S. currently spends too much on
foreign aid while 32% think it spends the right
amount. Only 9% think that the U.S. is currently
spending too little.

Gallup also presented Americans with a list
of foreign policy goals and asked them to indicate
how important they thought each was. A strong
majority thought each goal was at least somewhat
important, but two emerged as the most important: preventing the spread of nuclear weapons
(identified as very important by 82%) and securing adequate supplies of energy (79%). Further
down the list, respondents identified defending
our allies' security (62%), maintaining superior
military power worldwide (59%), and promoting
and defending human rights in other countries
(51%) as key goals.

The least important goals for the public are
those that appear more altruistic in nature: help-

ing to improve the standard of living in less developed nations (40%), protecting weaker nations against foreign aggression (39%), and building democracy in other countries (32%).

These results can be compared to the public's views about the United Nations' role in solving international problems, which are very similar. Slightly more think that the UN should take the leading role (19%) than the U.S. However, fewer say that the UN should take a major role (49%) in world affairs than the U.S. Combined, 68% think the UN should take a major or leading role in foreign affairs, while 73% say this about the U.S. In all, it appears Americans favor a foreign policy approach that is not dominated by one country or organization, but one in which the U.S. and the UN are prominent participants.

MARCH 12
ECONOMIC CONDITIONS/
MOST IMPORTANT PROBLEMS

Interview Dates: 3/5–7/01
Gallup Poll News Service
Survey #GO 132070

How would you rate economic conditions in this country today—excellent, good, only fair, or poor?

	Excellent, good	Only fair	Poor; no opinion
2001 Mar 5–7	46%	43%	11%
2001 Feb 1–4	51	36	13
2001 Jan 10–14	67	27	6

How likely do you think it is that there will be a recession in the country during the next twelve months—very likely, fairly likely, not too likely, or not at all likely?

	Very, fairly likely	Not too, not at all likely**
2001 Mar 5–7	49%	48%
2001 Feb 1–4	53	42

| 2000 Dec 2–4 | .45 | 50 |

*Based on part sample
**"No opinion" is omitted.

Do you think the economy is now in a recession, or not?

	Yes	No	No opinion
2001 Mar 5–7	31%	64%	5%
2001 Feb 1–4	44	49	7

*Based on part sample

What do you think is the most important problem facing this country today?

	2001 Mar 5–7*	2001 Jan 10–14*
Economic Problems	**29%**	**22%**
Economy in general	10	7
Taxes	7	5
Unemployment; jobs	4	4
Recession	3	4
Federal budget deficit; federal debt	2	1
High cost of living; inflation	2	1
Fuel; oil prices	1	2
Wage issues	1	1
Gap between rich and poor	1	1
Trade relations; deficit	**	**
Other specific economic	1	**
Noneconomic Problems	**76%**	**77%**
Education	16	12
Ethics; moral; religious; family decline; dishonesty; lack of integrity	11	13
Crime; violence	8	9
Poor health care; hospitals; high cost of health care	7	7
Children's behavior; way they are raised	6	3
Drugs	6	7
Dissatisfaction with government; Congress; politicians; candidates; poor leadership; corruption	5	9
Poverty; hunger; homelessness	5	4

School shootings; school violence 5	0
International issues; problems 4	4
Medicare; Social Security 4	3
Guns; gun control 4	1
Lack of military defense 2	2
Fear of war 2	**
Lack of energy sources 2	4
Race relations; racism 2	4
Environment; pollution 2	2
Care for the elderly 1	2
Lack of respect for each other 1	—
The media 1	1
Abortion .1	1
National security 1	—
Welfare 1	2
Foreign aid; focus overseas 1	**
Judicial system; courts; laws 1	1
Unifying the country 1	1
Overpopulation 1	1
Election; election reform . . . .**	2
Immigration; illegal aliens . . . . . .**	2
Advancement of computers; technology . . . .**	0
Child abuse . . . .—	1
AIDS . . . .—	**
Other noneconomic issues 1	3
No opinion 7	8

*Total adds to more than 100% due to multiple replies.
**Less than 1%

Next, I'm going to read a list of problems facing the country. For each one, please tell me if you personally worry about this problem a great deal, a fair amount, only a little, or not at all?

	Great deal, fair amount	Only a little, not at all*
Crime and violence 88%	12%
The availability and affordability of health care 84	16
Drug use .80	20
The availability and affordability of energy 77	22
Hunger and homelessness 79	21

The quality of the environment 77	22
The economy 77	23
Unemployment 63	48
Race relations 62	38
Illegal immigration 52	47

*"No opinion" is omitted.

Analysis: The latest Gallup measures of the economy are not much different from those obtained last month, suggesting a pause in the decline in consumer sentiment. Americans' ratings of current economic conditions are significantly below where they were as recently as January, and ratings of the direction of the economy are significantly below where they were as recently as last fall. Still, the rating of the current economy is about as high now as it was right before the 1996 presidential election, and nowhere near as low as it was in the early 1990s. Other measures also indicate at least a moderating of consumer pessimism, as the number expecting a recession within the next year has declined, as has the number who think the economy is in a recession right now.

The most recent poll on the economy was conducted March 5–7 and shows that 46% rate the economy as excellent or good, 43% as fair, and 10% as poor. Last month, the percentage who said excellent or good was slightly higher (51%) but the percentage saying poor was also slightly higher at 13%.

Other attitudes measured in the poll reinforce the interpretation that public economic sentiment has at least held steady over the past month, if not improved slightly. In February, Americans were more likely than not to think there would be a recession in the next year by an 11-point margin (53% to 42%). The most recent measure shows an almost evenly divided public, with 49% who think a recession is likely and 48% who think it unlikely. More dramatic is the change in the number who think the country is currently in a recession, from 44% who thought so last month to just 31% this month.

Another indication that the public still

views the economy as mostly positive is that only 29% identify some aspect of the economy as one of the most important problems facing the country today, while 76% identify some noneconomic aspect such as education, morality, crime, and health care. In January, the comparable figures were 22% and 77%, respectively, suggesting only a slight change over the past two months. Further, when asked specifically to rate how much they worry about each of ten problems, respondents ranked the economy seventh behind crime, health care, drugs, energy, homelessness, and the environment.

MARCH 13
INCOME TAX CUT

Interview Dates: 3/9–11/01
CNN/*USA Today*/Gallup Poll
Survey #GO 133198

As you may know, on Thursday, the House of Representatives passed a plan to cut federal income taxes that had been proposed by President Bush. Do you approve or disapprove of that vote?

Approve 61%
Disapprove 33
No opinion 6

The Senate now will consider the tax cut plan passed by the House. Do you think the Senate should pass the tax cut plan substantially as the House passed it, pass the tax cut plan but only with major changes, or reject the tax cut?

Pass tax cut as House passed it 41%
Pass tax cut but with major changes 35
Reject tax plan 17
No opinion 7

Looking ahead to the debate on the tax bill in the U.S. Senate, would you favor or oppose each of the following changes to the tax cut plan passed by the House:

Significantly lowering the total amount of the tax cuts?

Favor 59%
Oppose 36
No opinion 5

Stopping the tax cuts if it looks like they will create a budget deficit in the future?

Favor 63%
Oppose 33
No opinion 4

Adjusting the plan so that more of the tax cuts go to lower-income taxpayers?

Favor 75%
Oppose 22
No opinion 3

Do you think the federal government has enough money for education and Social Security, paying down the federal debt, as well as for the tax cut that the House of Representatives passed on Thursday?

Yes 51%
No 43
No opinion 6

If the tax cut plan is enacted, how likely is it that each of the following would happen— very likely, somewhat likely, not too likely, or not at all likely: *

It would cause a federal budget deficit?

	2001 Mar 9–11	2001 Feb 9–11
Very, somewhat likely	56%	53%
Not too, not at all likely	39	42
No opinion	5	5

It would take money away that is needed to protect Social Security?

	2001 Mar 9–11	2001 Feb 9–11
Very, somewhat likely	56%	57%

Not too, not at all likely 40   39
No opinion 4   4

It would mostly benefit the rich?

	2001 Mar 9–11	2001 Feb 9–11
Very, somewhat likely	75%	75%
Not too, not at all likely	22	22
No opinion	3	3

*Based on part sample

If the tax cut plan is enacted, how likely is it that each of the following would happen—very likely, somewhat likely, not too likely, or not at all likely:

It would provide you and your family money to spend and save?

Very, somewhat likely 62%
Not too, not at all likely 37
No opinion 1

It would provide others in the country money to spend and save?

Very, somewhat likely 73%
Not too, not at all likely 25
No opinion 2

It would help the economy?

Very, somewhat likely 68%
Not too, not at all likely 28
No opinion 4

*Based on part sample

For each of the following, please tell me whether it would or would not make you less likely to support the tax cut plan:

You thought it would cause a federal budget deficit?

Would 49%
Would not 47
No opinion 4

You thought it would take money away that is needed to protect Social Security?

Would 50%
Would not 48
No opinion 2

You thought it would mostly benefit the rich?

Would 47%
Would not 50
No opinion 3

*Based on part sample

For each of the following, please tell me whether it would or would not make you more likely to support the tax cut plan:

You thought it would provide you and your family money to spend and save?

Would 79%
Would not 19
No opinion 2

You thought it would provide others in the country money to spend and save?

Would 76%
Would not 20
No opinion 4

You thought it would help the economy?

Would 86%
Would not 11
No opinion 3

Analysis: A review of recent polling about President Bush's $1.6 trillion tax cut plan suggests that Americans are generally supportive of a tax cut bill being passed by Congress and signed into law, but are prepared to accept such a bill even if significantly modified in the deliberative process. While 61% think the House of Representatives did the right thing by passing it last week, the public is open to modifying the bill, and appears sympathetic to the arguments for and against the plan. These findings, coupled with the fact that tax cuts are a low priority for Americans, make it hard to imagine that the result will generate much public enthusiasm or uproar regardless of what ultimately happens to the bill.

When asked about it without qualification or reasons for opposition, it is no surprise that a majority react positively to the passage of President Bush's bill. A long-term Gallup trend has found more than 70% consistently favor a tax cut. In polls conducted over the past two months, respondents consistently have said that they favor Bush's tax cut proposals

Additionally, when asked about the bill, close to two-thirds think it is likely to provide their families more money to spend and save, nearly 75% think it will help others in this way, and 68% think it will help the economy. And most say these benefits are only "somewhat likely" to happen rather than "very likely."

Americans also tend toward the Republican argument that the government has sufficient funding for education, Social Security, debt reduction, and tax cuts. Fifty-one percent agree that the government has enough money to do all of these things simultaneously while 43% disagree.

Basic support for the Bush bill and belief that it will produce benefits do not mean that the public is opposed to Senate modifications. Despite the fact that a majority approve of the House of Representative's passage of the bill, only 41% think the Senate should approve the bill intact. Nearly as many (35%) think the Senate should pass it with modifications. Still, only 17% say they want the Senate to reject the tax cut bill outright. Seventy-six percent say that the Senate should pass some form of tax cuts, even if not exactly in the form handed to them by the House. Fifty-six percent agree that a tax cut would likely cause a federal budget deficit, 56% that it would take needed money away from Social Security, and 75% that it would mostly benefit the rich.

MARCH 14
"SURVIVOR" TELEVISION SHOW

Interview Dates: 3/9–11/01
CNN/*USA Today*/Gallup Poll
Survey #GO 133198

Have you yourself happened to watch "Survivor" this year?

Yes	37%
No	63

Asked of those who watched "Survivor": Now, thinking about the participants who are left on the show—Alicia, Elisabeth, Nick, Rodger, Amber, Colby, Jerri, Keith, and Tina—if you had a vote, who would you vote off the show next?

Jerri	27%
Colby	10
Tina	10
Alicia	7
Amber	4
Keith	2
Elisabeth	1
Nick	1
Rodger	1
Other	*
None	2
All	1
No opinion	34

*Less than 1%

As you may know, there have been several new reality-based programs on television recently like "Survivor" and "Temptation Island." How truthful do you think these reality-based programs are—they are as truthful as documentaries, they take some liberties but are essentially truthful, they show us only what they want us to see and present a distorted picture of events, or they are totally phony?

As truthful as documentaries	1%
Take some liberties, essentially truthful	12
Show only what they want us to see	57
Totally phony	23
No opinion	7

Analysis: More than one-third of the American public has watched the CBS Television program "Survivor" this year, an estimated 75 million adults. Among these viewers, there appears to be a developing consensus that Jerri should be the next participant to be kicked out of the dwindling group who are attempting to survive in the Australian outback. Most Americans seem aware that reality shows like "Survivor" are more show business than documentary, and about one out of four go so far as to say that they are totally phony.

The sequel to "Survivor" features contestants competing to see who can remain in the Australian Outback the longest in order to win the $1 million grand prize. "Survivor II" has been among the top-rated programs since its premiere following the Super Bowl on January 28. In fact, a Gallup Poll conducted March 9–11 shows that more than one-third of the public (37%) have watched the program this year.

Like its predecessor, this edition of "Survivor" revolves around the drama of one contestant being voted out of the contest each week by his or her peers. If the show's viewers (27%) had their way, Jerri (the bartender and actress from California) would be the next person voted out. No one else comes even close to Jerri in terms of having engendered the dislike of viewers. Colby and Tina follow as the participants viewers would most like to see removed, but each are named by only 10 percent. Alicia and Amber draw 7% and 4% of viewers naming them, respectively.

Recently, reality-based television shows have been all the rage on the airwaves, with as many as six such shows airing in 2000 or 2001, and even more currently in production. Basically, the public views reality-based programs more as fiction than fact as over one-half (57%) believe they "show only what they want us to see," and 23% think such programs are "totally phony." The March 9–11 survey also shows that 12% believes reality-based programs are "essentially truthful, but take some liberties," and just a miniscule 1% say they are as "truthful as documentaries."

MARCH 14
CLINTON'S PRESIDENTIAL
PARDONS

Interview Dates: 3/9–11/01
CNN/*USA Today*/Gallup Poll
Survey #GO 133198

Now, I have a few questions about the pardons that Bill Clinton granted in his final days as president. How important an issue do you think these pardons are to the nation—very important, somewhat important, not too important, or not important at all?

Very important 33%
Somewhat important 30
Not too important 17
Not important at all 17
No opinion 3

Which of the following statements best describes your view of Bill Clinton's actions relating to the pardons—Bill Clinton did something illegal, he did something unethical but not illegal, he did not do anything seriously wrong, or are you unsure?

Clinton did something illegal 18%
Clinton did something very unethical
  but not illegal 35
Clinton did something slightly unethical
  but not illegal 22
Clinton did not do anything seriously
  wrong 22
Not sure; no opinion 3

Overall, do you approve or disapprove of Bill Clinton's presidential pardon of financier Marc Rich?

	Approve	Dis-approve	No opinion
2001 Mar 5–7 . . . . . . .11%		75%	14%
2001 Feb 19–21* 20		62	18

*Based on half sample

Currently, congressional committees are holding hearings into Bill Clinton's pardon of financier Marc Rich—do you think these hearings should continue, or not?

Yes, should continue 49%

No, should not continue 43
No opinion 8

Analysis: According to a Gallup Poll—conducted March 9–11, the public has an overwhelmingly critical view of the pardons Bill Clinton gave just prior to leaving the presidency. As federal prosecutors in New York and congressional committees in Washington continue to probe the details of the pardons, only about one in five (18%) think Clinton did something illegal. An additional 57% think he did something unethical but not illegal. Combined, 75% have a negative view of the pardons that matches the 75% in a March 5–7 Gallup Poll who disapprove of the most controversial pardon, that of fugitive financier Marc Rich. Only 11% approve of the Rich pardon, down from 20% last month.

The fifty-seven percent who say Clinton did something unethical can be divided into two camps: 35% say he did something very unethical and 22% say his actions were only slightly unethical. Just 22% think he did nothing seriously wrong. Therefore, a majority (53%) rate his actions in rather seriously negative terms (as either illegal or very unethical), while fewer (44%) rate them less seriously by characterizing them as slightly unethical or not wrong at all.

At this point, it is unclear how far investigations into the pardons will go, but when asked in Gallup's March 5–7 survey about the status of congressional hearings into the Rich pardon, 49% felt the hearings should continue while 43% felt they should stop.

MARCH 15
STOCK MARKET DROP

Interview Date: 3/14/01
CNN/*USA Today*/Gallup Poll
Survey #GO 133237

As you may know, the Dow Jones Industrial Average of stocks lost more than 300 points and fell below the 10,000 mark today. Did the fall in the stock market affect your family's financial position in a major way, a minor way, or not at all?

	Major way	Minor way	Not at all; no opinion
National Adults			
2001 Mar 14 . . . . .7%		35%	58%
Stockholders			
2001 Mar 14 9		49	42
Nonstockholders			
2001 Mar 14 3		11	86

How concerned are you personally about the direction the stock market takes in the next year—very concerned, somewhat concerned, not too concerned, or not at all concerned?

	Very, somewhat concerned	Not too, not at all concerned	No opinion
National Adults			
2001 Mar 14 . . . . .59%		40%	1%
Stockholders			
2001 Mar 14 67		33	*
Nonstockholders			
2001 Mar 14 43		54	3

*Less than 1%

Next, please tell me whether the recent changes in the stock market have, or have not:

Made you feel less confident about the nation's economy?

Yes 51%
No 46
No opinion 3

Made you less likely to invest in the stock market?

Yes 40%
No 56
No opinion 4

Made you less confident that you will be able to live comfortably when you retire?

Yes 33%

No 58
No opinion 7

Made you feel less confident about your own personal financial situation?

Yes 29%
No 69
No opinion 2

Made you seriously consider canceling or postponing a big purchase, vacation, or other expenditure?

Yes 21%
No 77
No opinion 3

Made you less confident about your job situation?

Yes 15%
No 66
No opinion 19

What do you think will happen to the stock market in the next six months—the stock market will get better, the stock market will stabilize, or the stock market will get worse? And do you think the stock market will get much worse or get a little worse?*

	Better	Stabilize	Little, much worse**
National Adults			
2001 Mar 14 ....29%		50%	16%
Stockholders			
2001 Mar 14 29		54	14
Nonstockholders			
2001 Mar 14 29		43	19

*Combined replies
**"No opinion" is omitted.

Looking more broadly at the economy, what do you think will happen in the next six months—the economy will get better, the economy will stabilize, or the economy will

get worse? And do you think the economy will get much worse or get a little worse?*

	Better	Stabilize	Little, much worse**
National Adults			
2001 Mar 14 ....23%		49%	25%
Stockholders			
2001 Mar 14 19		53	26
Nonstockholders			
2001 Mar 14 30		43	23

*Combined replies
**"No opinion" is omitted.

As mentioned earlier, today the Dow Jones finished the day below the 10,000 mark. Do you consider this a significant economic milestone, or no big deal?

	Significant milestone	No big deal	No opinion
National Adults			
2001 Mar 14 ....37%		57%	6%
Stockholders			
2001 Mar 14 41		55	4
Nonstockholders			
2001 Mar 14 28		63	9

As you may know, people who think the market will rise are usually described as bulls and people who think the market will drop are usually described as bears. Would you currently describe yourself more as a bull or more as a bear?

	Bull	Bear	No opinion
National Adults			
2001 Mar 14 ....52%		38%	10%
Stockholders			
2001 Mar 14 59		35	6
Nonstockholders			
2001 Mar 14 41		42	17

Does today's drop in the stock market make you more likely to support a tax cut, make no difference in your support for a tax cut, or make you less likely to support a tax cut?

	More likely	No difference	Less likely*
National Adults			
2001 Mar 14 ....39%	42%	16%
Stockholders			
2001 Mar 14 44	38	15
Nonstockholders			
2001 Mar 14 29	50	17

*"No opinion" is omitted.

Do you personally, or jointly with a spouse, have any money invested in the stock market right now either in an individual stock, a stock mutual fund, or in a self-directed 401(k) or IRA?

	Yes	No	No opinion
2001 Mar 14 ....64%	35%	1%
2000 May 5–7 54	44	2
2000 Mar 10–12 61	37	2
2000 Jan 7–10 61	38	1

Analysis: According to a Gallup Poll conducted Wednesday night after the Dow Jones Industrial Average dropped more than 300 points during the day and closed at its lowest level in almost two years, Americans remain more bullish than bearish about the stock market. By a margin of 57% to 37%, they say the close of the index below the 10,000 mark is no big deal rather than a significant milestone and, by a somewhat smaller margin (52% to 38%), describe themselves as bulls rather than bears. Furthermore, by a margin of 29% to 16%, they expect the stock market to be better rather than worse in the next six months, with half expecting it to stabilize.

Still, the poll shows that a slight majority (51%) say that recent changes in the stock market have made them feel less confident about the nation's economy. Thirty-three percent feel less confident that they will be able to live comfortably when they retire, and 29% feel less confident about their own personal financial situation. In addition, 40% (42% among stockholders) say the recent changes in the stock market have made them less likely to invest in the stock market, while 21% say they are now seriously considering putting off a major purchase, vacation, or other expenditure. When predicting how the economy will fare over the next six months, Americans are more ambivalent about it than they are about the stock market, as one-half expect the economy to stabilize, 25% expect it to get worse, and 23% better. The most recent poll finds that 42% say their family's financial position has been affected by the current fall in the stock market (7% say in a "major" way, 35% in a "minor" way).

MARCH 16
ENERGY VS. THE ENVIRONMENT

Interview Dates: 3/5–7/01
Gallup Poll News Service
Survey #GO 132070

I'm going to read a list of problems facing the country. For each one, please tell me if you personally worry about this problem a great deal, a fair amount, only a little, or not at all:

Crime and violence?

Great deal; fair amount 88%
Only a little 9
Not at all; no opinion 3

The availability and affordability of health care?

Great deal; fair amount 84%
Only a little 11
Not at all; no opinion 5

Drug use?

Great deal; fair amount 80%
Only a little 13
Not at all; no opinion 7

The availability and affordability of energy?

Great deal; fair amount 77%
Only a little 16
Not at all; no opinion 7

Hunger and homelessness?

Great deal; fair amount 79%
Only a little 16
Not at all; no opinion 5

The quality of the environment?

Great deal; fair amount 77%
Only a little 17
Not at all; no opinion 6

The economy?

Great deal; fair amount 77%
Only a little 19
Not at all; no opinion 4

Unemployment?

Great deal; fair amount 63%
Only a little 24
Not at all; no opinion 13

Race relations?

Great deal; fair amount 62%
Only a little 23
Not at all; no opinion 15

Illegal immigration?

Great deal; fair amount 52%
Only a little 29
Not at all; no opinion 19

With which one of these statements about the environment and energy production do you more agree—protection of the environment should be given priority, even at the risk of limiting the amount of energy supplies; or development of U.S. energy supplies should be given priority, even if the environment suffers to some extent?

Protection of the environment 52%
Development of energy supplies 36
Both equally (vol.) .6

Neither; other (vol.) 2
No opinion 4

Next, I am going to read some specific environmental proposals. For each one, please say whether you generally favor or oppose it:

Setting higher emissions and pollution standards for business and industry?

Favor 81%
Oppose 17
No opinion 2

Spending more government money on developing solar and wind power?

Favor 79%
Oppose 19
No opinion 2

More strongly enforcing federal environmental regulations?

Favor 77%
Oppose 20
No opinion 3

Setting higher auto emissions standards for automobiles?

Favor 75%
Oppose 23
No opinion 2

Giving tax breaks to provide incentives for drilling for more oil and gas in the United States?

Favor 53%
Oppose 45
No opinion 4

Expanding use of nuclear energy?

Favor 44%
Oppose 51
No opinion 5

Opening up the Alaskan Arctic Wildlife Refuge for oil exploration?

Favor 40%
Oppose 56
No opinion 4

Setting legal limits on the amount of energy which average consumers can use?

Favor 35%
Oppose 62
No opinion 3

How serious would you say the energy situation is in the United States—very serious, fairly serious, or not at all serious?

Very serious 31%
Fairly serious 59
Not at all serious; no opinion 10

Which of the following approaches to solving the nation's energy problems do you think the United States should follow right now—emphasize production of more oil, gas, and coal supplies; or emphasize more conservation by consumers of existing energy supplies?

More production 33%
More conservation 56
Both equally (vol.) 8
Neither; other (vol.) 1
No opinion 2

Do you think that the United States is or is not likely to face a critical energy shortage during the next five years?

Is 60%
Is not 36
Already facing one (vol.) 1
No opinion 3

Overall, do you strongly favor, somewhat favor, somewhat oppose, or strongly oppose the use of nuclear energy as one of the ways to provide electricity for the United States?*

Strongly favor 20%
Somewhat favor 26
Somewhat oppose 28
Strongly oppose 20
No opinion 6

*Based on part sample

Overall, would you strongly favor, somewhat favor, somewhat oppose, or strongly oppose the construction of a nuclear energy plant in your area as one of the ways to provide electricity for the United States?*

Strongly favor 11%
Somewhat favor 23
Somewhat oppose 19
Strongly oppose 44
No opinion 3

*Based on part sample

Do you think George W. Bush will do a good job or a poor job handling each of the following issues as president:

Protecting the nation's environment?

Good job 51%
Poor job 38
Fair; mixed (vol.); no opinion 11

Improving the nation's energy policies?

Good job 58%
Poor job 29
Fair; mixed (vol.); no opinion 13

Keeping America prosperous?

Good job 66%
Poor job 23
Fair; mixed (vol.); no opinion 11

Increased efforts by business and industry to reduce air pollution might lead to higher prices for the things consumers buy. Would you be willing to pay $100 more each year in higher prices so that industry could reduce air pollution, or not?*

Yes 74%
No 24
No opinion 2

*Based on part sample

Increased efforts by business and industry to reduce air pollution might lead to higher prices for the things consumers buy. Would you be willing to pay $500 more each year in higher prices so that industry could reduce air pollution, or not?

Yes 63%
No 35
No opinion 2

*Based on part sample

Analysis: President Bush angered environmental groups this week with a decision to reverse his campaign pledge to regulate the amount of carbon dioxide emitted by energy producing plants. That, added to his previous decision to allow oil and gas drilling in the Arctic National Wildlife Refuge, has positioned Bush squarely on the probusiness side of the energy versus environmentalism divide.

At the root of these decisions is Bush's view that "We have a serious energy problem that demands a national energy policy," as expressed in his February 27 speech before a joint session of Congress. But a new Gallup Poll, focusing on the topic of energy, suggests a mixed reaction to the seriousness of energy issues among Americans today. Only 31% in the March 5–7 survey describe the energy situation today as "very serious." Most (59%) consider it only "fairly serious," while a handful (9%) discount the problem entirely.

At the same time, responses to a different question included in the poll show that almost one-half are personally worried about the nation's energy supply, and that these worries rank fairly high among other issues tested in the survey. Forty-six percent say they worry "a great deal" about the availability and affordability of energy. A similar number worry this much about hunger and homelessness, and environmental quality.

Still, crime, health care, and drug use rate as larger concerns for most. Respondents also differ from the new administration in their preferred approach to solving the nation's energy woes. Although the details are still being worked out, Bush's strategy is expected to emphasize increased production of domestic energy supplies. Several findings from the new poll suggest that Americans would prefer that he pursue energy conservation and other more proenvironmental alternatives. When asked which of two approaches the U.S. should use to solve the nation's current energy problems—more production of oil, gas and coal supplies or more conservation by consumers of existing supplies—Americans choose conservation over production 56% to 33%. And when asked which of two goals should prevail—environmental protection at the risk of limiting energy supplies, or the development of U.S. energy supplies such as oil, gas and coal at the risk of some environmental damage—respondents choose environmental protection over energy production 52% to 36%.

A majority (56%) opposes opening up the Alaskan Arctic Wildlife Refuge for oil exploration while just 40% favor it. Eighty-one percent favor setting higher emissions and pollution standards for business and industry, and just 17% are opposed. Seventy-seven percent favor more strongly enforcing federal environmental regulations, and 75% favor setting higher auto emissions standards for automobiles. Only 44% favor expanding the use of nuclear energy while 51% are opposed. And Americans favor instituting tax breaks to provide incentives for more oil and gas drilling in the U.S., but only by a slim margin: 53% versus 43%.

There are limits, however, on the extent to which Americans will back conservation. The new poll finds they are willing to pay higher prices for consumer items in order to pay for higher emissions controls. Three-quarters (74%) would be willing to pay $100 more in higher costs per year if it meant increased efforts by business and industry to reduce air pollution. Almost two-thirds (63%) would be willing to pay $500 more per year for this purpose.

At the same time, the new Gallup Poll finds only 35% of the public in favor of legal limits on the amount of energy that average consumers can use. Nearly two-thirds of (62%) oppose such limits. However, as of early March, Americans mainly were optimistic in their assessment of Bush's handling of both energy and the environment. At that time, roughly three out of five (58%) expected Bush to do a good job improving the nation's energy polices, and only 35% anticipate a fair or poor job. Nearly as many (51%) had positive expectations about his efforts to protect the nation's environment. A substantial minority (43%) expects Bush to do only a fair or poor job in this area.

One area where the public and the Bush administration seem to agree is renewable energy. The Bush budget reportedly will include new tax credits to encourage the use of solar and other renewable energy. The new poll finds 79% in favor of more government spending to develop solar and wind power.

MARCH 19
AMERICANS' FEARS

Interview Dates: 2/19–21/01
Gallup Poll News Service
Survey #GO 133064

Everybody has fears about different things, but some are more afraid of certain things than others. I'm going to read a list of some of these fears. For each one, please tell me whether you are afraid of it, or not. *

	Men	Women
Mice	.6%	33%
Snakes	.38	62
Spiders and insects	.15	38
Being closed in a small space	..25	42
Heights	.31	41
Thunder and lightning	.6	16
Flying on an airplane	.14	22
Public speaking in front of an audience	.37	44
Dogs	.7	14
The dark	.2	8
Crowds	.10	12
Needles and getting shots	.20	21

Going to the doctor	.11	8

*Totals add to more than 100% due to multiple replies.

Analysis: What scares Americans most? It isn't the dark, or thunder and lightning, or even flying on an airplane. What really strikes fear in the hearts of many are snakes. A recent Gallup Poll that asked adults what they were afraid of reveals that more people (51%) fear snakes than any other suggested possibility, including speaking in public in front of an audience (40%) and heights (36%). And while children are reputed to fear the dark, only 5% of surveyed adults do. Just 11% of adults fear thunder and lightning. Although the occasional airplane crash or threat of terrorism make for big news, only 18% are afraid to fly on an airplane; this, despite the fact, that 36% fear heights and 34% fear being closed in a small space.

When it comes to fears—or at least admitting to them—clear gender differences emerge. The survey reveals that women are more likely than men to be fearful of most of the situations tested, but in particular, women disproportionately fear reptiles, rodents, and insects.

In the poll, 62% of women say they fear snakes while just 38% of men claim to share this fear. Other living creatures frighten women more, too: 38% say they are afraid of spiders and insects, compared to 15% of men. Mice really scare women a lot more: 33% fear these rodents compared to just 6% of men. The only creatures that do not inspire fear in too many people are dogs: 14% of women fear canines and just 7% of men fear the animals famously said to be their best friends.

MARCH 20
CAMPAIGN FINANCE REFORM

Interview Dates: 3/9–11/01
CNN/*USA Today*/Gallup Poll
Survey #GO133198

When it comes to dealing with campaign finance reform, whose approach do you prefer—George W. Bush or John McCain?

Bush	.33%

McCain 43
Same; both (vol.) 1
Neither (vol.) 3
No opinion 20

Would you favor or oppose new federal laws limiting the amount of money that any individual or group can contribute to the national political parties? And do you feel strongly or moderately about that?

Strongly favor 51%
Moderately favor 25
Moderately oppose 10
Strongly oppose 9
No opinion 5

In general, if new campaign finance reform legislation were passed, do you think it would make our democratic form of government work much better than it does now, just a little better, about the same, just a little worse, or much worse than it does now?

Much better 22%
A little better 37
About the same 32
A little worse 3
Much worse 2
No opinion 4

How closely have you followed the debate over campaign finance—very closely, somewhat closely, not too closely, or not closely at all?

Very closely 10%
Somewhat closely 39
Not too closely 31
Not closely at all 20
No opinion ....*

*Less than 1%

Analysis: As the U.S. Senate begins debate this week on campaign finance reform, a review of Gallup Polls on the issue shows that Americans are dissatisfied with current campaign finance laws and generally support efforts to limit campaign contributions to political parties.

The debate in the next two weeks will be over several proposals, all of which limit, to some extent, the amount of money that Americans and American businesses can contribute to political parties—so-called "soft money"—that allows parties to indirectly support candidates running for office. One proposal by Senators John McCain (R) of Arizona and Russ Feingold (D) of Wisconsin would ban all such soft money contributions, while a proposal by Senator Chuck Hagel (R) of Nebraska would only limit the amount of such contributions. President George W. Bush has agreed to support campaign finance reform by banning soft money contributions from corporations and labor unions, but not individuals.

A recent Gallup Poll conducted March 9–11 shows widespread public support for some type of limit on campaign contributions. By a margin of 76% to 19%, Americans favor new federal laws limiting the amount of money that any individual or group can contribute to the national political parties, with 51% saying they favor the idea "strongly" and 25% "moderately." Also, 59% say that if new campaign finance reform legislation were passed, it would make our democratic form of government work better than it does now, while only 5% say worse and 32% say it would not matter.

In addition, McCain's efforts in the Senate may be bolstered by poll results showing that respondents are more likely to say they prefer McCain's approach to campaign reform over Bush's approach by 43% to 33%.

MARCH 21
VICE PRESIDENT CHENEY

Interview Dates: 3/9–11/01
CNN/*USA Today*/Gallup Poll
Survey #GO 133198

Are you concerned or not concerned that Vice President Dick Cheney's health problems will prevent him from serving effectively as vice president?

Concerned 39%
Not concerned 59
No opinion 2

Which comes closest to your view concerning Vice President Dick Cheney's health problems—Cheney should resign as vice president, Cheney should remain as vice president but cut back on his duties, or Cheney should remain as vice president and continue with his current duties with little or no change?

Should resign 11%
Cut back on duties 21
Continue duties 66
No opinion 2

Analysis: Americans seem to agree with Dick Cheney's boss that the vice president need not reduce his workload as a result of recent bouts with coronary heart disease. Even fewer agree with the handful of political observers who have publicly called for the vice president's resignation.

Last November, after Cheney suffered his fourth heart attack, only 30% of the public expressed concern that his health problems would prevent him from serving effectively as vice president should the Bush-Cheney ticket win. Now, after a new heart scare for Cheney requiring an emergency medical procedure, only slightly more (39%) say they are concerned while 59% are not, according to the March 9–11 Gallup Poll.

More to the point, only 11% think Cheney should resign and just 21% think he should cut back on his vice presidential duties. Most (66%) think Cheney should continue his current duties with little or no change. Perhaps Americans are taking the news of Cheney's health in relative stride today because he is only second in command, because he seemed to recover so quickly from each heart episode, or because medical treatment of heart disease has improved to the point it has today.

MARCH 22
ACADEMY AWARDS

Interview Dates: 3/15–18/01
Gallup Poll News Service
Survey #GO 133223

Do you plan on watching this year's Academy Awards broadcast on Sunday March 25, or not?

Yes 43%
No 51
No opinion 6

If it were up to you, who would you be most interested in watching host the Academy Awards ceremonies this year—Billy Crystal, Whoopi Goldberg, David Letterman, or Steve Martin?

Billy Crystal 37%
Whoopi Goldberg 22
Steve Martin 20
David Letterman 14
No opinion 7

Are you aware of any of the five movies nominated for the Academy Award for Best Picture this year? Any others? *

*Erin Brockovich*** 15%
*Gladiator*** 14
*Chocolat*** 9
*Crouching Tiger, Hidden Dragon*** 8
*Traffic*** 7
Castaway 5
Almost Famous 1
Hannibal 1
None (vol.) 40
Other (vol.) 3
No opinion 29

*Total adds to more than 100% due to multiple replies.
**Nominated films

Please tell me for each of these movies whether you have already seen it, if you haven't seen it but you expect to see it sometime, or if you do not expect to see it at all:

Chocolat?

Already seen it 6%
Not seen it, expect to .... .27
Not seen it, don't expect to .... .54
Not seen it, don't know (vol.) .... .13

Crouching Tiger, Hidden Dragon?

Already seen it 9%
Not seen it, expect to .... .29
Not seen it, don't expect to .... .54
Not seen it, don't know (vol.) 8

Erin Brockovich?

Already seen it .... .48%
Not seen it, expect to .... .19
Not seen it, don't expect to .... .28
Not seen it, don't know (vol.) 5

Gladiator?

Already seen it .... .41%
Not seen it, expect to .... .21
Not seen it, don't expect to .... .35
Not seen it, don't know (vol.) 3

Traffic?

Already seen it 7%
Not seen it, expect to .... .38
Not seen it, don't expect to .... .45
Not seen it, don't know (vol.) .... .10

At the Academy Awards ceremony this year, which one of the following movies would you like to see win the Oscar award for Best Picture of the Year: Chocolat, Crouching Tiger, Hidden Dragon, Erin Brockovich, Gladiator, *or* Traffic*?*

Erin Brockovich .... .32%
Gladiator .... .27
Crouching Tiger, Hidden Dragon .... .10
Traffic 8
Chocolat 5
No opinion .... .18

Analysis: Americans' choice for Best Picture in the upcoming Oscar awards is the drama *Erin Brockovich*, but among frequent moviegoers—a

group that might be closer in their views to the Motion Picture Academy members who vote for the award—the winner is *Gladiator.* One of the reasons for the popularity of these two pictures is that relatively few Americans have seen any of the other three nominated films: *Traffic, Chocolat,* and *Crouching Tiger, Hidden Dragon.* These and other findings are based on a new Gallup Poll conducted March 15–18 that examines several aspects of the motion picture industry including public opinion of the events, people, and awards associated with the seventy-third annual Academy Awards.

Among Americans, *Erin Brockovich* leads the Best Picture category with 32% of all mentions, followed by *Gladiator* with 27%. Of the remaining five nominated films, *Crouching Tiger, Hidden Dragon* is chosen by 10%, *Traffic* receives 8%, and *Chocolat* 5%.

The public's preference for Best Picture is very closely tied to the pictures they have actually seen. Forty-eight percent report having seen *Erin Brockovich* and 41% have seen *Gladiator,* while less than 10% has seen each of the other three nominated films. In fact, only 10% has seen three or more of the nominated films, and a very small percentage (2%) have seen four or five.

Awareness of this year's nominated films is low. Sixty-nine percent asked in an open-ended format to name any of the movies nominated for best picture this year could not come up with a single one. Respondents were most likely to mention *Erin Brockovich* or *Gladiator* as films that were nominated for Best Picture, named by 15% and 14%, respectively. The other nominated films all were mentioned by fewer than 10%: *Chocolat* (9%), *Crouching Tiger, Hidden Dragon* (8%), and *Traffic* (7%). Interestingly, the film *Castaway* was mentioned by 5% as a Best Picture nominee, even though it is not up for the award. Of course, the fact that *Erin Brockovich* and *Gladiator* are at the top of the average American's wish list for the Best Picture winner has no official bearing on what will be revealed Sunday night.

The Oscars often are regarded as one of the most important events in Hollywood. The event draws immense media attention but doesn't exactly capture Americans' collective attention.

This year, 43% indicate that they intend to watch the awards ceremony while 51% say they probably will not.

Actor/Comedian Steve Martin is slated to host the show this year. Gallup's survey shows he will have to work hard to overcome the popular legacy of previous hosts. When asked which of four personalities they would most like to see host the Academy Awards, Billy Crystal (who hosted in 2000 and several other times in the 1990s) tops the list with 37%, followed by Whoopi Goldberg at 22%, Steve Martin at 20%, and David Letterman at 14%.

MARCH 22
"MAD COW" DISEASE

Interview Dates: 3/9–11/01
CNN/*USA Today*/Gallup Poll
Survey #GO 133198

How much have you heard about a disease that affects the brains of cattle called mad cow disease—a great deal, a moderate amount, only a little, or nothing at all?

A great deal	.29%
A moderate amount	.43
Only a little	.24
Nothing at all	.3
No opinion	.1

How concerned are you personally about mad cow disease becoming a problem in the United States—very concerned, somewhat concerned, not too concerned, or not at all concerned?

Very concerned	.29%
Somewhat concerned	.36
Not too concerned	.24
Not at all concerned	.11

Analysis: Most Americans are aware of the news accounts about mad cow disease that has prompted the destruction of millions of animals in Great Britain. The disease forced the seizure of over 200 sheep at a Vermont farm by federal agents this week.

A Gallup Poll conducted March 9–11 showed that 72% of Americans had heard at least a moderate amount about the disease, including 29% who had heard a great deal. Asked about their concern over the disease, 65% said they were either somewhat or very concerned, another 24% said they were not too concerned, and just 11% said they were not at all concerned.

MARCH 22
UNITED NATIONS

Interview Dates: 2/1–4/01
Gallup Poll News Service
Survey #GO 132811

Do you think the United Nations is doing a good job or a poor job in trying solve the problems it has had to face?

	Good job	Poor job	No opinion
2001 Feb 1–4	54%	38%	8%
2000 May 18–21	52	43	5

Now thinking more specifically, which of the following roles would you like to see the United Nations play in world affairs today— should it play a leading role where all countries are required to follow UN policies; a major role, where the UN establishes policies but where individual countries still act separately when they disagree with the UN; or should it play a minor role, with the UN serving mostly as a forum for communication between nations, but with no policy making role?

Leading role	.19%
Major role	.49
Minor role	.28
Should not exist (vol.)	.*
Other (vol.)	.1
No opinion	.3

*Less than 1%

Analysis: On Friday, George W. Bush concludes a busy week of meetings with foreign leaders by hosting United Nations Secretary-General Kofi Annan at the White House. A recent Gallup Poll conducted February 1–4 shows that Americans, by a margin of 54% to 38%, believe the United Nations is doing a good, rather than a poor, job of handling the problems it has faced. An even larger number envisions a substantial role for the UN internationally, as either the leader or a major player in world affairs.

During the mid-1990s when the UN struggled with the situations in the former Yugoslavia, its image suffered, falling to a low of 35% in 1995. The organization's image has made a steady recovery since.

The poll also shows that Americans want the UN to be heavily involved in foreign policy, but not necessarily as the preeminent power. Overall, 19% say the UN should "play a leading role where all nations are required to follow UN policy," 49% say the UN should play "a major role where it establishes policies but other nations that disagree may act independently," and 28% say the UN should play a "minor role, where it mainly serves as a forum for communication among nations but with no policy-making role."

MARCH 23
MOVIES AND MOVIE STARS

Interview Dates: 3/16–18/01
Gallup Poll News Service
Survey #GO 133233

How many movies, if any, have you attended in a movie theater in the past twelve months?

None 34%
1 to 4 40
5 or more 26

Asked of those who have been to the movies in the past year: When did you last go to the movies—within the last seven days, within the last thirty days, between thirty days and six months ago, or more than six months ago?

Within last seven days 13%
Within last thirty days 35
Between thirty days and six months 41
More than six months 11

Does your household have a VCR or DVD player?

Yes 94%
No 6

Asked of those who have a VCR or DVD player: Do you have only a VCR, only a DVD player, or both?

VCR only 75%
DVD only 1
Both 24

Also asked of those who have a VCR or DVD player: How many movies do you view in an average month on your VCR or DVD player?

None 11%
One 12
Two 11
Three 10
Four 10
Five 5
Six 7
Seven 1
Eight 5
Nine . . . .*
Ten 10
Eleven to twenty .11
More than twenty .6
No opinion 1

*Less than 1%

Also asked of those who have a VCR or DVD player: Do you prefer to watch movies at a movie theater or at home on your VCR or DVD?

At movie theater 23%
At home 68
Both; neither (vol.) 9

Are there any movie stars you always make a special effort to see?

	Yes	No	No opinion
2001 Mar 16–18	58%	40%	2%
2000 Mar 17–19	52	47	1

What are their names? *

Julia Roberts	28%
Tom Hanks	13
Mel Gibson	11
Harrison Ford	7
Tom Cruise	7
Robert De Niro	5
Sean Connery	5
Nicholas Cage	4
Steven Seagal	4
Al Pacino	4
Sandra Bullock	4
Denzel Washington	4
Arnold Schwarzenegger	4
Brad Pitt	4
Clint Eastwood	3
Bruce Willis	3
Michael Douglas	2
Meg Ryan	2
Jackie Chan	2
Kevin Costner	2
Whoopi Goldberg	2
Keanu Reeves	2
Jim Carrey	2
Wesley Snipes	2
Russell Crowe	2
Meryl Streep	1
Anthony Hopkins	1
George Clooney	1
Chuck Norris	1
John Travolta	1
Richard Gere	1
Sylvester Stallone	1
John Wayne	1
Val Kilmer	1
Jack Nicholson	1
Tom Selleck	1
Jean-Claude Van Damme	1
Dustin Hoffman	1
Chris Rock	1
Robert Redford	1
Eddie Murphy	1
Robin Williams	1
Barbra Streisand	1
Tommy Lee Jones	1
Johnny Depp	1
Patrick Swayze	1
Paul Newman	1
Kevin Spacey	1
Sidney Poitier	1
Samuel L. Jackson	1
Morgan Freeman	1
Other	24
No opinion	2

*Total adds to more than 100% due to multiple replies.

Who is your favorite movie star of all time? *

John Wayne	12%
Julia Roberts	7
Clint Eastwood	7
Mel Gibson	5
Tom Hanks	5
Sean Connery	4
Harrison Ford	4
Robert De Niro	3
Al Pacino	3
Jimmy Stewart	3
Tom Cruise	3
Nicholas Cage	2
Arnold Schwarzenegger	2
John Travolta	2
Paul Newman	2
Steven Seagal	2
Denzel Washington	2
Sidney Poitier	2
Meg Ryan	1
Kevin Costner	1
Bruce Willis	1
Clark Gable	1
Jack Nicholson	1
Charlton Heston	1
Robert Redford	1
Cary Grant	1
Jackie Chan	1

Sandra Bullock 1
Katharine Hepburn 1
George Clooney 1
Patrick Swayze 1
Bette Davis 1
Humphrey Bogart 1
Michael Douglas 1
Richard Gere 1
Morgan Freeman 1
Samuel L. Jackson 1
Wesley Snipes 1
Kevin Spacey 1
Meryl Streep 1
Bing Crosby 1
Jean-Claude Van Damme 1
Jim Carrey 1
Elizabeth Taylor 1
Chris Rock 1
Shirley Temple 1
Barbra Streisand 1
Anthony Hopkins 1
Robert Mitchum 1
Chuck Norris 1
Spencer Tracy 1
Russell Crowe 1
Tom Selleck 1
Marilyn Monroe 1
Gary Cooper ....**
None 8
Other 20
No opinion 10

*Total adds to more than 100% due to multiple replies.
*Less than 1%

Analysis: Nearly six in ten Americans say they make a special effort to see movies featuring specific stars, with Julia Roberts easily having the greatest appeal for movie fans, according to a new Gallup Poll. Other stars with high "marquee value" include Tom Hanks, Mel Gibson, and Harrison Ford. When asked to name their favorite movie star of all time, Americans give the honor to John Wayne. About two-thirds say they have attended a movie within the last year, and have watched movies at home on videocassette recorders or DVD players even more frequently.

The poll shows that, by a large margin, Americans prefer to watch movies at home instead of going to the theater.

Following Julia Roberts at some distance is *Castaway* star and two-time Oscar winner Tom Hanks with 13%. Mel Gibson places third with 11%, followed by Harrison Ford (7%), Tom Cruise (7%), Robert De Niro (5%) and Sean Connery (5%).

When asked to indicate its favorite movie star of all time, the public accords this honor to John Wayne who starred in nearly 200 films and won a best actor Oscar for his performance in the 1969 film *True Grit*. Coming in second behind Wayne who was favored by 12%, are Julia Roberts and Clint Eastwood, each with 7% naming them the favorite movie star of all time. Mel Gibson and Tom Hanks rank next, followed by Sean Connery and Harrison Ford.

According to the latest poll, 66% have attended a movie at a theater in the last twelve months. In fact, most who have attended a movie have done so fairly recently, including 7% who did so within a week of the time they were interviewed, 23% who did so within the previous month, and 41% who did so within the previous six months.

More than nine in ten say they own a home video player such as a VCR or DVD, with 70% owning just a VCR, 1% owning just a DVD player, and 23% owning both. While movie attendance among Americans is high, they are more likely to watch movies at home. Eighty-three percent (and 88% of those with a VCR or DVD player) have seen a movie at home using one of these devices in the past month.

Gallup asked those who own either a VCR or a DVD player if they prefer to watch movies at home or at the theater. Given the above data showing how frequently people watch movies at home, it is not surprising that the overwhelming number of VCR and/or DVD owners say they prefer to watch movies at home (68%) rather than at the theater (23%).

MARCH 26
SCHOOL SHOOTINGS

Interview Dates: 3/9–11/01
CNN/*USA Today*/Gallup Poll
Survey #GO 133198

Asked of parents of children in Kindergarten through Grade 12: Thinking about your oldest child, when he or she is at school, do you fear for his or her physical safety?

	Yes	No	No opinion
2001 Mar 9–11	45%	54%	1%
2000 Aug 24–27	26	74	0
2000 Apr 7–9	43	57	0

Also asked of parents of children in Kindergarten through Grade 12: Have any of your school-aged children expressed any worry or concern about feeling unsafe at their school when they go to school?

	Yes	No	No opinion
2001 Mar 9–11	22%	77%	1%
2000 Aug 24–27	8	92	0

Thinking about the recent shootings at schools, in your opinion, how likely is it that these kinds of shootings could happen in your community—is it very likely, somewhat likely, somewhat unlikely, or very unlikely?

	Very, somewhat likely	Somewhat, very unlikely	No opinion
2001 Mar 9–11	65%	33%	2%
2000 Apr 7–9	66	31	3

Which of the following statements comes closer to your view of shootings like the recent ones that have occurred in schools— they are indications that there is something seriously wrong in the country today, or they are isolated incidents that do not indicate anything about the country in general?

Something seriously wrong 75%
Isolated incidents 22
Other (vol.); no opinion 3

Which of the following statements comes closer to your overall view—government and society can take action that will be effective in preventing shootings like the recent ones in schools from happening again, or shootings like the recent ones in schools will happen again regardless of what action is taken by government and society?

	Government and society can take action	Will happen again regardless	No opinion
2001 Mar 9–11	49%	47%	4%
2000 Apr 7–9	47	49	4

Analysis: With yet another school shooting incident involving students, this time in El Cajon, California, U.S. Attorney General John Ashcroft is calling for an end to the "ethic of violence" among youth in this country, suggesting that the news and entertainment industry, not tighter gun laws, could play a role in ending the crisis. Other observers are wondering whether there are any steps that government and society can take to prevent such incidents from happening again. A Gallup Poll conducted shortly after the incident in Santee, California, but before the most recently reported incident in El Cajon, suggests that the public also is divided on the issue. While large majorities of Americans believe that the incidents reflect "something seriously wrong in the country today," and that they could occur in their own communities, they are about evenly split on whether or not any actions can be taken to prevent such shootings from occurring again. Conducted March 9–11, the poll shows that 49% believe that government and society can take actions to prevent more shootings from happening, while 47% take the opposite point of view, saying that such incidents will occur regardless of what action might be taken. The poll also shows that about two-thirds believe such shooting incidents are likely to occur in their own community, with 31% saying very likely to happen, and another 34% somewhat likely. Another third believe that such incidents are not likely to occur in their community.

Responses to the poll suggest a widespread consensus (75% to 22%) that shootings such as the ones in Southern California, Colorado, and elsewhere, are indications that there is something seriously wrong in the country and are not just isolated incidents.

The more likely people are to think such incidents can happen in their own community, the more likely they are to say that government and society can take effective action, and that the incidents suggest something seriously wrong in America. Among people who say school shootings are very likely to happen in their community, 61% say effective action can be taken, while just 36% say it cannot. However, among those who say such incidents are only somewhat likely to occur, opinion is about evenly divided (50% to 48%). And among those who say shootings are not likely to occur in their communities, 57% say no effective action can be taken while only 39% disagree.

Similarly, about eight in ten people who say it is likely that shootings could occur in their communities also say that the incidents suggest there is something seriously wrong in America, while that view is expressed by just six in ten people who believe shootings are not likely to occur in their own community.

Among parents who currently have children in school, almost one-half (45%) personally fear for the physical safety of their children while at school. This number is up again after having fallen last August as children were returning to school for the new year. At that time, only 26% said they feared for their children's safety, significantly lower than the 43% recorded five months earlier. The largest percentage, (55%) was found in the spring of 1999, immediately after the Columbine High School shootings in Colorado. Additionally, about one in five parents say their children also have expressed worry about their safety at school, up from only 8% last August.

MARCH 27
PROMINENT SPEAKERS

Interview Dates: 2/19–21/01
Gallup Poll News Service
Survey #GO 133064

Regardless of your personal views of him, how interested would you be in hearing a live speech by each of the following if you could attend the speech in person—very interested, somewhat interested, not too interested, or not at all interested:

Colin Powell?

Very interested 49%
Somewhat interested 30
Not too interested 6
Not at all interested 13
No opinion 2

George W. Bush?

Very interested 38%
Somewhat interested 31
Not too interested 9
Not at all interested 21
No opinion 1

Jimmy Carter?

Very interested 31%
Somewhat interested 35
Not too interested 12
Not at all interested 21
No opinion 1

Oprah Winfrey?

Very interested 30%
Somewhat interested 29
Not too interested 11
Not at all interested 29
No opinion 1

Bill Clinton?

Very interested 28%
Somewhat interested 23
Not too interested 10
Not at all interested 39
No opinion . . . .*

Hillary Rodham Clinton?

Very interested 22%

Somewhat interested 26
Not too interested 12
Not at all interested 40
No opinion . . . .*

Al Gore?

Very interested 16%
Somewhat interested 29
Not too interested 13
Not at all interested 42
No opinion . . . .*

Jay Leno?

Very interested 13%
Somewhat interested 29
Not too interested 17
Not at all interested 39
No opinion 2

Regis Philbin?

Very interested 11%
Somewhat interested 30
Not too interested 16
Not at all interested 39
No opinion 4

*Less than 1%

Those Replying "Very Interested"
(By Politics)

	Republicans	Independents	Democrats
Colin Powell 62%		44%	39%
George W. Bush 64		31	17
Jimmy Carter 29		30	37
Oprah Winfrey 27		28	33
Bill Clinton 12		24	50
Hillary Rodham Clinton 10		21	37
Al Gore 8		11	32
Jay Leno 14		12	13
Regis Philbin 15		9	9

Analysis: A recent Gallup Poll asked Americans how interested they would be in attending speeches given by several prominent U.S. politicians and celebrities. Among the nine suggested speakers, current Secretary of State Colin Powell topped the list with 79% expressing interest in hearing him speak. In fact, interest in Powell exceeds that of his boss, President George W. Bush. Nearly seven out of ten (69%) expressed interest in a presidential speech by Bush. Following Bush were former President Jimmy Carter (66%), Oprah Winfrey (59%), and former President Bill Clinton (51%). Powell was a hit on the lecture circuit before taking his place in the Bush administration and the current poll suggests that his appeal continues.

Among the nonpoliticians measured in the new poll, Oprah Winfrey ranks as the most popular. The other two entertainers on the Gallup list received lower levels of interest. About four out of ten would be interested in speeches by either "Tonight Show" host Jay Leno or "Live" host Regis Philbin.

MARCH 30
MARCH MADNESS

Interview Dates: 3/26–28/01
Gallup Poll News Service
Survey #GO 133224

For each of the following, please say whether you are a fan of that sport or not:

Professional football?

Yes, a fan 54%
No, not a fan 37
Somewhat of a fan (vol.) 9

Professional baseball?

Yes, a fan 46%
No, not a fan 44
Somewhat of a fan (vol.) 10

College football?

Yes, a fan 44%
No, not a fan 47
Somewhat of a fan (vol.) 9

Figure skating?

Yes, a fan 40%
No, not a fan 50
Somewhat of a fan (vol.) 10

College basketball?

Yes, a fan 38%
No, not a fan 53
Somewhat of a fan (vol.) 9

Professional basketball?

Yes, a fan 36%
No, not a fan 56
Somewhat of a fan (vol.) 8

Auto racing?

Yes, a fan 31%
No, not a fan 61
Somewhat of a fan (vol.) 8

Professional golf?

Yes, a fan 27%
No, not a fan 64
Somewhat of a fan (vol.) 9

Professional ice hockey?

Yes, a fan 24%
No, not a fan 69
Somewhat of a fan (vol.) 7

Professional tennis?

Yes, a fan 19%
No, not a fan 72
Somewhat of a fan (vol.) 9

Professional wrestling?

Yes, a fan 12%
No, not a fan 85
Somewhat of a fan (vol.) 3

Analysis: Two weeks ago, sixty-five teams had a dream. Now, the dreamers are down to the Final Four. This weekend's NCAA men's basketball championship in Minneapolis is one of the most anticipated sporting events of the year, and millions will be watching as Duke, Arizona, Maryland, and Michigan State square off for bragging rights.

A new Gallup Poll conducted March 26–28 finds that nearly one-half of Americans (47%) consider themselves college basketball fans. While that percentage is smaller than the fan base for pro football (63%), pro baseball (56%), college football (53%), and figure skating (50%), it is larger than the fan base for pro basketball, auto racing, golf, hockey, and tennis.

APRIL 2
MAJOR LEAGUE BASEBALL

Interview Dates: 3/26–28/01
Gallup Poll News Service
Survey #GO 133224

Asked of those who follow sports: Which is your favorite major league baseball team?

New York Yankees 15%
Atlanta Braves 11
Boston Red Sox 5
St. Louis Cardinals 5
New York Mets 4
Los Angeles Dodgers 4
Chicago Cubs 4
Texas Rangers 3
Cleveland Indians .3
Chicago White Sox 3
Pittsburgh Pirates .3
Detroit Tigers 3
Cincinnati Reds 2
Philadelphia Phillies 2
Colorado Rockies .2
Oakland Athletics .2
Baltimore Orioles .2
San Francisco Giants 2
Minnesota Twins 2
Kansas City Royals 2
Seattle Mariners 1

Milwaukee Brewers .1
Anaheim Angels 1
Houston Astros 1
Arizona Diamondbacks 1
San Diego Padres . . . .*
Florida Marlins . . . .*
Tampa Bay Devil Rays . . . .*
Montreal Expos . . . .*
Toronto Blue Jays .0
None 12
No opinion 4

*Less than 1%

*Has the fact that the Yankees have won the World Series three years straight lessened your interest in big-league baseball?**

Yes 19%
No 75
No opinion 6

*Based on part sample

*Has the fact that the Yankees have won the World Series three years straight increased your interest in big-league baseball, decreased your interest, or has it had no effect?**

Increased 10%
Decreased 11
No effect 78
No opinion 1

*Based on part sample

Asked of those who follow sports: Do you think the owners of major league baseball teams should be allowed to put a "cap" on the total amount of money available for players' salaries, or shouldn't they be able to do that?

	Should	Should not	It depends (vol.); no opinion
National Adults			
2001 Mar 26–28 . . . . .77%		17%	6%
Baseball Fans			
2001 Mar 26–28 79		17	4

Also asked of those who follow sports: I am going to name some changes that major league baseball has seen over the past twenty or thirty years and want you to tell me whether you think each has been a change for the better, a change for the worse, or not made a difference:

The increases in the number of major league teams?

	National adults	Baseball fans
Better 53%		57%
Worse 18		18
No difference; no opinion 29		25

The increases in the average salary paid to players?

	National adults	Baseball fans
Better 21%		22%
Worse 56		58
No difference; no opinion 23		20

The designated hitter rule in the American League?

	National adults	Baseball fans
Better 37%		42%
Worse 21		24
No difference; no opinion 42		34

Playoffs in each league to determine who goes to the World Series?

	National adults	Baseball fans
Better 68%		72%
Worse 5		6
No difference; no opinion 27		22

The addition of a wild-card playoff team in each league?

	National adults	Base-ball fans
Better	.54%	58%
Worse	.13	15
No difference; no opinion	.33	27

Interleague play?

	National adults	Base-ball fans
Better	.53%	60%
Worse	.6	6
No difference; no opinion	.41	34

Who would you say is the greatest baseball player of all time?

Babe Ruth	.32%
Mickey Mantle	.6
Hank Aaron	.6
Joe DiMaggio	.4
Jackie Robinson	.4
Mark McGwire	.3
Lou Gehrig	.3
Ted Williams	.2
Nolan Ryan	.2
Willie Mays	.2
Pete Rose	.2
Ty Cobb	.2
Stan Musial	.1
Roberto Clemente	.1
Cal Ripken Jr.	.1
Sammy Sosa	.1
Satchel Paige	.1
Ken Griffey Jr.	.*
Honus Wagner	.—
Walter Johnson	.—
Christy Mathewson	.—
Carl Hubbell	.—
Dizzy Dean	.—
Other	.7
No opinion	.20

*Less than 1%

Analysis: The New York Yankees are America's favorite baseball team according to the latest Gallup Poll conducted March 26–28. And Babe Ruth, the Hall of Fame Yankee slugger of the 1920s and 1930s, is far and away recognized by Americans as the greatest baseball player of all time. As the new major league baseball season gets underway in earnest today, sports fans generally think that most of the recent changes to the game of baseball have been for the better, with the notable exception of the tremendous increase in player salaries, which is seen by the majority of fans as a change for the worse.

The New York Yankees, looking for a fourth consecutive World Series title, are the number one baseball team in the nation, based on fan preferences. Fifteen percent of sports fans name the Yankees as their favorite, with the Atlanta Braves coming in second at 11%. Several teams trail the Yankees and Braves at some distance, including the Boston Red Sox (5%), St. Louis Cardinals (5%), New York Mets (4%), Los Angeles Dodgers (4%), and Chicago Cubs (4%). Gallup last asked this question in February 1990, and at that point, there was no clear favorite. The Yankees, Mets, and Cubs tied for first with 7% each, with the Red Sox, Cardinals, and Dodgers all coming in at 6%.

Without a doubt, one of the reasons for the Yankees' continued success is that they have traditionally had one of the highest payrolls in the game. Baseball, unlike football and basketball, does not limit how much teams can spend on players. The result has been that teams in smaller markets spend far less money on players than the Yankees, putting them at what many believe is a severe competitive disadvantage. The vast majority of baseball fans (79%) think that major league baseball owners should be allowed to put a cap on the total amount of money available for players' salaries. These numbers have increased since a 1995 poll showed that 69% of those interested in baseball supported the idea of a salary cap.

The high level of support for the salary cap is not surprising, given that 56% of sports fans think the increases in average salaries paid to players are a "change for the worse" in the game of baseball, while only 21% think they have been a change for the better. However, fans believe that most of the other recent significant changes in the game have been for the better. A strong majority of sports fans (68%) think that having playoffs in each league to determine who goes to the World Series is a change for the better. A majority also think changes to the game such as the addition of a wild-card playoff team in each league (54%), interleague play (53%), and the increased number of teams in baseball (53%) have been for the better.

APRIL 3
FOREIGN NATIONS/CHINA

Interview Dates: 2/1–4/01
Gallup Poll News Service
Survey #GO 132811

*I'd like your overall opinion of some foreign countries. First, is your overall opinion of each of the following very favorable, mostly favorable, mostly unfavorable, or very unfavorabl⌐?**

	Very, mostly favorable	Mostly, very unfavorable	No opinion
Canada	90%	7%	3%
Australia	85	8	7
Great Britain	85	9	6
Italy	78	12	10
France	77	17	6
Germany	75	16	9
Israel	63	32	5
Japan	73	21	6
Mexico	67	26	7
Brazil	69	17	14
The Philippines	63	25	12
Egypt	65	23	12
South Africa	57	33	10
Taiwan	63	22	15
India	58	30	12
Colombia	30	59	11
Saudi Arabia	47	46	7
Vietnam	46	44	10
Russia	52	42	6
China	45	48	7
Cuba	27	68	5
The Palestinian Authority	22	63	15
North Korea	31	59	10
Iran	12	83	5
Iraq	9	85	6
Libya	11	75	14

*Based on part sample

What one country anywhere in the world do you consider to be America's greatest enemy today?

Iraq	38%
China	14
Iran	8
Russia	6
Libya	4
Saudi Arabia	4
North Korea	2
Middle East	2
Cuba	2
Japan	1
The Palestinian Authority	1
Israel	*
Afghanistan	*
None	2
Other	4
No opinion	11

*Less than 1%

Analysis: As the Chinese and U.S. authorities deal with the tense situation surrounding Sunday's collision between a U.S. Navy spy plane and a Chinese fighter plane, a review of past Gallup Polls about China suggests that the American public is currently divided between positive and negative views of that country. About one-fifth consider the most populous country in the world to be an "enemy" of the United States, while about three in ten consider it friendly, and another one-fifth have little idea of how to characterize relations between the two countries. A recent Gallup Poll also shows that a little less than one-half of the U.S. public has a favorable opinion of China, putting it into the bottom third of a list of countries respondents were asked to rate in the poll.

The most recent February poll finds that one in seven Americans (14%) places China second as the country representing "America's greatest enemy today," behind Iraq (identified by 38% as the greatest enemy). Third on the list is Iran with 8%, followed by Russia (6%), Libya (4%), Saudi Arabia (4%), and North Korea (2%). The Palestinian Authority came in at 1%.

APRIL 4
AIRLINE STRIKES

Interview Dates: 3/26–28/01
Gallup Poll News Service
Survey #GO 133224

If airline workers decided to strike, which side would you favor—the airline workers or the airlines?

Airline workers 56%
Airlines 19
Both sides (vol.) 4
Neither (vol.) 8
No opinion 13

Do you think President Bush should or should not use his emergency powers to prevent airline workers from striking?

Should 37%
Should not 54
No opinion 9

If there is an airline strike by employees of one or more airlines in the near future, would it be a major inconvenience to you, a minor inconvenience to you, or would it not affect you much at all?

Major inconvenience 11%
Minor inconvenience 27
Would not effect 62

Analysis: This could be a long year for frequent fliers with labor problems threatening to lead to strikes at several of the nation's major airlines.

Comair (Delta Connection) pilots are already on strike and Delta pilots could walk off the job at the end of April. United Airlines flight attendants have voted to authorize a strike and President Bush has already intervened to keep Northwest Airlines mechanics from striking. A new Gallup Poll conducted March 26–28 shows that a majority of Americans side with the workers in their disputes with airline management. Fifty-six percent would support airline workers should they strike while 19% side with the airlines. As might be expected, those who are members of labor unions overwhelmingly support the airline workers (74%), but airline workers also enjoy support from a majority of nonunion members (53%). Perhaps somewhat surprising, a slight majority who describe themselves as politically conservative also support the workers (51%) while 24% back management. This question about support for workers versus management provides an instructive first glance at the reaction of the public to possible strikes in the airline industry, but these attitudes could change depending on the circumstances surrounding an actual prolonged, highly publicized strike.

In addition to using his emergency powers to intervene in the Northwest Airlines talks with the International Association of Machinists, President Bush also has pledged to keep workers on the job at other airlines, though he has yet to step into the Comair strike. Fifty-four percent of Americans say Bush should not intervene in the strikes while 37% say he should.

Nearly two out of three Americans say they would not be affected at all if airline workers do go on strike, largely because most Americans take a limited number of trips by air each year. However, 11% say strikes at one or more airlines would be a major inconvenience for them, and another 27% say the strikes would be only a minor inconvenience.

APRIL 4
PRESIDENT BUSH

Interview Dates: 3/26–28/01
Gallup Poll News Service
Survey #GO 133224

Do you approve or disapprove of the way George W. Bush is handling his job as president?

	Approve	Dis-approve	No opinion
2001 Mar 26–28	53%	29%	18%
2001 Mar 9–11	58	29	13
2001 Mar 5–7	63	22	15
2001 Feb 19–21	62	21	17
2001 Feb 9–11	57	25	18
2001 Feb 1–4	57	25	18

Asked of those who approve of Bush: Why do you approve of the way Bush is handling his job as president?

Satisfied; doing good job	22%
Honest; trustworthy; man of integrity	10
Agree with his tax plan	8
Approve of his style; balance; moderate approach	8
Fulfilling his promises	7
Voted for him; Republican	6
Accomplishing things; getting things done	5
Better than Bill Clinton	4
Appears confident; in control	4
Agree with his policies in general	4
Agree with his economic policies	3
Chose good advisors; Cabinet	3
Concerned for people	1
No scandals	1
None (vol.)	3
Other (vol.)	4
No opinion	7

Asked of those who disapprove of Bush: Why do you disapprove of the way Bush is handling his job as president?

Disagree with his tax plan	13%
Don't agree with his policies in general	11
Dissatisfied; doing a poor job	10
Disapprove of his economic policies	9
Failing to fulfill his campaign promises	8
Disapprove of his environmental policies	8
Caters to the rich; big business	7
Didn't vote for him; Democrat	7
Not knowledgeable	5
Disapprove of his foreign policy	3
Elected in a flawed election	3
Untrustworthy	2
Hasn't accomplished much	1
None	*
Everything	1
Other	6
No opinion	6

Analysis: Three out of ten Americans disapprove of President George W. Bush's job performance, according to a new Gallup Poll, and are most likely to cite objections to specific policies and positions as the basis for their negative evaluations. Those who approve, on the other hand, are more likely to cite general approval of his leadership style, Cabinet appointments, and character. Twenty-nine percent of Americans now say they disapprove of the way Bush is handling his job while 18% have no opinion.

This Gallup Poll included an effort to investigate what is on Americans' minds at this early stage in the Bush administration when asked to evaluate their new president. After indicating whether they approved or disapproved of Bush's job performance, respondents were asked to explain their answer in their own words. The results were categorized, then further grouped into broad categories.

It is apparent that those who approve of Bush's performance are somewhat less likely to speak in very specific terms than are those who disapprove. This is, to some degree, a natural function of the fact that approval (or having no opinion) is a logical default response of Americans when asked the job approval question. In essence, they give a new president the benefit of the doubt.

Those who feel strongly enough to tell an interviewer that they disapprove of the president's job performance are more likely to have developed specific reasons for their position at this point. Over one-half of those who disapprove of Bush's job performance cite aspects of the policy positions he has taken, including mentions of his tax plan, foreign, environmental, and economic policies. Five percent say that they disapprove because they think that Bush is not knowledgeable. Interestingly, despite the tremendous visibility given to the Florida recount situation after the election and the fact that Bush actually lost the popular vote, only 3% base their negative response on the fact that he gained office "in a flawed election."

APRIL 5
SCHOOL SHOOTINGS

Interview Dates: 3/26–28/01
Gallup Poll News Service
Survey #GO 133224

How important do you think each of the following is as a cause of the school shootings that have been occurring—extremely important, very important, somewhat important, not too important, or not at all important:

The home life students have today, including their relationship with their parents?

Extremely important 57%
Very important 35
Somewhat, not too, not at all important;
 no opinion 8

The availability and ease of obtaining guns by students?

Extremely important 46%
Very important 31
Somewhat, not too, not at all important;
 no opinion 23

The portrayal of violence and use of guns in today's entertainment and music?

Extremely important 38%
Very important 30
Somewhat, not too, not at all important;
 no opinion 32

The way schools discipline their students?

Extremely important 31%
Very important 36

Somewhat, not too, not at all important;
 no opinion 33

The coverage given to school shootings by the news media?

Extremely important 32%
Very important 32
Somewhat, not too, not at all important;
 no opinion 36

Bullying and teasing of students at school?

Extremely important 29%
Very important 33
Somewhat, not too, not at all important;
 no opinion 38

The size of high schools today in terms of the number of students who attend?

Extremely important 20%
Very important 29
Somewhat, not too, not at all important;
 no opinion 51

The fact that families move around and students don't have roots in one specific town?

Extremely important 17%
Very important 26
Somewhat, not too, not at all important;
 no opinion 57

In your opinion, what is the single most important thing that could be done to prevent another incidence of school shootings by students like the recent ones in California?

Parent involvement, responsibility 31%
More security at schools 14
Better gun control; laws; issues 11
Better education; students; parents 6
Control media violence; video games;
 Internet 5
Lift laws on disciplining children 4
Put prayer back in school, home 3
Raise morals, people's standards 3

Better communication between students,
    parents, teachers 3
Monitor, watch students more closely 3
Stop bullies, bullying 2
More counselors; counseling; teachers 2
Stricter punishment on children; laws 2
Report threats; take threats more seriously . . .1
Dress codes; uniforms . . . .*
None 1
Other 2
No opinion 7

*Less than 1%

Overall, do you feel the news media have acted responsibly or irresponsibly in this situation?

Responsibly 57%
Irresponsibly 37
No opinion 6

Analysis: As experts ponder what actions, if any, can be effective in curbing the rash of school shootings that have occurred in the United States over the past several years, a new Gallup Poll finds that the American public would recommend focusing primarily on students' family situations. More people identify a student's home life than any other reason as an extremely or very important factor in causing school shootings. And when asked to describe in their own words what would be the "single most important thing that could be done to prevent another incidence of school shootings," Americans are most likely to mention greater parental involvement and responsibility. But the poll also shows that the public sees many other causes for the school shootings, especially the easy availability of guns and the portrayal of violence in the entertainment industry.

The poll was conducted March 26–28 and shows that 57% say that the "home life students have today, including their relationship with their parents" is an extremely important cause of the school shootings, with another 35% citing it as a very important cause. This 92% who rate the student's home life as at least very important, is the highest number giving this rating among the eight factors measured in the poll. Seventy-seven percent give the same rating to the availability and

ease of obtaining guns by students, followed by 68% for the portrayal of violence and use of guns in today's entertainment and music, 67% for the way schools discipline their students, 64% for the coverage given to school shootings by the news media, and 62% for the bullying and teasing of students at school. The least important reasons are the size of the high school (rated as extremely important by just 49%), and the lack of community roots that some students experience because they move frequently (43%).

In a separate question, respondents were asked to describe what single action would be the most effective in preventing another school shooting incident. More than three in ten (31%) mention greater parental involvement and responsibility, while 14% say more security at school and 11% cite the need for stricter gun control. An additional 6% say better education among parents, students, and teachers, reinforcing the central role that parents are seen to have in any effort to reduce school violence.

The news media appear to be held at least partially responsible for the shootings because of extensive coverage devoted to the incidents. More than six in ten say that such coverage is either extremely (32%) or very (32%) important in causing other shooting incidents. However, when asked directly about news coverage of the incidents, respondents appear to give a more positive rating as 57% say the news media have acted responsibly while just 37% say irresponsibly.

APRIL 6
AMERICANS' SECOND LANGUAGES

Interview Dates: 3/26–28/01
Gallup Poll News Service
Survey #GO 133224

How important is it that Americans learn to speak a second language other than English— is it essential, important but not essential, not too important, or not at all important?

Essential 19%
Important 50

Not too important 18
Not at all important 12
No opinion 1

How important is it that immigrants living in the United States learn to speak English—is it essential, important but not essential, not too important, or not at all important?

Essential 77%
Important 19
Not too important 2
Not at all important 1
No opinion 1

Do you personally speak a language other than English well enough to hold a conversation?

Yes 26%
No 74

Asked of those who speak a foreign language: Which foreign language do you speak?

Spanish 55%
French 17
German 10
Italian 3
Chinese 2
Other 13

Analysis: A new Gallup Poll conducted March 26–28 reveals that about one-fourth of the country can speak a language other than English well enough to hold a conversation. Spanish is the most frequently spoken second language, followed by French and German. The poll also shows that most Americans believe a second language is a valuable, although not necessarily essential, skill. More than three-quarters say it is essential for new immigrants into this country to learn to speak English, perhaps as a result of the cultural diversity created by recent waves of immigration. At the same time, respondents are much less likely to feel that the average American needs to speak a language other than English.

About one in five (9%) believe that it is essential to speak a second language in general, and an additional 50% believe that knowledge of a foreign language is a valuable skill but is not necessarily essential. Nearly one-third (30%) feel that it is not too important or not important at all to speak a second language.

APRIL 9
THE ENVIRONMENT/
GLOBAL WARMING

Interviewing Dates: 3/5–7/01
Gallup Poll News Service
Survey #GO 132070

I'm going to read you a list of environmental problems. As I read each one, please tell me if you personally worry about this problem a great deal, a fair amount, only a little, or not at all:

The "greenhouse effect" or global warming?

	Great deal; fair amount	Only a little	Not at all; no opinion
2001 Mar 5–7	.63%	22%	15%
2000 Apr 3–9	.72	15	13
1999 Apr 13–14	.68	18	14
1999 Mar 12–14	.59	23	18
1997 Oct 27–28	.50	29	21
1991 Apr 11–14	.62	22	16
1990 Apr 5–8	.57	20	23
1989 May 4–7	.63	18	19

Damage to the Earth's ozone layer?

	Great deal; fair amount	Only a little	Not at all; no opinion
2001 Mar 5–7	.75%	16%	9%
2000 Apr 3–9	.78	14	8
1999 Apr 13–14	.76	15	9
1997 Oct 27–28	.60	25	15
1991 Apr 11–14	.73	16	11

1990 Apr 5–8 71	15	14
1989 May 4–7 77	13	10

ENVIRONMENTAL PROBLEMS
(Personally Worry About)

	Great deal	Fair amount
Pollution of drinking water 64%		24%
Pollution of rivers, lakes, and reservoirs 58		29
Contamination of soil and water by toxic waste 58		27
Contamination of soil and water by radioactivity from nuclear facilities 49		22
Air pollution 48		34
The loss of natural habitat for wildlife 48		33
Damage to the Earth's ozone layer 47		28
The loss of tropical rain forests . . .44		32
Ocean and beach pollution 43		34
Extinction of plant and animal species 43		30
Urban sprawl and loss of open spaces 35		34
The "greenhouse effect" or global warming 33		30
Acid rain 28		28

Next, thinking about the issue of global warming (sometimes called the "greenhouse effect"), how well do you feel you understand this issue—would you say very well, fairly well, not very well, or not at all?

Very well 15%
Fairly well 54
Not very well 24
Not at all well 6
No opinion 1

Which of the following statements reflects your view of when the effects of global warming will begin to happen—they have already begun to happen, they will start happening within a few years, they will start

happening within your lifetime, they will not happen within your lifetime but they will affect future generations, or they will never happen?

Already begun 54%
Within a few years .4
Within your lifetime 13
Will affect future generations 18
Will never happen .7
No opinion 4

Just your impression, which one of the following statements do you think is most accurate—most scientists believe that global warming is occurring, most scientists believe that global warming is not occurring, or most scientists are unsure about whether global warming is occurring or not?

Is occurring 61%
Is not occurring 4
Unsure if occurring 30
No opinion 5

Do you think that global warming will pose a serious threat to you or to your way of life in your lifetime?

Yes 31%
No 66
No opinion 3

Thinking about what is said in the news, in your view is the seriousness of global warming generally exaggerated, generally correct, or is it generally underestimated?

Exaggerated 30%
Correct 34
Underestimated 32
No opinion 4

And from what you have heard or read, do you believe increases in the Earth's temperature over the last century are due more to the effects of pollution from human activi-

ties, or natural changes in the environment that are not due to human activities?

Human activities 61%
Natural causes 33
No opinion 6

Analysis: Since taking office, President Bush seems to have rebuffed environmentalist concerns about global warming, first by retracting his support for regulating carbon dioxide emissions at power plants and, more recently, by announcing the U.S. will not implement the limits on carbon dioxide emissions called for in the international Kyoto global warming treaty.

The American public is not terribly concerned, according to a special Gallup environmental survey conducted last month. Most believe the effects of global warming are already occurring or likely to occur in their lifetime. They also believe the problem is caused by human activities, something scientists and politicians are still debating. However, barely one-third predicts global warming will pose a serious threat to their way of life.

Gallup's March 5–7 poll asked respondents to characterize the amount they worry about thirteen different environmental issues as either "a great deal," "a fair amount," "only a little," or "not at all." Only 33% told Gallup they personally worry about the "greenhouse effect" or global warming a great deal. Concern about damage to the Earth's ozone layer—a related problem—is somewhat higher, with 47% saying they worry a great deal about it. However, public concern about both of these ranks well below several other environmental issues rated in the survey, particularly water pollution, air pollution, and toxic waste. Global warming ranks twelfth out of the thirteen issues tested, ahead of only "acid rain." Ozone damage ranks seventh.

This constancy in public concern about global warming is interesting in light of the fact that Americans now claim to have a somewhat better understanding of the issue than was the case nine years ago. In January 1992, 53% said that they understood the issue either fairly well or

very well, while today that percentage has risen to 69%. Still, even today, only 15% say they understand it very well.

There is little controversy about the fact that the average temperature of the Earth has risen slightly over the past century; thus, global warming per se is not in dispute. Rather, the global warming debate is over the seriousness of its impact and whether it is the result of human activities (specifically auto exhaust and other carbon dioxide emissions) or natural climactic changes. Six in ten respondents (61%) tell Gallup they believe increases in the Earth's temperature are due more to the effects of pollution from human activities while only 33% believe they are the result of natural changes in the environment not due to human activities.

Along with increasing reported awareness of the global warming issue, Gallup has seen an increase in the percentage who believe the impact of global warming is already being felt: 54% today, up from 48% in 1997. Another 17% believe the effects will be felt at some point in their lifetime whereas an additional 18% today believe the effects will be delayed until future generations. However, only a handful (7%) believe the effects of global warming will never happen.

There has been an even sharper increase in the percentage who are under the impression that scientists believe global warming is occurring (61%). Consistent with this, a majority think that news reports of the seriousness of global warming are either correct (34%) or underestimated (32%), while only 30% believe they are exaggerated. Despite this, and despite widespread agreement among Americans that global warming will be evident in their lifetime, only 31% think global warming will pose a serious threat to themselves or to their way of life, while 66% disagree.

APRIL 10
CHINA

Interview Dates: 4/6–8/01
Gallup Poll News Service
Survey #GO 132071

Do you approve or disapprove of the way George W. Bush is handling his job as president?

	Approve	Dis-approve	No opinion
2001 Apr 6–8	59%	30%	11%
2001 Mar 26–28	53	29	18
2001 Mar 9–11	58	29	13
2001 Mar 5–7	63	22	15

As you may know, a U.S. Navy plane was involved in a midair collision with a Chinese plane, and had to land in Chinese territory. The plane and its twenty-four crew members are currently being held by China. Do you approve or disapprove of the way George W. Bush is handling this situation?

Approve	61%
Disapprove	31
No opinion	8

The government in China says it will not return the twenty-four crew members until the United States officially apologizes for the incident. Do you think the United States should or should not officially apologize to China?

Yes, should apologize	41%
No, should not	54
No opinion	5

Thinking only about the flight and the midair collision with the Chinese plane, do you think the United States is or is not at fault for what happened?

Is at fault	13%
Is not at fault	68
No opinion	19

Finally, do you consider the twenty-four U.S. crew members to be hostages of China, or has the situation not yet reached the point where they can be described as hostages?

Yes, consider them hostages	55%
No, not yet	43
No opinion	2

Analysis: A new Gallup Poll conducted this past weekend shows that a majority of Americans (54%) do not believe the U.S. should officially apologize to China for the midair collision that took place last week, and led to the detainment of twenty-four U.S. crew members and their aircraft. Only 13% think the United States is at fault for the matter; nevertheless, 41% think the U.S. should apologize. A majority consider the U.S. crew members to be hostages. Americans generally approve of the way President Bush is handling the situation with China. The Chinese government has said it will not return the twenty-four crew members it is holding until the United States officially apologizes for the incident. To date, Bush has offered his "regrets" to the Chinese government but has indicated he will not apologize. Sixty-one percent approve of the way Bush is handling the situation with China, while 31% disapprove.

The poll also shows that just 13% of the public thinks the U.S. is at fault for the collision, while 68% do not and 19% have no opinion on the matter. Predictably, those who think the U.S. is at fault favor an apology to China: 85% favor and 15% oppose an apology. Among those who do not think the U.S. is at fault, 28% favor an apology while 69% are opposed.

Neither the president nor the Chinese government has referred to the twenty-four Americans held in China as "hostages." A majority (55%) do consider them hostages and 43% do not.

APRIL 11
ECONOMIC CONDITIONS

Interview Dates: 4/6–8/01
Gallup Poll News Service
Survey #GO 132071

Turning to the economy, how would you rate economic conditions in this country today—excellent, good, only fair, or poor?

	Excellent; good	Only fair; poor	No opinion
2001 Apr 6–8	.45%	55%	*
2001 Mar 5–7	.46	53	1
2001 Feb 1–4	.51	49	*
2001 Jan 10–14	.67	33	*

*Less than 1%

Right now, do you think that economic conditions in the country as a whole are getting better or getting worse?

	Better	Worse	Same (vol.); no opinion
2001 Apr 6–8	.24%	63%	13%
2001 Mar 5–7	.28	61	11
2001 Feb 1–4	.23	66	11
2001 Jan 10–14	.32	56	12
2000 Dec 2–4	.39	48	13
2000 Nov 13–15	.50	38	12
2000 Oct 6–9	.54	34	12

Asked of those who thought economic conditions were getting worse: How long do you think it will be before the economy starts to get better—up to three months, up to six months, up to a year, or longer than a year?

Up to three months 2
Up to six months 11
Up to a year 19
Longer than a year 36
Getting better now (vol.) 24
No opinion 8

Has the economic news you've heard or read about recently been mostly good or mostly bad?

	Mostly good	Mostly bad	Mixed (vol.); no opinion
2001 Apr 6–8	.16%	75%	9%
2000 Apr 7–9	.71	19	10

Do you think the economy is now in a recession, or not?

	Yes	No	No opinion
2001 Apr 6–8	.42%	52%	6%
2001 Mar 5–7*	.31	64	5
2001 Feb 1–4*	.44	49	7

*Based on part sample

Analysis: The latest Gallup measures of the economy suggest that, compared with last month, public confidence has declined slightly. In March, Americans' ratings of current economic conditions, and their projections for the future, both leveled off after significant declines the previous month and a persistent downward trend since October. But this month, both measures are slightly worse than last month, suggesting continuing economic worries.

Gallup's most recent poll on the economy was conducted April 6–8, and shows that 45% of Americans rate the economy as excellent or good, and 55% as only fair or poor. Last month, the percentage who said excellent or good was only a point higher, at 46%, but the percentage saying poor was somewhat lower at 10%.

Americans' expectations about the direction of the economy continue to be more negative than positive, as 63% say that economic conditions are getting worse, while just 24% say better. These numbers are slightly worse than those measured last month, when respondents said they thought the economy was getting worse rather than better by a 61%-to-28% margin.

While only 24% of Americans say that economic conditions are getting better now, another 32% say they will get better within at least a year: 2% within the next quarter, 11% within the next six months, and 19% by the end of a year. Over a majority (56%) expect the economy to start getting better within a year, leaving just over one-third (36%) who think it will take more than a year before improvement begins. The vast majority today are hearing mostly bad news about the economy whereas a year ago, they indicated they were hearing mostly positive news. No doubt the change in news content over the year helps to explain why Americans view the economy so poorly this year compared with last.

The poll also shows that 42% say the economy is now in a recession, while 52% disagree. This measure has been volatile over the past three months, with about the same number saying the country was in a recession in February (44%) as are saying it now. However, last month, the percentage dropped to 31%, perhaps in a temporary response to suggestions that the Federal Reserve Board was about to cut interest rates significantly, with some financial analysts predicting a three-quarter percentage point cut (75 basis points) instead of the half-point cut (50 basis points) that actually occurred. Whatever the reasons for the March drop on the Gallup recession measure, it was not accompanied by an equally significant improvement in the public's rating of the economy.

APRIL 11
DEATH PENALTY

Interview Dates: 3/26–28/01
Gallup Poll News Service
Survey #GO 133224

As you may know, Illinois has instituted a moratorium, or temporary halt, on the use of the death penalty until it can be better determined if the death penalty is being administered accurately and fairly in that state. Would you say you favor or oppose such a moratorium on the death penalty in all other states with the death penalty?

Favor 53%
Oppose 40
No opinion 7

Which comes closer to your view—there should be a moratorium, or temporary halt, on the death penalty until it can be better determined if the death penalty is being administered accurately and fairly in this country; or there should not be a moratorium, or temporary halt, on the death

penalty because there are already sufficient safeguards in the current justice system to prevent the execution of innocent people?

Should be a moratorium 42%
Should not be a moratorium 55
No opinion 3

Analysis: Last spring, Illinois Governor George Ryan made headlines by imposing a moratorium on the death penalty in his state as several death row inmates were discovered to be innocent of the crimes for which they were found guilty. The state of Maryland's attempt to institute a moratorium of its own failed at the close of its legislative session last Monday. Supreme Court Justice Ruth Bader Ginsburg publicly endorsed the legislation in a speech on Monday, hours before the legislative session ended.

The public's opinion is divided on death penalty moratoriums. A March 26–28 Gallup Poll experiment posed the issue of a moratorium to Americans in two different ways, the results of which revealed that attitudes about such an action are tentative at this point. The public's support for a moratorium ranges between 53% and 42%, depending on exactly how the concept is presented to them.

The first question was asked as follows: "As you may know, Illinois has instituted a moratorium, or temporary halt, on the use of the death penalty until it can be better determined if the death penalty is being administered accurately and fairly in that state. Would you say you favor or oppose such a moratorium on the death penalty in all other states with the death penalty?" Note that the question only provides reasons in favor of a moratorium but no reasons to oppose it. Therefore, the question wording generally tilts responses toward a moratorium. The results show that a majority (53%) favors the moratorium while 40% oppose it.

However, when asked a slightly different question, which does provide a reason to oppose a moratorium, less than one-half supports it. This question was worded: "Which comes closer to your view—there should be a moratorium, or temporary halt, on the death penalty until it can be better determined if the death penalty is being administered accurately and fairly in this country; or there should not be a moratorium, or temporary halt, on the death penalty because there are already sufficient safeguards in the current justice system to prevent the execution of innocent people?" According to this phrasing, 42% think there should be a moratorium on the death penalty while 55% do not.

These differences in results based on question construction are quite normal in survey research. They give a good indication of the degree to which Americans are open to argument on an issue. In this situation, the results suggest that, while a majority may support the idea of a moratorium on the death penalty at first glance, that support can be lowered considerably if strong arguments against such a moratorium are effectively carried to the people.

It also should be noted that when the first question was posed this February, the public was asked a follow-up question probing whether they felt strongly or not about the death penalty moratorium. About three out of ten said they did not have a strong opinion on the matter, indicating that their view is open to change.

APRIL 11
THE JFK ASSASSINATION

Interview Dates: 3/26–28/01
Gallup Poll News Service
Survey #GO 133224

Do you think that one man was responsible for the assassination of President Kennedy, or do you think that others were involved in a conspiracy?

	One man	Others involved	No opinion
2001 Mar 26–28	13%	81%	6%
1993 Nov 15–16	15	75	10
1992 Feb*	10	77	13
1983 Oct*	11	74	15
1976 Dec**	11	81	9
1966 Dec**	36	50	15
1963 Nov**	29	52	19

*Question wording included *one man, Lee Harvey Oswald*.
**Slight variations in wording from 2001 questions

Analysis: The vast majority of Americans believes the 1963 assassination of President John F. Kennedy, one of the most infamous events in American history, was a conspiracy. A Gallup Poll from March of this year shows that over eight in ten Americans (81%) believe that other people were involved in a conspiracy to assassinate President Kennedy. Only 13% believe that just one man (Lee Harvey Oswald) acted alone. These recent results match the high point of those believing in a conspiracy, a percentage that has increased since the 1960s.

Gallup first asked about a possible conspiracy shortly after the assassination in November 1963. At that time, 52% thought others were involved in the assassination. A similar percentage (50%) believed in a conspiracy three years later in December 1966. When Gallup revisited the subject in 1976, the percentage believing others were involved had increased considerably: 81% thought others were involved in the killing of President Kennedy. It is likely that this large increase in belief in a conspiracy was related to the highly publicized findings of the 1976 House Select Committee on Assassinations (HSCA), which concluded that Kennedy was probably killed as a result of a conspiracy. The percentage believing in a conspiracy decreased slightly, by 7%, in 1983 (74%). Support of the conspiracy theory remained high in 1992 (77%) and 1993 (75%), following the release of the popular Oliver Stone film *JFK* in 1991, which presented a variety of assassination conspiracy theories.

APRIL 12
FEDERAL INCOME TAX ATTITUDES

Interview Dates: 4/6–8/01
Gallup Poll News Service
Survey #GO 132071

Do you consider the amount of federal income tax you have to pay as too high, about right, or too low?

	Too high	About right	Too low*
2001 Apr 6–8 ......65%		31%	1%
2000 Apr 7–9 63		33	1
1999 Sep 10–14 68		28	1
1999 Jul 16 60		37	**
1999 Apr 6–7 65		29	2
1998 Apr 66		31	1
1997 Mar 58		38	1
1996 Apr 64		33	1
1994 Dec 66		30	1
1994 Apr 56		42	**
1993 Mar 55		41	2
1992 Mar 56		39	2
1991 Mar 55		37	2
1990 Mar 63		31	2
1985 Jun 63		32	1
1973 Feb 65		28	1
1969 Mar 69		25	**
1967 Mar 58		38	1
1966 Feb 52		39	–
1964 Feb 56		35	1
1963 Jan 52		38	1
1962 Jun 63		32	1
1962 Feb 48		45	–
1961 Feb 46		45	1
1957 Apr 61		31	**
1953 Feb 59		37	**
1952 Feb 71		26	**
1951 Feb 52		43	1
1950 Feb 57		40	–
1949 Mar 43		53	1
1948 Mar 57		38	1
1947 Nov 63		32	–
1947 Mar 54		40	–
1997 Mar 51		43	6
1946 Nov 60		34	6
1946 Feb 62		38	–
1945 Mar 85		15	–
1944 Mar 87		13	–
1944 Feb 90		10	–
1943 Feb 85		15	–

*"No opinion" is omitted.
**Less than 1%

Do you regard the income tax which you will have to pay this year as fair, or not?

	Yes	No	No opinion
2001 Apr 6–8 ......51%	46%	3%
1999 Apr 6–7 45	49	6

All in all, which of the following best describes how you feel about doing your income taxes—you love it, you like it, you dislike it, or you hate it?

	Love it; like it	Dislike it; hate it	None (vol.); no opinion
2001 Apr 6–8 ......24%	66%	10%
2000 Apr 7–9 18	71	11
1991 Mar 28–30 24	65	11
1990 Mar 8–11 22	63	14

Now we have a few questions about your 2001 income tax filing with the IRS for what you earned in 2000. Have you used or will you or your family use a computer program to help you prepare your taxes, or not?

	Yes	No	No opinion
2001 Apr 6–8 ......29%	69%	2%
1999 Apr 6–7 26	67	7
1997 Mar 24–26 36	59	5
1991 Mar 9–12 14	83	3
1990 Mar 14–17 9	87	4

Are you planning to or did you already send your tax return to the IRS by mail, or electronically by computer?

	Mail	Electronically	Not sure; does not apply (vol.); no opinion
2001 Apr 6–8 ......62%	28%	10%
1999 Apr 6–7 66	20	14
1997 Mar 24–26 77	15	8

Analysis: It's tax time again, and, perhaps not surprisingly, Americans continue to think that the amount of taxes they pay is too high. Perceptions that taxes are too high has been a consistent finding in Gallup Polls conducted for more than fifty years. The average "too high" rating over that period of time has been 59%, just slightly below the current reading of 65% obtained in a Gallup Poll completed Sunday. President Bush's emphasis on the need for an across-the-board tax cut certainly resonates with the general perceptions that Americans have held for many years, but there is little evidence that this year marks an unusual high point in viewing taxes as a burden. Despite the fact that two-thirds complain that their taxes are too high, only a little less than one-half say they are unfair. The poll also shows that respondents have very negative reactions to the annual ritual of filling out and sending in tax returns. Almost one-third say they hate it. One out of three will be filing their taxes electronically this year, double the number from just four years ago.

Gallup has been asking about taxes since 1947. An analysis of 33 different surveys, when the public has been asked if the amount of taxes they pay is too high, about right, or too little, shows that on average, 59% have said their taxes are "too high." This year, in a Gallup Poll conducted April 6–8, 65% say their taxes are too high, 31% say they are about right, and 1% say they are too low.

From a long-term perspective, the current figure is not extraordinary. The percentage saying their taxes are "too high" is somewhat up from 1991 to 1994, but is similar to readings obtained in the late 1960s, in 1973, in 1985, and in 1990. The high point was 71% saying "too high" in February 1952.

Rarely has the percentage who say their taxes are too high fallen below 50%. One such time was in 1949 when just 43% chose the "too high" response. Another more positive period came in the early 1960s, after John F. Kennedy's election to the presidency. The period from late 1991 to 1994 also appeared to be a little more positive with the percentage choosing the "too high" alternative in the mid-50% range.

A majority don't like doing their income taxes, a fact that presumably does not come as a great shock to most observers. Given a choice of four words to describe their reaction to doing taxes, 35% of Americans say they "dislike" doing them and another 31% "hate" it. At the other end of the spectrum, 21% say they "like" doing their taxes and—perhaps strangest of all—3% actually choose the word "love" to describe their attitude toward taxes. Gallup has asked this question four times, twice at the beginning of the 1990s, once last year, and again this year. There has been relatively little change. Between 63% and 71% of those interviewed have given the negative reaction each time.

Americans appear to make a distinction between feeling that their taxes are too high and the perception that their payment of taxes is fair. While 65% say they pay too much in the way of taxes, just 46% say that the income tax they are paying this year is not fair.

In 1990, just 9% said that they used a computer program to help them prepare their taxes. That number jumped to 36% in 1997, but has actually been lower the last two years at 26% in 1999 and 29% this year. On the other hand, the electronic filing of income taxes has gone up more consistently over the past four years. In 1997, just 15% said they would be filing electronically. This year that number is up to 28%.

APRIL 13
RELIGION/CHURCH ATTENDANCE

Interview Dates: 2/19–21/01
Gallup Poll News Service
Survey #GO 133064

How important would you say religion is in your own life—very important, fairly important, or not very important?

	Very important	Fairly important	Not very important*
2001 Feb 19–21 . . . . .55%	30%	15%
2000 Aug 24–27 57	31	12
2000 Mar 17–19 61	27	12

*"No opinion" is omitted.

At the present time, do you think religion as a whole is increasing its influence on American life or losing its influence?

	Increasing its influence	Losing its influence	Same (vol.)*
2001 Feb 19–21	.39%	55%	3%
2000 Aug 24–27	.35	58	4
2000 Mar 17–19	.37	58	–

*"No opinion" is omitted.

Do you happen to be a member of a church or synagogue?

	Yes	No
2001 Feb 19–21	.65%	35%
2000 Aug 24–27	.68	32
2000 Mar 17–19	.68	32

Did you, yourself, happen to attend church or synagogue in the last seven days, or not?

	Yes	No
2001 Feb 19–21	.41%	59%
2000 Aug 24–27	.43	57
2000 Mar 17–19	.44	56

How often do you attend church or synagogue—at least once a week, almost every week, about once a month, seldom, or never?

	At least once a week; almost every week	Once a month	Seldom; never*
2001 Feb 19–21	.42%	15%	42%
2000 Aug 24–27	.44	15	38
2000 Mar 17–19	.47	13	40

*"No opinion" is omitted.

Would you describe yourself as "born-again" or evangelical?

	Yes	No	No opinion
2001 Feb 19–21	.45%	49%	6%
2000 Aug 24–27	.44	50	6
2000 Mar 17–19	.46	47	7

Do you believe that religion can answer all or most of today's problems, or that religion is largely old-fashioned and out of date?

	Can answer	Old-fashioned	No opinion
2001 Feb 19–21	.63%	22%	15%
2000 Aug 24–27	.63	17	20
2000 Mar 17–19	.66	21	13

Which of the following statements comes closest to describing your views about the Bible—the Bible is the actual word of God and is to be taken literally, word for word; the Bible is the inspired word of God but not everything in it should be taken literally; or the Bible is an ancient book of fables, legends, history, and moral precepts recorded by man?

Actual word 27%
Inspired word 49
Fables 20
No opinion 4

Analysis: As Americans celebrate the Easter and Passover season this year, a review of Gallup polling reveals a religious nation, one in which over six in ten adults claim to be a member of a church or synagogue, and in which over half say that religion is a very important part of their lives. A substantial majority says that religion can answer all or most of life's questions, although well under one-half attend church regularly.

Gallup Polls over the past decade suggest that about four in ten attended a religious service in any given week, and about three in ten regularly attend services every week. These numbers have varied over the years, ranging from a low of 35% who indicated attendance during the previous week in August 1997, to a high of 49% measured in 1955 and 1958. Still, there has been no persistent upward or downward trend over the past six decades.

The fact that church attendance has remained fairly stable over time points to the perhaps surprising resilience of organized religion at a time when modern societal trends could be expected to undermine attachment to formal religion.

According to the latest numbers, about two in three (65%) claim to be a member of a church or synagogue. This is down slightly from the past few years when the percentages who said they were members of a church or synagogue were closer to 70%.

Gallup's latest numbers show 55% say that religion is a "very important" part of their lives. The current figure of 55% represents the low end of the range on this question, which for several decades has seldom been lower than the mid- to high-50s. More than six in ten (63%) think religion "can answer all or most of today's problems," while 22% think it is "largely old-fashioned and out of date."

Americans on the whole believe that the Bible is heavily influenced by God. While only 27% think it is the literal word of God, 49% think it is the inspired word of God, but that not everything in it should be taken literally. Only 20% think it is an ancient book of fables. However, the percentage who think it is a book of fables is the highest Gallup has ever recorded and the percentage who think it is the literal word of God is the lowest ever recorded.

APRIL 16
EARTH DAY AND THE ENVIRONMENT

Interviewing Dates: 3/5–7/01
Gallup Poll News Service
Survey #GO 132070

How would you rate the overall quality of the environment in this country today— excellent, good, only fair, or poor?

Excellent	.5%
Good	.41
Only fair	.47
Poor	.6
No opinion	.1

Right now, do you think the quality of the environment in the country as a whole is getting better or getting worse?

Getting better	.36%
Getting worse	.57
Same (vol.)	.5
No opinion	.2

How much progress have we made in dealing with environmental problems in the past few decades, say, since 1970—would you say we have made a great deal of progress, only some progress, or hardly any progress at all?

	Great deal	Some	Hardly any*
2001 Mar 5–7	.25%	64%	9%
2000 Apr 3–9	.26	64	9
1999 Apr 13–14	.36	55	8
1995 Apr 17–19	.24	61	14
1991 Apr 11–14	.18	61	19
1990 Apr 5–8	.14	63	21

*"No opinion" is omitted.

How much optimism do you have that we will have our environmental problems well under control in twenty years, that is, by about 2020—a great deal of optimism, only some optimism, or hardly any optimism at all?

	Great deal	Only some	Hardly any*
2001 Mar 5–7	.15%	65%	19%
2000 Apr 3–9	.18	60	21
1999 Apr 13–14	.18	62	18
1991 Apr 11–14	.19	60	18
1990 Apr 5–8	.18	58	22

*"No opinion" is omitted.

Thinking specifically about the environmental movement, do you think of yourself as an active participant in the environmental movement, sympathetic toward the movement but not active, neutral, or unsympathetic toward the environmental movement?

Active participant	.18%
Sympathetic, not active	.50
Neutral	.25
Unsympathetic	.5
No opinion	.2

For each of the following, please say whether you think they are doing too much, too little, or about the right amount in terms of protecting the environment:

The federal government?

Too much 11%
Too little 55
Right amount 31
No opinion 3

U.S. corporations?

Too much 4%
Too little 68
Right amount 23
No opinion 5

The American people?

Too much 2%
Too little 65
Right amount 30
No opinion 3

All in all, which of the following best describes how you feel about the environmental problems facing the Earth—life on Earth will continue without major environmental disruptions only if we take additional, immediate, and drastic action concerning the environment; we should take some additional actions concerning the environment; or we should take just the same actions we have been taking on the environment?

Immediate drastic action 27%
Some additional actions 56
Same actions 15
No opinion 2

Next, I am going to read some specific environmental proposals. For each one, please say whether you generally favor or oppose it:

Setting higher emissions and pollution standards for business and industry?

Favor 81%
Oppose 17
No opinion 2

Spending more government money on developing solar and wind power?

Favor 79%
Oppose 19
No opinion 2

More strongly enforcing federal environmental regulations?

Favor 77%
Oppose 20
No opinion 3

Setting higher auto emissions standards for automobiles?

Favor 75%
Oppose 23
No opinion 2

Giving tax breaks to provide incentives for drilling for more oil and gas in the United States?

Favor 53%
Oppose 43
No opinion 4

Expanding use of nuclear energy?

Favor 44%
Oppose 51
No opinion 5

Opening up the Alaskan Arctic Wildlife Refuge for oil exploration?

Favor 40%
Oppose 56
No opinion 4

Setting legal limits on the amount of energy that average consumers can use?

Favor 35%
Oppose 62
No opinion 3

Increased efforts by business and industry to reduce air pollution might lead to higher prices for the things consumers buy. Would you be willing to pay $100 more each year in higher prices so that industry could reduce air pollution, or not?

Yes 74%
No 24
No opinion 2

Increased efforts by business and industry to reduce air pollution might lead to higher prices for the things consumers buy. Would you be willing to pay $500 more each year in higher prices so that industry could reduce air pollution, or not?

Yes 63%
No 35
No opinion 2

Analysis: A variety of results from Gallup's Earth Day Poll conducted March 5–7 with 1,060 national adults suggest that only a quarter or so of Americans are highly troubled about environmental conditions. About one-half could be described as complacent, while the remaining majority is concerned about the environment but only moderately so.

At the same time, the Bush administration's emphasis on energy production and the economy over environmental concerns seems to be at odds with Americans' consistent preference for making environmental protection the priority. In general terms, the public says the environment should take precedence over economic as well as energy needs. And on specific issues such as regulating industrial emissions, drilling in the Alaskan wilderness, and the Kyoto global warming treaty, the public opposes the administration's positions.

A key question in this year's survey asks respondents to describe the current state of environ-

mental conditions in the United States. Overall, Americans are closely divided in their assessment with 46% viewing conditions as "good" or "excellent" and 53% considering them "only fair" or "poor." A different question finds that only 42% worry "a great deal" about the quality of the environment. Not surprisingly, only one-third who rate the environment in positive terms (as excellent or good) say they worry a great deal about it. But the rate of worry is also subdued (51% saying they worry "a great deal") among those who rate the environment more negatively (as only fair or poor). Combining these ratings, only 27% fall into the highly concerned camp, rating the environment in negative terms and indicating a great deal of concern about it. Just 14% rate the environment positively and express little to no worry about it while 57% fall somewhere in between.

A different question yields a similar result. When Americans are asked what steps are necessary to address the Earth's environmental problems, 27% say "immediate and drastic" action is needed. Only 15% think current actions are sufficient while the majority (56%) favors the moderate approach of "some additional" actions.

Eighteen percent of respondents describe themselves as an "active participant" in the environmental movement and 50% say they are "sympathetic but not active." Another 25% are "neutral," while only 5% say they are "unsympathetic." Three-quarters (74%) would be willing to pay an additional $100 per year for consumer products to pay for higher industrial emissions standards. Almost two-thirds (63%) would be willing to pay an additional $500 per year.

Americans' continuing support for environmental protection also is apparent in their responses to a list of eight environmental policy proposals being discussed in various policy circles. Three-quarters or more favor "setting higher emissions and pollution standards for business and industry" (81%), "spending more government money on developing solar and wind power" (79%), "more strongly enforcing federal environmental regulations" (77%), and "setting higher auto emissions standards for automobiles" (75%). In contrast, only 53% favor "giving tax breaks to provide incentives for drilling for more oil and gas in the U.S.," while "expanding use of nuclear energy" and "opening up the Alaskan Arctic Wildlife Refuge for oil exploration" are opposed by majorities of 51% and 56%, respectively. The least-favored proposal is one that would set "legal limits on the amount of energy that average consumers can use," opposed by 62% and favored by only 35%.

A pair of questions focusing specifically on "willingness to pay" for air-pollution control reveals somewhat greater support for environmental activism. When Americans were told that "increased efforts by business and industry to reduce air pollution might lead to higher prices," and were then asked if they would be willing to pay more so that industry could reduce air pollution, solid majorities replied in the affirmative to two differing scenarios. Half of the sample were asked if they would be willing to pay "$100 more each year in higher prices"; nearly three-quarters (74%) said yes. When the figure was raised to $500 for the other half of the sample, the percentage saying yes dropped to 63%, but still greatly exceeded the 35% saying no.

APRIL 17
THE ENVIRONMENT

Interview Dates: 4/6–8/01
Gallup Poll News Service
Survey #GO 132071

Do you think George W. Bush will do a good job or a poor job in handling each of the following issues as president:

Protecting the nation's environment?

	2001 Apr 6–8	2001 Mar 5–7
Good job	49%	51%
Poor job	41	38
Fair; mixed (vol.); no opinion	10	11

Improving the nation's energy policy?

	2001 Apr 6–8	2001 Mar 5–7
Good job	54%	58%

Poor job	36	29
Fair; mixed (vol.); no opinion	10	13

Keeping America prosperous?

	2001 Apr 6–8	2001 Mar 5–7
Good job	60%	66%
Poor job	30	23
Fair; mixed (vol.); no opinion	10	11

When it comes to environmental protection, which of these do you think is most likely to happen over the next four years under the Bush administration—the nation's environmental protection policies will be strengthened, the nation's environmental protection policies will be kept about the same, or the nation's environmental policies will be weakened?*

Strengthened	13%
Kept about the same	48
Weakened	34
No opinion	5

*Based on part sample

President Bush recently announced that the United States will not adhere to the Kyoto international treaty, which sets voluntary limits on the production of carbon dioxide and other global warming-related gases. Bush said that the treaty places too much of an economic burden on the United States while demanding little of developing countries. Do you approve or disapprove of Bush's decision for the United States not to adhere to the Kyoto treaty?

Approve	41%
Disapprove	48
No opinion	11

Analysis: From reversing new standards on arsenic in drinking water to abandoning the Kyoto global warming treaty, the Bush administration has announced a series of policies over the past month that have environmentalists seeing red and Democrats seeing a political opportunity. Despite the fact that Americans are at odds with many of these specific environmental actions, Gallup Polls show that the public maintains an overall positive view of President Bush's environmental policies.

Gallup's baseline rating of Bush on the environment was recorded in early March, just before the flurry of White House proposals on environmental issues were announced. These proposals included the retraction of a campaign promise to control carbon dioxide emissions from power plants, the decision to drop out of the Kyoto global warming agreement, and the rescission of many Clinton administration environmental proposals. A follow-up survey completed April 6–8 showed little substantive change in the public's ratings of the president on the environment.

The original March 5–7 survey found Americans somewhat optimistic in their environmental expectations for Bush. A slight majority (51%) predicted he would do a good job of protecting the nation's environment and just 38% said he would do a poor job. Gallup repeated the question in the April survey—after the controversial environmental policies made headlines—and the results were identical: 49% vs. 41%.

When the public is asked to prognosticate about Bush administration environmental protection, they show even less concern about his policies. Only one-third (34%) believe environmental protection will be weakened under Bush. While that clearly outnumbers the 13% who expect that environmental protection policies will be strengthened, the plurality (48%) thinks that environmental protection will be kept about the same during Bush's tenure in office.

A slight plurality disagree with the president's announcement that the U.S. will not adhere to the 1997 international Kyoto treaty (the treaty calls for limits on carbon dioxide and other gases that are believed to contribute to global warming). According to the early April poll, 48% disapprove of this position while 41% approve. And while Bush has pledged to open the Arctic National Wildlife Refuge in Alaska for oil exploration, only 40% support this and 56% are opposed.

Eighty-one percent of respondents favor setting higher emissions and pollution standards for business and industry, in contrast to Bush's policy decision. Three-quarters (77%) favor stronger enforcement of federal environmental regulations. In contrast, Bush policy advocates increasing the acceptable level of arsenic in drinking water, relaxing pollution rules on blending corn-based ethanol with gasoline to expand the fuel supply, and delaying a ban on road construction and logging in a third of all federal forest land. Nearly four in five Americans (79%) favor spending more government money on developing solar and wind power, something the Bush 2002 budget proposes to do.

APRIL 19
JOB OPTIMISM

Interview Dates: 4/6–8/01
Gallup Poll News Service
Survey #GO 132071

How would you describe business conditions in your community—would you say they are very good, good, not too good, or bad?

Very good	13%
Good	54
Not too good	25
Bad	6
No opinion	2

Asked of employed adults: How well is the company or organization that you work for doing—would you say business conditions there are very good, good, not too good, or bad?

Very good	28%
Good	53
Not too good	14
Bad	4
Doesn't apply (vol.); no opinion	1

Also asked of employed adults: Thinking about the next twelve months, how likely do you think it is that you will lose your job or be laid off—is it very likely, fairly likely, not too likely, or not at all likely?

Very likely 5%
Fairly likely 7
Not too likely 36
Not at all likely 52
No opinion . . . .*

*Less than 1%

Also asked of employed adults: If you were to lose your job, how likely is it that you would find a job just as good as the one you have now—very likely, somewhat likely, not very likely, or not at all likely?

Very likely 37%
Somewhat likely 33
Not too likely 23
Not at all likely 7
No opinion . . . .*

*Less than 1%

Also asked of employed adults: If you were to lose your job, how many months could you go without a job before experiencing significant financial hardship?

None 6%
Less than one month 7
One month 21
Two months 15
Three months 13
Four months 5
Five months 1
Six months 14
Seven to eleven months 2
Twelve months 3
More than a year 8
Indefinitely; don't need job (vol.) 4
No opinion 1

Asked of employed but not self-employed adults: Have you, personally, received a pay raise from your employer in the past twelve months?

Yes 72%
No 28

Also asked of employed but not self-employed adults: Do you expect to receive a pay raise from your employer in the next twelve months?

Yes 76%
No 22

Analysis: One result of the current "profits recession" has been a seemingly endless barrage of new layoff announcements. As many companies announced their lower earnings for the first quarter of 2001 and warn about continued earnings pressures in the months ahead, they also let Wall Street know that they would be reducing costs and laying off a significant number of workers.

Given this atmosphere of continuous layoff announcements, one might expect that many workers would fear for their jobs. According to a new Gallup Poll conducted April 6–8, however, this is not the case. Only one out of twenty workers (5%) say that they feel it is "very likely" that they will lose their job or be laid off during the next twelve months, while another 7% think it is "fairly likely." This total of 12% who express some fear for their jobs is the same as it was the last time Gallup asked this question, in 1998 when economic conditions were generally perceived to be much better than they are today.

Worker optimism about job security may be a significant key to understanding the current economic data that show that there has been only a small drop-off in consumer spending (down 0.2% during March). The fact that relatively few workers feel that today's record number of layoff announcements will actually impact them provides reason to be optimistic that consumers will continue to spend in the months ahead, thereby keeping the current slowdown/recession from becoming much worse.

During April 2001, eight out of ten workers (81%) describe business conditions where they work as either "very good" (28%) or "good" (53%). This may explain, at least in part, why most workers do not fear layoffs in spite of all the layoff announcements. The fact is that most workers feel that the business they work for is doing well and, therefore, have little to fear.

Seventy-two percent surveyed also say that they had received a pay raise during the past twelve months. Given the public's expectations of rapidly deteriorating economic conditions during 2001, it seems highly counterintuitive that so many workers should expect to continue to receive pay raises in the year ahead.

Unfortunately, most workers are not financially prepared to handle being out of work for any length of time. When asked how many months they could go without a job before experiencing significant financial hardship, about one-half (49%) could last less than three months. Another third (33%) could handle things for between three and six months. Only 17% say they could go for more than six months without encountering significant financial hardships.

It clearly is good news for the economy that workers are optimistic about their jobs and their prospects for getting a raise in the next twelve months. If worker optimism is misplaced, however, Gallup's polling suggests that workers are not financially ready to handle even a relatively brief period of unemployment. If worker optimism turns out to be a bubble that bursts, then the current slowdown and/or recession could become something much more significant.

APRIL 25
PRESIDENT BUSH

Interview Dates: 4/20–22/01
CNN/*USA Today*/Gallup Poll
Survey #GO 133357

Do you approve or disapprove of the way George W. Bush is handling his job as president?

	Approve	Dis-approve	No opinion
2001 Apr 20–22	62%	29%	9%
2001 Apr 6–8	59	30	11
2001 Mar 26–28	53	29	18
2001 Mar 9–11	58	29	13
2001 Mar 5–7	63	22	15

Do you approve or disapprove of the way Dick Cheney is handling his job as vice president?

Approve	63%
Disapprove	21
No opinion	16

Do you think the policies being proposed by George W. Bush will move the country in the right direction or the wrong direction?

	Right direction	Wrong direction	No opinion
National Adults			
2001 Apr 20–22	55%	34%	11%
2001 Jan 15–16*	56	36	8
2000 Aug 18–19	55	36	9
2000 Apr 7–9	51	31	18
1999 Oct 8–10	64	27	9
Registered Voters			
2001 Jan 15–16*	57	36	7
2000 Oct 20–22	53	38	9
2000 Sep 28–30	51	36	13
2000 Sep 8–10	49	36	15
2000 Sep 7–9	49	33	18

*Question wording varies from Bush as candidate to Bush as sitting president

Next, I have some questions about the Bush administration which took office in January. Whether or not you support Bush, do you think the Bush administration will or will not be able to do each of the following:

	Will
Cut your taxes	49%
Increase respect for the presidency	61
Improve moral values in the United States	55
Improve quality of the environment	42
Improve race relations	44
Improve health-care system	46
Improve respect for America abroad	58
Heal political divisions in this country	41
Keep federal budget balanced	50
Improve education	66
Ensure long-term strength of the Social Security system	50
Keep America prosperous	63

Whether or not you support Bush, do you think the Bush administration will or will not be able to do each of the following:

	Will	Will not*
Improve education	68%	28%
Increase respect for the presidency	68	28
Keep America prosperous	64	30
Improve respect for America abroad	62	34
Improve moral values in United States	62	35
Cut your taxes	59	36
Keep federal budget balanced	53	42
Ensure long-term strength of Social Security system	52	41
Improve health-care system	51	42
Improve race relations	49	44
Improve quality of the environment	48	47
Heal political divisions in this country	45	49

*"No opinion" is omitted.

Do you think George W. Bush's political views are too conservative, about right, or too liberal?

	Too conservative	About right	Too liberal*
2001 Apr 20–22	35%	41%	16%
2000 Aug 18–19**	40	41	12
2000 Aug 4–5**	30	50	13
2000 Jul 25–26**	30	45	12
2000 Mar 10–12**	30	47	14
2000 Feb 25–27**	33	38	16
2000 Jan 17–19**	27	45	12
1999 Oct 8–10**	27	50	16

*"No opinion" is omitted.
**Based on part sample

Have George W. Bush's policies since he became president been more conservative than you thought they would be, or not?*

Yes, more conservative 36%
No 56

No opinion 8
*Based on part sample

Do you think President Bush is or is not working hard enough to be an effective president?

Is 70%
Is not 26
No opinion 4

Which of the following comes closer to your view—George W. Bush is personally making the decisions in his administration that a president should make, or other people aside from George W. Bush are making the decisions in his administration that a president should make?

Bush 51%
Other people 43
No opinion 6

Do you think that big business does or does not have too much influence over the decisions made by the Bush administration?

Yes 63%
No 30
No opinion 7

Analysis: April 30th will be George W. Bush's 100th day in office as president of the United States. A new Gallup Poll takes stock of Americans' assessment of several dimensions of their new president; namely, his policies, his politics, and his personal style. Overall, the April 20–22 survey finds that Bush has held on to the mostly positive image he enjoyed shortly before taking office on January 20, and in a few cases, has improved on it. The areas in which the public rates Bush lowest are generally those that were his relative weaknesses before he took office, reinforcing the overall conclusion that in the first 100 days in office, Bush has generally sprung no surprises on the public. Across a wide variety of measures, the public now perceives Bush as no better or no worse than they did before his January 20 inauguration.

Bush's job approval rating is currently 62%, roughly the same as Gallup's first measurement of his job rating in early February when 57% approved. Also, by a 55%-to-34% margin, Americans think the policies Bush has proposed will generally move the country in the right, rather than the wrong, direction. This assessment, too, has held steady over the past 100 days. In short, after having had over three months to watch their president in action, respondents have just about the same viewpoint on Bush's job performance and the direction in which he is leading the country as they did when he started.

Additionally, Americans have maintained, or in some instances increased, their confidence that Bush will be able to accomplish a series of specific goals in his administration. We asked them in mid-January to assess whether or not Bush would be able to achieve each of twelve specific goals, and asked the same question again this past weekend. The public has not downgraded Bush's likelihood of achieving any of these goals. On several items, there has been little change, and on four of the objectives—cutting taxes, increasing respect for the presidency, improving moral values, and the environment—the percentage saying that Bush will succeed has increased by 6 percentage points or more.

Perhaps one surprising change can be seen in views on Bush's ability to improve the quality of the environment. In mid-January, just 42% said that he would succeed in this area. Since then, Bush has been widely criticized for several environmental policy decisions, including proposed drilling for oil on public lands in Alaska, deciding the U.S. would not adhere to limits on carbon dioxide emissions called for in the Kyoto global warming treaty, and deciding not to regulate carbon dioxide emissions standards in power plants. Despite this criticism, the public's feeling that Bush can improve the environment has actually gone up, by 6 percentage points, to 48% in the weekend poll. On a relative basis, the environment continues to be one of Bush's weak points, ranking near the bottom of the list of twelve policy goals, but it appears that, so far, his actions as president have actually improved rather than worsened his position on this issue.

The biggest improvement in Bush's issue ratings has come in the area of taxes. Fifty-nine percent now believe he will succeed in cutting taxes compared to 49% 100 days ago. Bush has made a tax-cut plan a centerpiece of his administration's first months in office, including his February 27 address to the nation in which he called for a major tax cut. Perhaps most important, both houses of Congress have already passed some form of tax cut plan, no doubt increasing the public's view that the odds of getting some sort of tax cut signed into law have improved. Currently, 56% favor Bush's proposed federal income taxes, and a majority has consistently supported these throughout his tenure in office. Thirty-five percent are opposed to the Bush tax cuts. Americans also have become somewhat more confident that Bush will increase respect for the presidency and improve moral values in the U.S.

The rank ordering of the public's assessment of Bush's likelihood to accomplish each of the twelve objectives measured in January and last weekend has remained relatively constant. The public is most confident that Bush will be able to improve education, increase respect for the presidency, keep America prosperous (interestingly, given the worsening economy), improve respect for the U.S. abroad, improve moral values in America, and cut taxes. The public is least optimistic that Bush will heal political divisions and improve the quality of the environment.

A good deal of discussion about Bush, before his election and since he took office in January, has focused on the views of some that he has turned out to be too conservative in his policy decisions and actions, and the views of others—from the right—that he has not been conservative enough. The latest poll shows that about one in three (35%) thinks Bush has been too conservative while 41% say his views are "about right." These numbers have changed very little since the presidential campaign when 30% to 40% thought Bush the candidate was too conservative. The latest poll shows 16% saying Bush is "too liberal."

A separate question addressed the matter more directly by asking Americans if Bush has been more conservative than they thought he would be. A majority (56%) says he has not but 36% say he has.

One of Bush's most significant potential problems is the perception by some that he is too tied into corporate America and big business, an accusation that surfaced most recently in relation to several of the Bush administration decisions on the environment. Asked about this directly, the public strongly tends to concur with this criticism. Almost two-thirds agree that "big business has too much influence over the decisions made by the Bush administration." While the public generally agrees with that criticism of Bush, respondents generally do not agree with two others. Americans overwhelmingly believe that Bush is in fact "working hard enough to be an effective president," a view expressed by 70% in the latest poll. Only 26% think that he is not working hard enough. In addition, a majority (51%) currently thinks that Bush "is making the decisions a president should make," while 43% think others are making the decisions he should make. While it is significant that four out of ten still agree that he is not as much in charge as he should be, there has been a shift in this sentiment within his first 100 days in office. A January 15–16 poll showed that 52% thought others would make the decisions a president should make while 45% thought Bush would. The current perceptions, as noted, have shifted, and now a slight majority believes that he is adequately in charge.

APRIL 25
CRIMES AGAINST PREGNANT WOMEN

Interview Dates: 4/20–22/01
CNN/*USA Today*/Gallup Poll
Survey #GO 133357

Suppose for a moment that a violent crime is committed against a pregnant woman, and the unborn child is harmed or killed. Do you think the criminal should or should not face additional charges for harming the unborn child as well as the woman? *

Should face additional charges 93%
Should not 5
No opinion 2
*Based on part sample

Suppose for a moment that a violent crime is committed against a pregnant woman, and the fetus is harmed or killed. Do you think the criminal should or should not face additional charges for harming the fetus as well as the woman? *

Should face additional charges 86%
Should not 9
No opinion 5

*Based on part sample

Analysis: The U.S. Congress takes up legislation this week to criminalize certain violent acts causing injury or death to a fetus or unborn child. The issue is highly controversial in Congress where members apparently are divided in their support for the "Unborn Victims of Violence Act of 2001" (H.R. 503, sponsored by Rep. Lindsey Graham). Supporters of the bill argue that it is necessary to fill a hole in current federal law, whereby a violent act that results in minimal injury to a pregnant woman but kills her fetus or unborn child, is subject only to the penalties for the harm done to the woman.

A new Gallup Poll finds that Americans overwhelmingly support the concept that the perpetrator of violence against a pregnant woman should be held legally responsible for causing harm to a fetus or unborn child, as well as to the pregnant mother. Widespread support for imposing stiffer penalties on such violent acts is found both when the word "fetus" is used as well as when the phrase "unborn child" is used. In an April 20–22 Gallup survey of national adults, one-half of respondents were asked: "Suppose for a moment that a violent crime is committed against a pregnant woman, and the unborn child is harmed or killed. Do you think the criminal should or should not face additional charges for harming the unborn child as well as the woman?" In response, 93% say the suspect should face additional charges while just 5% disagree. The second half of survey respondents were asked the same question, but the word "fetus" replaced the phrase "unborn child." The results were similar as 86% favor additional charges and just 9% oppose them.

APRIL 26
CAREERS

Interview Dates; 3/26–28/01
Gallup Poll News Service
Survey #GO 133224

Supposing a young woman came to you for advice on choosing a line of work or career. What kind of work or career would you recommend?

	2001	1998	1950
Computers	16%	16%	–
Doctor; medical field	15	11	2
Something she likes; depends on the person; finish school	13	15	–
Business; self-employed; sales	8	5	–
Technology	8	2	–
Nursing	7	4	28
Teaching	6	7	16
Lawyer; attorney	3	2	–
Secretary; clerical	2	3	8
Stay home; homemaker; wife; mother	2	2	–
Something with people; helping others; social work . . .	2	2	7
Engineering	1	1	–
Military	1	–	–
Government career	1	–	–
Actress	–	–	3
Airline stewardess	–	–	4
Beautician	–	–	2
Dept. store sales clerk . .	–	–	1
Dietician; home economics	–	–	8
Dressmaker; fashion . . .	–	–	4
Journalism	–	–	3
Librarian	–	–	2
Modeling	–	–	2
Musician	–	–	2
Other (vol.)	5	14	3
Nothing (vol.)	–	2	–
Anything (vol.)	–	3	–
No opinion	10	11	5

Analysis: April 26th marks the ninth annual "Take our daughters to work day," an event focused on introducing young women to the workplace in an effort to expand their horizons and build confidence. A recent Gallup Poll asked Americans what career they would advise women people to pursue. The top two suggestions are computers and medicine, 16% and 15%, respectively. Technology and business or sales comprise the next three suggested professions.

The last time Gallup asked this question, in 1998, computers topped the list of suggested professions for young women. A comparison of this year's results with those from 1950, the first time Gallup asked about a young woman's career options, highlights the sweeping cultural change that has taken place over the last fifty years. At that time, the top response was nursing (28%), followed by teaching (16%) and secretary/clerical (8%).

MAY 1
INCOME TAX CUTS

Interview Dates: 4/20–22/01
CNN/*USA Today*/Gallup Poll
Survey #GO 133357

Based on what you have read or heard, do you favor or oppose the federal income tax cuts President Bush has proposed?

	Favor	Oppose	No opinion
2001 Apr 20–22	56%	35%	9%
2001 Mar 5–7	56	34	10
2001 Feb 19–21	53	30	17
2001 Feb 9–11	56	34	10

Whether or not you support Bush, do you think the Bush administration will or will not be able to cut your taxes?

	2001 Apr 20–22	2001 Jan 15–16
Will	.59%	49%
Will not	.36	46
No opinion	.5	5

Do you approve or disapprove of the way George W. Bush is handling taxes?

	2001 Apr 20–22	2001 Mar 9–11
Approve	.54%	56%
Disapprove	.39	35
No opinion	.7	9

Analysis: A Gallup Poll conducted last week shows little change in the public's support for a tax cut over the past four months, although expectations that a cut will be enacted appear to have risen. The good news for President Bush is that this centerpiece of his legislative agenda appears to have substantial public support, with 56% of Americans saying they favor the tax cuts he has proposed and just 35% saying they are opposed. Furthermore, by a 54%-to-39% margin, respondents approve of the way Bush is handling the issue of taxes.

MAY 2
McVEIGH EXECUTION

Interview Dates: 4/20–22/01
CNN/*USA Today*/Gallup Poll
Survey #GO 133357

Thinking about Timothy McVeigh, the man convicted of murder in the Oklahoma City bombing case and sentenced to death, which comes closest to your view—I generally support the death penalty and believe McVeigh should be executed, I generally oppose the death penalty but believe McVeigh should be executed in this case, or I generally oppose the death penalty and do not believe McVeigh should be executed?

Support death penalty, McVeigh should be executed	.59%

Oppose death penalty, McVeigh should be executed	.22
Oppose death penalty, McVeigh should be executed	.16
Other (vol.)	.1
No opinion	.2

Which comes closest to your view about televising the scheduled execution of Timothy McVeigh on May 16—it should not be shown on television at all, it should be shown on closed circuit television only for the families of the victims to watch, or it should be shown on national television for anyone to watch?

Not on television at all	.43%
On television for victims' families only	.39
On television for anyone to watch	.17
No opinion	.1

If the execution of Timothy McVeigh were to be broadcast on national television, would you watch his execution, or not?

Would	.23%
Would not	.76
No opinion	.1

Asked of those who would not watch the execution on television: If your family member had been a victim in the Oklahoma City bombing, would you watch his execution in that case, or not?

Would	.27%
Would not	.68
No opinion	.5

Analysis: In two weeks, Timothy McVeigh is scheduled to be executed for the deaths of 168 people in the April 1995 bombing attack on the Alfred P. Murrah Federal Building in Oklahoma City. A Gallup Poll conducted April 20–22 shows that the vast majority of Americans—including those who generally oppose the death penalty—believes McVeigh should be executed. The public is strongly opposed to televising the execution "for anyone to watch," a position favored by just 17%. Most believe it should only be shown on closed circuit television for the victims' families to watch (39%) or believe it should not be televised at all (43%). Only about one in four would watch the execution if they had the opportunity, but an additional 21% would watch if one of their family members had been a victim of the bombing. According to the poll, 81% believe McVeigh should be executed, while 16% think he should not.

Since McVeigh was sentenced to death, there has been much discussion about whether or not his execution should be televised. A small number of witnesses, including representatives of the victims' families, are required by federal law to observe the execution. United States Attorney General John Ashcroft recently decided that the execution would be televised by closed circuit for all of the victims' families to watch if they so choose. A federal judge rejected an Internet company's appeal to broadcast the execution over the Internet.

The public is divided as to whether or not the McVeigh execution should be televised. Forty-three percent think it should not be televised at all, 39% think it should be televised only for the victims' families, and 17% think it should be on television for anyone to watch. Americans do not seem overly interested in viewing the execution if it were televised. When asked if they would watch, only 23% would while 76% would not. However, an additional 21% say they would watch if one of their family members had been a victim in the bombing.

MAY 4
WORKING PARENTS

Interview Dates: 4/20–22/01
CNN/*USA Today*/Gallup Poll
Survey #GO 133357

Considering the needs of both parents and children, which of the following do you see as the ideal situation for a family in today's society—both parents work full time outside the home; one parent works full time outside

the home, the other works part time; one parent works full time outside the home, the other works at home; or one parent stays at home solely to raise the children?

Both parents work full time 13%
One parent full time, one part time 24
One parent full time, one works at home 17
One parent stays at home to raise children . .41
No opinion 5

Asked of those who think one parent should work part time or at home: Which parent do you think should work full time outside the home—the husband, the wife, or doesn't it make any difference?

Husband 30%
Wife 1
No difference 69
No opinion 0

Asked of those who think one parent should stay at home solely to raise the children: Which parent do you think should stay home solely to raise the children—the husband, the wife, or doesn't it make any difference?

Husband 1%
Wife 43
No difference 55
No opinion 1

Analysis: Americans have reasonably strong opinions about issues concerning child care and ideal working situations. According to a Gallup Poll conducted April 20–22, only 13% say the ideal situation is for both parents to work full time outside the home, but 41% say it is ideal for one parent to work either part time or at home. An additional 41% believe it is best for one parent to stay at home solely to raise the children while the other parent works.

Nearly seven in ten (69%) who think the ideal situation is to have one parent working at home or part time outside of the home believe that it does not matter which parent remains the full-time worker. Another 30% say the man should work full time. This represents a substantial shift from the last time Gallup posed this question in July 1991. At that time, a smaller majority (55%) agreed that it did not make any difference which parent worked full time and 44% felt that the father should work full time outside the home. In the intervening ten years, it appears that a portion who felt the father was responsible for working full time outside the home have changed their opinion to reflect a growing acceptance of more flexible gender roles in parenting. However, traditions based on gender apparently do not die easily. In both 1991 and 2001, only 1% of those who said one parent should work part time or at home nominated the mother to work full time outside the home.

Of those who believe one parent should stay at home solely to raise the children, 55% feel it does not make any difference which parent stays home. But the views of those who have a preference skew heavily toward a scenario in which the mother stays home. More than four in ten (43%) believe the mother should stay home, and only 1% believes the father should stay home. Again, there has been a noticeable shift in these percentages since this question was last asked. At that time, a substantially greater percentage of the public believed that the mother should stay home solely to raise the children (63% in 1991, compared to 43% in 2001).

MAY 8
SOCIAL SECURITY INVESTMENT

Interview Dates: 3/26–28/01
Gallup Poll News Service
Survey #GO 133224

Asked of nonretired persons: Do you think the Social Security system will be able to pay you a benefit, or not, when you retire?

	Yes	No	Doesn't apply (vol.); no opinion
2001 Mar 26–28	.52%	41%	7%
2000 Aug 11–12	.49	42	9

George W. Bush has made a proposal that would allow people to put a portion of their Social Security payroll taxes into personal retirement accounts that would be invested in private stocks or bonds. Do you favor or oppose this proposal?*

	Favor	Oppose	No opinion
2001 Mar 26–28	.54%	36%	10%
2001 Jan 5–7	.60	36	4
2000 Jun 6–7	.59	31	10

*Based on part sample

A proposal has been made that would allow people to put a portion of their Social Security payroll taxes into personal retirement accounts that would be invested in private stocks and bonds. Do you favor or oppose this proposal?*

	Favor	Oppose	No opinion
2001 Mar 26–28	.63%	30%	7%
2000 Jun 6–7	.65	30	5

*Based on part sample

Analysis: Last week, President George W. Bush made his first major announcement on Social Security and appointed a bipartisan commission to study the issue. The commission is sure to consider a proposal that would allow Americans to invest a portion of their Social Security contributions in private stocks and bonds, something Bush strongly favors. Despite recent drops in the value of stocks, Americans continue to support the idea of investing a portion of their Social Security contributions in the stock market. A recent Gallup Poll conducted March 26–28 shows 63% favor the proposal while 30% are opposed. The numbers are virtually unchanged from a poll conducted in June of last year, when 65% of Americans favored this particular reform proposal and 30% opposed it.

The proposal was a major part of Bush's campaign for president, and his preferred way to ensure the long-term strength of Social Security.

Gallup also finds majority support for the idea of private investment of Social Security funds when the question associates the proposal with Bush, but not as high as when he is not mentioned. In this version of the question, the proposal is favored by 54%, with 36% opposed. The 54% support is lower than two previous measurements that linked Bush to the proposal. In June of last year, 59% favored the Bush proposal and in January 2001, 60% did.

Given that the proposal without the Bush affiliation has shown little change over time, the drop in the proposal's favorability may be due to lower evaluations of Bush rather than changes in perceptions about the proposal itself. The March 26–28 poll marked the low point in Bush's overall job approval to date.

MAY 9
FINANCIAL CONCERNS

Interview Dates: 4/6–8/01
Gallup Poll News Service
Survey #GO 132071

*Please tell me how concerned you are right now about each of the following financial matters, based on your current financial situation—are you very worried, moderately worried, not too worried, or not worried at all?**

	Very, moderately worried
Not having enough money for retirement	53%
Not being able to pay medical costs in the event of serious illness or accident	50
Not being able to pay medical costs for normal health care	44
Not being able to maintain the standard of living you enjoy	43
Not having enough to pay your normal monthly bills	32
Not being able to pay your rent, mortgage, or other housing costs	24
Not being able to make the minimum payments on your credit cards	18

*Total adds to more than 100% due to multiple replies.

Analysis: With the U.S. economy teetering between a recession and a "soft landing," the financial well-being of a third of Americans may just hang in the balance. A recent Gallup Poll suggests that many are living so close to the edge financially that a prolonged economic downturn could put them in a serious financial squeeze.

Nearly one-third (32%) told Gallup in an April 6–8 survey that they worry about not having enough money to pay their normal monthly bills. Having enough money for retirement emerged as the number one concern. Fifty-three percent are either very or moderately worried about this. Whether for a serious illness or for standard medical bills, paying for health care ranks next, with 50% and 44% worried, respectively.

A substantial portion (43%) worry about their ability to maintain their standard of living. Thirty-two percent worry about paying their normal monthly bills. Meeting housing costs (such as rent and mortgage) and paying credit card bills rank as lower concerns, with 24% and 18%, respectively, worried about these expenditures.

MAY 10
CREDIT CARDS

Interview Dates: 4/6–8/01
Gallup Poll News Service
Survey #GO 132071

Thinking about all credit cards including department stores and retail chain stores as well as general bank credit cards such as VISA and MasterCard, how many credit cards do you have?

None	22%
One to two	33
Three to four	23

Five to six 11
Seven or more 9
No opinion 2

Mean (including zero)	**3.10**
Median (including zero)	**2.00**
Mean (excluding zero)	**4.00**
Median (excluding zero)	**3.00**

Asked of those with at least one credit card: How do you generally pay your credit card(s) each month—do you always pay the full amount, do you usually pay the full amount but not always, do you always pay as much as you can but usually leave balances, do you usually pay the minimum amount due but not much more, or do you sometimes pay less than the minimum amount due?

Always pay full amount 42%
Usually pay full amount 16
Always pay as much as you can 29
Usually pay minimum amount 11
Pay less than minimum 1
Other (vol.) 1

Analysis: Credit cards have become one of the most important means of financial transactions in modern American life, providing people with immediate cash and credit, although often at a steep price. The poll was conducted April 6–8, and shows that 22% say they have no credit card while 33% have from one to two cards, 23% have three to four cards, and 20% have five or more cards. The average number of cards reported by respondents is 3.1.

The poll also shows that only 42% of Americans who have credit cards say they always pay the full amount of their credit card balances each month, while another 16% say they usually do. That leaves 41% of credit card owners—almost a third—who regularly leave some part of the balance to roll over to the next month, including 29% who say they pay as much of the balance as they can, although they usually leave some balance; 11% who usually pay only the minimum

balance due; and 1% who sometimes pay less than the minimum amount due.

MAY 11
ENERGY SITUATION

Interview Dates: 5/7–9/01
Gallup Poll News Service
Survey #GO 133629

How serious would you say the energy situation is in the United States—very serious, fairly serious, or not at all serious?

	Very serious	Fairly serious	Not at all serious; no opinion
2001 May 7–9	58%	36%	6%
2001 Mar 5–7	31	59	10

Do you think the current rise in gas prices represents a temporary fluctuation in prices, or a more permanent change in prices?*

	Temporary fluctuation	More permanent change	No opinion
2001 May 7–9	40%	56%	4%
2000 Jun 22–25	57	39	4
2000 May 23–24	45	50	5
2000 Mar 30–Apr 2 ...	60	37	3
2000 Mar 10–12	63	34	3

*Based on part sample

Looking ahead to one month from now, do you think gas prices at that time will be higher than they are today, about the same, or lower than they are today?*

	Higher	About the same	Lower**
2001 May 7–9	83%	13%	3%
2000 Jun 22–25	38	39	22
2000 May 23–24	51	33	14

| 2000 Mar 10–12 | .74 | 16 | 9 |

*Based on part sample
**"No opinion" is omitted.

*Looking ahead to six months from now, do you think gas prices at that time will be higher than they are today, about the same, or lower than they are today?**

	Higher	About the same	Lower**
2001 May 7–9	.38%	37%	24%
2000 Jun 22–25	.20	28	50
2000 May 23–24	.24	25	49
2000 Mar 10–12	.37	26	34

*Based on part sample
**"No opinion" is omitted.

Have recent price increases in gasoline caused any financial hardship for you or your household?

	Yes	No
2001 May 7–9	.47%	53%
2000 Jun 22–25	.44	56
2000 May 23–24	.36	64
2000 Mar 30–Apr 2	.39	61
2000 Mar 10–12	.41	59

Will the price of gas cause you to drive less than you might have otherwise this summer, or not?

	Yes	No	No opinion
2001 May 7–9	.58%	41%	1%
2000 Jun 22–25	.50	49	1
2000 May 23–24	.41	57	2

Analysis: Well over half of Americans now say the energy situation in this country is very serious, one out of two say the increasing cost of energy has caused them financial hardship, and almost six out of ten say the rising price of gasoline will force them to cut back on their summer travel plans. These and other findings from a new Gallup Poll underscore the impact that the rising cost and diminished availability of energy are having.

Perhaps the most telling sign of the energy situation's increasing significance for Americans comes from the response to a simple question that Gallup first asked back in 1977: "How serious would you say the energy situation is in the United States—very serious, fairly serious, or not at all serious?" The question was asked twice this year. In just the last two months, there has been a significant increase in the percentage who say the energy situation in the United States is very serious: from 31% at the beginning of March to 58% in the May 7–9 poll.

The poll also shows that about one-half say the recent price increases in gasoline have caused financial hardship for their households. And what about the possible impact of high gas prices on the summer travel season? Fifty-eight percent say they will be driving less this summer.

The public is apparently settling in for a possible long-term increase in gas prices. A majority (56%) say the recent rise in gas prices is more permanent, and not just a temporary fluctuation. This fear that gas price increases are permanent is echoed in respondents' responses to two questions about whether they expect gas prices to go up, go down, or stay the same over the next month, and over the next six months. Only 3% say that prices will be lower in one month, and only 24% are willing to venture the guess that they will be lower in six months. In addition, respondents are decidedly pessimistic when they are asked to look forward just one month and guess the direction gas prices will take. Over eight out of ten (83%) believe gas prices will be even higher one month from now, the most pessimistic response to this question measured in the four times it has been asked.

Asked to look ahead six months, Americans become decidedly more positive, at least on a relative basis. Thirty-eight percent say gas prices will be higher, and 37% about the same. However, only 24% say they will be lower.

MAY 11
MOTHER'S DAY

Interview Dates: 5/7–9/01
Gallup Poll News Service
Survey #GO 133629

Is your mother living today?

	Yes	No
2001 May 7–9	64%	36%
2000 May 5–7	64	36

Asked of those whose mother is living today: How would you characterize your relationship with your mother today—is it very positive, somewhat positive, neither positive nor negative, somewhat negative, or very negative?

	Very, somewhat positive	Neither positive nor negative	Somewhat, very negative*
National Adults			
2001 May 7–9	93%	4%	3%
2000 May 5–7	92	4	4
Men			
2001 May 7–9	94	4	1
2000 May 5–7	92	5	3
Women			
2001 May 7–9	92	4	4
2000 May 5–7	91	3	3

*"No opinion" is omitted.

Also asked of those whose mother is living today: Which, if any of the following are you likely to do for your mother on Mother's Day this year?

	Likely	Not likely*
Send or give your mother a card	89%	11%
Buy your mother a gift	76	23
Call your mother on the telephone	70	29
Visit your mother	68	30
Send your mother flowers	40	58

*"Nothing; other" are omitted.

Analysis: As Americans celebrate Mother's Day this weekend, a new Gallup Poll conducted May 7–9 shows nine out of ten enjoy a positive relationship with their mothers. Among the 64% whose mothers are still living, 76% describe their relationship with their mother as "very positive" while 17% term it "somewhat positive." Just 4% describe the relationship as neutral—"neither positive nor negative"—while only 3% say the relationship is negative.

Cynics suggest that the greeting card industry was responsible for the creation of Mother's Day, and if those cynics are correct, then the card makers should be very successful again this year. Nearly nine out of ten (89%) plan to send or give their mothers a card for the holiday while 76% will buy a gift. Seven out of ten will telephone their mothers, 68% plan to visit in person, and just 40% plan to send flowers.

MAY 14
McVEIGH EXECUTION

Interview Dates: 5/7–9/01
Gallup Poll News Service
Survey #GO 133629

How closely have you followed the news about the scheduled execution of Timothy McVeigh, the man convicted of murder in the Oklahoma City bombing case and sentenced to be executed on May 16th—very closely, somewhat closely, not too closely, or not at all?

Very closely	14%
Somewhat closely	45
Not too closely	27
Not at all	14

How interested are you in watching the live news coverage of the McVeigh execution on the morning of May 16th—very interested, somewhat interested, not too interested, or not at all interested?

Very interested	9%
Somewhat interested	10

Not too interested 15
Not at all interested 66

*Just your opinion, do you think the execution
of McVeigh will or will not act as a deterrent to future acts of violence and murder?*

Will 30%
Will not 66
No opinion 4

*Just your opinion, do you think the execution
of McVeigh will or will not help the families
of the victims cope with the tragedy and
reach "closure"?*

Will 53%
Will not 40
No opinion 7

*Just your opinion, do you think the execution
of McVeigh will or will not make McVeigh a
martyr in the eyes of some Americans?*

Will 46%
Will not 46
No opinion 8

*Has the effect of the scheduled McVeigh ex-
ecution been to increase your support of the
death penalty, increase your opposition to
the death penalty, or has it made no difference to you?*

Increase support 22%
Increase opposition 8
No difference 68
No opinion 2

Analysis: On Friday, Attorney General John
Ashcroft delayed the execution of convicted
Oklahoma City bomber Timothy McVeigh until
June 11 so that newly discovered FBI files on his
case can be reviewed. The execution has been
one of the biggest news stories of the year.
Regardless of when the execution finally takes
place, Gallup polling suggests that the public

does not appear to think the event represents a
pivotal moment in the history of the American
justice system. Respondents say they are not interested in watching live news coverage of it, and
do not think the execution will have much of an
effect on death penalty attitudes or on future acts
of violence in the U.S.

The latest Gallup Poll conducted May 7–9
shows that just 19% of Americans are "very" or
"somewhat interested" in watching news coverage of McVeigh's execution. Fully two-thirds are
"not at all interested." To date, the public has
paid only a moderate amount of attention to
McVeigh's execution. Fifty-nine percent have
followed the news about this story closely (14%
very closely).

McVeigh's case is unusual in several respects.
His attack on the Alfred P. Murrah Federal
Building in April 1995 caused more deaths than
any other act of terrorism on American soil. He
also will be the first person executed by the federal
government since 1963. One key question is what
effect, if any, the McVeigh execution will have on
the country. Just over one-half (53%) say that it
will help the victims' families cope with the
tragedy and reach "closure," although 40% disagree. The public is evenly divided over whether
McVeigh will be seen as a martyr by some, with
46% predicting he will and 46% predicting he will
not. Americans are far less optimistic that
McVeigh's death will act as a deterrent to future
acts of violence, as only 30% think it will while
66% think it will not.

According to the poll, 68% say the scheduled execution will make no difference in their
opinion on the death penalty, although among the
rest, more say it has increased their support than
say it has increased their opposition. Overall,
22% say the effect of the scheduled execution has
been to increase their support for the death
penalty, while 8% say the effect has been to increase their opposition.

**MAY 15
ENERGY CONSERVATION
VERSUS PRODUCTION**

Interview Dates: 5/7–9/01
Gallup Poll News Service
Survey #GO 133629

Which of the following approaches to solving the nation's energy problems do you think the United States should follow right now—emphasize production of more oil, gas, and coal supplies or emphasize more conservation by consumers of existing energy supplies?

	2001 May 7–9	2001 Mar 5–7
More production	35%	33%
More conservation	47	56
Both equally (vol.)	14	8
Neither; other (vol.)	2	1
No opinion	2	2

Here are some things that can be done to deal with the energy situation. For each one, please say whether you generally favor or oppose it:

Investments in new sources of energy such as solar, wind, and fuel cells?

Favor	91%
Oppose	6
No opinion	3

Mandating more energy-efficient appliances such as air conditioning, clothes driers, and water heaters?

Favor	87%
Oppose	12
No opinion	1

Mandating more energy-efficient new buildings?

Favor	86%
Oppose	12
No opinion	2

Mandating more energy-efficient cars?

Favor	85%
Oppose	14
No opinion	1

Investing in new power-generating plants?

Favor	83%
Oppose	13
No opinion	4

A federal government partnership with the auto industry working toward energy-efficient cars?

Favor	76%
Oppose	22
No opinion	2

Investing in more electrical transmission lines?

Favor	69%
Oppose	23
No opinion	8

Investing in more gas pipelines?

Favor	64%
Oppose	29
No opinion	7

Drilling for natural gas on federal lands?

Favor	63%
Oppose	33
No opinion	4

Increasing the use of nuclear power as a major source of power?

Favor	48%
Oppose	44
No opinion	8

Opening up the Alaskan Arctic Wildlife Refuge for oil exploration?

Favor	38%

Oppose 57
No opinion 5

Analysis: In his radio address to the nation last Saturday, President Bush said that conservation was a key element in his administration's energy strategy, which will be presented to the public this week. A Gallup Poll conducted May 7–9 shows that the president's new emphasis on conservation is likely to appeal to the public. Americans express widespread support for several measures to deal with the current energy situation, including both new production and conservation initiatives. But when asked to make a trade-off between the two approaches, more choose conservation than new production. Still, the margin in favor of conservation has declined by half over the past two months.

The poll also shows that while there is much support for steps to mandate more energy-efficient products such as appliances, cars, and buildings, there is less support for additional investments in some of the infrastructures that would be needed to produce more power. Also, respondents are divided over whether to increase the use of nuclear power and remain opposed to opening up the Arctic National Wildlife Refuge for oil exploration.

According to the poll, 35% of Americans favor an emphasis on the production of more oil, gas, and coal supplies as a way to solve the nation's energy problems, while 47% favor emphasizing more conservation. An additional 14% volunteer that they would like an emphasis on both approaches.

Among eleven approaches to deal with the country's energy problems covered in the poll, respondents are most supportive of the general concept of investing in new sources of energy such as solar, wind, and fuel cells (91%). Almost as strong is the support for mandating more energy-efficient appliances (87%), buildings (86%), and cars (85%). A government partnership with the auto industry to manufacture more efficient cars is favored by 76%.

While Americans also favor investing in new power-generating plants (83%), support for investing in more electrical transmission lines

(69%) and more gas pipelines (64%) is considerably lower, as is support for drilling for natural gas on federal lands (63%). Respondents are about evenly divided over increasing the use of nuclear power as 48% favor and 44% oppose that proposal. And they remain opposed to drilling in the Arctic National Wildlife Refuge, with 57% against it and 38% in favor.

MAY 16
INCOME TAX CUTS

Interview Dates: 5/7–9/01
Gallup Poll News Service
Survey #GO 133629

How important is it that the Bush administration cuts taxes—is it a top priority, high priority, low priority, or not a priority at all?

	Top, high priority	Low priority	Not a priority; no opinion
2001 May 7–9	60%	29%	11%
2001 Feb 9–11	67	25	8
2001 Jan 5–7	65	26	9

Based on what you have heard or read, do you favor or oppose Congress including a substantial tax cut in this year's federal budget?

Favor 60%
Oppose 30
No opinion 10

Which of the following would you prefer— the original tax cut of $1.6 trillion proposed by President Bush, or the tax cut of $1.25 trillion proposed by some in Congress?

Tax cut of $1.6 trillion 38%
Tax cut of $1.25 trillion 49
No opinion 13

Looking ahead to the debate on the tax bill in the U.S. Senate and in the U.S. House of

Representatives, would you favor or oppose each of the following provisions that could be put into the tax bill when it becomes law:

Providing a $100 billion tax cut effective immediately this year?

Favor 61%
Oppose 31
No opinion 8

Reducing the amount of payroll taxes for Social Security and Medicare that the average taxpayer has to pay?

Favor 55%
Oppose 40
No opinion 5

Giving larger tax cuts to lower- and middle-income taxpayers, and smaller tax cuts to upper-income taxpayers?

Favor 74%
Oppose 24
No opinion 2

Analysis: President Bush aims to sign a federal tax cut bill into law by Memorial Day. To date, both the Senate and House of Representatives have passed tax cut bills, and the Senate Finance Committee is currently working on a compromise bill they hope will quickly reach the president's desk. Americans generally favor the idea of a tax cut. According to a May 7–9 Gallup Poll, 60% support a substantial tax cut in this year's federal budget while 29% are opposed.

When asked which tax cut they prefer—the $1.6 trillion proposal made by President Bush or a smaller $1.3 trillion proposal similar to the compromise bill the Senate is currently considering—a near majority (49%) favors the smaller tax cut while 38% prefer Bush's proposal. And 61% favor an immediate tax cut of $100 billion for this year while 31% are opposed.

MAY 17
ECONOMIC CONDITIONS

Interview Dates: 5/10–14/01
Gallup Poll News Service
Survey #GO 132072

How would you rate economic conditions in this country today—excellent, good, only fair, or poor?

	Excellent; good	Only fair	Poor*
2001 May 10–14	40%	45%	15%
2001 Apr 6–8	45	41	14
2001 Mar 5–7	46	43	10
2001 Feb 1–4	51	36	13
2001 Jan 10–14	67	27	6

*"No opinion" is omitted.

Right now, do you think that economic conditions in the country as a whole are getting better or getting worse?

	Getting better	Getting worse	Same (vol.); no opinion
2001 May 10–14	25%	63%	12%
2001 Apr 6–8	24	63	13
2001 Mar 5–7	28	61	11
2001 Feb 1–4	23	66	11
2001 Jan 10–14	32	56	12

Do you think the economy is now in a recession, or not?

	Yes	No	No opinion
2001 May 10–14	33%	62%	5%
2001 Apr 6–8	42	52	6
2001 Mar 5–7*	31	64	5
2001 Feb 1–4*	44	49	7

*Asked of half sample

Analysis: Gallup's most recent poll on the economy was conducted May 10–14 and shows that 40% of Americans rate the economy as excellent or good, 45% as fair, and 15% as poor. Last month, the percentage who said excellent or good was five points higher, at 45%, and the percentage saying it is poor was one point lower, at 14%.

Expectations about the direction of the economy remain quite negative. Sixty-three percent say that economic conditions are getting worse while just 25% say better. These numbers are virtually identical to those measured last month, when respondents thought the economy was getting worse rather than better by a 63%-to-24% margin.

The May poll also shows that 62% say the economy is not now in a recession while 33% disagree. This measure has been volatile over the past several months, with about the same number saying the country was not in a recession in March (64%) as are saying it is now. However, last month the percentage decreased to 52%, similar to its February percentage (49%).

MAY 17
MOST IMPORTANT PROBLEM

Interview Dates: 5/10–14/01
Gallup Poll News Service
Survey #GO 132072

*What do you think is the most important problem facing this country today?**

	2001 May 10–14	2001 Mar 5–7
Economic Problems	*31%*	*29%*
Economy in general	10	10
Fuel, oil prices	9	1
Unemployment; jobs	6	4
Taxes	4	7
Gap between rich and poor	1	1
High cost of living; inflation	1	2
Federal budget deficit; federal debt	1	2
Wage issues	**	1
Trade relations, deficit	**	**
Recession	**	3
Other specific economic	2	1
Noneconomic Problems	*68%*	*76%*
Lack of energy sources	12	2
Education	9	16
Ethics; moral, religious, family decline; dishonesty; lack of integrity	8	11
Crime; violence	7	8
Drugs	5	6
Dissatisfaction with government, Congress, politicians, candidates; poor leadership; corruption	5	5
Poverty; hunger; homelessness	4	5
Poor health care, hospitals; high cost of health care	4	7
Children's behavior; way they are raised	4	6
Foreign aid; focus overseas	3	1
Environment; pollution	3	2
Medicare, Social Security issues	3	4
Situation, conflict with China	2	—
Lack of money	2	—
Race relations; racism	2	2
Guns; gun control	1	4
Abortion	1	1
Judicial system; courts; laws	1	1
Unifying the country	1	1
Lack of respect for each other	1	1
Lack of military defense	1	2
Welfare	1	1
Immigration; illegal aliens	1	**
International issues, problems	**	4
Overpopulation	**	1
Child abuse	**	—
Fear of war	**	2
Care for the elderly	**	1
The media	**	1
School shootings; school violence	**	5
Election; election reform	**	*
National security	**	1
Cancer; diseases	—	—
Advancement of computers; technology	—	**
AIDS	—	—
Other noneconomic	6	1
No opinion	6	7

*Totals add to more than 100% due to multiple replies.
**Less than 1%

Analysis: The American public now perceives the energy issue to be one of the most important problems facing the nation, representing a re-markable surge in the perceived importance of energy concerns in just one month. The latest Gallup Poll conducted May 10–14 shows that 21% now mention some aspect of energy in response to Gallup's traditional "what is the most important problem facing the nation" question. More specifically, 12% now spontaneously mention the lack of adequate energy sources as the country's most important problem, and another 9% mention the high cost of fuel, gas, and oil.

MAY 18
PRESIDENT BUSH/MOOD OF AMERICA

Interview Dates: 5/10–14/01
Gallup Poll News Service
Survey #GO 132072

Do you approve or disapprove of the way George W. Bush is handling his job as president?

	Approve	Dis-approve	No opinion
2001 May 10–14	56%	31%	13%
2001 May 7–9	53	33	14
2001 Apr 20–22	62	29	9
2001 Apr 6–8	59	30	11
2001 Mar 26–28	53	29	18
2001 Mar 9–11	58	29	13
2001 Mar 5–7	63	22	15
2001 Feb 19–21	62	21	17
2001 Feb 9–11	57	25	18
2001 Feb 1–4	57	25	18

In general, are you satisfied or dissatisfied with the way things are going in the United States at this time?

	Satisfied	Dis-satisfied	No opinion
2001 May 10–14	46%	50%	4%
2001 Apr 6–8	50	47	3
2001 Mar 5–7	53	44	3
2001 Feb 1–4	51	45	4
2001 Jan 10–14	56	41	3

Analysis: Gallup's satisfaction measure has been trending downward for a number of months. As

George W. Bush took over in January, satisfaction was at 56%, but fell to 50% by April, and in the latest poll—conducted May 10–14—it is down to 46%, while 50% say they are dissatisfied. This 46% rating is the lowest recorded in four years.

President Bush's current 56% job approval rating is a little below the average for his still-young term.

MAY 21
SOCIAL SECURITY AND RETIREMENT

Interview Dates: 4/6–8/01
Gallup Poll News Service
Survey #GO 132071

Asked of those who are employed or whose spouse/partner is employed: Which of the following statements best describes your household's retirement situation—you are saving enough for retirement; you are saving some for retirement, but should be saving a little more; you are saving some for retirement, but should be saving a lot more; you have some savings for retirement, but are not currently adding to it; or you have no savings for retirement?

Saving enough for retirement	21%
Should be saving a little more	33
Should be saving a lot more	21
Some savings, not adding to it	8
No savings for retirement	16
No opinion	1

Also asked of those who are employed or whose spouse/partner is employed: When you retire, how much do you expect to rely on each of the following sources for money—will it be a major source of income, a minor source of income, or not a source at all:

A 401(k), IRA, Keogh, or other retirement savings account?

Major source	58%
Minor source	26

Not a source 15
No opinion 1

A work-sponsored pension plan?

Major source 34%
Minor source 28
Not a source 37
No opinion 1

Social Security?

Major source 28%
Minor source 57
Not a source 14
No opinion 1

Individual stock or stock mutual fund investments?

Major source 24%
Minor source 39
Not a source 36
No opinion 1

Other savings such as a regular savings account or CDs?

Major source 16%
Minor source 51
Not a source 32
No opinion 1

Part-time work?

Major source 10%
Minor source 52
Not a source 36
No opinion 2

Annuities or insurance plans?

Major source 7%
Minor source 34
Not a source 58
No opinion 1

Money from an inheritance?

Major source 7%
Minor source 29
Not a source 63
No opinion 1

Rent and royalties?

Major source 5%
Minor source 22
Not a source 72
No opinion 1

Expected Sources of Retirement Income
(Based on Personal Savings Rates)

	Saving enough; need a little more	Saving some; need a lot more	Not saving
401(k), Retirement Savings Plans	69%	56%	26%
Work Pension	39	35	10
Stocks; Mutual Funds	30	20	14
Social Security	22	32	40
Savings Account; CDs	17	12	22
Inheritance	9	7	1
Annuities; Insurance	6	10	3
Part-time Work	5	14	21
Rent; Royalties	4	5	6

Analysis: The importance of ensuring the long-term solvency of the U.S. Social Security system is clear in a recent Gallup Poll dealing with Americans' personal finances. Roughly one in four nonretired adults (28%) told Gallup in an April 6–8 survey that they are counting on the system to be a major source of income in their retirement.

Gallup asked about a variety of possible retirement income sources in the recent survey. Retirement savings instruments such as 401(k) accounts, IRAs, and Keogh plans emerged as the real workhorses of Americans' long-term financial planning. Close to three in five (58%) tell Gallup that these types of accounts will provide them with a major source of income after they retire. No other savings mechanism comes close to this, but work-sponsored pensions rank second with 34%. Social Security follows in third place, mentioned as a major source by 28%. About a quarter expects stock investments—either individual stocks or stock mutual funds—to be a major source of their retirement funds. Other savings, such as regular savings accounts or certificates of deposit, rank fifth, with 16% describing these as a major potential source. Only 10% expect to rely on part-time work as a major source of income when they retire, and even smaller numbers expect to receive substantial resources from annuities or an insurance plan, an inheritance, or rent or royalties of any kind.

MAY 22
INCOME TAX CUTS

Interview Dates: 5/18–20/01
CNN/*USA Today*/Gallup Poll
Survey #GO 133631

Based on what you have heard or read, do you favor or oppose Congress including a substantial tax cut in this year's federal budget?

	2001 May 18–20	2001 May 7–9
Favor	67%	60%
Oppose	27	30
No opinion	6	10

In the next several days, Congress may pass a plan that would cut taxes more than $1 trillion over the next ten years. If the tax cut is enacted, do you think President Bush will or will not have fulfilled his campaign promise to include a significant tax cut in his budget?

Will have	73%
Will not have	19
No opinion	8

If the tax cut is enacted, do you think this will be a major accomplishment for President Bush, a minor accomplishment, or not an accomplishment at all?

Major accomplishment	49%
Minor accomplishment	33
Not an accomplishment	15
No opinion	3

If the tax cut is enacted, do you think it will mostly help the economy, hurt the economy, or do you think it will not make much difference? And will this help or hurt the economy a lot or a little?

Help the economy a lot	25%
Help the economy a little	24
Not much difference	34
Hurt the economy a little	6
Hurt the economy a lot	9
No opinion	2

If the tax cut is enacted, do you think it will mostly help you and your family, hurt you and your family, or do you think it will not make much difference? And will this help or hurt you and your family a lot or a little?

Help you and your family a lot	17%
Help you and your family a little	20
Not much difference	49
Hurt you and your family a little	5
Hurt you and your family a lot	6
No opinion	3

Analysis: With the Congress apparently on the verge of passing one of the largest tax cuts in history, a new Gallup Poll finds Americans solidly in favor of a substantial tax cut in this year's federal budget. However, most doubt the tax cut will have much positive impact on them personally, and only about one-quarter thinks such a cut will help the economy a lot. Whatever their doubts about the impact of the new legislation, most believe that if the tax cut is enacted, President George W. Bush will have fulfilled his campaign promise on the issue.

The poll conducted May 18–20 shows that by a margin of 67% to 27%, Americans favor rather than oppose a substantial tax cut. And by an even larger margin (73% to 19%), they say that if the tax cut is enacted, Bush will have fulfilled his campaign pledge on this issue. Moreover, more than eight in ten believe that enactment of the tax cut will reflect favorably on Bush: 49% say it would be a major accomplishment, and another 33% say it would be a minor accomplishment. Only 15% say it would not represent an accomplishment at all.

The poll also shows that respondents are divided on whether the new legislation would have much of a positive impact. About half (49%) say the tax cut would help the economy, while the same number say it would either make little difference (34%) or actually hurt the economy (15%). More specifically, 25% say the tax cut, if enacted, would help the economy "a lot" while another 24% say it would help "a little." The public is less optimistic that the tax cut would help them personally. Seventeen percent say it would help "a lot" and another 20% say "a little." Forty-nine percent say the tax cut would make no difference to them at all while 11% expect it to actually hurt them.

MAY 24
THE MOVIES

Interview Dates : 3/16–18/01
Gallup Poll News Service
Survey #GO 133223

Do you think movies, in general, are getting better or getting worse?

Getting better 45%
Getting worse 43
No opinion 12

Now, thinking about some specific aspects of going to the movies in theaters today, please say whether you are generally satisfied or dissatisfied with each one:

The price of the ticket?

Satisfied 42%
Dissatisfied 53
No opinion 5

The price of the food and drink at the concession stand?

Satisfied 5%
Dissatisfied 78
No opinion 7

The variety of food and drink available at the concession stand?

Satisfied 69%
Dissatisfied 21
No opinion 10

The behavior of the audience around you as you watch the movie?

Satisfied 77%
Dissatisfied 16
No opinion 7

The overall entertainment value of the movies you see these days?

Satisfied 69%
Dissatisfied 24
No opinion 7

The quality and cleanliness of seating in the theater?

Satisfied 81%
Dissatisfied 12
No opinion 7

The courtesy of the movie theater employees?

Satisfied 85%
Dissatisfied 8
No opinion 7

We'd like to know how you would feel about certain types of content in movies. If you happened to go to a movie and it included any of the following, would you find that extremely offensive, very offensive, only somewhat offensive, not too offensive, or not offensive at all:

Negative racial stereotypes?

Extremely, very offensive 48%
Only somewhat offensive 23
Not too, not at all offensive 26
No opinion 3

Homosexual sexual activity?

Extremely, very offensive 46%
Only somewhat offensive 22
Not too, not at all offensive 30
No opinion 2

Frequent profanity, meaning swear language?

Extremely, very offensive 40%
Only somewhat offensive 27
Not too, not at all offensive 32
No opinion 1

Graphic violence?

Extremely, very offensive 40%
Only somewhat offensive 26
Not too, not at all offensive 33
No opinion 1

Anti-religious imagery?

Extremely, very offensive 39%
Only somewhat offensive 25
Not too, not at all offensive 33
No opinion 3

Negative gender stereotypes?

Extremely, very offensive 32%
Only somewhat offensive 29
Not too, not at all offensive 32
No opinion 7

Heterosexual sexual activity?

Extremely, very offensive 28%
Only somewhat offensive 24
Not too, not at all offensive 46
No opinion 2

Nudity?

Extremely, very offensive 21%
Only somewhat offensive 24
Not too, not at all offensive 53
No opinion 2

Analysis: The summer months signal the crescendo of the movie-watching season as Hollywood rolls out its blockbuster films in the hope of capturing the attention of America's collective consciousness. As the public braces for the expected onslaught of epics, thrillers, romances, and comedies, a review of a recent Gallup Poll appraises the public's opinion of the movies, their satisfaction with aspects of going to the movies, and how offensive they find various types of movie content.

When asked whether movies are getting better or getting worse, the public is evenly split. Currently, 45% say that movies are getting better while 43% say they are getting worse, and another 12% have no opinion.

Overall, Americans are most dissatisfied with the costs of going to movie theaters: 53% say they are dissatisfied with the price of movie theater tickets, and an even larger 78% are dissatisfied with the price of food and drink concessions at the theater. Aside from price, they are generally satisfied with the other aspects of movie attendance. Eighty-five percent are satisfied with the courtesy of theater employees and 81% with the cleanliness of the theater. Nearly eight in ten (77%) are satisfied with the behavior of those in the audience, 69% with the variety of food and drink available in the theater, and 69% with the overall entertainment value of movies.

The poll also asked respondents to rate how offended they were over eight different types of content that could appear in movies. Less than a majority found each of the eight contents tested to be "extremely" or "very" offensive.

Negative racial stereotypes top the list of material the public finds offensive, with 48% saying such content is extremely or very offensive, 23% saying it is only somewhat offensive, and 26% saying it is either not too offensive or not offensive at all.

The public is equally offended by content that involves homosexual sexual activity. Forty-six percent find this content extremely or very offensive, 22% only somewhat offensive, and 30% are not too offended or not offended at all.

Frequent profanity, graphic violence, and anti-religious imagery in movies are rated as extremely or very offensive by about four in ten. Heterosexual sexual activity and nudity in movies rate as the least offensive forms of risqué content as they are the only two items measured where significantly more found such material not too offensive or not at all offensive than said they thought is was very or extremely offensive. For heterosexual sexual activity, 28% said they think it is very or extremely offensive, and only 21% find nudity in movies to be very or extremely offensive.

MAY 24
MORALITY AND MARRIAGE

Interview Dates: 5/10–14/01
Gallup Poll News Service
Survey #GO 132072

What do you think is the ideal number of children for a family to have?

None to two	52%
Three or more	38
No opinion	10

Do you think it is, or is not, morally wrong for a couple to have a baby if they are not married?

Is	40%
Is not	57
No opinion	3

There is a lot of discussion about the way morals and sexual attitudes are changing in this country. What is your opinion about this—do you think it is wrong for a man and a woman to have sexual relations before marriage, or not?

Yes, wrong	38%
No, not wrong	60
No opinion	2

Do you personally think that it is morally acceptable or morally unacceptable for an unmarried man and woman to live together?

Morally acceptable	52%
Morally unacceptable	41
It depends on situation (vol.)	3
Not a moral issue (vol.)	2
No opinion	2

Regardless of whether or not you think that the following two issues should be legal, for each one, please tell me whether you personally believe that in general it is morally acceptable or morally wrong:

Sex between an unmarried man and woman?

Morally acceptable	53%
Morally unacceptable	42
It depends on situation (vol.)	3
Not a moral issue (vol.)	1
No opinion	1

Divorce?

Morally acceptable	59%
Morally unacceptable	28
It depends on situation (vol.)	12
Not a moral issue (vol.)	*
No opinion	1

*Less than 1%

Analysis: Today, according to a May 10–14 Gallup Poll, only 38% of U.S. adults say it is wrong for a man and a woman to have sexual relations before marriage, while 60% disagree. A slightly different question on the same subject yielded a similar result. When Gallup asked in the same survey whether sex between an unmarried man and woman is morally acceptable or morally wrong, the majority (53%) said it is acceptable while 42% said it is wrong.

Respondents even go a step further, with a majority (52%) sanctioning "living together" as a morally acceptable lifestyle. Less than half (41%) say it is morally unacceptable for an unmarried couple to live together; 3% think it depends on the situation, and 2% say it is not a moral issue.

In addition to liberalized sexual mores taking away some of the urgency to marry, there has been an important long-term change in family size expectations that may partially account for people marrying later in life. According to the poll, the majority (52%) say that less than three children is ideal, while 38% prefer larger families of three or more children.

For better or worse, when married couples run into hard times today there appears to be relatively little social pressure to force them to stay together. Nearly three in five (59%) think divorce is morally acceptable, and another 12% say it depends on the situation. Only 28% feel divorce is morally unacceptable.

MAY 25
SENATOR JEFFORDS

Interview Date: 5/24/01
CNN/*USA Today*/Gallup Poll
Survey #GO 133748

Jim Jeffords, a U.S. Senator from Vermont, announced today that he is leaving the Republican Party and becoming an independent. How closely have you been following the news about Jeffords's decision—very closely, somewhat closely, not too closely, or not at all closely?

Very closely 16%
Somewhat closely .34
Not too closely 18
Not at all closely .31
No opinion 1

As you may know, Jeffords's decision to become an independent will now give Democrats control of the Senate. Overall, do you think Jeffords's decision will be good or bad for the country?

Good 43%
Bad 35
No opinion 22

How much of a difference do you think Jeffords's decision will make to the country— a major difference, a minor difference, or no difference at all?

Major difference 36%
Minor difference 42
No difference 15
No opinion 7

As you may know, Senator Jeffords just won reelection for six years after running as a Republican. Now that he has decided to become an independent, what comes closer to your point of view—Jeffords should resign immediately and run for reelection as an independent, or Jeffords should remain in office and fulfill his six-year term with whatever party he chooses?

Resign 35%
Remain in office 58
No opinion 7

As a result of this, what do you think will happen between the Republicans and Democrats in Washington—do you think there will be more cooperation, more gridlock, or will there be no change?

Cooperation 15%
Gridlock 50
No change 30
No opinion 5

Senator Jeffords said one reason that he left the Republican Party is that the party has become too conservative under President Bush. Do you agree or disagree?

Agree 50%
Disagree 42
No opinion 8

Do you think it is better for the country to have a president who comes from the same political party that controls Congress, or do you think it is better to have a president from one political party and Congress controlled by another?

Same party 36%
Different party 42
No difference (vol.); no opinion 22

Analysis: The immediate reaction of the American public to Thursday's defection of Vermont Senator James Jeffords from the Republican Party is muted. A snapshot Gallup Poll conducted Thursday night shows that just about half the country is following the story closely at this point. A slight plurality feel the move will be good for the country rather than bad, but only a little more than one-third says it will make a major difference either way. There is some suggestion in the poll that Americans fear more gridlock will result from Jeffords's move, and mixed feelings about the overall philosophic implications of having one-party control of government.

Asked directly whether the decision will be good or bad for the country, 43% of those interviewed on Thursday night's May 10 poll say "good," 35% say "bad," and 22% have not yet formed an opinion. What will the impact of the Jeffords defection be on the country? There is no groundswell of feeling among Americans that this is a momentous turning point. Only about one-third (36%) says the resulting change in party control of the Senate will make a major difference while 42% say it will make a minor difference. One out of five either says it will make no difference or do not yet have an opinion.

Senator Jeffords was reelected last fall to the Senate as a Republican, and thus has more than five years to serve in his current term. Asked about the suggestion that—given the switch in party—Jeffords should resign immediately and run for reelection as an independent, respondents say "no need." Just 35% endorse that course, while 58% say it is fine for Jeffords to serve out his term "with whatever party he chooses."

One-night polls like this one provide an excellent portrait of the immediate reaction of the public to breaking news. Quite often, the overall impact of the decision on Americans' view of their government and the current political situation in

Washington will change in the days and weeks to come as they are exposed to news media interpretations and the usual political "spin" on the events.

MAY 25
ARMED FORCES VETERANS

Interview Dates: 5/18–20/01
CNN/*USA Today*/Gallup Poll
Survey #GO 133631

Are you personally a veteran of the Armed Forces?

Yes 16%
No 84

Asked of veterans: Would you say you have or have not received the respect and thanks you deserve for serving in the Armed Forces?

Yes 73%
No 24
No opinion 3

Just off the top of your head, which of the four major branches of the Armed Forces in this country would you say is the most prestigious and has the most status in our society today—the Air Force, the Army, the Navy, or the Marines?

Air Force 32%
Army 11
Navy 14
Marines 36
All the same (vol.) .4
No opinion 3

Just off the top of your head, which of the four major branches of the Armed Forces in this country would you say is the most important to our national defense today—the Air Force, the Army, the Navy, or the Marines?

Air Force 42%
Army 18
Navy 15

Marines 14
All the same (vol.) .9
No opinion 2

Analysis: As the United States pauses this Memorial Day to honor its war dead, a new Gallup Poll finds that most veterans of the Armed Forces feel they have been adequately thanked and appreciated for their service to their country. The poll also reveals an interesting variation in the reputation of the Armed Services. The Marines are the branch with the most status and prestige, while the Air Force is considered to be the most important to the nation's defense.

MAY 29
ENERGY SITUATION

Interview Dates: 5/18–20/01
CNN/*USA Today*/Gallup Poll
Survey #GO 133631

Thinking about the cost and availability of electricity, gasoline, natural gas, and other forms of energy, would you say the country is in a state of crisis, has major problems, has minor problems, or has no problems at all?

State of crisis 12%
Major problems 59
Minor problems 25
No problems 3
No opinion 1

Would you say in the United States, that each of the following is in a state of crisis, is a major problem, is a minor problem, or is not a problem at all:

Price of gasoline?

State of crisis 19%
Major problem 60
Minor problem 17
Not a problem 3
No opinion 1

Shortages of electricity?

State of crisis 17%
Major problem 52
Minor problem 19
Not a problem 10
No opinion 2

Price of natural gas or home heating oil?

State of crisis 14%
Major problem 58
Minor problem 17
Not a problem 6
No opinion 5

Price of electricity?

State of crisis 11%
Major problem 50
Minor problem 28
Not a problem 9
No opinion 2

Please tell me whether you think each of the following deserves a great deal of blame, some blame, not much blame, or no blame at all for the country's current energy problems:

The current Bush administration?

Great deal 20%
Some blame 34
Not much 18
No blame at all 26
No opinion 2

The Clinton administration?

Great deal 28%
Some blame 40
Not much 14
No blame at all 15
No opinion 3

Congress?

Great deal 31%
Some blame 51

Not much 9
No blame at all 6
No opinion 3

U.S. oil companies?

Great deal 52%
Some blame 35
Not much 6
No blame at all 5
No opinion 2

U.S. electric companies?

Great deal 42%
Some blame 43
Not much 8
No blame at all 5
No opinion 2

Environmental laws and regulations?

Great deal 23%
Some blame 47
Not much 14
No blame at all 12
No opinion 4

Foreign countries that produce oil?

Great deal 44%
Some blame 37
Not much 9
No blame at all 8
No opinion 2

American consumers?

Great deal 22%
Some blame 47
Not much 13
No blame at all 17
No opinion 1

Which comes closer to your view—Americans can retain their lifestyle and the country's current energy problems can still be solved, or Americans must make real changes in their lifestyle in order for the country's current energy problems to be solved?

Can retain lifestyle .30%
Must make changes .67
No opinion 3

Analysis: A recent Gallup Poll shows that, while relatively few Americans view the current energy situation as a "crisis," seven in ten believe the availability and high cost of energy are at least a major problem for the country. Americans are most likely to blame oil and electric companies for the current energy problems, rather than politicians or consumers. Still, two-thirds believe that Americans must make real changes to their lifestyle to help resolve the energy problems.

The poll conducted May 18–20 shows that 12% think the availability and high prices of electricity, gasoline, natural gas, and other energy sources constitute a crisis. Additionally, 59% think limited availability and higher energy prices represent a major problem, 25% a minor problem, and only 3% no problem at all.

The poll asked respondents how much blame each of several groups deserves for the country's current energy problems. Generally, businesses receive the greatest amount of blame from the public. Nearly nine in ten believe that U.S. oil companies deserve at least some blame for the energy problems, which includes a majority who think they deserve a great deal of blame. Eighty-five percent perceives U.S. electric companies as worthy of blame, including 42% who think they deserve a great deal of blame. Americans also assign responsibility to foreign countries that produce oil, with 81% believing they deserve at least some blame.

Respondents place less blame on their own government. Even though more than eight in ten think Congress deserves at least some blame for the current energy situation, only 31% believe it deserves a great deal of blame. About seven in ten blame the Clinton administration, but only about one-half thinks the current Bush administration deserves blame. In fact, the Bush administration is seen as least responsible among the eight entities tested.

MAY 31
McVEIGH STAY OF EXECUTION

Interview Dates: 5/18–20/01
CNN/*USA Today*/Gallup Poll
Survey #GO 133631

Which comes closest to your view—I generally support the death penalty and believe Timothy McVeigh should be executed, I generally oppose the death penalty but believe McVeigh should be executed in this case, or I generally oppose the death penalty and do not believe McVeigh should be executed?

	2001 May 18–20	2001 Apr 20–22
Support death penalty, McVeigh should be executed	57%	59%
Oppose death penalty, McVeigh should be executed	23	22
Oppose death penalty, McVeigh should not be executed	16	16
Other (vol.)	2	1
No opinion	2	2

As you may know, the FBI recently discovered documents that were related to the McVeigh court case but that were not previously made available to his defense lawyers. Which comes closer to your view—the FBI knowingly withheld evidence in the McVeigh case, or the FBI made an honest mistake?

Knowingly withheld evidence 42%
Made honest mistake 52
No opinion 6

Which comes closer to your view—the federal government should delay the McVeigh execution as long as necessary to properly review these files, or the federal government should not delay the McVeigh execution beyond the June 11 date it already set?

Should delay 52%
Should not delay .47
No opinion 1

Still thinking about the recently discovered documents, which comes closest to your view—you were convinced McVeigh was guilty before and you still are, you were convinced McVeigh was guilty before but now you have doubts, or you have never been convinced McVeigh was guilty?

Convinced McVeigh was guilty
before and still are 86%
Convinced McVeigh was guilty before
but now have doubts 8
Never been convinced McVeigh
was guilty 2
Other (vol.) 1
No opinion 3

Analysis: If convicted Oklahoma City bomber Timothy McVeigh decides to ask for a stay of his pending execution currently scheduled for June 11, it may be the first time since he was sentenced to death that public opinion will be on his side, at least in one narrow respect.

A recent Gallup Poll finds that a slim majority of Americans (52%) believe McVeigh's execution should be delayed as long as necessary to properly review newly discovered FBI files concerning his case, while 47% believe the federal government should not postpone it any further. McVeigh's original execution date was May 16, but Attorney General John Ashcroft moved it to June 11 once it was discovered that the FBI had failed to turn over all evidentiary documents to McVeigh's lawyers prior to his trial.

The FBI blunder, although extremely embarrassing for the agency, has not changed the public's view that McVeigh deserves the death penalty for his role in the bombing, which left 168 dead at the Alfred P. Murrah Federal Building in Oklahoma City on April 19, 1995. According to the May 18–20 Gallup Poll, 80% of Americans believe that McVeigh should be executed, nearly identical to the 81% who felt this way a month earlier (and several weeks before the problem with the missing FBI files was revealed). Only 16% oppose the execution.

News of the FBI files also has not changed the public's view that McVeigh is guilty. Eighty-six percent "were convinced McVeigh was guilty before and still are." Only 8% say they were previously convinced of his guilt but now have doubts because of the FBI file issue. A miniscule 2% say they have never been convinced that McVeigh was guilty.

The public's support for delaying McVeigh's execution may stem in part from a basic respect for due process of the law, but it also could be a result of concerns that what is contained in the previously withheld documents could be relevant to the McVeigh defense. The FBI maintains that their failure to turn certain files over to McVeigh's attorneys was unintentional, but the public seems a bit skeptical. While a slim majority (52%) believe that the omission of files was "an honest mistake," a sizeable number (42%) believe that the FBI "knowingly withheld evidence in the McVeigh case."

JUNE 4
HOMOSEXUALS AND HOMOSEXUALITY

Interview Dates: 5/10–14/01
Gallup Poll News Service
Survey #GO 132072

Do you think homosexual relations between consenting adults should or should not be legal?

Legal 54%
Not legal 42
No opinion 4

As you may know, there has been considerable discussion in the news regarding the rights of homosexual men and women. In general, do you think homosexuals should or should not have equal rights in terms of job opportunities?

Should 85%
Should not 11
It depends (vol.); no opinion 4

Do you think homosexuals should or should not be hired for each of the following occupations:

Salespersons?

Should 91%
Should not 6
It depends (vol.); no opinion 3

Members of the Armed Forces?

Should 72%
Should not 23
It depends (vol.); no opinion 5

Doctors?

Should 78%
Should not 18
It depends (vol.); no opinion 4

Clergy?

Should 54%
Should not 39
It depends (vol.); no opinion 7

Elementary schoolteachers?

Should 56%
Should not 40
It depends (vol.); no opinion 4

High school teachers?

Should 63%
Should not 33
It depends (vol.); no opinion 4

Members of the president's Cabinet?

Should 75%
Should not 21
It depends (vol.); no opinion 4

Do you feel that homosexuality should be considered an acceptable alternative lifestyle or not?

Acceptable 52%
Not acceptable 43
No opinion 5

In your view, is homosexuality something a person is born with or is homosexuality due to other factors such as upbringing or environment?

Born with 40%
Upbringing or environment 39
Both; neither (vol.); no opinion 21

Would you favor or oppose a law that would allow homosexual couples to legally form civil unions, giving them some of the legal rights of married couples?

	2001 May 10–14	2000 Oct 25–28*
Favor	.44%	42%
Oppose	.52	54
No opinion	.4	4

*Question wording: *Would you vote for or against a law . . .*

Analysis: A Gallup Poll conducted May 10–14 reveals a continuation of a gradual, but to some degree steady, increase in the liberalization of public opinion about homosexuality. Americans still exhibit ambivalence about the overall acceptability of homosexuality in society today, and substantial numbers say that homosexual relations should be neither acceptable nor legal. But there have been changes in these attitudes over time.

Gallup has recorded a gradual increase in adherence to the belief that homosexuality is an acceptable alternative lifestyle. Agreement with this proposition has risen from 38% in 1992 to 52% today. There also has been a shift in attitudes about the legality of homosexuality, with a majority (54%) now saying that "homosexual relations between consenting adults" should be legal, compared to 43% who felt this way in 1977.

One of the more significant changes in public opinion on gay and lesbian issues has been the increase in the perception that homosexuality is genetic—something a person is born with—as opposed to other factors such as upbringing and environment. For the first time in twenty-four years, as many people in Gallup's most recent poll say homosexuality is genetic as say it is environmental. This represents a major shift from 1977 when environment was seen as the more prevalent factor by more than a four-to-one ratio.

In terms of specific issues, a majority remains opposed to the extension of marriage benefits to gay and lesbian partners joined in civil unions. And about four in ten think that gays and lesbians should not be allowed to work as members of the clergy or as elementary school teachers. However, only a minority are uncomfortable with gays and lesbians having a number of other professions and jobs.

There has been greater change in attitudes about employment rights for homosexuals. The Gallup question asks, "As you may know, there has been considerable discussion in the news regarding the rights of homosexual men and women. In general, do you think homosexuals should or should not have equal rights in terms of job opportunities?" The percentage saying yes has risen from 56% in 1977 to a significantly higher 85% today. The question about equal opportunity, on the other hand, may invoke the public's attitudes about discrimination, fair play, and equal treatment.

The widespread acceptance of equal opportunity for homosexuals in the general sense is contradicted somewhat when respondents are asked whether or not homosexuals should be hired for a number of specific positions. Although a substantial majority has no problem with gays and lesbians being hired as salespeople, doctors, presidential Cabinet members, or serving in the Armed Forces, the number accepting homosexuals as clergy or elementary school teachers is just above the 50% level. It should be noted that this question does not ask about the legality of refusing to hire individuals for these professions because of their sexual orientation. Instead, the question asks more generally whether or not they "should" be hired, thereby tapping into the basic, underlying attitude.

JUNE 4
BLACK AND HISPANIC POPULATIONS

Interview Dates: 3/26–28/01
Gallup Poll News Service
Survey #GO 133224

Just your best guess, what percentage of the U.S. population today would you say is black?

Less than 10% 3%
Between 10% and 14% 7
Between 15% and 19% 8
Between 20% and 29% 19
Between 30% and 39% 23
Between 40% and 49% 16
50% or more 17
No opinion 7

Just your best guess, what percentage of the U.S. population today would you say is Hispanic?

Less than 5% 2%
Between 5% and 9% 3
Between 10% and 19% 22
Between 20% and 29% 25
Between 30% and 49% 26
50% or more 14
No opinion 8

Analysis: The latest U.S. Census findings on the increasing diversity of America have received considerable attention this year. Americans seem to realize that the U.S. is a diverse nation, but recent polling suggests the public thinks the nation is more diverse than it actually is. Respondents generally overestimate, to a significant degree, the percentage of the U.S. population that is either black or Hispanic. According to the U.S. Census Bureau, 12.3% of the U.S. population is black and 12.5% is Hispanic. Gallup Poll results from March 26–28, however, show that slightly less than one in ten can accurately identify that the population of either blacks or Hispanics in this country falls between 10% and 14%. The typical American estimates the percentages of blacks and Hispanics in this country to be more than twice as high as they actually are.

On average, respondents say that 33% of the U.S. population is black. In fact, a majority (56%) estimates that the percentage of blacks in this country stands at 30% or higher. As many as

17% say the percentage of blacks is 50% or greater. Only 7% accurately state that the percentage of blacks falls between 10% and 14% of the entire population.

Impressions about the percentage of Hispanics in this country are somewhat more accurate than those about the percentage of blacks. Americans, on average, say that 29% of the U.S. population is Hispanic, slightly more than twice the actual percentage. About two in five say Hispanics constitute 30% or more of the population. Just 10% accurately estimate that between 10% and 14% of the population is Hispanic.

JUNE 7
VICE PRESIDENT CHENEY

Interview Dates: 5/18–20/01
CNN/*USA Today*/Gallup Poll
Survey #GO 133631

Do you approve or disapprove of the way Dick Cheney is handling his job as vice president?

Approve 60%
Disapprove 26
No opinion 14

Based on what you know about Dick Cheney, do you think he is qualified to serve as president if it becomes necessary, or not?

Yes 62%
No 28
No opinion 10

If you had to choose, who do you think is more qualified to be president—George W. Bush or Dick Cheney?*

Bush 46%
Cheney 34
Both (vol.) 3
Neither (vol.) 11
No opinion 6

*Based on part sample

Do you think Dick Cheney has too much, too little, or about the right amount of power in the Bush administration?

Too much 13%
Too little 16
About the right amount 61
No opinion 10

Analysis: Dick Cheney's role as the crucial tie-breaking vote in the U.S. Senate is now gone, with Senator James Jeffords's defection from the Republican Party, giving the Democrats a 50–49 advantage. Nevertheless, Americans have a positive view of Cheney according to a recent Gallup Poll. Sixty percent approve of the job Cheney is doing as vice president while just 26% disapprove, according to the survey conducted May 18–20. The numbers are better than George W. Bush's presidential job approval measured in the same poll, in which 56% approved and 36% disapproved of the president.

Some critics have argued that Cheney has too much influence in the Bush administration, viewing Bush as more of a hands-off leader and with Cheney making the key decisions. This criticism resurfaced recently, as Cheney had a prominent role in designing and promoting the administration's energy plan. However, the public does not agree with the critics, as only 13% think Cheney has too much power. The majority (61%) thinks he has the right amount of power, and about one in six thinks he has too little power. And 62% think Cheney is qualified to be president if it becomes necessary.

JUNE 7
HUMAN CLONING

Interview Dates: 5/10–14/01
Gallup Poll News Service
Survey #GO 132072

Do you think the cloning of animals should or should not be allowed?

Should 32%
Should not 64
No opinion 4

If it becomes possible, do you think the cloning of humans should or should not be allowed?

Should 9%
Should not 89
No opinion 2

Analysis: As the House Judiciary Committee prepares for oversight hearings today on the issue of human cloning, a recent Gallup Poll shows that roughly nine in ten Americans (89%) say that the cloning of humans—if it becomes possible—should not be allowed. While polling about human cloning shows widespread public opposition to the issue, respondents seem somewhat less opposed to the cloning of animals. The May 10–14 Gallup Poll indicates that nearly two-thirds (64%) say the cloning of animals should not be allowed.

JUNE 8
PSYCHIC AND PARANORMAL PHENOMENA

Interview Dates: 5/10–14/01
Gallup Poll News Service
Survey #GO 132072

For each of the following items I am going to read you, please tell me whether it is something you believe in, something you're not sure about, or something you don't believe in:

Psychic or spiritual healing, or the power of the human mind to heal the body?

Believe 54%
Not sure 19
Don't believe 26
No opinion 1

ESP or extrasensory perception?

Believe 50%
Not sure 20
Don't believe 27
No opinion 3

That houses can be haunted?

Believe 42%
Not sure 16
Don't believe 41
No opinion 1

That people on Earth are sometimes possessed by the devil?

Believe 41%
Not sure 16
Don't believe 41
No opinion 2

That ghosts, or spirits of dead people, can come back in certain places and situations?

Believe 38%
Not sure 17
Don't believe 44
No opinion 1

Telepathy, or communication between minds without using the traditional five senses?

Believe 36%
Not sure 26
Don't believe 35
No opinion 3

That extraterrestrial beings have visited Earth at some time in the past?

Believe 33%
Not sure 27
Don't believe 38
No opinion 2

Clairvoyance, or the power of the mind to know the past and predict the future?

Believe 32%
Not sure 23
Don't believe 45
No opinion . . . .*

*Less than 1%

That people can hear from or communicate mentally with someone who has died?

Believe 28%
Not sure 26
Don't believe 46
No opinion . . . .*

*Less than 1%

Astrology, or the position of the stars and planets can affect people's lives?

Believe 28%
Not sure 18
Don't believe 52
No opinion 2

Witches?

Believe 26%
Not sure 15
Don't believe 59
No opinion . . . .*

*Less than 1%

Reincarnation, that is, the rebirth of the soul in a new body after death?

Believe 25%
Not sure 20
Don't believe 54
No opinion 1

Channeling, or allowing a "spirit-being" to temporarily assume control of a human body during a trance?

Believe 15%
Not sure 21
Don't believe 62
No opinion 2

Analysis: What exactly do Americans believe in when it comes to the paranormal, the occult, and "out-of-this-world" experiences? The Gallup Poll recently updated its audit of the public's beliefs in a variety of these types of phenomena. The results suggest a significant increase in belief in a number of these experiences over the past decade, including in particular such Halloween-related issues as haunted houses, ghosts, and witches.

Only one of the experiences tested has seen a drop in belief since 1990: devil possession. Overall, one-half or more believes in two of the issues: psychic or spiritual healing, and extrasensory perception (ESP); and one-third or more believes in such things as haunted houses, possession by the devil, ghosts, telepathy, extraterrestrial beings having visited Earth, and clairvoyance.

The list of thirteen experiences tested in the poll is eclectic, ranging from Halloween- and occult-oriented phenomena such as ghosts and witches, to mental experiences such as ESP, clairvoyance, and psychic or spiritual healing. Overall beliefs in the experiences tested range from a slight majority who believes in the power of the human mind to heal the body, to a low of 15% who believe in the New Age concept of channeling or allowing a "spirit-being" to assume control of a body during a trance.

JUNE 12
McVEIGH EXECUTION

Interview Dates: 6/8–10/01
CNN/*USA Today*/Gallup Poll
Survey #GO 133811

Thinking about Timothy McVeigh, the man convicted of murder in the Oklahoma City bombing case and sentenced to death, which comes closest to your view—you generally support the death penalty and believe McVeigh should be executed, you generally oppose the death penalty but believe McVeigh should be executed in this case, or you generally oppose the death penalty and do not believe McVeigh should not be executed?

	2001 June 8–10	2001 May 18–20	2001 April 20–22
Support death penalty, McVeigh should be executed	59%	57%	59%
Oppose death penalty, McVeigh should be executed	19	23	22
Oppose death penalty, do not believe McVeigh should not be executed	17	16	16
Other (vol.)	3	2	1
No opinion	2	2	2

Which comes closer to your view—McVeigh has not revealed the names of everyone who helped him in the Oklahoma City bombing, or everyone involved in the Oklahoma City bombing has been caught or apprehended?

McVeigh has not revealed names 65%
Everyone involved has been caught 23
No opinion 12

As you may know, the FBI recently discovered documents that were related to the Oklahoma City bombing court case that were not previously made available to defense lawyers. Do you think the federal government should or should not hold a new trial for Terry Nichols, the man convicted of helping Timothy McVeigh make the bomb?

Should 33%
Should not 59
No opinion 8

Analysis: Prior to his execution on June 11 for the 1995 bombing of the federal building in Oklahoma City that resulted in the deaths of 168 people, Timothy McVeigh denied that he needed the help of any "unknown" collaborators to commit his deed. But according to the latest Gallup Poll conducted June 8–10, most Americans (65%) believe that there were other collaborators whose names were never revealed by McVeigh. Just 23% agree with the position of the FBI that everyone involved in the bombing has been apprehended.

The poll also shows that over the past three months, there has been little change in the public's support for the execution of McVeigh. The weekend poll shows that about eight in ten (78%) supported the death penalty for McVeigh, similar to the percentages recorded by Gallup Polls in April (80%) and May (81%). Among the supporters, 59% said they generally favor the death penalty, while 19% said they usually oppose it, but felt that McVeigh should be an exception.

Since mid-May the courts have ruled that there was no evidence in the files the FBI failed to previously turn over to McVeigh's defense lawyers that would justify a new trial for him, and the public apparently feels the same judgment applies to Terry Nichols, the man convicted of helping McVeigh make the bomb. Just 33% say the federal government should not hold a new trial for Nichols, while 59% say it should.

JUNE 13
PRESIDENT BUSH

Interview Dates: 6/8–10/01
CNN/*USA Today*/Gallup Poll
Survey #GO 133811

We'd like to get your overall opinion of one of the people in the news. Please say if you have a favorable or unfavorable opinion of George W. Bush, or if you have never heard of him?

	Favorable	Unfavorable	No opinion; never heard of
2001 Jun 8–10	62%	36%	2%
2001 Apr 20–22	65	32	3
2001 Mar 9–11	63	32	5
2001 Mar 5–7	69	28	3
2001 Feb 19–21	67	27	6
2001 Feb 1–4	64	33	3
2001 Jan 15–16	62	36	2

Please tell me whether you agree or disagree that George W. Bush has the personality and leadership qualities a president should have?

	Agree	Disagree	No opinion
National Adults			
2001 Jun 8–10	54%	42%	4%

2000 Aug 18–19	64	32	4
2000 Aug 11–12	65	28	7
2000 Aug 4–5	70	26	4
2000 Jul 25–26	62	32	6
2000 Apr 7–9	61	30	9
2000 Jan 17–19	65	28	7
Registered Voters			
2001 Jun 8–10	54	42	4
2000 Oct 20–22	57	39	4
2000 Sep 28–30	56	38	6
2000 Sep 8–10	57	37	6
2000 Sep 7–9	58	35	7
2000 Aug 18–19	64	32	4
2000 Aug 11–12	66	27	7
2000 Aug 4–5	71	25	4
2000 Jul 25–26	62	32	6
2000 Apr 7–9	62	30	8
2000 Jan 17–19	65	29	6

Do you think George W. Bush does a good job representing America to the world, or not?

Yes	56%
No	39
No opinion	5

Do you think leaders of other countries around the world have respect for George W. Bush, or do you think they don't have much respect for him?

Respect him	40%
Don't have much respect for him	46
No opinion	14

What do you think will be best for the United States in the long run—to strengthen our ties with Western Europe, to continue our relations with Western Europe about as they are now, or to reduce our ties with Western Europe?

Strengthen ties	47%
Continue as now	31
Reduce our ties	13
No opinion	9

Analysis: Much of the buzz surrounding President Bush's five-nation European tour this week concerns his reportedly poor image over-seas. A Gallup survey conducted in the United Kingdom in April found only 26% of the British hold a favorable view of Bush while 51% view him unfavorably. This contrasts sharply with Americans' view of their own president: 62% view him favorably.

These contrasts seem symptomatic of Bush's larger image problem throughout Europe, but according to a new Gallup Poll conducted June 8–10, a majority of Americans (56%) thinks Bush does a good job of representing the United States to the world. Only 39% disagree and just 5% are unsure. But despite the fact that a major-ity thinks Bush does a good job representing the country abroad, they are skeptical about how for-eign leaders perceive him. Just 40% believe lead-ers of other countries around the world respect George W. Bush while 46% think they "don't have much respect for him." And 54% think Bush has the leadership qualities it takes to be president while 42% disagree.

JUNE 13
THE BUSH DAUGHTERS

Interview Dates: 6/8–10/01
CNN/*USA Today*/Gallup Poll
Survey #GO 133811

As you may know, President Bush's 19-year-old daughters were issued citations by po-lice in connection with attempts to buy alcohol with false identification. Do you think the news media should or should not have reported this matter?*

Should 45%
Should not 54
No opinion 1

*Based on part sample

Overall, do you feel the news media have acted responsibly or irresponsibly in this situation?*

Responsibly 42%

Irresponsibly 54
No opinion 4

*Based on part sample

Do you think the Bush daughters' behavior has been worse than most college students their age, about the same as most college students their age, or not as bad as most col-lege students their age?

Worse than most 4%
About the same 79
Not as bad as most 15
No opinion 2

Analysis: Almost two weeks since the press first reported that President Bush's twin 19-year-old daughters—Jenna and Barbara—were cited by police in connection with attempts to buy alcohol with false identification, a new Gallup Poll shows that Americans overwhelmingly believe what President Bush's daughters did was no worse than the behavior of most other college students. A slight majority also feels that the news media acted irresponsibly in reporting this story.

The June 8–10 poll asked respondents how the behavior of Bush's daughters compares to other college students their age. An overwhelm-ing 79% feel Bush's daughters are acting about the same as their peers. Fifteen percent say Bush's daughters are not behaving as badly as most college students their age, and only 4% say their behavior is worse.

The latest also poll asked the American pub-lic two questions about the handling of the Bush daughters' story by the news media. One-half of respondents were asked whether or not the news media should have reported this matter; the other half were asked if the media acted responsibly or irresponsibly in its handling of the situation. Results are similar, with 54% saying the media should not have reported this matter and the same percent responding that the media acted irrespon-sibly in this situation. Forty-five percent feel the media should have reported these incidents, and 42% say the media acted responsibly.

CONGRESSIONAL JOB APPROVAL

Interview Dates: 6/8–10/01
CNN/*USA Today*/Gallup Poll
Survey #GO 133811

Do you approve or disapprove of the way the following are handling their job:

The Republicans in Congress?

	Approve	Dis-approve	No opinion
2001 Jun 8–10	.49%	43%	8%
2000 Aug 18–19	.45	44	11
2000 Jul 25–26	.46	39	15
2000 Apr 28–30	.42	46	12

The Democrats in Congress?

	Approve	Dis-approve	No opinion
2001 Jun 8–10	.54%	37%	9%
2000 Aug 18–19	.56	34	10
2000 Jul 25–26	.51	36	13
2000 Apr 28–30	.46	42	12

Whom do you want to have more influence over the direction the nation takes in the next year—George W. Bush or the Democrats in Congress?*

Bush	.48%
Democrats in Congress	.41
Both; neither (vol.)	.6
No opinion	.5

*Based on part sample

Whom do you want to have more influence over the direction the nation takes in the next year—the Republicans in Congress or the Democrats in Congress?*

Republicans in Congress	.39%
Democrats in Congress	.47
Both; neither (vol.)	.8
No opinion	.6

*Based on part sample

Next, how important is it to you that the president and Congress deal with each of the following issues in the next year—is it extremely important, very important, moderately important, or not that important?

	Ex-tremely, very important
Education	.93%
Prescription drugs for older Americans	.85
Increased energy conservation	.79
Patients' bill of rights	.77
Increased oil and gas production	.70
Price caps on electricity	.65
Raising the minimum wage	.63
Missile defense	.54
Campaign finance reform	.40

As you may know, Jim Jeffords, a U.S. senator from Vermont, left the Republican Party and became an independent. Jeffords's decision to become an independent has now given the control of the Senate to the Democrats. Do you approve or disapprove of Jeffords's decision to become an independent?

Approve	.58%
Disapprove	.34
No opinion	.8

Now that the Democrats control the Senate and the Republicans control the House of Representatives, do you think Congress will be more likely or less likely to deal with the major issues facing the nation today?

More likely	.47%
Less likely	.43
No difference (vol.)	.5
No opinion	.5

If the elections for Congress were being held today, which party's candidate would you vote for in your congressional district—the Democratic Party's candidate, or the Republican Party's candidate? [As of today, do you lean more toward the Democratic Party's candidate, or the Republican Party's candidate?]

	National adults	Registered voters
Democratic	.50%	49%
Republican	.43	45
Undecided; other	.7	6

Analysis: The year 2001 has been an eventful one in Congress, with speedy passage of a large tax cut and major proposals on education and energy currently making their way through the legislative process. A closely divided Senate has already witnessed two changes in partisan control, from a brief initial period of Democratic control in January (while Vice President Al Gore still had the tie-breaking vote) to Republican control following the inauguration of Vice President Dick Cheney, and now from Republicans to Democrats after Senator Jim Jeffords decided to leave the Republican Party and become an independent. The latest Gallup Poll conducted June 8–10 finds 54% of Americans approve and 37% disapprove of the job the Democrats in Congress are doing, slightly better than the 49%-to-43% rating given the Republicans. Democrats also fare slightly better in an early reading on the 2002 midterm elections, which shows that 49% of registered voters say they would vote for the Democratic candidate in their Congressional district, while 45% say they would vote for the Republican.

Although 58% approve of Jeffords's decision to leave the Republican Party and become an independent, the public is almost evenly divided as to whether Congress—with the Senate now controlled by the Democrats and the House by the Republicans—will be more likely (47%) or less likely (43%) to deal with the major issues facing the nation today.

Similarly, the public shows mixed views on who should have more influence over the direction the nation takes in the next year. When asked to choose between President Bush and the Democrats in Congress, Bush gets the nod by 48% to 41%. However, when the choice is between the Democrats and Republicans in Congress, the Democrats are favored by 47% to 39%. Typically, the public has generally favored the president over the opposition party in Congress when confronted with this choice, perhaps deferring to the president's informal role as the "chief legislator" of the nation.

JUNE 14
TIGER WOODS

Interview Dates: 6/8–10/01
CNN/*USA Today*/Gallup Poll
Survey #GO 133811

We'd like to get your overall opinion of one of the people in the news. Please say if you have a favorable or unfavorable opinion of Tiger Woods, or if you have never heard of him?

	2001 Jun 8–10	2000 Jun 22–25
Favorable	.84%	88%
Unfavorable	.9	5
No opinion; never heard of	.7	5

In your opinion, who is the greatest athlete active in the world of sports today?

Tiger Woods	.38%
Michael Jordan	.6
Allen Iverson	.4
Shaquille O'Neal	.3
Kobe Bryant	.1
Lance Armstrong	.1
Jeff Gordon	.1
Ray Bourque	.1
Mark McGwire	.1
Derek Jeter	.1
Venus Williams	.1
Andre Agassi	.1
Cal Ripken	.*
Sammy Sosa	.*
Other (vol.)	.14

None 1
Don't know (vol.) .25
No opinion 1

*Less than 1%

Who do you think is the better golfer—Tiger Woods today, or Jack Nicklaus in his prime?

Woods 69%
Nicklaus 19
Same (vol.) 3
No opinion 9

Analysis: When Tiger Woods tees off at this year's U.S. Open tournament at the Southern Hills Country Club in Tulsa, Oklahoma, he will be trying for an unprecedented fifth straight major tournament title. Woods is the first player to hold all of golf's four major titles at the same time, a feat that signals the total domination of a sport where it is rare for one player to win tournaments consistently.

The public has obviously taken notice of Woods's greatness, and overwhelmingly names him as the "greatest athlete active in the world of sports today." In the June 8–10 Gallup Poll, 38% name Tiger Woods when asked who is the world's greatest active athlete, far outdistancing anyone else. Michael Jordan (who is no longer actively playing basketball) comes in second with 6%. Allen Iverson and Shaquille O'Neal, who are both currently competing in the NBA Finals, follow with mentions by 4% and 3%, respectively.

Tiger Woods's perceived mastery of the sport of golf becomes even clearer when the public is asked to rate him in comparison to one of the sport's other icons. When asked who they think is better, Tiger Woods or Jack Nicklaus when he was in his prime, 69% choose Woods, and only 19% choose Nicklaus.

JUNE 15
RUSSIAN PRESIDENT PUTIN

Interview Dates: 6/8–10/01
CNN/*USA Today*/Gallup Poll
Survey #GO 133811

Do you consider Russian President Vladimir Putin to be an ally of the United States, friendly but not an ally, unfriendly, an enemy of the United States, or don't you know enough to say?

Ally 7%
Friendly, not an ally 36
Unfriendly 9
Enemy 5
Don't know enough 43

Analysis: On June 9, President George W. Bush will hold his first meeting with Russian President Vladimir Putin in the small country of Slovenia, formerly part of Yugoslavia. The talks are expected to focus on Bush's stated intentions of building a missile defense system in the United States, in direct violation of the 1972 Anti-Ballistic Missile Treaty between the Soviet Union and the U.S. Recent Gallup Polls suggest that the general public holds a more favorable view of Russia than it did two years ago—during the fighting in Kosovo—when Russia's President Boris Yeltsin was one of the country's severest critics.

According to a Gallup Poll conducted June 8–10, Americans are more likely to consider Putin friendly than unfriendly by 43% to 14%, while another 43% have no opinion. The friendly group includes 7% who say Putin is an ally, and another 36% who say he is a friend but not an ally. The unfriendly group includes 5% who think Putin is an enemy with the other 9% saying just unfriendly.

JUNE 19
ECONOMIC CONDITIONS

Interview Dates: 6/11–17/01
Gallup Poll News Service
Survey #GO 132073

How would you rate economic conditions in this country today—excellent, good, only fair, or poor?

	Excellent, good	Only fair	Poor*
2001 Jun 11–17	42%	45%	13%

	Getting better	Getting worse	Same (vol.); no opinion
2001 May 10–14	.40	45	15
2001 Apr 6–8	.45	41	14
2001 Mar 5–7	.46	43	11
2001 Feb 1–4	.51	36	13
2001 Jan 10–14	.167	27	6

*"No opinion" is omitted.

Right now, do you think that economic conditions in the country as a whole are getting better or getting worse?

	Getting better	Getting worse	Same (vol.); no opinion
2001 Jun 11–17	.29%	60%	11%
2001 May 10–14	.25	63	12
2001 Apr 6–8	.24	63	13
2001 Mar 5–7	.28	61	11
2001 Feb 1–4	.23	66	11
2001 Jan 10–14	.32	56	12

Analysis: The latest monthly Gallup Poll on public sentiment toward the economy shows little change from last month and, in fact, little change over the past several months. About four out of ten give the economy a positive rating, and expectations for the economy's performance in the immediate future show widespread pessimism.

This month's poll on the economy was conducted June 11–17 and shows that 42% rate the economy as excellent or good, 45% as fair, and 12% as poor. These results are within a few percentage points of the results found last month and represent no significant change. In January of this year, 67% rated the economy as excellent or good, and just 6% as poor.

Expectations about where the economy is headed continue to be more negative than positive, as 60% say that economic conditions are getting worse while just 29% say better. Over the past five months, the negative sentiment about the immediate future of the economy has remained steady but highly negative. The percentage saying the economy is getting worse has fluctuated between 60% and 66%, while the percentage saying better has fluctuated in the 23%-to-29% range.

JUNE 20
PATIENTS' BILL OF RIGHTS

Interview Dates: 6/8–10/01
CNN/*USA Today*/Gallup Poll
Survey #GO 133811

How important is it to you that the president and Congress deal with a patients' bill of rights in the next year—is it extremely important, very important, moderately important, or not that important?

Extremely important	.40%
Very important	.37
Moderately important	.16
Not that important	.5
No opinion	.2

Thinking for a moment about health care overall, whom do you have more confidence in when it comes to the issue of a patients' bill of rights—President Bush, or the Democratic leaders in the Senate?

Bush	.34%
Democrats in Senate	.49
Both; neither (vol.)	.6
No opinion	.11

Analysis: As Democrats and Republicans begin their public relations battle over a "patients' bill of rights," a new Gallup Poll shows that more than three in four Americans say such a bill is either "extremely" or "very" important to them. Both parties in Congress support some form of a patients' bill of rights, and the Senate is ready to debate the two different measures, one backed by President Bush and the Republican leaders in the Senate, the other by Senate Democratic leaders. While most people may not know the details of the two bills, the poll shows that, by a margin of 49% to 34%, respondents have more confidence in the Democratic leaders than in President Bush on this issue. The poll, conducted June 8–10, shows that 40% say it is "extremely" important, and another 37% "very" important, that Congress and the president address the issue of a patients' bill of rights this year.

JUNE 21
GOVERNMENT APPROVAL BY RACE

Interview Dates: 6/11–18/01
Gallup Poll News Service
Survey #GO 132073

Do you approve or disapprove of the way George W. Bush is handling his job as president?

	Approve	Dis-approve	No opinion
National Adults	55%	33%	12%
Men	61	31	8
Women	49	34	17
Whites	58	31	11
Blacks	36	50	14
Hispanics	59	28	13

Do you approve or disapprove of the way Congress is handling its job?

	Approve	Dis-approve	No opinion
National Adults	51%	34%	15%
Men	55	34	11
Women	47	35	18
Whites	50	35	15
Blacks	49	39	12
Hispanics	55	32	13

Do you approve or disapprove of the way the Supreme Court is handling its job?

	Approve	Dis-approve	No opinion
National Adults	62%	25%	13%
Men	61	29	10
Women	63	22	15
Whites	63	24	13
Blacks	52	36	12
Hispanics	48	39	13

Analysis: A June Gallup Poll shows that Hispanics and whites are just as likely to approve of the job being done by President George W. Bush and Congress, but Hispanics are much more negative in their assessment of the Supreme Court. Blacks, on the other hand, give Bush much lower job approval ratings than do either whites or Hispanics, but share Hispanics' more critical view of the Supreme Court. Overall, among the three branches of government, Americans rate the Supreme Court most positively and Congress most negatively.

The new poll conducted June 11–17 included larger samples of both blacks and Hispanics, allowing for attitude comparisons across racial and ethnic groups. (All data for "whites" and "blacks" in this analysis exclude those who say they are of Hispanic ethnicity.)

The new Gallup Poll shows Bush with an overall job approval rating of 55%, consistent with his last several ratings. Thirty-three percent disapprove of the job Bush is doing. The data from the poll show that a higher percentage of both blacks and Hispanics currently approve of the job Bush is doing in office than voted for him on Election Day. Bush gets a 36% approval rating among blacks, which is significantly lower than he gets among whites (58%), but is much higher than the 9% of blacks who voted for him for president. Similarly, 59% of Hispanics now approve of Bush after only 35% of Hispanics chose him in the presidential election contest.

Currently, 51% of Americans approve of the job Congress is doing and 34% disapprove. Whites, blacks, and Hispanics show little difference in their ratings of Congress. Fifty percent of whites and 49% of blacks approve of Congress, though blacks are a little more likely to disapprove (39% compared to 35% of whites). Hispanics give Congress slightly higher marks, as 55% approve and 32% disapprove.

Of the three branches of government, Americans give the Supreme Court the highest job approval rating at 62%. One in four disapproves of the Supreme Court's performance. Sixty-three percent of whites approve of the job the Supreme Court is doing, but blacks and Hispanics are much less likely to approve of the nation's highest court. Fifty-two percent of blacks and just 48% of Hispanics say they approve of the job the Supreme Court is doing. Substantial proportions of each racial group disapprove of the Supreme Court's work, including 36% of blacks and 39% of Hispanics.

Race and ethnicity are not the only characteristics that are associated with differing evaluations of the three branches of government. For example, men and women differ considerably in their evaluation of Bush, as 61% of men but only 49% of women approve of the job he is doing as president, reflecting the gender gap that has been apparent in partisan politics for many years. Men are slightly more likely to approve of Congress (55%) than are women (47%), but men and women do not differ in their ratings of the Supreme Court (61% of men and 63% of women approve).

JUNE 22
QUALITY OF LIFE BY RACE

Interview Dates: 6/11–18/01
Gallup Poll News Service
Survey #GO 132073

We'd like to know how satisfied you are with each of the following aspects of your life—very satisfied, somewhat satisfied, somewhat dissatisfied, or very dissatisfied:

Your community as a place to live in?

	Very, somewhat satisfied	Somewhat, very dissatisfied	No opinion
National Adults	88%	12%	*
Men	88	11	1
Women	87	13	*
Whites	90	10	*
Blacks	80	19	1
Hispanics	84	16	*

Your current housing?

	Very, somewhat satisfied	Somewhat, very dissatisfied	No opinion
National Adults	93%	7%	*
Men	95	4	1
Women	90	10	*
Whites	93	7	*

Blacks	84	16	*
Hispanics	81	19	*

Your education?

	Very, somewhat satisfied	Somewhat, very dissatisfied	No opinion
National Adults	87%	12%	1%
Men	88	11	1
Women	87	12	1
Whites	88	11	1
Blacks	82	18	0
Hispanics	79	20	1

Your family life?

	Very, somewhat satisfied	Somewhat, very dissatisfied	No opinion
National Adults	94%	5%	1%
Men	97	2	1
Women	92	7	1
Whites	94	5	1
Blacks	91	8	1
Hispanics	94	6	0

Your financial situation?

	Very, somewhat satisfied	Somewhat, very dissatisfied	No opinion
National Adults	77%	22%	1%
Men	80	20	*
Women	76	24	*
Whites	79	21	*
Blacks	62	37	1
Hispanics	70	30	*

Your personal health?

	Very, somewhat satisfied	Somewhat, very dissatisfied	No opinion
National Adults	89%	11%	*

Men 91	9	0
Women 87	13	*
Whites 88	12	*
Blacks 89	10	1
Hispanics 87	13	0

Your safety from physical harm or violence?

	Very, some- what satisfied	Some- what, very dis- satisfied	No opinion
National Adults 88%	11%	1%
Men 92	7	1
Women 85	15	*
Whites 90	10	*
Blacks 78	21	1
Hispanics 79	20	1

The opportunities you have had to succeed in life?

	Very, some- what satisfied	Some- what, very dis- satisfied	No opinion
National Adults 86%	13%	1%
Men 89	10	1
Women 83	15	2
Whites 86	13	1
Blacks 83	16	1
Hispanics 80	18	2

Your job, or the work you do?

	Very, some- what satisfied	Some- what, very dis- satisfied	No opinion
National Adults 89%	11%	0%
Men 89	11	0
Women 88	12	0
Whites 88	12	0
Blacks 83	16	1
Hispanics 86	14	0

*Less than 1%

Do you feel that racial minorities in this country have equal job opportunities with whites, or not?

	Yes	No	No opinion
National Adults 48%	50%	2%
Men 51	48	1
Women 45	52	3
Whites 53	45	2
Blacks 18	79	3
Hispanics 46	51	3

Asked of blacks or Hispanics: We have a question about your own experiences as a black or Hispanic. How often do you feel discriminated against in public life or employment because you are black or Hispanic—every day, every week, about once a month, a few times a year, less than once a year, or never?

	Every day; every week	Once a month; few times a year	Less than once a year; never*
All blacks 24%	36%	39%
Black men 24	40	35
Black women 24	32	43
All Hispanics 18	33	47
Hispanic men 11	41	48
Hispanic women 25	26	47

*"No opinion" is omitted.

Analysis: A Gallup Poll addressing minority rights and relations in the U.S. finds that the nation's two largest minority groups—blacks and Hispanics—have markedly different perceptions of their quality of life in certain respects. According to the June 11–17 Gallup survey, the two groups express similar levels of satisfaction with their housing, health, education, and opportunities to succeed in life. Blacks, however, are less satisfied with their family life, personal safety, jobs, and their community as a place in which to live. Also, blacks are much more likely than Hispanics to consider race discrimination in employment to be a problem.

Despite these concerns, the overall assessment from blacks about their lives is positive.

Close to nine in ten blacks and Hispanics say they are either very or somewhat satisfied with their lives, while only 12% are dissatisfied. Looking just at the percentage "very satisfied," however, blacks are less positive with only 42% very satisfied, compared to 49% of Hispanics and 54% of whites.

The vast majority of blacks and Hispanics say they are at least somewhat satisfied with every specific dimension of their personal lives measured in the new survey. The distinctions between the two groups are seen in the generally lower rate of high satisfaction among blacks.

A majority of blacks is very satisfied with only two of the nine areas measured: their family life (59% are very satisfied) and their personal health. By contrast, a majority of Hispanics are very satisfied with four items: their community and their job in addition to family life and health. The white majority adds housing and physical safety to the list of areas with which it is highly satisfied, leaving only three about which whites are less content: their opportunities to succeed, their education, and their finances.

The largest differences between blacks and Hispanics in the new survey are seen in attitudes related to employment. Among Hispanics who currently work full or part time, 51% say they are very satisfied with their job or the work they do, compared to only 36% of employed blacks who feel this way, a 15-point gap.

Even more dramatic is the difference in the two groups' perceptions of race discrimination in the job market or workplace: only 18% of blacks believe that racial minorities have job opportunities equal to those of whites while 79% disagree. By contrast, 46% of all Hispanics—not far from the 53% recorded among whites—perceive that there are equal job opportunities, while 51% disagree.

The poll did not find this same difference between blacks and Hispanics in terms of their personal experiences with discrimination. About two-thirds of Hispanics (64%) say they occasionally feel discriminated against in public life or employment because of their ethnicity, compared to three-quarters (76%) of blacks who feel discriminated against because of their race. The gap

is similar in terms of the percentage who often feel subject to discrimination (that is, on a monthly or more frequent basis): 39% of blacks and 31% of Hispanics.

Another important distinction between blacks and other groups in society is blacks' lower satisfaction with their safety from physical harm or violence. Only 33% of blacks say they are very satisfied with their level of safety. Another 45% are somewhat satisfied while 10% are somewhat dissatisfied, and 11% are very dissatisfied. By contrast, 47% of Hispanics and 59% of whites are very satisfied with their safety.

A related concern for blacks is their community, with only 42% of blacks feeling very satisfied with their community as a place to live, compared to 53% of Hispanics and 61% of whites. A majority of blacks indicate strong contentment with their family life, but the percentage is substantially smaller than that among Hispanics: 59% for blacks versus 73% for Hispanics.

Blacks and Hispanics are fairly similar in their responses to questions about housing, personal health, education, their financial situation, and the opportunities they feel they've had to succeed in life. The last three elicit the lowest levels of satisfaction of all nine items measured, with less than a majority of blacks, Hispanics, and whites saying they are very satisfied with each. Only one-quarter of all Americans (26%), including 29% of whites, 23% of Hispanics, and 15% of blacks, say they are very satisfied with their finances.

JUNE 25
CONFIDENCE IN INSTITUTIONS

Interview Dates: 6/8–10/01
CNN/*USA Today*/Gallup Poll
Survey #GO 133811

I am going to read you a list of institutions in American society. Please tell me how much confidence you, yourself, have in each one— a great deal, quite a lot, some, or very little?

	Great deal, quite a lot
The military	.66%
The church or organized religion	.60
The police	.57
The U.S. Supreme Court	.50
The presidency	.48
Banks	.44
The medical system	.40
Public schools	.38
Faith-based charitable organizations	.37
Newspapers	.36
Television news	.34
Electric power utilities	.28
Big business	.28
Organized labor	.26
Congress	.26
Health maintenance organizations (HMOs)	.15

Confidence by Political Party
("Great Deal, Quite a Lot")

	Republicans	Democrats
The military	75%	61%
The church or organized religion	68	53
The police	65	53
The U.S. Supreme Court	60	44
The presidency	73	27
Banks	47	42
The medical system	43	38
Public schools	34	43
Faith-based charitable organizations	46	33
Newspapers	31	41
Television news	32	37
Electric power utilities	32	24
Big business	38	20
Organized labor	24	20
Congress	30	26
Health maintenance organizations (HMOs)	17	14

Analysis: Two-thirds of Americans have a high degree of confidence in the military, and about six in ten have a high degree of confidence in organized religion and the police, according to Gallup's annual confidence in institutions survey, putting these three institutions at the top of the list of sixteen institutions tested. At the same time, less than one-third has a high degree of confidence in electric power utilities, big business, Congress, organized labor, and HMOs. There have been few significant changes in these levels of confidence over the past year, but Americans generally have less confidence in many institutions now than they did in the 1970s when Gallup first began testing them. The major exception is the military, which has gained in confidence over the past thirty years so that it is now the single institution tested in which the American public has the most confidence.

The results from this year's survey conducted June 8–10 show that the military, organized religion, and the police are given high confidence ratings (defined as the percentage saying they have a great deal or quite a lot of confidence) by over one-half of the public. The U.S. Supreme Court and the presidency also generate high confidence ratings from about one-half. The rest range below that level, with the bottom position taken by health maintenance organizations in which only 15% have confidence. Of the three branches of government, Congress gets significantly lower ratings than either the presidency or the U.S. Supreme Court.

Two institutions tested for the first time this year do not get exceptional confidence ratings. Electric power utilities, much in the news as a result of the energy problems in California, generate high confidence from only 28%, while faith-based charitable organizations get high confidence ratings from only 37%.

JUNE 28
INTERNET PRIVACY

Interview Dates: 6/14–26/01
Gallup Poll News Service
Survey #GO 133802

How concerned are you personally about the privacy of personal information you give out on the Internet, as well as privacy regarding what you do on the Internet?

Very concerned 28%
Somewhat concerned 50
Not too concerned .18
Not at all concerned 3
No answer 1

How concerned are you personally about each of the following: *

Misuse of your credit card information that you give out on the Internet?

Very concerned 46%
Somewhat concerned 36

Companies that keep records on your Internet usage, which they then use for marketing purposes?

Very concerned 35%
Somewhat concerned 38

Internet "cookies" that track where you go on the Internet?

Very concerned 31%
Somewhat concerned 40

Your Internet service provider monitoring your use of Internet and e-mail?

Very concerned 29%
Somewhat concerned 32

Someone forwarding your e-mails to people you did not want to read them?

Very concerned 19%
Somewhat concerned 31

Your business or company monitoring your use of Internet and e-mail?

Very concerned 16%
Somewhat concerned 23

*"Not too, not at all concerned," "No answer" are omitted.

Do you think the Federal government should pass more laws to ensure citizens' privacy online, or are the current laws sufficient?

Yes, should pass more laws 66%
No, current laws sufficient 33
No answer 1

Please indicate how comfortable you feel about giving the following information out over the Internet:

Date of birth?

Very comfortable 13%
Somewhat comfortable 34
Not too comfortable 23
Not at all comfortable 30
No answer . . . .*

*Less than 1%

Credit card number?

Very comfortable 5%
Somewhat comfortable 28
Not too comfortable 30
Not at all comfortable 37
No answer 0

Social Security number?

Very comfortable 1%
Somewhat comfortable 10
Not too comfortable 16
Not at all comfortable 73
No answer . . . .*

*Less than 1%

Street address?

Very comfortable 11%
Somewhat comfortable 38
Not too comfortable 24
Not at all comfortable 27
No answer . . . .*

*Less than 1%

Home phone number?

Very comfortable 7%
Somewhat comfortable 28
Not too comfortable 28
Not at all comfortable 37
No answer . . . .*

*Less than 1%

Work phone number?

Very comfortable 17%
Somewhat comfortable 36
Not too comfortable 19
Not at all comfortable 24
No answer 4

E-mail address?

Very comfortable 34%
Somewhat comfortable 44
Not too comfortable 19
Not at all comfortable 3
No answer 0

In general, how confident are you that if you use a credit card to pay for something on the Internet, the credit card number will be secure and not stolen or misused in some way—completely confident, very confident, somewhat confident, not too confident, or not at all confident?

Completely confident 2%
Very confident 20
Somewhat confident 48
Not too confident .16
Not at all confident 14
No answer . . . .*

*Less than 1%

Analysis: Nearly eight in ten e-mail users are at least somewhat concerned about the privacy of personal information that they give out on the Internet, but a new online Gallup Poll of e-mail users indicates that just 28% are "very concerned."

The poll, conducted via the Internet June 14–26, shows that e-mail users are most worried about misuse of their credit card information, and feel least comfortable giving out their Social Security number and credit card numbers online. Two-thirds think that the federal government should pass more laws to ensure citizens' privacy online, while 33% think the current laws are sufficient.

In addition to general concern, the survey also measured concern about a series of specific privacy risks encountered while using the Internet, including those associated with credit card information, Internet "cookies," and privacy of online communication. More than eight in ten (82%) are "very concerned" or "somewhat concerned" about the misuse of credit card information given out on the Internet. The percentage of respondents who are very concerned is just a little under one-half of those surveyed.

Marketing activities and the use of Internet "cookies" also make e-mail users uneasy: 73% are concerned about companies keeping records on their Internet usage, and 71% are concerned about Internet "cookies" that track where they go on the Internet.

Attitudes about monitoring Internet and e-mail use apparently depend on who is doing the monitoring. Sixty-one percent indicate that they are concerned about their Internet service provider monitoring their use of the Internet and e-mail, while just 39% say they are concerned about their business or company doing the same thing. They are evenly divided in their views about having their e-mails forwarded to someone whom they did not want to read them, with 50% concerned and 50% not concerned.

The poll asked e-mail users how comfortable they are giving out several different types of personal information. Overall, they are least comfortable giving out their Social Security number as only 11% are comfortable while 73% say they are "not comfortable at all" giving out this apparently vital piece of information. They also are quite uncomfortable giving out their credit card information, as only 33% say they are comfortable sharing this information online. A related question shows that just 22% are "completely" or "very confident" that their credit card information will be secure and not misused in some way if they pay for something on the Internet using their credit card.

E-mail users also are quite reluctant to give out their home phone number. Just 35% are comfortable doing so, but are much more comfortable giving out their work phone number (53% say they are comfortable doing this). About one-half feels comfortable giving out their date of birth or street address online. Respondents are most comfortable (78%) giving out their e-mail address, which might be expected since they agreed to share their e-mail address with Gallup.

JUNE 29
JOB EQUITY FOR WOMEN

Interview Dates: 6/11–18/01
Gallup Poll News Service
Survey #GO 132073

If you were free to do either, would you prefer to have a job outside the home, or would you prefer to stay at home and take care of the house and family?

	Job outside home	Stay home	Both (vol.)*
National Adults	62%	35%	2%
Men	73	24	2
Women	53	45	2
Whites	61	36	2
Blacks	69	29	2
Hispanics	58	40	2

*"No opinion" is omitted.

Do you feel that women in this country have equal job opportunities with men, or not?

	Yes	No	No opinion
National Adults	42%	57%	1%
Men	53	46	1
Women	32	67	1
Whites	43	56	1
Blacks	35	64	1
Hispanics	51	45	4

Do you feel that racial minorities in this country have equal job opportunities with whites, or not?

	Yes	No	No opinion
National Adults	48%	50%	2%
Men	51	48	1
Women	45	52	3
Whites	53	45	2
Blacks	18	79	3
Hispanics	46	51	3

Do you consider yourself a feminist, or not?

	Yes	No	No opinion
National Adults	23%	73%	4%
Men	20	75	5
Women	25	72	3
Whites	22	74	4
Blacks	20	74	6
Hispanics	40	50	10

Analysis: The National Organization for Women (NOW) will soon meet in Philadelphia for its annual national conference, with organizers under pressure to combat what they call the "anti-feminist Bush administration." The latest Gallup Poll conducted June 11–17 suggests that most women do not share this negative reaction to the new president: only 34% of women disapprove of the job George W. Bush is doing, similar to the 31% of men who disapprove. However, the survey—which focuses on minority and gender rights—does find that, among American women, there are pockets of dissatisfaction with the way society treats them, particularly in the area of employment. A substantial gender gap exists on this issue, with men far less likely than women to perceive job discrimination based on gender.

Only one-quarter of women considers themselves "feminists," the term widely associated with the women's rights movement in this country.

When it comes to employment, the new Gallup survey finds women to be critical of society, with only 32% saying they believe men and women enjoy equal job opportunities in the United States and two-thirds disagreeing. A majority of men (53%), on the other hand, believes women do have equal job rights, creating a significant gender gap in perceptions about employment.

Do more women than men prefer to stay home because they are frustrated with the lack of fairness in employment, or do women engender different treatment because they are more likely to leave the job market to care for family? It is a delicate issue. In either case, the differential pull of family on men and women is evident in the Gallup survey in the answers to this question: If you were free to do either, would you prefer to have a job outside the home, or would you prefer to stay at home and take care of the house and family? Only 53% of women, compared to 73% of men, would prefer to work outside the home. Close to one-half of women (45%), compared to just one-quarter of men (24%), say they would rather stay home.

JULY 3
PRESIDENT BUSH

Interview Dates: 6/28–7/1/01
Gallup Poll News Service
Survey #GO 133787

Do you approve or disapprove of the way George W. Bush is handling his job as president?

	Approve	Dis-approve	No opinion
2001 Jun 28–Jul 1	52%	34%	14%
2001 Jun 11–17	55	33	12
2001 Jun 8–10	55	35	10
2001 May 18–20	56	36	8
2001 May 10–14	56	31	13
2001 May 7–9	53	33	14
2001 Apr 20–22	62	29	9
2001 Apr 6–8	59	30	11
2001 Mar 26–28	53	29	18
2001 Mar 9–11	58	29	13
2001 Mar 5–7	63	22	15
2001 Feb 19–21	62	21	17
2001 Feb 9–11	57	25	18
2001 Feb 1–4	57	25	18

Analysis: The evolving political consensus seems to be that George W. Bush is in trouble, but an analysis of the trend in his job performance ratings over the little more than five months during which he has been president suggests caution in assuming that the tide of public opinion has turned dramatically away from him. According to the most recent Gallup Poll conducted June 28–July 1, a majority of Americans (52%) approves of the job Bush is doing as president, while only one-third (34%) disapproves. This represents a continuation of approval ratings that are lower than his average from the first months of his presidency, but is little changed over the past two months.

Bush's current 52% approval rating could be interpreted to mean that he is still 4 points ahead of the game. However, in a political environment where the political balance hovers around 50%—in the popular and electoral vote for president, as well as in the division of the U.S. House and Senate—approval ratings for Bush in the low to mid 50s also are an indication of how narrow his political advantage is in Washington. At a time when many say Bush needs to build his political base, he has failed to do so, thereby, perhaps, losing the expectations game.

The public's evaluation of Bush has declined from the start of his presidency, but only moderately, and not at a consistent rate that would indicate steady erosion of public support for him. Rather, the greatest change Gallup has seen in support for Bush occurred this spring, after which public attitudes have been fairly stable.

Gallup's first measurement of Bush's job performance, in early February, found 57% of respondents approving and 25% disapproving. Bush's approval score rose to a high of 63% in the weeks following a presidential address to the nation in late February, during which he outlined his tax cut plan and other priorities. At one point in late March, however, his job approval was at 53%, essentially what it is today. Support for Bush remained fairly high in April, but fell to the low- to mid-50s in May where it has remained since. In fact, Bush's current rating is nearly identical to one recorded by Gallup in early May when 53% approved and 33% disapproved.

Averaging Bush's approval ratings by month, he garnered a 59% approval score for February, enjoyed similar ratings in March (58%), jumped to 61% in April, fell to 55% in May, and remained at roughly that level (54%) in June. If any pattern can be identified, it is of recent stability in the public's reaction to Bush after a drop in May. The current rating of 52% approval is within the margin of error of the 55% ratings recorded recently, but it may be premature to guess whether this represents a more permanent downward shift in Bush's approval score or not.

JULY 3
VICE PRESIDENT CHENEY

Interview Dates: 6/28–7/1/01
Gallup Poll News Service
Survey #GO 133787

Are you concerned or not concerned that Vice President Dick Cheney's health problems will prevent him from serving effectively as vice president?

	2001 Jun 29– Jul 1	2001 Mar 9–11
Concerned	34%	39%
Not concerned	64	59
No opinion	2	2

Which comes closest to your view concerning Vice President Dick Cheney's health problems—Cheney should resign as vice president, Cheney should remain as vice president but cut back on his duties, or Cheney should remain as vice president and continue with his current duties with little or no change?

	2001 Jun 29– Jul 1	2001 Mar 9–11
Resign	12%	11%
Cut back	20	21
Continue current duties	65	66
No opinion	3	2

Analysis: Vice President Dick Cheney is back at work after a Saturday operation, during which he received a pager-sized version of the defibrillator used in emergencies to shock a patient's heart back into normal rhythm. The vice president's heart problems have been a source of concern for some ever since his selection as George W. Bush's running mate a year ago, but a new Gallup Poll conducted the weekend of June 29–July 1 shows a majority of Americans do not believe his health will affect his ability to carry out his duties.

When asked whether they are concerned that Cheney's health problems would prevent him from serving effectively as vice president, 64% of those surveyed are not concerned while 34% are. This represents a slightly lower level of concern than that found earlier this year in a March Gallup Poll when 39% were concerned about the effect of the vice president's health on his performance in office.

Just 12% believe the vice president's health problems are serious enough to justify his resignation from office while 20% say he should cut back on his workload. Nearly two out of three, however, say there is no reason why Cheney should not carry on with his regular duties.

JULY 3
FOURTH OF JULY

Interview Dates: 6/28–7/1/01
Gallup Poll News Service
Survey #GO 133787

Which of the following, if any, do you think you will do this Fourth of July:

Give or attend a barbecue, picnic, or cookout?

Will do	78%
Will not do	20
No opinion	2

Get together with family members?

Will do	76%
Will not do	23
No opinion	1

Display an American flag?

Will do 66%
Will not do 33
No opinion 1

Attend a fireworks display?

Will do 63%
Will not do 36
No opinion 1

Watch a Fourth of July parade?

Will do 32%
Will not do 66
No opinion 2

Fire off your own fireworks?

Will do 26%
Will not do 73
No opinion 1

As far as you know, what specific historical event is celebrated on July 4th?

Signing of the Declaration of
   Independence 61%
America's Independence;
   Independence Day 24
Birth of the United States 2
Family get-togethers 1
Honoring veterans 1
Other 4
No opinion 7

As far as you know, from what country did America gain its independence following the Revolutionary War?

England; Great Britain; United Kingdom ...76%
France 2
United States 1
Mexico 1
Europe ....*
Other 1
No opinion 19

*Less than 1%

Overall, do you think the signers of the Declaration of Independence would be pleased or disappointed by the way the United States has turned out?

Pleased 54%
Disappointed 42
No opinion 4

Analysis: This week Americans will celebrate the signing of the Declaration of Independence, the event that sparked the American Revolution and led to the eventual creation of the United States of America. Whether they know the origins of the holiday or not, Americans will celebrate in a variety of ways. The results of a new Gallup Poll show that the holiday will likely be filled with barbecues, family, fireworks, and flags. Nearly eight in ten (78%) will attend a picnic or barbecue, the most popular Fourth of July activity among those tested. Most (76%) will celebrate with family. Other common activities include displaying an American flag (66%) and attending fireworks displays (63%). Watching a parade and firing off their own fireworks were the least mentioned activities in the June 28–July 1 poll (32% and 26%, respectively).

As Americans gather for fireworks, food, and fun this Fourth of July, the majority will be doing so with an understanding of the day's significance. Gallup asked the public what specific event is celebrated on this holiday. Sixty-one percent gave the correct answer (Signing of the Declaration of Independence) and another 26% gave answers that are essentially correct (America's independence and birth of the United States). However, 13% either gave incorrect answers or did not have an answer at all.

Another question probed respondents on their knowledge of the American Revolution, asking, "As far as you know, from what country did America gain its independence following the Revolutionary War?" Again, Americans generally pass the test. The majority (76%) correctly answered England, Great Britain, or the United Kingdom. Almost a quarter (24%) either gave an incorrect answer or did not have an answer.

The United States has undergone vast changes in the more than 200 years since its founding, and one final question asked Americans whether they thought the signers of the Declaration would be pleased with the way the United States turned out. A majority (54%) thinks America's forefathers would be pleased, while 42% say they would be disappointed.

JULY 5
BUSH'S ENERGY PLAN

Interview Dates: 6/28–7/1/01
Gallup Poll News Service
Survey #GO 133787

How serious would you say the energy situation is in the United States—very serious, fairly serious, or not at all serious?

	Very, fairly serious	Not at all serious	No opinion
2001 Jun 28–Jul 1	90%	8%	2%
2001 May 7–9	94	4	2
2001 Mar 5–7	90	9	1

How closely have you been following the news about President Bush's energy plan—very closely, somewhat closely, not too closely, or not at all?

Very closely	11%
Somewhat closely	35
Not too closely	32
Not at all	22

Based on what you have heard or read, do you favor or oppose President Bush's plan to deal with the country's current energy problems?

Favor	38%
Oppose	32
No opinion	30

Asked of those who oppose Bush's energy plan: What is the main reason why you op-pose Bush's plan to deal with the country's current energy problems?

Not environmentally friendly; oppose drilling in Alaska	20%
Would only benefit oil companies	13
Disagree with all of Bush's policies	11
Plans don't go far enough; too limited	8
No solution is being offered; nothing is being done	7
Too much emphasis on drilling, not enough on conservation	6
Not enough emphasis on finding alternate energy sources	6
Bush doesn't know enough about problem	3
Nothing is being done to lower prices	3
Don't believe there really is an energy problem	3
California's energy problems aren't being addressed	2
Need more regulation of the energy industry	2
No one reason	1
Other	6
No opinion	9

Analysis: Americans have become somewhat less concerned about the seriousness of the energy situation over the last two months, and although a third now have no opinion on the matter, the remainder is closely divided on President Bush's controversial new energy plan. A new Gallup Poll also shows that the public is not currently paying a great deal of attention to the energy plan.

The new poll conducted June 28–July 1 finds that just 47% say the energy situation in the U.S. at this time is "very serious." Another 43% say it is fairly serious while only 8% say it is not at all serious. In historical perspective, this puts the current perception of energy as a problem at a lower level than at any point previous to this year during the quarter century that Gallup has asked this question.

Forty-six percent of respondents say they are following news about Bush's energy plan either very or somewhat closely. And 38% favor Bush's plan, 34% oppose it, and 30% have no opinion. Overall, however, paying attention to the issue has little basic relationship to how one stands on the plan. Those who are paying close attention favor it by a 48%-to-43% margin, while those who are not paying attention favor it by a 30%-to-23% margin. In other words, those who claim to-be following the plan are more likely to have an opinion, but the nature of those opinions—roughly split down the middle—is no different from the opinion of those not paying a lot of attention.

JULY 5
MICROSOFT ANTITRUST CASE

Interview Dates: 6/28–7/1/01
Gallup Poll News Service
Survey #GO 133787

Thinking about Microsoft, the computer software company that produces Windows and other products—do you have a favorable or unfavorable opinion of the Microsoft Corporation?

Favorable 60%
Unfavorable 17
No opinion 23

How closely have you been following the news about the Justice Department lawsuit against Microsoft—very closely, somewhat closely, not too closely, or not at all closely?

Very, somewhat closely 39%
Not too, not at all closely 61
No opinion . . . .*

*Less than 1%

As you may know, last year, a district court judge ruled that Microsoft should be split into two companies. This past Thursday, an appeals court overturned the ruling and ordered the whole case sent to a different judge because the original judge had been biased against Microsoft. What do you think the federal government should do now—drop the case against Microsoft altogether, seek a settlement with Microsoft, or go forward with the case against Microsoft in

front of a new judge, or don't you have an opinion on this matter?

Drop the case 34%
Seek a settlement .22
Go forward with new judge 22
No opinion 22

All in all, would you say the fact that Microsoft dominates its software markets has been positive or negative for:

The economy?

Positive 68%
Negative 19
No opinion 13

Consumers?

Positive 63%
Negative 24
No opinion 13

The computer industry?

Positive 62%
Negative 25
No opinion 13

Analysis: Last week, an appeals court judge overturned a lower court ruling that would have divided Microsoft into two companies. One would develop and market the operating system used by the vast majority of personal computers in the country, and the other would develop and market other kinds of software. Citing biased comments by the district judge who originally heard the Justice Department's lawsuit against the software company, the appeals court remanded the case to a new judge to determine what penalties should be assessed to Microsoft, which, the appeals court agreed, had abused its monopoly of the operating system.

In the wake of this decision, a new Gallup Poll finds public sentiment about Microsoft little changed over the past several years. While relatively few have followed the case closely, most

Americans hold a favorable view of the company and think that Microsoft's domination of the software markets has been mostly good for the economy, consumers, and the computer industry. These views are even more positive among the "attentive public" who say they have followed the case closely.

As for the suit itself, respondents show no clear consensus about what should be done. About a third want the federal government to drop the case altogether, while the rest are evenly divided among those who want the government to pursue a settlement, those who want the case to go forward with a new judge, and those who have no opinion on the matter. The good news for Microsoft is that it appears a majority do not favor breaking up the company, but the bad news is that a majority is not willing to see the lawsuit dropped altogether.

JULY 6
RACE RELATIONS/TREATMENT
OF VARIOUS GROUPS

Interview Dates: 6/11–17/01
Gallup Poll News Service
Survey #GO 132073

We'd like to know how you feel about the way various groups in society are treated. For each of the following groups, please say whether you are very satisfied, somewhat satisfied, somewhat dissatisfied, or very dissatisfied with the way they are treated:

Immigrants?

	Very, some-what satisfied	Some-what, very dis-satisfied	No opinion
National Adults	54%	41%	5%
Men	60	36	4
Women	48	46	6
Whites	58	37	5
Blacks	35	57	8
Hispanics	36	60	4

Women?

	Very, some-what satisfied	Some-what, very dis-satisfied	No opinion
National Adults	70%	29%	1%
Men	80	19	1
Women	61	37	2
Whites	73	26	1
Blacks	47	51	2
Hispanics	60	38	2

Blacks?

	Very, some-what satisfied	Some-what, very dis-satisfied	No opinion
National Adults	61%	37%	2%
Men	66	32	2
Women	58	40	2
Whites	64	34	2
Blacks	39	60	1
Hispanics	50	44	6

Hispanics?

	Very, some-what satisfied	Some-what, very dis-satisfied	No opinion
National Adults	60%	35%	5%
Men	67	30	3
Women	54	40	6
Whites	64	32	4
Blacks	41	51	8
Hispanics	45	54	1

Asians?

	Very, some-what satisfied	Some-what, very dis-satisfied	No opinion
National Adults	69%	23%	8%
Men	74	21	5
Women	64	26	10

Whites 71	22	7
Blacks 53	38	9
Hispanics 51	35	14

Analysis: The National Association for the Advancement of Colored People (NAACP) plans to use its upcoming annual convention, being held in New Orleans July 7–13, to address the challenges it sees facing "communities of color" nationwide. Some of these challenges are evident in a recent Gallup Poll focusing on minority rights and relations.

The nationwide survey, conducted June 11–18, included larger-than-normal samples of blacks and Hispanics in order to study the views of these groups more closely than is ordinarily possible. A review of survey's results underscores first and foremost that a significant perceptual gap continues between the way whites view the situation for blacks in American society today and the way blacks themselves view it.

Six in ten blacks are dissatisfied with the way people of their own race are treated by society, including 32% who are very dissatisfied and another 28% who are somewhat dissatisfied. Only 39% of blacks nationwide are satisfied, including just 8% who are very satisfied. In contrast, almost two-thirds of whites (64%) say they are personally satisfied with the way blacks are treated in society while only 34% are dissatisfied.

Blacks' appraisal of their current situation in U.S. society is just slightly more negative than Hispanics' assessment of their own treatment: 45% of Hispanics are satisfied with the way they are treated and 54% are dissatisfied.

There is, on the other hand, no difference between whites' perceptions of Hispanics' situation in society and their perceptions of blacks' situation. Sixty-four percent of whites say they are satisfied with the way Hispanics are treated, the exact percentage of whites who say they are satisfied with the way blacks are treated. In short, the majority of whites apparently feel that the treatment of blacks and Hispanics in American society today is acceptable, while the majority of both of these latter two groups disagree.

JULY 9
MORALITY AND MARRIAGE

Interview Dates: 5/10–14/01
Gallup Poll News Service
Survey #GO 132072

In general, do you think it is wrong or not wrong for a man and a woman to have sexual relations when they are not married?

Yes, wrong 32%
No, not wrong 64
No opinion 4

What is your opinion about a married person having sexual relations with someone other than their marriage partner—is it always wrong, almost always wrong, wrong only sometimes, or not wrong at all?

Always, almost always wrong 91%
Sometimes wrong .6
Not wrong; no opinion 3

Analysis: A Gallup Poll conducted May 10–14 found that 91% of Americans consider it to be either always or almost always wrong for married people to have sexual relations with someone other than their spouses, and in response to a separate but related question, 89% say that "married men and women having an affair" is morally unacceptable.

Unlike many sexual mores in American society, intolerance of infidelity has actually grown over the last two decades. In 1973 a survey done by the University of Chicago's National Opinion Research Center found that 84% considered extramarital sex to be wrong. In contrast, a 1969 Gallup Poll found that 68% thought it wrong for couples to engage in sexual relations before marriage, although that sentiment has changed. Now only 38% say it is wrong for a man and a woman to have sexual relations before marriage.

Despite the apparent stigma, many Americans seem to be aware of the inherent conflict between a moral ideal and actual behavior. Gallup polling shows that more than one-half of respondents know someone who has taken part in an extramarital affair, and a 1997 poll shows that

64% believe that half or more of all married men have had an affair.

JULY 9
PATIENTS' BILL OF RIGHTS

Interview Dates: 6/28–7/1/01
Gallup Poll News Service
Survey #GO 133787

When you hear about a patients' bill of rights, what does that mean to you?*

Patient is allowed to sue; take legal action against provider	12%
Rights of a patient; rights a patient has (unspecified)	11
Provides for a person's right to medical care	10
Patient can choose own doctor, hospital	10
Gives patient a voice in own health care	8
Rights regarding insurance, HMOs (unspecified)	5
Provides for protection of patients	3
Provides for patient confidentiality	3
Patient/doctor, not insurance company, would decide on care	2
Good idea; would make things better	2
Right of a patient to be kept informed	2
Holds doctors, insurance companies more accountable	2
Bad idea; would make things worse	2
Right of a patient to be treated fairly	1
Government interference would increase	1
Ensure fair costs are being charged	1
Places limits on amount a patient can sue	1
All patients treated equally	**
None	8
Other	3
No opinion	18

*Total adds to more than 100% due to multiple replies.
**Less than 1%

Recently, there has been some discussion in the news about a patients' bill of rights.

How closely have you been following the news about this—very closely, somewhat closely, not too closely, or not at all?

Very closely	7%
Somewhat closely	29
Not too closely	29
Not at all	34
No opinion	1

Based on what you have heard or read, do you favor or oppose Congress passing a patients' bill of rights?

Favor	58%
Oppose	11
No opinion	31

There are two versions of a patients' bill of rights currently being considered in the Senate: one sponsored mostly by Republicans, although with some Democratic support; and one sponsored mostly by Democrats, although with some Republican support. How much would you say you know about the differences between the two approaches—a lot, a little, or are you unsure what the differences are?

A lot	5%
A little	23
Unsure of differences	66
No opinion	6

Even if you don't know all of the details, in general, whose approach to a patients' bill of rights would you be more likely to trust—the Republicans' or the Democrats'?

Republicans'	34%
Democrats'	44
Neither; both (vol.)	12
No opinion	10

Analysis: According to a recent Gallup Poll, Americans support a "patients' bill of rights" by a margin of better than 5 to 1, although relatively few have followed the issue closely and can say for sure what such a bill would entail. Even fewer say they are aware of the differences between the two major bills that were recently being considered by the U.S. Senate, one sponsored and supported mostly by Republicans, the other sponsored and supported mostly by Democrats. Still, the results of an open-ended question that asked respondents to describe what they would envision in a patients' bill of rights show that many Americans correctly expect that such a bill would provide consumers with more rights in their dealings with their health care providers. Respondents also express moderately more trust in the Democratic Party than in the Republican Party to deal with a patients' bill of rights.

The poll, conducted June 28–July 1, as the Senate was passing the Democratic version of the patients' bill of rights legislation (which will now be considered by the U.S. House of Representatives), shows that just 36% say they have closely followed the news about this issue, while 7% say "very closely" and 29% "somewhat closely."

When asked to describe what a patients' bill of rights means to them, 29% gave no response, while just 12% mentioned the most salient part of both bills considered by the Senate: that patients would have the right to sue their health care insurer. Other comments, although less specific, are essentially correct. Eight percent said a patients' bill of rights would give patients more of a voice in their own health care and 2% said it would hold insurance companies more accountable for decisions that are made. But most of the other comments were more vague, referring to unspecified rights or protections for patients, suggesting that most people have less than a precise grasp of what the bills before Congress would provide.

Given the title—a patients' bill of rights—as well as the fact that political leaders of both major parties support some version of the legislation, it is not surprising that few Americans are opposed to it. The poll shows that 58% support Congress passing such legislation, 11% are opposed, and an unusually large number (31%) express no opinion. Most of this last group are people who earlier indicated that they have paid little attention to the issue and are unsure what such legislation entails.

Although both bills before the U.S. Senate called for a patient's right to sue the health care providers, the Democratic version generally allows for higher penalties and for lawsuits in state, as well as federal, courts. Only 5% indicate they have "a lot" of knowledge about the differences between the two versions, and another 23% know "a little" about the differences. That leaves over seven in ten unsure about what the differences are. Still, when asked which party they would be more likely to trust in enacting a patients' bill of rights, the public favors Democrats over Republicans by a 10-point margin (44% to 34%) with 22% expressing no preference.

JULY 10
AMERICANS AS IMMIGRANTS

Interview Dates: 6/11–17/01
Gallup Poll News Service
Survey #GO 132073

Were you born in the United States or in another country?

	Another country	In U.S.
National Adults	7%	93%
Men	8	92
Women	7	93
Whites	3	97
Blacks	13	87
Hispanics	47	53

Were either of your parents born in another country, or were both of your parents born in the United States?

	Another country	In U.S.
National Adults	18%	82%
Men	19	81
Women	17	83
Whites	13	87
Blacks	18	82
Hispanics	73	27

Were any of your grandparents born in another country, or were all of your grandparents born in the United States?

	Another country	In U.S.	Unsure; refused to answer
National Adults	40%	59%	1%
Men	43	56	1
Women	37	61	2
Whites	38	61	1
Blacks	21	78	1
Hispanics	83	14	3

Analysis: According to a June 11–17 Gallup Poll, the majority of Americans (56%) is at least the third generation of their family to be born in the United States, saying that they, their parents, and their grandparents were all born in this country. By contrast, only 7% are immigrants to the U.S., while just 12% say one or both of their parents were immigrants. Another quarter says that at least one grandparent came from another country.

There is wide variation in this measure according to racial and ethnic backgrounds. Almost half of all Hispanics living in the United States today (47%) indicate they were born in another country, compared to 13% of black Americans and just 3% of whites. Additionally, just 27% of Hispanics say their parents were born in the United States, compared to 82% of blacks and 87% of whites. Thus, the majority of Hispanic Americans (71%) are either the first generation or are immigrants themselves, compared to 20% of blacks and 14% of whites. Moreover, blacks are more likely than either whites or Hispanics to be third-generation Americans. Seventy-five percent of black Americans indicate that they are at least the third generation born in the United States, compared to 58% of whites and 13% of Hispanics.

JULY 11
SHARING GENETIC INFORMATION

Interview Dates: 6/28–7/1/01
Gallup Poll News Service
Survey #GO 133787

Do you think that medical insurance companies should or should not have access to this information in deciding about health care coverage for individuals?*

Should	21%
Should not	74
No opinion	5

*Based on part sample

Do you think that employers should or should not have access to this information in deciding whether or not to hire someone?*

Should	19%
Should not	76
No opinion	5

*Based on part sample

Analysis: The House Subcommittee on Commerce, Trade, and Consumer Protection begins hearings about the potential for discrimination based on predictive genetic tests by health insurance companies. Many are concerned that insurers would deny health coverage to individuals with a genetic predisposition toward serious diseases such as cancer, or that employers may refuse to hire someone with such a genetic predisposition. A new Gallup Poll finds widespread public opposition to giving medical insurance companies and employers access to genetic information.

Amid the medical promise that new advances in genetic mapping offer are risks associated with access to that information. The Gallup Poll conducted June 28–July 1 asked half of the respondents if medical insurance companies should have access to information about the genetic makeup of individuals when they decide about health care coverage for individuals. The other half of the sample was asked whether employers should have access to genetic information when making hiring decisions. Results for both questions were essentially the same: 74% say that medical insurance companies should not have access to this information when deciding about health coverage, and 76% say employers should not have access to this information when making hiring decisions. Only about one in five feels that employers and medical insurance companies should be given access to this information.

JULY 12
CELLULAR PHONES AND DRIVING

Interview Dates: 6/28–7/1/01
Gallup Poll News Service
Survey #GO 133787

Thinking for a moment about driving, which of the following have you ever done?*

Talked on a cellular phone while driving . . .49%
Shouted, cursed, or made gestures to
   other drivers whose driving upset you 49
Eaten a complete meal while driving 34
Read a road map while driving 33
Slept overnight in your car 29
Put on makeup or shaved with an
   electric razor while driving 13
Read a book, magazine, or
   newspaper while driving 7

*Total adds to more than 100% due to multiple replies.

Do you currently own a cellular phone, or not?

Yes 55%
No 45

Asked of cellular phone users: And how often do you use a cellular phone while driving— every day, several times a week, about once a week, less frequently, or never?

Every day 23%
Several times a week 16
About once a week 14
Less frequently 26
Never 21

How dangerous is it when drivers use a cellular phone while driving—very dangerous, somewhat dangerous, not too dangerous, or not dangerous at all?

Very dangerous 56%
Somewhat dangerous 36
Not too dangerous .6
Not dangerous at all 1
No opinion 1

Do you think your state government should or should not pass a law making it illegal to use a cellular phone while driving?*

Should 62%
Should not 32
Already illegal in state (vol.) 1
No opinion 5

*Based on part sample

Do you think your state government should or should not pass a law making it illegal to use hand-held cellular phones while driving?*

Should 70%
Should not 24
Already illegal in state (vol.) 1
No opinion 5

*Based on part sample

If your state banned cellular phone use while driving, would it be a major inconvenience for you, a minor inconvenience, or not an inconvenience at all?

Major inconvenience 10%
Minor inconvenience 22
Not an inconvenience 67
No opinion 1

Asked of cellular phone users: Have you, personally, been in a situation in which your own driving was dangerous or unsafe because you were using a cellular phone while driving, or not?

Yes 12%
No 88

Analysis: Last month New York became the first state to enact a law banning the use of hand-held cellular phones while driving. The bill, however, would allow for the use of "hands-free" phones. A recent Gallup Poll conducted June 28–July 1 shows that an overwhelming majority of Americans supports the idea of such cell phone laws. Seventy percent of those interviewed think that their state government should pass a law making it illegal to use hand-held cellular phones while driving while only 24% think that they should not. Additionally, 62% say their state should pass a ban on all cell phone use while driving while 32% believe that they should not. Americans who currently admit to using cell phones while driving, however, are less enthusiastic: just 49% support a total ban on cell phone use while driving.

New York enacted the law because of the state legislature's conviction that the practice of talking while driving poses a significant threat to public safety. The public agrees, as the majority (56%) says using a cell phone while driving is "very dangerous," and another 36% believe that it is "somewhat dangerous." The poll also asked cellular phone users if they ever felt their own driving was dangerous or unsafe due to their using a cellular phone while at the wheel. Twelve percent of cell phone users agreed that their own personal use of a cell phone had made their driving unsafe.

The poll shows that the use of cell phones while driving is a fairly common practice in America today. A little more than half of respondents own a cell phone, and, of this group, four in ten (39%) say they use a cell phone while driving either "every day" or "several times a week." Another 14% say they use them "about once a week." Approximately half of cell phone users (47%) use their phone while driving "less frequently" or "never."

The convenience of staying in touch with people while traveling is seemingly the chief benefit of talking while driving. But the majority of the public (67%) and half of cell phone users (52%) think a ban on cell phone use in their state would "not be an inconvenience to them at all." Looking just at those cell phone users who say they use their phones while driving at least once a week or more, however, shows a more negative reaction: just 31% say the passage of a law ban-

ning cell phone use in cars would not be an inconvenience to them at all.

The laws regarding the use of cellular phones have brought to bear the larger topic of distracted drivers. The Gallup Poll shows that respondents participate in a variety of activities while driving, many of which could dangerously distract them from the task of operating a motor vehicle. Very little is apparently off limits to some while driving, even eating meals and reading.

Almost one-half admits to talking on the phone while driving, up sharply from the last time Gallup measured this in 1996 (reflecting the increased prevalence of cell phones). The same percentage (49%) admits to having shouted at or made gestures to other drivers while driving, and approximately one-third has eaten a complete meal while driving (34%), read a road map while driving (33%), or slept overnight in their car (29%). Finally, 13% say they have either put on makeup or shaved with an electric razor while driving the car, and another 7% have read a book, magazine, or newspaper while at the wheel.

JULY 13
CONGRESSMAN CONDIT AND
CHANDRA LEVY

Interview Dates: 7/10–11/01
CNN/*USA Today*/Gallup Poll
Survey #GO 134222

I have a few questions about the case of Chandra Levy, the twenty-four-year-old Washington intern who disappeared more than two months ago. How closely have you been following the news concerning the investigation into the disappearance of Chandra Levy—very closely, somewhat closely, not too closely, or not at all?

Very closely	.20%
Somewhat closely	.43
Not too closely	.22
Not at all	.15

Do you think the case involving the disappearance of Chandra Levy will ever be solved, or not?

Will 51%
Will not 35
No opinion 14

Now, I have a few questions concerning Gary Condit, the California congressman who, according to some reports, had an extramarital affair with Chandra Levy. How likely do you think it is that Gary Condit was directly involved in the disappearance of Chandra Levy—very likely, somewhat likely, not too likely, or not at all likely?

Very likely 28%
Somewhat likely 37
Not too likely 13
Not at all likely 7
No opinion 15

Do you think Gary Condit should or should not take a lie detector test in this matter?

Should 83%
Should not 13
No opinion 4

If your representative from Congress were involved in a matter like this, would this make you less likely to vote for that person, or would it have no effect?

Less likely 71%
No effect 24
More likely (vol.) ....*
No opinion 5

*Less than 1%

Overall, do you feel the news media have acted responsibly or irresponsibly in this situation?

Responsibly 61%
Irresponsibly 30
No opinion 9

Suppose you had a daughter in her early twenties who asked your advice on whether

she should move to Washington, DC, to become a government intern. Would you advise her to accept the internship in Washington, or not?

Would 53%
Would not 43
No opinion 4

Analysis: Washington, DC, police completed a search of U.S. Representative Gary Condit's apartment in the continuing investigation into the disappearance of former Washington intern Chandra Levy. A week ago, Condit reportedly admitted to police that he had had an affair with the twenty-four-year-old woman, but police still maintain that this is not a criminal investigation and that Condit is not a suspect in her disappearance.

A new Gallup Poll, however, shows that more than six in ten Americans think it is likely that Condit was "directly involved" in the disappearance of Levy, including 28% who say it is "very likely." Twenty percent do not think it is likely that Condit was involved and 15% have no opinion.

Among those who say they are following the case "very closely," almost one-half (47%) thinks it is very likely that Condit was involved in Levy's disappearance, and another 30% say it is somewhat likely. Additionally, 83% think Condit should take a lie detector test in this matter, as Chandra Levy's parents and police investigators have requested.

This missing-person case has attracted nationwide attention. Sixty-three percent of Americans say they are closely following the story, including 20% who say they are following it "very closely," which ranks the story near the middle of a list of more than 90 news events Gallup has tested over the past decade. The public gives the media credit for the way they have handled coverage of the story, with 61% saying they have acted responsibly and only 30% saying they have acted irresponsibly.

At this point, a slight majority (51%) thinks the case will be solved, 35% think it will not, and the rest have no opinion. Those who are following the news about this story closely are somewhat more hopeful, with 59% saying it will be solved.

If the constituents in Condit's district are like most Americans across the country, the controversy could seriously harm his political future. The vast majority (71%) would be less likely to vote for their representative from Congress if he or she "were involved in a matter like this," with only 24% saying it would have no effect on their vote.

The Levy case, coupled with the extraordinary visibility generated by the Bill Clinton-Monica Lewinsky affair, raises the issue of whether it is advisable for young women to serve as government interns in the nation's capital. When respondents were asked in the poll whether they would advise their daughter to accept a government internship in Washington, DC, 53% said they would, but a substantial number (43%) said they would not.

JULY 16
PRESIDENT BUSH

Interview Dates: 7/10–11/01
CNN/*USA Today*/Gallup Poll
Survey #GO 134222

Do you approve or disapprove of the way George W. Bush is handling his job as president?

	Approve	Dis-approve	No opinion
2001 Jul 10–11	57%	35%	8%
2001 Jun 28–Jul 1	52	34	14
2001 Jun 11–17	55	33	12
2001 Jun 8–10	55	35	10
2001 May 18–20	56	36	8
2001 May 10–14	56	31	13
2001 May 7–9	53	33	14

Do you approve or disapprove of the way George W. Bush is handling:

Education?

Approve 63%
Disapprove 25
No opinion 12

Taxes?

Approve 60%
Disapprove 33
No opinion 7

The economy?

Approve 54%
Disapprove 36
No opinion 10

Foreign affairs?

Approve 54%
Disapprove 33
No opinion 13

Prescription drugs for older Americans?

Approve 52%
Disapprove 28
No opinion 30

Patients' bill of rights?

Approve 51%
Disapprove 28
No opinion 21

Social Security?

Approve 49%
Disapprove 35
No opinion 16

The environment?

Approve 46%
Disapprove 42
No opinion 12

Government support for faith-based organizations?

Approve 46%
Disapprove 32
No opinion 22

Energy?

Approve 45%

Disapprove 44
No opinion 11

Campaign finance reform?

Approve 37%
Disapprove 40
No opinion 23

Analysis: According to the latest Gallup Poll, the American public generally approves of President George W. Bush's performance in office, both overall and on most of the specific issues measured in the poll. The survey was conducted July 10–11, and the results give little support to recent commentary, suggesting that the president is in serious trouble with the American people.

While Bush's approval rating did fall to 52% at the end of June and has rebounded to 57% in the current poll, the basic trend has remained fairly stable since he assumed office. The June rating is the lowest Bush has received, but it was only one point lower than two of his other ratings: one at the end of March and another at the beginning of May. Overall, his ratings have fluctuated within an 11-point range (between 52% and 63%) averaging 57% since the first measurement last February, the exact level where it is now. The average job approval ratings in May and June were 55% and 54%, respectively, down slightly from averages of 59%, 58%, and 61% in February, March, and April

The poll also shows that a clear plurality, if not a majority, approves of Bush's handling of most of the issues measured, with divided feelings expressed on the rest of the issues. For the most part, these views reflect few differences from those stated in earlier polls, contributing to the picture of a president who has not gone through a major crisis with the public, but rather one who has maintained a fairly steady base of support.

Respondents express their greatest level of approval on Bush's handling of education and taxes, two issues where Bush has focused some of his most intensive legislative efforts. The tax cut has already been passed and signed into law, and the education bill appears likely to be enacted

into law sometime this summer. Bush also receives high marks for the economy and foreign affairs, suggesting that uncertain predictions about the health of the economy have not taken a toll on his support, and that the public views his overseas diplomatic efforts positively.

Americans give the president relatively high approval ratings on prescription drugs for older Americans, the patients' bill of rights, Social Security, and government support for faith-based organizations. These ratings must be viewed cautiously, however, as it is likely that most Americans are not aware of specific actions Bush has taken on these issues, and that they give him good ratings on these issues mostly because of their overall positive feelings about the president.

On three issues—the environment, energy, and campaign finance—opinion is about evenly divided between approval and disapproval. Slightly greater numbers of Americans say they approve rather than disapprove of Bush's handling of environmental issues (46% to 42%). On the other hand, slightly greater numbers say they disapprove rather than approve of Bush on campaign finance (40% to 37%). But these differences are small and within the poll's margin of error. Similarly, the public is about evenly divided on energy, with 45% approving of Bush on the issue and 44% disapproving.

JULY 17
THE PRESIDENTIAL ELECTION DISPUTE

Interview Dates: 7/10–11/01
CNN/*USA Today*/Gallup Poll
Survey #GO 134222

*Which comes closest to your view of the way George W. Bush won the 2000 presidential election: he won fair and square, he won but only on a technicality, or he stole the election?**

	Won fair and square	Won on technicality	Stole the election**
2001 Jul 10–11 . . . . . .48%		33%	17%
2001 Apr 20–22 50		29	19

2001 Jan 15–16 45	31	24
2000 Dec 15–17 48	32	18

*Based on half sample
**"No opinion" is omitted.

Thinking about the circumstances surrounding last year's presidential election, which of the following describes your view of whether President Bush is a legitimate president—I accept him as the legitimate president, I don't accept him as the legitimate president now but might in the future, or I will never accept him as the legitimate president?

Accept as legitimate president 73%
Don't accept but might in future 15
Will never accept as legitimate 11
No opinion 1

Analysis: A *New York Times* story, analyzing the postelection count of overseas absentee ballots in Florida, has stirred up another controversy over the 2000 presidential election. A recent Gallup Poll, however, finds most Americans satisfied that George W. Bush is the "legitimate" president, and only 17% believe he "stole" the election. The poll, conducted July 10–11 (prior to the *Times* story), shows that almost one-half (48%) feels Bush won the election "fair and square" while one-third says he won, but only on a technicality. While seven out of ten accept Bush as president, 15% do not accept Bush as the legitimate president now, but might in the future, and 11% will never accept Bush as the legitimate president.

Gallup has asked Americans about the nature of Bush's victory since December 2000, when Bush was finally declared the winner of the presidential race. Results have been roughly similar since this question was first asked. Almost one-half of the public says Bush won the election fairly. The percentage of Americans who say Bush stole the election has also remained essentially the same, except on the eve of his inauguration in January, when the percentage of those who felt Bush stole the election increased slightly.

JULY 17
PRESIDENT BUSH

Interview Dates: 7/10–11/01
CNN/*USA Today*/Gallup Poll
Survey #GO 134222

Apart from whether you approve or disapprove of the way George W. Bush is handling his job as president, what do you think of Bush as a person—would you say you approve or disapprove of him?

Approve 70%
Disapprove 25
No opinion 5

Thinking about each of the following characteristics and qualities, please say whether you think it applies or doesn't apply to George W. Bush:

Is tough enough for the job?

Applies 69%
Doesn't apply 28
No opinion 3

Is honest and trustworthy?

Applies 66%
Doesn't apply 31
No opinion 3

Is a strong and decisive leader?

Applies 57%
Doesn't apply 40
No opinion 3

Cares about the needs of people like you?

Applies 57%
Doesn't apply 40
No opinion 3

Shares your values?

Applies 56%

Doesn't apply 40
No opinion 4

Would you say President Bush is in touch or out of touch with the problems ordinary Americans face in their daily lives?

In touch 47%
Out of touch 50
No opinion 3

Which of the following are most important to you when you decide whether the president is doing a good job—where he stands on issues that matter to you, or the leadership skills and vision you think he has as president?

Stance on issues 40%
Leadership skills, vision 48
Both; equally (vol.) 9
No opinion 3

Do you think big business does, or does not, have too much influence over the decisions made by the Bush administration?

Yes, does 67%
No, does not 26
No opinion 7

Regardless of how you feel about his political views, would you say you respect President Bush, or don't you feel that way?

Yes, respect him 78%
No 20
No opinion 2

How would you rate the job President Bush has done so far in explaining his policies and plans for the future to the American people—very good, good, poor, or very poor?

Very good 14%
Good 57
Poor 21

Very poor 6
No opinion 2

Analysis: The American public has a generally positive impression of President George W. Bush, according to the latest Gallup Poll. Almost eight in ten say that, regardless of how they feel about his political views, they respect Bush; seven in ten approve of him as a person; and substantial majorities give him positive ratings on several personal characteristics measured in the poll. The ratings on these characteristics have changed very little since Bush was inaugurated six months ago. In addition, most say Bush is doing a good job in explaining his policies to the American people. On the downside, about half say the president is out of touch with the problems faced by ordinary Americans, and two-thirds say big business has too much influence over the decisions made by his administration.

The July 10–11 poll shows that 57% of Americans approve of the way Bush is handling his job as president, but an even larger number (70%) approve of him as a person. This is 5 points higher than it was last February, shortly after his inauguration, and 10 points higher than what he received in January before he took office.

President Bush also fares quite well on five personal characteristics measured in the current poll. Most respondents say Bush is tough enough for the job (69%), is honest and trustworthy (66%), is a strong and decisive leader (57%), "cares about the needs of people like you" (57%), and "shares your values" (56%). There are only minor differences in these ratings from what Bush received in February, shortly after he took office.

The poll shows that most Americans (78%) respect President Bush, and 71% say he is doing a good job in explaining his policies and plans for the future to the American people. Only 20% say they do not respect the president, and just 27% say he is doing a poor job in explaining his policies to the public.

While the poll shows a public that is mostly positive about the president, it finds that two-thirds think big business has too much influence over the decisions made by the Bush administration. Also, the public is about evenly divided over whether Bush is out of touch with the problems ordinary Americans face in their daily lives: 50% say he is, but 47% disagree.

JULY 18
IMMIGRATION

Interview Dates: 6/11–17/01
Gallup Poll News Service
Survey #GO 132073

Thinking about immigrants, that is, people who come from other countries to live here in the United States, in your view should immigration be kept at its present level, increased, or decreased?

	Present level	In- creased	De- creased*
National Adults 42%	14%	41%
Men 41	15	41
Women 43	12	42
Whites 42	10	45
Blacks 42	24	31
Hispanics 38	33	25

*"No opinion" is omitted.

On the whole, do you think immigration is a good thing or a bad thing for this country today?

	Good thing	Bad thing	Mixed (vol.)*
National Adults 62%	31%	5%
Men 68	28	2
Women 57	33	7
Whites 62	32	4
Blacks 61	28	7
Hispanics 73	18	2

*"No opinion" is omitted.

On the whole, do you think immigration has been a good thing or a bad thing for the United States in the past?

	Good thing	Bad thing	Mixed (vol.)*
National Adults 75%	19%	4%

Men 81	15	3
Women 69	23	5
Whites 75	19	4
Blacks 63	27	7
Hispanics 75	17	2

*"No opinion" is omitted.

Which do you think is better for the United States—to encourage immigrants to blend into American culture by giving up some important aspects of their own culture, or to encourage immigrants to maintain their own culture more strongly, even if that means they do not blend in as well?

	Blend in	Maintain culture	Both equally (vol.)*
National Adults 58%	34%	5%
Men 59	34	4
Women 57	34	5
Whites 61	31	5
Blacks 48	43	4
Hispanics 45	49	2

*"No opinion" is omitted.

For each of the following areas, please say whether immigrants to the United States are making the situation in the country better or worse, or not having much effect:

The overall quality of life?

	Better	Worse	Not having much effect*
National Adults 30%	24%	41%
Men 35	19	41
Women 26	28	41
Whites 28	27	41
Blacks 27	25	44
Hispanics 58	10	27

*"No opinion" is omitted.

The quality of public schools?

	Better	Worse	Not having much effect*
National Adults	18%	40%	37%
Men	19	38	38
Women	17	42	35
Whites	16	43	36
Blacks	20	36	40
Hispanics	48	22	24

*"No opinion" is omitted.

The crime situation?

	Better	Worse	Not having much effect*
National Adults	7%	50%	38%
Men	8	48	39
Women	6	52	37
Whites	5	54	37
Blacks	9	44	41
Hispanics	12	47	33

*"No opinion" is omitted.

Job opportunities for you and your family?

	Better	Worse	Not having much effect*
National Adults	15%	31%	50%
Men	17	29	49
Women	13	34	51
Whites	12	32	53
Blacks	20	38	41
Hispanics	42	18	37

*"No opinion" is omitted.

Food, music, and the arts?

	Better	Worse	Not having much effect*
National Adults	58%	8%	29%
Men	63	6	25
Women	55	9	32
Whites	59	8	28
Blacks	54	10	33
Hispanics	72	3	23

*"No opinion" is omitted.

The economy in general?

	Better	Worse	Not having much effect*
National Adults	32%	32%	31%
Men	38	26	32
Women	26	38	30
Whites	29	34	32
Blacks	27	39	31
Hispanics	42	23	29

*"No opinion" is omitted.

Taxes?

	Better	Worse	Not having much effect*
National Adults	12%	46%	34%
Men	16	41	35
Women	9	51	32
Whites	10	48	34
Blacks	12	50	32
Hispanics	40	26	25

*"No opinion" is omitted.

Politics and government?

	Better	Worse	Not having much effect*
National Adults	23%	24%	47%
Men	24	22	48
Women	21	26	47
Whites	20	26	48
Blacks	23	27	43
Hispanics	42	16	32

*"No opinion" is omitted.

Social and moral values?

	Better	Worse	Not having much effect*
National Adults	25%	26%	45%
Men	26	24	47
Women	23	27	44
Whites	22	29	45
Blacks	26	20	50
Hispanics	45	17	34

*"No opinion" is omitted.

Analysis: The White House is considering several new proposals on immigration. One that has drawn considerable attention would grant permanent legal resident status to some three million Mexicans who immigrated to the United States illegally. A recent Gallup Poll shows that most Americans believe immigration is good for the country in general but can cite few specific areas in which immigration makes the country better. Additionally, the public is more likely to say that immigration levels in this country should be decreased or kept at their present level, rather than being increased. Hispanics living in the U.S. express more positive views on immigration than do blacks or whites, but even among Hispanics only 33% believe immigration levels should be increased.

According to the poll conducted June 11–17, and including larger samples of blacks and Hispanics, 62% of Americans think that immigration is a good thing for this country while 31% think it is a bad thing. Hispanics are more inclined to say immigration is good for the country (73%) than are blacks (61%) or whites (62%).

Respondents are even more positive about immigration when contemplating the past. Seventy-five percent say immigration has been a good thing for the U.S. in the past and less than one in five thinks it has been a bad thing. In this regard, whites are as positive about immigration as are Hispanics while blacks are much less so.

Despite these positive general assessments, Americans are fairly critical about the effect immigration has had on the country in several areas. Among nine areas tested, on only one—food,

music, and the arts—do a majority say that immigration has made the situation better. In every other area, more say that immigration has made the situation worse rather than better, although a significant number also say that immigration has had no effect. The perception of a negative impact is strongest with respect to crime, the quality of public schools, taxes, and job opportunities. Americans are more divided on immigration's effect on the economy, politics, and government, and on social and moral values.

In stark contrast to whites and blacks, Hispanics think immigration has improved the situation in the U.S. in all areas except crime, and in general are much more positive in their assessment of immigration than are blacks and whites. Whites and blacks generally see things similarly, but whites are slightly more critical of the effects of immigration on crime, public schools, and social and moral values. Blacks think immigration has had a positive influence on social and moral values. Blacks, however, are more likely to see immigration as having a negative effect on the economy.

Ironically, despite the credit Americans give to immigrants for their cultural contributions, a majority (58%) feels immigrants should be encouraged to blend into American culture rather than maintain their own culture. Opinion on this matter varies by racial and ethnic group. Whites are most in favor of immigrants blending into American culture by a 61%-to-31% margin. Blacks are more likely to believe that immigrants should maintain their own culture, but still a plurality say that immigrants should adopt American culture (48% to 43%). Among Hispanics, however, more believe that immigrants should maintain their own culture (49%) than blend into American culture (45%).

The poll also shows a division in sentiment about immigration levels. Forty-two percent believe immigration should be kept at its present level and 41% favor a decrease. Only 14% say it should be increased. There has been little change in this sentiment in recent years, but in the mid-1990s, a majority of respondents preferred decreases in immigration levels. In 1993 and 1995, about two-thirds of the public, substantially more than the current 41%, wanted immigration decreased.

Hispanics are most likely to say that immigration levels should be increased (33%), but a plurality of Hispanics (38%) believes that the current level should be maintained, and one in four Hispanics thinks immigration levels should be decreased (25%). Among blacks, a plurality (42%) thinks that immigration levels should be kept as they are, while 31% think they should be decreased and 24% think they should be increased. A slight plurality of whites (45%) says that immigration levels should be decreased, while 42% think they should be kept at their current level and only 10% think they should be increased.

JULY 20
STEM CELL RESEARCH

Interview Dates: 7/10–11/01
CNN/*USA Today*/Gallup Poll
Survey #GO 134222

As you may know, the federal government is considering whether to fund certain kinds of medical research known as "stem cell research." How closely have you followed the debate about government funding of stem cell research—very closely, somewhat closely, not too closely, or not closely at all?

Very closely 9%
Somewhat closely .29
Not too closely 28
Not closely at all .32
No opinion 2

Do you think the federal government should or should not fund this type of research, or don't you know enough to say?

Should 30%
Should not 13
Don't know enough to say 57

The kind of stem-cell research the government is considering involves human embryos that have been created in medical clinics by fertilizing a woman's egg outside the womb.

An embryo may be implanted into a woman's womb to develop into a baby. If an embryo is not implanted into a woman's womb to develop into a baby, it may be destroyed, either by being discarded or by being used for medical research. Some scientists believe this type of medical research could lead to treatments for diseases such as Alzheimer's, diabetes, heart disease, and spinal cord injuries. Given this information, do you think the federal government should or should not fund this type of research?

Should 54%
Should not 39
No opinion 7

Which comes closest to your view of this kind of stem cell research—it is morally wrong and is unnecessary, it is morally wrong but may be necessary, it is not morally wrong and may be necessary, or it is not morally wrong but is unnecessary?

Morally wrong, unnecessary 20%
Morally wrong, may be necessary 34
Not morally wrong, may be necessary 35
Not morally wrong, unnecessary 4
No opinion 7

For each of the following, please tell me if it is very important, somewhat important, not too important, or not at all important to you personally:

Medical researchers finding cures for diseases such as Alzheimer's, diabetes, heart disease, and spinal cord injury?

Very important 82%
Somewhat important 16
Not too important 1
Not at all important 1
No opinion . . . .*

*Less than 1%

Preventing human embryos from being used in medical research?

Very important 30%
Somewhat important 29
Not too important 20
Not at all important 16
No opinion 5

One of the issues involved in this type of research is whether or not the embryos used were developed specifically for stem cell research. Do you think the federal government should or should not allow scientists to fertilize human eggs specifically for the purpose of creating new stem cells?

Should 38%
Should not 54
No opinion 8

At least one other country currently allows scientists to create human embryos specifically for stem cell research. How concerned are you that other countries will gain a competitive advantage over the United States if the government does not allow U.S. scientists to do the same—are you very concerned, somewhat concerned, not too concerned, or not at all concerned?

Very concerned 12%
Somewhat concerned 21
Not too concerned .33
Not at all concerned 33
No opinion 1

Analysis: President Bush is reported to be weighing conflicting advice about federal funding of embryonic stem cell research, and the pope will most likely lobby him on the subject when the two meet in Europe next week. This is one area about which the president will find little immediate guidance from the American public, however. The reason is that most Americans tell Gallup they are not following the issue closely and do not know enough about the facts involved to render an opinion.

The issue before Bush is whether the federal government should fund medical research using cells obtained from human embryos in the first few days after fertilization (often obtained from fertility clinics); it is controversial because the embryos are destroyed in the process. As a presidential candidate, Bush committed to eliminating this funding, but pressure on him to reverse that stance has been building, most recently from a report issued by the National Institutes of Health (NIH).

Only 38% of Americans, according to a July 10–11 Gallup Poll, are following the stem cell research issue very or somewhat closely. As a result, a clear majority (57%) says they "don't know enough to say" when asked whether the federal government should fund the particular kind of stem cell research being debated. Of the remainder, 30% say the government should fund it while 13% disagree.

While respondents admit to being unfamiliar with the issue, they do have opinions about some aspects of the stem cell debate. The new poll asks for their personal reaction to the importance of two key issues at stake, and suggests that the critics of the use of embryos in this research could face an uphill battle in convincing the public to embrace their position.

The overwhelming majority says that finding cures or medical treatments for Alzheimer's, diabetes, heart disease, and spinal cord injury is very important: 82% feel this way, and another 16% say it is somewhat important. At the same time, only 30% consider it very important to prevent human embryos from being used in medical research. Another 29% say this is somewhat important, but more than one-third (36%) says this concern is not important to them. Critics of embryonic stem cell research say it is immoral because it destroys human life, and they argue that there are alternative uses for the embryos.

A different question in the new poll suggests that Americans' desire to see diseases cured may take precedence over their moral concerns about stem cell research. When they are asked which of four positions comes closest to their own, a majority (54%) indicates that embryonic stem cell research is morally wrong. Nevertheless, 69% indicate the research may be necessary. Specifically, only 20% believe the research is morally wrong and unnecessary, a position held by many critics of the research, who believe that stem cells obtained from umbilical cords or adults may lead to the same cures. Another 34% also believe the research is morally wrong, but say it may be necessary. About one-third (35%) is in agreement with most proponents of the research, saying it may be necessary and is not morally wrong. Only 4% hold the view that the research is neither necessary nor morally wrong.

The new NIH report cites two major bases for its support of embryonic stem cell research: that adult stem cells are not as useful as are embryonic stem cells, and that a large number of embryonic stem cells can be generated in the laboratory. The current poll suggests that while the public may be persuaded by the first argument—that stem cells obtained from embryos may be uniquely valuable for this research—the second argument is more controversial. Gallup finds a majority of Americans (54%) opposed to the fertilization of human eggs specifically for the purpose of generating stem cells. Only 38% are in favor.

Another argument that does not appear to have much currency with the public is that if this country does not allow the creation of human embryos specifically for research, others will. Only one-third says they are concerned that other countries will gain a competitive advantage over the U.S. if the government does not allow embryos to be created specifically for research. Sixty-six percent say they are "not too" or "not at all concerned" about this.

If Americans do pay more attention to the embryonic stem cell research issue in the future, it is possible these arguments will suppress their support for it. However, as of today, the subset of those who are closely following the issue support it by a wide margin: 55% of the currently attentive group favor it and just 24% are opposed.

JULY 23
THE INTERNET AND E-MAIL

Interview Dates: 6/14–25/01
Gallup Poll News Service
Survey #GO 133802

On average, how many hours per week do you use the Internet?

Less than 1 hour 2%
1 to 2 hours 8
3 to 4 hours 13
5 to 6 hours 17
7 to 8 hours 12
9 to 10 hours 11
11 to 15 hours 12
16 to 20 hours 12
21 to 30 hours 5
31 to 40 hours 3
40 hours or more 5

Which of the following activities do you do most when you are online?

Send and read e-mail 52%
Send and read Instant Messages 2
Search the Internet for information
  on topics that interest you 32
Make transactions such as buying
  products, paying bills, or checking
  financial accounts 4
Other 10

Would you say the Internet has generally made your life better or worse?

Better 96%
Worse 2
No answer 2

Thinking about e-mail, do you use e-mail at home?

Yes 90%
No 10

Asked of full or part time employed adults: Do you use e-mail at work?

Yes 83%
No 16
No answer 1

How many separate e-mail addresses do you personally have for sending and receiving e-mail messages, including those for personal and business use?

One 23%
Two 33
Three 14
Four 7
Five or more 22
No answer 1

Mean 7.5
Median 2

Would you say e-mail has generally made your life better or worse?

Better 97%
Worse 2
No answer 1

What percentage of the e-mail you receive each week is "spam," or unsolicited bulk e-mail that promotes a product or service?

10% or less 30%
11 to 20% 16
21 to 30% 15
31 to 40% 11
41 to 50% 10
51 to 60% 6
61 to 70% 4
71 to 80% 5
81 to 90% 2
91 to 100% 1
No answer . . . .*

*Less than 1%

Would you say you hate spam, find spam an annoyance but do not hate it, have no strong feelings either way about spam, sometimes find the information in spam interesting and useful, or really like to receive spam?

Hate spam 42%
Find spam an annoyance but do not
  hate it 45
Have no strong feelings 9

Sometimes find information in spam
  interesting and useful 4
Really like to receive spam 0
No answer . . . .*

*Less than 1%

Which of the following do you find more annoying—"spam," or unsolicited e-mail promoting a product or service; or Internet "pop-up" ads that promote a product or service and appear when you visit certain Web pages?

Spam 34%
Internet "pop-up" ads 65
No answer 1

How has your use of e-mail affected your use of the telephone?

Now use the phone a great deal less 18%
Now use the phone somewhat less 34
Now use the phone a little bit less 16
No decrease in use of the phone 32

How has your use of e-mail affected your use of the U.S. mail provided by the Postal Service?

Now use U.S. mail a great deal less 19%
Now use U.S. mail somewhat less 28
Now use U.S. mail a little bit less 19
No decrease in use of U.S. mail 34

From the list below, please indicate the method of communication you would be least willing to sacrifice if you had to stop using one.

Telephone 63%
E-mail 12
Mobile or cellular phone 10
U.S. mail 15

From the list below, please indicate the method of communication you would be most willing to sacrifice if you had to stop using one.

Telephone 7%
E-mail 16
Mobile or cellular phone 55
U.S. mail 21
No answer 1

Asked of adults who use e-mail at work: How often do you check your e-mail when you are at work?

All the time, continuously 32%
At least once per hour 19
A couple of times a day 33
About once a day 11
A couple of times a week 3
About once a week 0
Less than once a week 2
No answer ....*

*Less than 1%

Asked of adults who use e-mail at work: How many e-mails would you say you receive at work each day?

5 or less 27%
6 to 10 19
11 to 15 13
16 to 20 10
21 to 30 12
31 to 40 2
41 to 50 8
More than 50 6
No answer 3

Mean   23.8
Median 12

Also asked of adults who use e-mail at work: How many e-mails would you say you send at work each day?

5 or less 48%
6 to 10 16
11 to 15 11

16 to 20 5
21 to 30 8
31 to 40 4
41 to 50 2
More than 50 2
No answer 4

Mean   12.8
Median 6

Asked of adults who use e-mail at home: How often do you check your e-mail when you are at home?

All the time, continuously 3%
At least once per hour 3
A couple of times a day 30
About once a day 41
A couple of times a week 16
About once a week 5
Less than once a week 1
No answer 1

Also asked of adults who use e-mail at home: How many e-mails would you say you receive at home each day?

5 or less 42%
6 to 10 28
11 to 15 10
16 to 20 9
21 to 30 6
31 to 40 1
41 to 50 2
More than 50 2
No answer ....*

*Less than 1%

Mean   11.4
Median 8

Also asked of adults who use e-mail at home: How many e-mails would you say you send at home each day?

5 or less 79%
6 to 10 7
11 to 15 2

```
16 to 20  . . . . . . . . . . . . . . . . . . . . . . . . . . .1
21 to 30  . . . . . . . . . . . . . . . . . . . . . . . . . . .1
31 to 40  . . . . . . . . . . . . . . . . . . . . . . . . . . .0
41 to 50  . . . . . . . . . . . . . . . . . . . . . . . . . . .*
More than 50  . . . . . . . . . . . . . . . . . . . . . . .0
No answer  . . . . . . . . . . . . . . . . . . . . . . . . .10
```

Mean 4.0
Median 3

Who would you say is the one person you e-mail most often, either at home or at work?

```
Spouse or significant other  . . . . . . . . . . . . . .6%
Brother or sister  . . . . . . . . . . . . . . . . . . . . . . .9
Mother or father . . . . . . . . . . . . . . . . . . . . . . .5
Your own child  . . . . . . . . . . . . . . . . . . . . . . .9
Another relative such as an aunt, uncle,
    grandparent, or cousin . . . . . . . . . . . . . . . .4
Friend . . . . . . . . . . . . . . . . . . . . . . . . . . . . . .28
Coworker, business associate, professional
    associate, client . . . . . . . . . . . . . . . . . . . . .39
No answer  . . . . . . . . . . . . . . . . . . . . . . . . . . .0
```

Which of the following best describes your use of Instant Messages, or IMs?

```
Use every time I am online  . . . . . . . . . . . . . . .3%
Use frequently, but not every time  . . . . . . . .8
Use occasionally  . . . . . . . . . . . . . . . . . . . . . .31
Never use IMs when I am online . . . . . . . . .58
No answer  . . . . . . . . . . . . . . . . . . . . . . . . . . .*
```

*Less than 1%

Analysis: A recent Gallup Poll of e-mail users finds that more than nine in ten say that both e-mail (97%) and the Internet (96%) have made their lives better. The typical e-mail user is on the Internet seven to eight hours each week, and 37% indicate they use it more than ten hours per week. Sending and reading e-mail is the most common activity for people when online, much more so than searching for information, paying bills, or using Instant Messages (IMs). Nine in ten use e-mail at home, and more than eight in ten say they use it at work. While a majority of e-mail users say they use the telephone and U.S. mail less often now, most are not willing to sacrifice these older methods of communication just yet.

The poll, conducted by means of the Internet June 14–25, included respondents who had e-mail addresses and were part of random samples of national adults in earlier Gallup telephone polls. The results show a wide range in the amount of time e-mail users spend online. Many spend fewer than five hours per week on the Internet, but about one in eight spends twenty hours or more online. A typical e-mail user spends seven to eight hours online (half spend more time online and half spend less).

A majority (52%) of e-mail users says that sending and receiving e-mail is their most common online activity. Thirty-two percent spend most of their time online searching the Internet for information on topics that interest them. Very few make financial transactions such as buying products, paying bills, and checking financial accounts (4%), or send and receive Instant Messages (2%) more often than they send e-mail or search for information.

Ninety percent of e-mail users say they use e-mail at home and 83% at work. Fifty-three percent use e-mail at both places, and, not surprisingly, most have more than one e-mail address (23% have only one). In fact, 33% have two e-mail addresses, 14% have three, 7% have four, and 22% have five or more.

E-mail use differs between home and work. Those who use it at work check it much more often and send and receive many more e-mails. A majority (51%) of those who use e-mail at work checks it at least once an hour, including 32% who say they check it "continuously." An additional 33% say they check e-mail at work a couple of times a day, and 11% check it about once a day. Only 5% check it less often than once a day. At home, only 6% say they check e-mail at least once an hour, including just 3% who check it continuously. Most people check their e-mail at home either a couple of times a day (30%) or about once a day (41%), but 22% check it less often.

The typical e-mail user receives twelve e-mails at work each day, and 28% receive twenty or more e-mails at work each day. Sending e-mail is less common, as the typical user sends just six e-mails at work each day, and just 16% send twenty or more messages per day.

At home, a typical e-mail user will receive just eight messages each day and send three. Only 11% say they receive more than twenty e-mail messages each day at home, and only 1% send that many from home. Because e-mails are sent and received more frequently at work, it is not surprising that respondents cite coworkers and business associates as the people they e-mail most often (39%). Thirty-three percent e-mail family members most often, and 28% indicate that they e-mail friends more frequently.

E-mail has given people another way to communicate with friends, family, and coworkers, one that is generally cheaper or faster than more established means of communication. A majority of e-mail users say they now use the telephone and U.S. mail less often, and about one in five indicates they use the telephone and U.S. mail "a great deal less." Just one in three e-mail users say that e-mail has not decreased their use of the telephone or the U.S. mail.

Despite the fact that e-mail messages are frequently used as alternatives to telephone calls or postal mail, most e-mail users do not see it as indispensable. When asked which of four communication modes they would be least willing to sacrifice, e-mail users say they are least willing to do without the telephone (63%). U.S. mail trails at 15%, followed by e-mail (12%) and cellular phones (10%).

Even though most would keep their telephone if they had to choose, e-mail users are in no rush to get rid of their e-mail. Of these four methods of communication, e-mail users are most willing to sacrifice cellular phones (55%), followed by U.S. mail (21%), e-mail (16%), and the telephone (7%).

The widespread use of e-mail has led to the rise of "spam," or unsolicited bulk e-mail that promotes products or services. Most e-mail users say that three out of every ten e-mail messages they receive are spam, and 39% say they receive more than that, including 18% who say that at least half their e-mail is spam. When asked their opinion on spam, 42% of e-mail users say they "hate it," 45% say they find it "an annoyance, but do not hate it," while the rest have no strong feelings either way (9%), or sometimes find the information contained in spam useful (4%).

While spam is a bother to most e-mail users, Internet pop-up ads are apparently worse. Asked which they find more annoying, by a 65%-to-34% margin, e-mail users choose pop-up ads. All subcategories of e-mail users show roughly equal disdain for Internet pop-up ads.

JULY 24
INCOME TAX REBATE

Interview Dates: 7/10–11/01 and 7/19–22/01
CNN/*USA Today*/Gallup Poll and
  Gallup Poll News Service
Surveys #GO 134222 and 132074

If you receive a tax rebate, what will you do with that money—spend it, save or invest it, pay off bills, or donate it to charity?

Spend it 17%
Save, invest it 32
Pay off bills 47
Donate to charity 2
No opinion 2

Do you approve or disapprove of the way George W. Bush is handling taxes?

	Approve	Dis-approve	No opinion
2001 Jul 10–11	60%	33%	7%
2001 Apr 20–22*	54	39	7
2001 Mar 9–11	56	35	9

*Based on half sample

*As you may know, Congress passed and President Bush signed a law that would cut tax rates over the next ten years. As part of the law, most taxpayers will receive a rebate check of $300 to $600 from the federal government in the next few months. How much of a difference will this tax rebate check make to you and your family—a big difference, some difference, only a little difference, or no difference at all?**

Big difference 11%

Some difference 21
Only a little difference 30
No difference 33
Won't receive a rebate (vol.) 4
No opinion 1

*Based on half sample

Do you think that the new tax cut law will be a good thing for the country, will not make much difference, or will be a bad thing for the country? *

Good thing 40%
Not much difference 39
Bad thing 18
No opinion 3

*Based on half sample

Analysis: One of the arguments many legislators made as they considered the $300 to $600 tax rebate, which the federal government will send to most Americans beginning this week, was that the money would help stimulate the economy. That may happen, of course, but a Gallup Poll conducted July 10–11 suggests that the stimulus may not be as great as economists might prefer.

Ideally, to stimulate the economy, most Americans would spend the money for new purchases, but the poll shows that just 17% expect to do that with their rebates, at least directly. Another 47% say they will pay off bills, while 32% expect to save or invest it. Two percent say they expect to give their rebate to charity. It is possible that by virtue of having paid off bills or invested the money, respondents will feel freer to spend other money on consumer products or services, but the poll's results provide no evidence for that possibility.

A new Gallup Poll conducted July 19–22 shows that Americans are somewhat ambivalent about the impact of the tax cut on the country, with four in ten thinking it will be a good thing, another four in ten saying it will make no difference, and two in ten saying it will be a bad thing. That poll also finds that only 11% think the $300 to $600 rebate will make a big difference to them and their families while 21% say it will make "some" difference. A clear majority (63%) says it will make lit-

tle or no difference to them (30% only a little difference, and another 33% no difference).

Despite these views about the potential benefits of the tax cut to the country and to individuals, the July 10–11 poll shows that six in ten approve of the way Bush has been handling the tax issue. The percentage is up 6 points from last April, before the tax cut bill became law.

JULY 25
PRESIDENT BUSH

Interview Dates: 7/19–22/01
Gallup Poll News Service
Survey #GO 132074

Do you approve or disapprove of the way George W. Bush is handling his job as president?

	Approve	Dis-approve	No opinion
2001 Jul 19–22	56%	33%	11%
2001 Jul 10–11	57	35	8
2001 Jun 28–Jul 1	52	34	14
2001 Jun 11–17	55	33	12
2001 Jun 8–10	55	35	10
2001 May 18–20	56	36	8
2001 May 10–14	56	31	13
2001 May 7–9	53	33	14

Do you think George W. Bush does a good job representing America to the world, or not? *

	Yes	No	No opinion
2001 Jul 19–22	58%	36%	6%
2001 Jun 8–10	56	39	5

*Based on part sample

Do you think leaders of other countries around the world have respect for George W. Bush, or do you think they don't have much respect for him? *

	Respect him	Don't respect him	No opinion
2001 Jul 19–22	45%	47%	8%
2001 Jun 8–10	40	46	14

2001 Feb 1–4 49   38   13

*Based on part sample

*As you may know, George W. Bush has decided that the United States should withdraw its support from the global warming agreement adopted in Kyoto, Japan, in 1997. Do you approve or disapprove of this decision?**

Approve 32%
Disapprove 51
No opinion 17

*Based on part sample

*Recently, there has been some discussion about the possibility of the United States building a defense system against nuclear missiles. Do you think the government should or should not spend the money that would be required for research and possible development of such a system, or are you unsure?**

Should 41%
Should not 28
Unsure 31

*Based on part sample

Analysis: President Bush concluded his week-long trip to Europe, which included meetings with other national leaders and a visit with Pope John Paul II. As he returns to the U.S., a new Gallup Poll shows that 56% of Americans approve of the job he is doing as president, a number similar to his previous ratings. In general, respondents say Bush does a good job representing America to the world, but the public is divided in its thinking on whether foreign leaders respect Bush. Bush used the trip to discuss global warming and missile defense with leaders of other developed nations, and to discuss stem cell research with Pope John Paul II. Gallup Poll results show that a majority disapproves of the Bush administration's decision to withdraw its support from the multinational global warming treaty agreed to in 1997 at Kyoto, Japan. A majority does not have an opinion on stem cell research, but among those who express an opinion,

more favor it than oppose it. Similarly, many Americans do not have a firm opinion on missile defense, but 41% favor spending the money necessary to build one. The latest poll, conducted July 19–22 while Bush was in Europe, shows no change in Bush's overall job approval rating. Currently, 56% approve of the job he is doing as president, while 33% disapprove and 11% have no opinion. Bush's approval rating has ranged between 52% and 57% since the beginning of May, following his high point of 62% in April during the spy plane incident with China.

A majority of Americans (58%) says Bush does a good job representing America to the world while 36% think he does not. Despite the fact that most Americans feel Bush represents the country well, the public is divided as to whether they believe foreign leaders respect Bush: 45% think they do and 47% say they do not. Gallup measured this sentiment on two previous occasions, with differing results, suggesting the public does not have very firm opinions on this matter. In February, at the beginning of his presidency, 49% thought foreign leaders respected Bush, 38% did not, and 13% had no opinion. By June, opinion had shifted: only 40% thought foreign leaders respected Bush and a plurality (46%) thought Bush was not respected.

Bush used the European meetings as an opportunity to promote his plan for a missile defense shield for the U.S., a proposal many foreign leaders, especially Russian President Vladimir Putin, oppose. The latest Gallup Poll shows that 41% of respondents believe the U.S. should spend the resources necessary to develop a missile defense system, 28% think it should not, and 31% are unsure. Opinion on this issue has not changed much from earlier this year, even though the system tested successfully this month.

One of the more publicized stops on Bush's trip was a meeting with Pope John Paul II. The pope discussed his opposition to stem cell research with the president. Bush will soon have to decide whether the government will fund certain types of stem cell research, a controversial decision he has struggled to make. A recent Gallup Poll suggests that Bush will receive little guidance on this decision from the American people, as a majority (57%) does not have an opinion on government funding of stem cell research. Thirty percent say they favor government funding of stem cell research, and 13% are opposed.

JULY 25
SECONDHAND SMOKE

Interview Dates: 7/19–22/01
Gallup Poll News Service
Survey #GO 132074

In general, how harmful do you feel second-hand smoke is to adults—very harmful, somewhat harmful, not too harmful, or not at all harmful?

Very, somewhat harmful 85%
Not too, not at all harmful 14
It depends (vol.); no opinion 1

What is your opinion regarding smoking in public places—should they set aside certain areas, should they totally ban smoking, or should there be no restrictions on smoking in:

Hotels and motels?

Set aside areas 66%
Totally ban 27
No restrictions; no opinion 7

Workplaces?

Set aside areas 58%
Totally ban 38
No restrictions; no opinion 4

Restaurants?

Set aside areas 52%
Totally ban 44
No restrictions; no opinion 4

Analysis: A study published by the Journal of the American Medical Association indicates that nonsmokers exposed to secondhand cigarette smoke may be at risk for circulatory problems. The study has renewed debate over the allowance of smoking in public places such as restaurants,

bars, and workplaces. A new Gallup Poll on this topic shows that roughly one-half of the American public (52%) believes secondhand cigarette smoke is "very harmful." This percentage is up significantly from when the question was first asked in 1994. At that time, 36% believed secondhand smoke was very harmful. The current numbers are actually a few points lower than the high point in 1997 when 55% said secondhand smoke was very harmful.

When it comes to smoking in public places, Americans favor setting aside places rather than an absolute ban. For hotels, 66% say they would prefer that areas be set aside for smoking, while just 27% say they want a total ban. For work-places, setting areas aside is favored over a ban (58% to 38%). The narrowest gap in public preference is recorded for restaurants, in which 52% favor setting aside areas for smoking while 44% say a total ban is in order. In all three situations, the percentage of Americans favoring a total ban has increased substantially since 1987, when Gallup first asked about the issue.

JULY 26
ECONOMIC CONDITIONS/
PERSONAL FINANCES

Interview Dates: 7/19–22/01
Gallup Poll News Service
Survey #GO 132074

How would you rate economic conditions in this country today—excellent, good, only fair, or poor?

	Excellent, good	Only fair	Poor*
2001 Jul 19–22	41%	47%	11%
2001 Jun 11–17	42	45	12
2001 May 10–14	40	45	15
2001 Apr 6–8	45	41	14
2001 Mar 5–7	46	43	10
2001 Feb 1–4	51	36	13
2001 Jan 10–14	67	27	6

*"No opinion" is omitted.

Right now, do you think that economic conditions in the country as a whole are getting better or getting worse?

	Getting better	Getting worse	Same (vol.)*
2001 Jul 19–22	.35%	53%	9%
2001 Jun 11–17	.29	60	8
2001 May 10–14	.25	63	9
2001 Apr 6–8	.24	63	9
2001 Mar 5–7	.28	61	7
2001 Feb 1–4	.23	66	8
2001 Jan 10–14	.32	56	8

*"No opinion" is omitted.

Next, we are interested in how people's financial situation may have changed. Would you say that you are financially better off now than you were a year ago, or are you financially worse off now?

	Better off	Worse off	Same (vol.)*
2001 Jul 19–22	.39%	36%	25%
2001 Jun 11–17	.42	37	20
2001 Apr 6–8	.42	36	22
2001 Feb 1–4	.46	30	23
2001 Jan 10–14	.49	30	21

*"No opinion" is omitted.

Looking ahead, do you expect that at this time next year you will be financially better off than now, or worse off than now?

	Better off	Worse off	Same (vol.)*
2001 Jul 19–22	.64%	18%	13%
2001 Jun 11–17	.62	22	11
2001 Apr 6–8	.62	18	15
2001 Feb 1–4	.61	19	16
2001 Jan 10–14	.63	21	13

*"No opinion" is omitted.

Analysis: The latest Gallup Poll offers some indication that the American public's mediocre assessment of the nation's economy may be on the mend. Of Gallup's two key ratings of the economy—how Americans rate current economic conditions and whether they think it is getting better or getting worse—the latter has shown small but steady improvement over the past two months.

Thirty-five percent of the nation's adults, according to Gallup's July 19–22 telephone survey, now believe the economy is getting better, up from 29% in mid-June and from 25% in mid-May. Over the same three months, perceptions of economic conditions have remained flat, with 40% to 42% saying the economy is in excellent or good shape, and 57% to 60% characterizing it as only fair or poor.

The recent improvement in Americans' economic outlook is notable because a slump in the rating earlier this year seemed to foreshadow the sharp decline in public evaluations of economic conditions that ensued a month later. As a result, the current finding of two months of slight improvement in the public's economic outlook is a hopeful sign. While not a definitive indication that consumer confidence in the economy will soon increase, it suggests that if Americans' economic outlook continues to improve, improved perceptions about the current state of the economy may follow.

Through the first half of last year, both of Gallup's economic indicators were fairly robust. As recently as August 2000, 74% characterized national economic conditions as "excellent" or "good," and 60% thought the economy was "getting better." However, by January 2001, the percentage who were optimistic about the direction of the economy had fallen 28 points to just 32%, while positive ratings of current economic conditions had fallen just 7 points to 67%. A month later, in February 2001, public perceptions of the current economy also nosedived, dropping to 51% at the same time that the percentage of the public thinking the economy was getting better tumbled further to 23%. Since then, both measures have remained low, with ratings of economic conditions sinking further into the low 40s, but with the forward-looking optimism measure creeping upward to its current 35%.

AUGUST 6
BIOTECH FOOD

Interview Dates: 7/19–22/01
Gallup Poll News Service
Survey #GO 132074

Do you feel confident or not confident that the food available at most grocery stores is safe to eat?

	Confident	Not confident	No opinion
2001 Jul 19–22	89%	10%	1%
2001 Mar 26–28	81	18	1
2000 Mar 30–Apr 2	80	18	2

Do you feel confident or not confident that the food served at most restaurants is safe to eat?

	Confident	Not confident	No opinion
2001 Jul 19–22	77%	21%	2%
2001 Mar 26–28	68	29	3

How much confidence do you have in the federal government to ensure the safety of the food supply in the United States—would you say you have a great deal, a fair amount, not much, or none at all?

	Great deal; fair amount	Not much; none at all	No opinion
2001 Jul 19–22	82%	17%	1%
2001 Mar 26–28	79	20	1

As you may know, some food products and medicines are being developed using new scientific techniques. The general area is called "biotechnology" and includes tools such as genetic engineering and genetic modification of food. How much have you heard or read about this issue—a great deal, some, not much, or nothing at all?

	Great deal	Some	Not much; nothing at all*
2001 Jul 19–22	16%	43%	40%
2000 Mar 30–Apr 2	14	37	49

*"No opinion" is omitted.

As you may know, some food products and medicines are being developed using new scientific techniques. The general area is called "biotechnology" and includes tools such as genetic engineering and genetic modification of food. How closely have you been following the news about this issue—very closely, somewhat closely, not too closely, or not at all?

Very closely 11%
Somewhat closely 34
Not too closely 33
Not at all 21
No opinion 1

Overall, would you say you strongly support, moderately support, moderately oppose, or strongly oppose the use of biotechnology in agriculture and food production?

	Strongly, moderately support	Moderately, strongly oppose	No opinion
2001 Jul 19–22	52%	38%	10%
2000 Mar 30–Apr 2	48	31	11

From what you know or have heard, do you believe that foods that have been produced using biotechnology pose a serious health hazard to consumers, or not?

	Do	Do not	No opinion
2001 Jul 19–22	30%	53%	17%
2000 Mar 30–Apr 2	30	51	19

Analysis: With benefits such as higher crop yields, lower costs, and better pesticide control, genetically modified varieties of corn, soy, and other agricultural products that eventually wind up in the human food supply have reportedly been quickly adopted by U.S. farmers. While the potential health risks of so-called biotech foods are hotly debated in scientific and environmental circles, a recent Gallup Poll finds that the issue has yet to ignite much interest or concern among the public at large.

According to Gallup's July 19–22 nationwide telephone survey, Americans' basic reaction to the use of biotechnology in agriculture and food production is fairly positive. A bare majority (52%) supports this application of biotechnology and a similar number (53%) are doubtful it poses a serious health hazard to consumers. Opposition to the technology hovers around one-third (38%) who generally oppose the use of biotechnology in food production and 30% who fear biotech foods pose a health risk. It should be noted that while the supporters of biotechnology outnumber its detractors, the greater intensity of feeling is on the opposing side: just 9% strongly support the use of biotechnology in food production while 14% strongly oppose it.

Despite the concerns expressed about biotech food when respondents are asked about it specifically, the fact remains that close to nine in ten (89%) feel confident that the food available at most grocery stores is safe to eat, even higher than the 80% who felt this way two years ago. Similarly, most (82%) express confidence in the federal government to ensure the safety of the U.S. food supply, while just 17% express serious doubts about it. Both of these measures were asked in the July Gallup survey before the topic of biotechnology was presented in the course of the interview.

Only 11% say they are following the news about the biotech food issue "very closely" and only 16% admit to having heard "a great deal" about the subject overall. Slightly larger numbers report having heard either a great deal or "some" about the issue (59%) but 40% continue to say they have heard "not much" or "nothing at all" on the subject.

Is a consumer backlash against biotechnology inevitable if and when the public becomes more familiar with it? As of today, familiarity does not seem to breed concern. Americans who report that they have heard a great deal or fair amount on the subject are no more critical of the technology than are others. For instance, 31% of this informed group believe that biotech foods pose a serious health risk while 58% disagree, resulting in a 27% net positive rating for the technology. Among those who have heard little to nothing about biotech foods, 24% believe they pose a risk while 46% disagree, resulting in a 22% net positive rating.

AUGUST 7
BUSH'S VACATION PLANS

Interview Dates: 8/3–5/01
CNN/*USA Today*/Gallup Poll
Survey #GO 134369

President Bush will spend the next thirty days at his ranch in Crawford, Texas. Do you think this is, or is not, too much time to spend away from the White House?

Is	55%
Is not	42
No opinion	3

Just your opinion, how many weeks of vacation should a president take each year?

No vacation	3%
One week or less	5
Two weeks	22
Three weeks	18
Four weeks	31
Five weeks	3
Six weeks	9
More than six weeks	5
No opinion	4

Mean (excluding no opinion)   3.5 weeks

Do you approve or disapprove of the way George W. Bush is handling his job as president?

	Approve	Dis-approve	No opinion
2001 Aug 3–5	55%	35%	10%
2001 Jul 19–22	56	33	11
2001 Jul 10–11	57	35	8
2001 Jun 28–Jul 1	52	34	14
2001 Jun 11–17	55	33	12
2001 Jun 8–10	55	35	10

Analysis: With President Bush off to his ranch in Crawford, Texas, for a month of what he calls a "working vacation," a new Gallup Poll finds the public somewhat critical of the president's long absence from the White House. Still, Bush's job approval and personal favorability ratings remain steady and, by a substantial margin, Americans are more likely to characterize the first six months of Bush's presidency as a success than as a failure.

Most Americans may not be aware of the fact that Bush is spending the next month in Texas, but when they are given that information, they express more opposition than support. The poll conducted August 3–5 shows that 55% say that thirty days is too much time for the president to spend away from the White House while 42% think it is not.

Among people who approve of the way Bush is handling his job as president, opinion on this matter is about evenly divided. Forty-eight percent say that thirty days is too long for the president to be away from the White House while 50% disagree. Among those who disapprove of Bush's job performance, however, 69% say that a month is too long while just 29% disagree.

On the broader question of how much vacation time a president should take in general, the average time suggested is 3.5 weeks. About one-half (48%) says a president should not take more than three weeks, while the other half says he should be able to take at least four weeks. Most people (79%) agree that a president should not take more than four weeks.

Whatever the public's reaction to the president's vacation schedule, Bush's job approval and personal favorability ratings remain steady. The poll shows that 55% of Americans approve of the way Bush is handling the presidency, not significantly different from the 57% rating measured in a Gallup Poll two weeks ago. And 60% say they have a favorable opinion of the president, again essentially the same as the 62% rating measured by Gallup in early June.

AUGUST 8
CONGRESS

Interview Dates: 8/3–5/01
CNN/*USA Today*/Gallup Poll
Survey #GO 134369

Do you approve or disapprove of the way Congress is handling its job?

	Approve	Dis-approve	No opinion
2001 Aug 3–5 . . . . . . .47%	47%	42%	11%
2001 Jul 19–22 49	49	37	14
2001 Jun 11–17 51	51	34	15
2001 May 10–14 49	49	34	17
2001 Apr 6–8 55	55	32	13
2001 Mar 5–7 55	55	28	17
2001 Feb 1–4 53	53	32	15
2001 Jan 10–14 50	50	40	10

Next, we'd like to get your overall opinion of some people in the news. As I read each name, please say if you have a favorable or unfavorable opinion of this person, or if you have never heard of him:

House Democratic Leader Dick Gephardt?

	Favor-able	Unfavor-able	No opinion; never heard of
2001 Aug 3–5 . . . . . . .39%	39%	24%	37%
2000 Oct 25–28 42	42	19	39

Speaker of the House Dennis Hastert?

	Favor-able	Unfavor-able	No opinion; never heard of
2001 Aug 3–5 . . . . . . .29%	29%	15%	56%
2000 Oct 25–28 28	28	9	63

Do you approve or disapprove of the way the following are handling their job:

The Republicans in Congress?

	Approve	Dis-approve	No opinion
2001 Aug 3–5 . . . . . . .49%	49%	40%	11%
2001 Jun 8–10 49	49	43	8
2000 Aug 18–19 45	45	44	11
2000 Jul 25–26 46	46	39	15
2000 Apr 28–30 42	42	46	12

The Democrats in Congress?

	Approve	Dis-approve	No opinion
2001 Aug 3–5	.52%	38%	10%
2001 Jun 8–10	.54	37	9
2000 Aug 18–19	.56	34	10
2000 Jul 25–26	.51	36	13
2000 Apr 28–30	.46	42	12

Do you think the country would be better off if the Republicans controlled Congress, or if the Democrats controlled Congress?

	Repub-licans	Demo-crats	Neither, same (vol.); no opinion
2001 Aug 3–5	.34%	43%	23%
2001 Apr 20–22	.41	43	16
2001 Jan 5–7	.39	41	20

Do you consider the first six months of this year's session of Congress to be a success or a failure?

Success. 49%
Failure 33
Too soon to tell (vol.) 6
No opinion 12

Do you consider the first six months of the Bush administration to be a success or a failure?

Success. 56%
Failure 32
Too soon to tell (vol.) 7
No opinion 5

Next, thinking about the major pieces of legislation which the House or Senate passed this year, please say how much of a difference each of the following will make to you and your family as a law—a major difference, a minor difference, or no difference at all:

A Patients' Bill of Rights?

Major difference 42%
Minor difference 35
No difference 17
No opinion 6

President Bush's energy plan?

Major difference 40%
Minor difference 32
No difference 20
No opinion 8

The tax cuts passed by Congress earlier this year?

Major difference 36%
Minor difference 39
No difference 23
No opinion 2

An education bill?

Major difference 42%
Minor difference 27
No difference 24
No opinion 7

Analysis: Congress began its recess on August 3, and a new Gallup Poll shows that, by a comfortable margin, more Americans rate the first six months of the 107th Congress positively than negatively. In addition to enacting a large tax cut earlier this summer, one or both houses have passed some form of legislation regarding a patients' bill of rights, energy, and education. About four in ten think each of these will make a major difference to them and their families. In evaluating Congress, the public gives the Democrats in Congress slightly higher marks than they do the Republicans.

According to the poll conducted August 3–5, 49% rate Congress's first six months as a success and 33% call it a failure. When asked to rate the Bush administration, 56% say the first six months have been a success and 32% say they have been a failure.

This year Congress has addressed several issues that are high on President Bush's agenda, including a tax cut (signed into law in June), an education bill, a patients' bill of rights, and an energy bill. About four in ten say these policy initiatives will make a major difference to them and their families. Forty-two percent say that a patients' bill of rights and an education bill will make a major difference, 40% say this about Bush's energy plan, and 36% say this about the tax cut.

The debates on key issues have apparently done little to raise the profile of congressional leaders. A majority of respondents (56%) has either no opinion or no awareness of Republican Speaker of the House Dennis Hastert, although this has improved since last fall, when 63% could not rate him. On balance, though, Hastert's ratings are more positive than negative, with 29% rating him favorably and 15% rating him unfavorably. This represents a slight increase in his negative ratings from last fall, with no change in his positive scores.

House Minority Leader Dick Gephardt is better known by the public, as 63% are able to rate him, 39% positively and 24% negatively. Only 37% are unable to rate Gephardt. Like Hastert, Gephardt's favorable ratings have remained stable since last fall, but his negative ratings have increased by 5 percentage points.

AUGUST 9
CONGRESSMAN CONDIT AND
CHANDRA LEVY

Interview Dates: 8/3–5/01
CNN/*USA Today*/Gallup Poll
Survey #GO 134369

How closely have you been following the news concerning the investigation into the disappearance of Chandra Levy—very closely, somewhat closely, not too closely, or not at all?

	Very, somewhat closely	Not too closely	Not at all; no opinion
2001 Aug 3–5	69%	20%	11%
2001 Jul 19–22	62	25	13
2001 Jul 10–11	63	22	15

Do you think the case involving the disappearance of Chandra Levy will ever be solved, or not?

	Will	Will not	No opinion
2001 Aug 3–5	39%	51%	10%
2001 Jul 19–22	51	38	11
2001 Jul 10–11	51	35	14

How likely do you think it is that Gary Condit was directly involved in the disappearance of Chandra Levy—very likely, somewhat likely, not too likely, or not at all likely?

	Very, somewhat likely	Not too likely	Not at all likely; no opinion
2001 Aug 3–5	65%	17%	18%
2001 Jul 19–22	64	16	20
2001 Jul 10–11	65	13	22

Should Gary Condit resign from Congress immediately, or not?

Yes	43%
No	51
No opinion	6

Overall, do you feel that the news media have acted responsibly or irresponsibly in this situation?

	Responsibly	Irresponsibly	No opinion
2001 Aug 3–5	53%	39%	8%
2001 Jul 10–11	61	30	9

Analysis: As the Chandra Levy mystery enters its fourth month, a new Gallup Poll shows that Americans are becoming less optimistic that the case of the missing intern will ever be solved. The survey, conducted the weekend of August 3–5, shows that 51% of those surveyed believe the case will not be solved while 39% believe there will eventually be a resolution. This represents a shift in public opinion from two previous Gallup

Polls conducted in July, when 51% in each poll were optimistic that the case would be solved.

Americans still continue to follow the Levy story; in fact, more say they are following the story in the most recent poll than did so last month. Currently, 69% are following details of the disappearance "very or somewhat closely." In a mid-July Poll, 62% expressed the same level of interest.

California Representative Gary Condit has maintained his lack of knowledge about details of Levy's disappearance, and his attorney claims a privately conducted polygraph test supports that claim. Washington police have repeatedly said Condit is not a suspect in what is still officially described as a "missing persons case." However, a majority continues to believe that Condit was involved in Levy's disappearance. The new poll shows that 65% believe it is "very likely" or "somewhat likely" that Condit was directly involved. This is consistent with the findings from two Gallup Polls conducted in July.

Condit and the missing intern have been linked romantically, although the California Democrat has never acknowledged that relationship publicly. Even so, respondents are split on whether Condit's ties to the case should lead to his resignation from Congress. Forty-three percent believe that he should resign immediately, while 51% say he should not. However, among those who have been following the case closely, the split is much narrower; 48% support Condit's immediate resignation and 50% oppose it.

The Levy case has been a daily fixture on all-news cable networks and nightly network newscasts as well as in the supermarket tabloids. While a majority have been following the case closely, their satisfaction with the media's handling of the case is starting to drop. The latest Gallup Poll shows that 53% say the media have acted responsibly in covering the Levy story while 39% say the media are acting irresponsibly. This represents a drop from mid-July, when 61% said the media were acting responsibly and just 30% said the media were acting irresponsibly. Among those who are following the case closely in the latest poll, 60% think that the media are acting responsibly and just 37% say irresponsi-

bly. Those who are not following the case closely are more negative in their evaluations of the media (45% irresponsible and 38% responsible).

AUGUST 9
SHOPPING HABITS

Interview Dates: 4/6–8/01
Gallup Poll News Service
Survey #GO 132071

Thinking about money for a moment, are you the type of person who more enjoys spending money, or who more enjoys saving money?

Spending money 45%
Saving money 48
No opinion 7

Not counting grocery shopping, how often, if ever, do you shop in each of the following ways—at least once a week, several times a month, a few times a year, about once a year, less often than that, or never:

Going to malls, department stores, or other shopping areas?

Once a week 21%
Several times a month 34
Few times a year .34
About once a year .6
Less often 1
Never 4
No opinion . . . .*

*Less than 1%

Online using the Internet?

Once a week 3%
Several times a month 9
Few times a year .17
About once a year .7
Less often 3
Never 60
No opinion 1

By telephone when watching home-shopping channels on television?

Once a week 1%
Several times a month 1
Few times a year 6
About once a year .4
Less often 5
Never 83
No opinion . . . .*

*Less than 1%

By catalog?

Once a week 1%
Several times a month 7
Few times a year 31
About once a year .15
Less often 7
Never 39
No opinion . . . .*

*Less than 1%

Analysis: Americans can be divided fairly evenly into two camps according to their relationship with money: 45% describe themselves as people who more enjoy spending money and 48% say they more enjoy saving it.

Gallup's April 6–8 national telephone survey found that going to malls, department stores, or other shopping areas (excluding grocery shopping) is a nearly universal experience for Americans. Ninety-six percent report that they do this at one time or another: 21% shop weekly at stores, 34% several times a month, 34% a few times a year, 6% about once a year, and 1% do so less than once a year. Only 4% say they "never" shop at stores.

Shopping by catalog ranks second to store shopping among respondents, with roughly six in ten (61%) saying they use catalogs at least sometimes. By comparison, only 40% ever shop on the Internet and just 17% ever shop through television home shopping channels. While most Americans tend to shop in stores on a weekly or monthly basis, few who use catalogs, the Internet, or television home shopping do so more than a few times a year.

AUGUST 10
STEM CELL RESEARCH

Interview Date: 8/9/01
CNN/*USA Today*/Gallup Poll
Survey #GO 134456

As you may know, the federal government is considering whether to fund certain kinds of medical research known as "stem cell research." How closely have you followed the debate about government funding of stem cell research—very closely, somewhat closely, not too closely, or not closely at all?

	2001 Aug 3–5
Very closely	18%
Somewhat closely	37
Not too closely	22
Not closely at all	23
No opinion	*

*Less than 1%

Do you think the federal government should or should not fund this type of research?

Should 55%
Should not 29
It depends (vol.) 3
No opinion 13

How important is the issue of stem cell research to you—very important, somewhat important, not too important, or not at all important?

Very important 25%
Somewhat important 37
Not too important 21
Not at all important 12
No opinion 5

Now I would like to ask about a few specific types of research on stem cells developed from human embryos that have been created outside a woman's womb. This kind of stem cell research destroys the embryos but may help find treatments for major diseases. As you may know, fertility clinics increase a woman's chance to have a child by fertilizing several embryos, but only a few are implanted in her womb to enable her to have a baby. Some stem cells are developed from the remaining embryos that the fertility clinics usually discard. Do you think the federal government should or should not fund research on stem cells from this kind of embryo?

	2001 Aug 3–5
Should	55%
Should not	40
It depends (vol.)	2
No opinion	3

Some stem cells are developed from embryos that are created in laboratories specifically for the purpose of conducting this research and not to help women have a child. Do you think the federal government should or should not fund research on stem cells from this kind of embryo?

Should	46%
Should not	49
It depends (vol.)	1
No opinion	4

Some stem cells may be developed from embryos produced by cloning cells from a living human being rather than by fertilizing a woman's egg. Do you think the federal government should or should not fund research on stem cells from this kind of embryo?

Should	28%
Should not	66
It depends (vol.)	5
No opinion	1

There is another kind of research using stem cells that come just from adults and do not come from embryos at all. The research results in no injury to the person from whom the stem cells are taken. Do you think the federal government should or should not fund research on this kind of stem cells?

Should	68%
Should not	26
It depends (vol.)	1
No opinion	5

Analysis: In a nationwide address, President George W. Bush announced that he would authorize federal government funding for embryonic stem cell research using only those stem cells that have already been extracted from embryos. The government would not fund research, he said, on stem cells that have yet to be extracted from embryos, rejecting the argument made by some proponents of such research that many of those embryos will be destroyed anyway.

A Gallup Poll conducted immediately after completion of Bush's August 9 speech finds that one-half of the public approves of the decision, one-fourth disapproves, and another one-fourth is unsure. Overall, 50% of Americans approve of Bush's decision.

While Bush will not allow the federal government to fund embryonic stem cell research on "extra" embryos that are produced in fertility clinics, a Gallup Poll conducted August 3–5 finds that a majority would approve of such research. When respondents were told that embryos are created as part of a process to help a woman's chances of having a baby, and that the "stem cells are developed from the remaining embryos that the fertility clinics usually discard," 55% said the federal government should fund research on stem cells from this kind of embryo, while 40% said it should not.

Among people who were following the issue closely, representing just over one-half (55%), support for this research was somewhat higher. By a margin of 59% to 37%, the relatively attentive public supported government funding for this type of embryonic stem cell research, while those who were not closely following the issue expressed support by a narrower margin of 50% to 44%.

Despite its support for stem cell research on embryos that will be discarded, the public is divided over federal government funding for stem cell research that uses embryos created expressly for research purposes. Overall, 49% say the government should not fund such research, 46% take the opposite point of view, and 5% express no opinion.

Some researchers have obtained stem cells from embryos that have been cloned from cells of human beings. Americans oppose government funding of that kind of stem cell research by 66% to 28%. And some stem cell research uses stem cells from adults. There is little political controversy over whether the government should fund this type of research—except if the funds for adult stem cell research divert funds that could be used in embryonic stem cell research. Obtaining the stem cells from adults does not harm the person from whom they are taken, and many opponents of embryonic stem cell research point to adult stem cell research as an alternative. In his speech Thursday evening, Bush included this type of stem cell research among those that the federal government would continue to fund.

The public may not fully realize the issues involved, however, as 26% express opposition to government funding for such research, while 68% express support. Whether the opposition comes from those who generally do not want the government to fund any kind of research, or whether there is some concern specifically about adult stem cells, is unclear.

AUGUST 13
DEMOCRATIC FAVORITES/
PRESIDENTIAL TRIAL HEAT

Interview Dates: 8/3–5/01
CNN/*USA Today*/Gallup Poll
Survey #GO 134369

Asked of Democrats and those leaning Democratic: I'm going to read a list of people who may be running in the Democratic primary for president in the next election. After I read all the names, please tell me which of those candidates you would be most likely to support for the Democratic nomination for president in the year 2004—former Vice President Al Gore, New York Senator

Hillary Rodham Clinton, Delaware Senator Joe Biden, Massachusetts Senator John Kerry, Connecticut Senator Joe Lieberman, North Carolina Senator John Edwards, House Democratic Leader Dick Gephardt, former New Jersey Senator Bill Bradley, or Senate Democratic Leader Tom Daschle?

Al Gore	.34%
Hillary Rodham Clinton	.21
Bill Bradley	.12
Joe Lieberman	.9
Dick Gephardt	.9
John Kerry	.6
Tom Daschle	.2
John Edwards	.1
Joe Biden	.1
Other	.*
No one	.2
No opinion	.3

*Less than 1%

Who would be your second choice if Al Gore does not run—New York Senator Hillary Rodham Clinton, Delaware Senator Joe Biden, Massachusetts Senator John Kerry, Connecticut Senator Joe Lieberman, North Carolina Senator John Edwards, House Democratic Leader Dick Gephardt, former New Jersey Senator Bill Bradley, or Senate Democratic Leader Tom Daschle?

	National adults	Registered voters
Hillary Rodham Clinton	.34%	36%
Dick Gephardt	.17	20
Joe Lieberman	.17	19
John Edwards	.6	5
Bill Bradley	.5	3
Joe Biden	.4	5
John Kerry	.3	2
Tom Daschle	.3	3
Other	.3	3
No one	.*	1
No opinion	.8	3

*Less than 1%

Suppose that the presidential election were being held today, and it included George W. Bush as the Republican candidate and Al Gore as the Democratic candidate. Would you vote for George W. Bush, the Republican, or Al Gore, the Democrat? [As of today, do you lean toward George W. Bush, the Republican, or Al Gore, the Democrat?]

	National adults	Registered voters
George W. Bush	.48%	49%
Al Gore	.48	48
Other (vol.); no opinion	.4	3

Do you want Al Gore to run for president in 2004, or not?

	National adults	Registered voters
Yes	.45%	42%
No	.48	51
No opinion	.7	7

Analysis: The contest for the presidency is never-ending, it seems, as potential Democratic candidates are already visiting Iowa and New Hampshire, meeting with local party leaders, and testing the waters for a possible run in 2004 for the highest elected office in the country. At this stage of the process, at least among the general electorate, name recognition is a crucial element in any measure of potential support. And, according to a recent Gallup Poll, two of the most prominent names in the Democratic Party garner the most support for their party's presidential nomination: former Vice President Al Gore, and former First Lady and now New York Senator Hillary Rodham Clinton.

Al Gore is the clear leader, with 34% of all Democrats saying they would support the party's 2000 nominee. Hillary Rodham Clinton comes in second, favored by 21% of the party, followed by former New Jersey Senator Bill Bradley with 12% support. The Democratic Party's vice presidential nominee in 2000, Connecticut Senator Joe Lieberman, draws 9% support, as does House Minority Leader Dick Gephardt. Massachusetts Senator John Kerry receives 6% of the vote, followed by Senate Majority Leader Tom Daschle with 2%, and Senators John Edwards from North Carolina and Joe Biden from Delaware with 1% each.

There has been some speculation in the news that Gore may not run; in that case, the leading candidate would be Clinton with 33% of support among the party faithful. Lieberman and Gephardt tie for second, each with 15% of the vote, followed by Bill Bradley with 13% and Kerry with 7%. Daschle, Edwards, and Biden all receive 3% of the vote or less.

Just as the 2000 election provided a photo finish with Gore winning the popular vote by half a percentage point, the poll suggests that if the 2004 election were held today, it, too, would provide a very close race. A hypothetical contest between the two major candidates who ran in 2000 ends in a dead heat with 48% each choosing George W. Bush and Al Gore. Among registered voters, Bush has a 1-point advantage (49% to 48%) but that difference is well within the margin of error of the poll, leaving the race too close to call.

The poll asked respondents if Gore should run for president again in 2004. Forty-five percent said he should while 48% said he should not. Another 7% expressed no opinion either way. Among registered voters, the margin was 42% in favor and 51% opposed, also with 7% expressing no opinion. These results show that slightly more people would actually support Gore if he decided to run than indicate they want Gore to run in the first place. About a quarter of those who prefer Gore not to run would still support him, while about a fifth of those who want him to run would vote for Bush.

AUGUST 15
PRESIDENT BUSH

Interview Dates: 8/10–12/01
CNN/*USA Today*/Gallup Poll
Survey #GO 134457

Do you approve or disapprove of the way George W. Bush is handling his job as president?

	Approve	Dis-approve	No opinion
2001 Aug 10–12	.57%	35%	8%
2001 Aug 3–5	.55	35	10
2001 Jul 19–22	.56	33	11
2001 Jul 10–11	.57	35	8

Analysis: There is little evidence that President Bush's recent high-profile decision regarding stem cell research has made a difference in his image among Americans—for better or worse. Americans approve of his decision to allow limited federal funding of stem cell research, but his job approval rating is little different from recent weeks. Other dimensions measured in a weekend CNN/*USA Today*/Gallup Poll also show little change from previous points in time.

In the poll conducted the previous weekend, before Bush's August 9 stem cell announcement, the president's job approval was 55%. This past weekend, after the speech, it was 57%, statistically unchanged. Indeed, Gallup has conducted eighteen surveys measuring Bush's job approval during his administration, and his average rating across those surveys has been 57%. In other words, Bush is now performing almost precisely at the average level for his administration.

All this is in spite of the fact that Bush presented the stem cell decision as one of the most significant of his administration. He spent weeks studying the issue and then preempted prime time programming on August 9 to announce his decision to the nation and to the world (by the weekend poll, 45% said that they had watched his speech). The media have given the issue enormous attention in recent days. Weekend polling shows that Americans' general reaction to the president's decision was positive. Still, it is apparent that his stem cell decision made little difference in how the public rates Bush's job performance.

AUGUST 16
MIDDLE EAST

Interview Dates: 8/10–12/01
CNN/*USA Today*/Gallup Poll
Survey #GO 134457

Do you think there will or will not come a time when Israel and the Arab nations will be able to settle their differences and live in peace?

	Will	Will not	No opinion
2001 Aug 10–12	.32%	64%	4%
2001 Feb 1–4	.41	56	3
2000 Jan 25–26	.49	45	6

In the Middle East situation, are your sympathies more with the Israelis or more with the Palestinian Arabs?

	Israelis	Palestinian Arabs	Both; neither (vol.)	No opinion
2001 Aug 10–12	.41%	13%	25%	21%
2001 Feb 1–4	.51	16	21	12
2000 Oct 13–14	.41	11	27	21
2000 Jul 6–9	.41	14	23	22
2000 Jan 25–26	.43	13	26	18

Which comes closer to your view about the situation in the Middle East between the Israelis and the Palestinian Arabs—the United States should take an active role in attempting to find a diplomatic solution to the violence in the Middle East, or the United States should encourage the two sides to find a solution on their own but should not take an active role?

Active role 32%
Not an active role 65
No opinion 3

Analysis: As mounting violence between the Palestinians and Israelis dominates news headlines, a new Gallup Poll finds the public decidedly pessimistic about the long-term chances of peace in the Middle East, and reluctant to see the U.S. take an active diplomatic role in trying to find a solution to the violence there. The poll also shows that Americans continue to be more likely to sympathize with the Israelis than with the

Palestinian Arabs, although almost one-half expresses no preference for either side.

The poll was conducted August 10–12 and finds that only about one-third wants the U.S. to take an active role in trying to find a diplomatic solution to the violence in the Middle East. The other two-thirds believe that the U.S. should encourage the Israelis and Palestinian Arabs to find a solution on their own, but that the country should not take an active role in that process.

The poll also finds that by a similar 2-to-1 margin (64% to 32%), respondents believe that there will not come a time when Israel and the Arab nations will be able to settle their differences and live in peace. These results represent an increase in pessimism since last February, when the margin was 56% to 41% against the likelihood of eventual peace, and show the highest level of pessimism across the six times that Gallup has asked this question since 1997.

By little more than a 3-to-1 margin (41% to 13%), Americans say their sympathies are more with the Israelis than with the Palestinian Arabs in the Middle East situation. That leaves close to one-half (46%) who indicate no preference between the two sides, 7% who say their sympathies are with both sides equally, 18% whose sympathies are with neither side, and 21% who have no opinion on the matter.

AUGUST 17
INCOME TAX REFUND

Interview Dates: 8/10–12/01
CNN/*USA Today*/Gallup Poll
Survey #GO 134457

What did you do with your tax cut check—did you spend it on something you wouldn't have otherwise bought, spend it on everyday items such as groceries or movie tickets, pay off bills, invest it, something else, or haven't you decided what to do with it?

Pay off bills 30%
Invest it 28
Spend it on everyday items 15
Spend it on something not
   otherwise bought .11

Gave some, all to charity (vol.) 2
Other 4
Haven't decided what to do with it 8
Unsure 2

How much credit do you give each of the following for the fact that the government is sending tax cut checks to most taxpayers—a lot of credit, some credit, not much credit, or none at all:

President Bush?

A lot of credit 44%
Some credit 33
Not much credit 10
None at all 11
No opinion 2

Republicans in Congress?

A lot of credit 25%
Some credit 48
Not much credit 11
None at all 12
No opinion 4

Democrats in Congress?

A lot of credit 11%
Some credit 44
Not much credit 21
None at all 20
No opinion 4

Analysis: Despite hopes from economists and retailers that advance refund checks on this year's tax payments would lead to a nationwide spending spree, a new Gallup Poll finds that most of those who have already received their checks are using the money to pay off bills or build up their savings accounts. The poll conducted the weekend of August 10–12 also shows that only one out of four Americans has received a tax cut check thus far.

Of that group, 30% have used their refund to pay off bills while 28% have invested it. Another 15% have spent their check on everyday items such as groceries or entertainment, while 11%

have spent refund checks to buy consumer goods that they would not have purchased otherwise.

Right or wrong, President Bush has tried to maximize the political benefit from the unprecedented tax cut checks. The new poll shows this effort may well succeed, as 44% of those surveyed give Bush "a lot of credit" for the checks and another 33% say he deserves some credit. The Republicans in Congress also may benefit, but to a lesser extent: just 25% say they deserve "a lot of credit" while 48% say they deserve "some credit."

At the time the law was passed, the Democratic leadership was heavily critical of the tax cut check plan, claiming that lower-than-expected budget surpluses could lead to "raids" on the Social Security and Medicare programs. This may help explain in part why the public gives the Democrats in Congress significantly less credit than it gives Bush or the Republicans. Just 11% give the Democrats in Congress "a lot of credit" and 44% give them "some credit." The percentage of those who give the Democrats "not much credit" or "none at all" (41%) is nearly double that of those who express that opinion about President Bush (21%) or the Republicans in Congress (23%).

AUGUST 20
STOCK MARKET

Interview Dates: 8/3–5/01
CNN/*USA Today*/Gallup Poll
Survey #GO 134369

Do you personally or jointly with a spouse have any money invested in the stock market right now either in an individual stock, a stock mutual fund, or in a self-directed 401 (k) or IRA?

	Yes	No	No opinion
2001 Aug 3–5	61%	38%	1%
2001 Apr 6–8	62	36	2
2001 Mar 14*	64	35	1
2000 May 5–7	54	44	2
2000 Apr 7–9	62	37	1
2000 Mar 10–12	61	37	2
2000 Jan 7–10	61	38	1

*Based on one-night poll

Asked of those who have money invested in the stock market right now: Thinking about how your stocks have performed over the past year, would you say your investments made money, lost money or stayed about even over the past year?

Made money	17%
Lost money	48
Stayed even	33

Also asked of those who have money invested in the stock market right now: Which of the following do you trust most for information or advice on your investments in the stock market—yourself, your broker or financial advisor, independent stock analysts who work for investment firms, or the media?

Yourself	37%
Broker/adviser	40
Stock analysts	12
Media	6
Other (vol.)	2
No opinion	3

Analysis: After more than five years of sustained growth in stock prices, the value of most stocks has been flat or even declined in the past year. A recent Gallup Poll shows that only a small minority of stock market investors—one in six—says their stock investments have made money in the last year. Almost one-half of investors reports losses in the value of their investments. Those who report such losses are most likely to blame themselves, but about one in five blames the media and slightly fewer blame stock analysts or financial advisors. When it comes to investing, stock market investors are equally as likely to say they trust themselves most as they are to say they trust stockbrokers most for information and advice.

According to the poll conducted August 3–5, six in ten Americans have money invested in the stock market now, in an individual stock, a mutual fund, or 401(k) or IRA. Nearly one-half of investors (48%) says their stock market investments lost money in the last year. One in three says the value of their investments stayed even and just 17% report that they made money in the stock market. This is in sharp contrast to the previous time Gallup asked this question, in July 1997, when 76% of investors said their investments had made money in the past year, 20% said they stayed even, and only 2% said their investments lost money.

Investors who lost money in the stock market in the past year were asked which source of information they blame most for their losses. The most frequent response, mentioned by one in three, was themselves. About one in five (19%) blames the media and 13% blame independent stock analysts who work for investment firms. Just 12% blame their stockbroker or financial advisor, while 17% place the blame on some other source of information.

When it comes to finding information or advice on investing, investors tend to trust themselves or a stockbroker or financial advisor the most. The poll finds that 40% say they trust a stockbroker or financial advisor most for information on investing, while 37% trust themselves the most. Only 12% say independent stock analysts are their most trusted source of information and just 6% say this about the media.

AUGUST 21
ECONOMIC CONDITIONS/
PERSONAL FINANCES

Interview Dates: 8/16–19/01
Gallup Poll News Service
Survey #GO 132075

How would you rate economic conditions in this country today—excellent, good, only fair, or poor?

	Excellent; good	Only fair	Poor*
2001 Aug 16–19	36%	49%	14%
2001 Jul 19–22	41	47	11

2001 Jun 11–17	42	45	12
2001 May 10–14	40	45	15
2001 Apr 6–8	8	41	14
2001 Mar 5–7	3	43	10
2001 Feb 1–4	7	36	13
2001 Jan 10–14	11	27	6

*"No opinion" is omitted.

Right now, do you think that economic conditions in the country as a whole are getting better or getting worse?

	Getting better	Getting worse	Same (vol.); no opinion
2001 Aug 16–19	27%	59%	14%
2001 Jul 19–22	35	53	12
2001 Jun 11–17	29	60	11
2001 May 10–14	25	63	12
2001 Apr 6–8	24	63	13
2001 Mar 5–7	28	61	11
2001 Feb 1–4	23	66	11
2001 Jan 10–14	32	56	12

Next, we are interested in how people's financial situation may have changed—would you say that you are financially better off now than you were a year ago, or are you financially worse off now?

	Better off	Worse off	Same (vol.); no opinion
2001 Aug 16–19	37%	41%	22%
2001 Jul 19–22	39	36	25
2001 Jun 11–17	42	37	21
2001 Apr 6–8	42	36	22
2001 Feb 1–4	46	30	24
2001 Jan 10–14	49	30	21

Looking ahead, do you expect that at this time next year you will be financially better off than now, or worse off than now?

	Better off	Worse off	Same (vol.); no opinion
2001 Aug 16–19	66%	18%	16%

2001 Jul 19–22 64	18	18
2001 Jun 11–17 62	22	16
2001 Apr 6–8 62	18	20
2001 Feb 1–4 61	19	20
2001 Jan 10–14 63	21	16

Has the economic news you've heard or read about recently been mostly good or mostly bad?

	Mostly good	Mostly bad	Mixed (vol.); no opinion
2001 Aug 16–19 . . . . .22%		66%	12%
2001 Apr 6–8 16		75	9
2000 Apr 7–9 71		19	10

Analysis: The Federal Reserve is widely expected to lower interest rates for the seventh time this year. The results of the Gallup Poll's August audit on consumer attitudes toward the economy and business suggest that such an attempt to continue to stimulate the economy is warranted.

American consumers' ratings of both the national economy and their own financial situation show no signs of improvement. As measured in the August 18–19 Gallup Poll, the ratings of the national economy remain negative. Any hint of the optimism found in previous months' ratings of future economic conditions has been erased. Only a little more than one-third now rates the economy as either excellent or good, and six out of ten say it is getting worse instead of better. Two-thirds say the economic news they hear is negative.

More respondents say their own financial situations are worse today than they were in 2000. Gallup first asked this question in 1976 and never has the response been so negative.

The August 16–19 Gallup Poll shows that 36% rate the economy positively (either "excellent" or "good"). This represents a decline from July, when 41% rated the economy positively. Positive ratings have leveled off in the low- to mid-40s since the spring, after steeper declines from late 2000 and early 2001. As recently as January, 67% of Americans rated the economy positively, and in February, a majority still

thought economic conditions were either excellent or good. At the same time, the public remains reluctant to rate the current economy as "poor." Only 14% give such a rating. A near majority (49%) rate the economy as "only fair" in the poll.

The public's responses to the optimism/pessimism question had shown a glint of optimism. The percentage thinking things would get better had steadily increased from 24% in April to 35% in July. However, that positive view of the future economy seems to have subsided. Just 27% now believe things are getting better. A majority of Americans continues to believe that things are getting worse, as has been the case since January of this year. Last fall, however, the optimists outnumbered the pessimists by a significant margin.

In the latest poll, 41% say their own personal financial situation is worse now compared to one year ago while 37% say it is better. This 41% figure is the highest Gallup has ever recorded on this measure, stretching back to 1976. The number is also nearly double what it was last October, when just 21% said their personal financial situation was worse compared to a year ago. The fact that the economy has changed so dramatically from last year, a time of highly visible and sustained economic growth to a time of very minimal growth, may help explain why negative assessments on this "compared to a year ago" measure are at an all-time high.

Despite the generally pessimistic comparisons of this year's financial situation and negative views about the future of the national economy, Americans remain optimistic that their own financial situation will improve in the next twelve months. Currently, 66% believe that their personal financial situation will be better this time next year. The number has remained in the 60% range throughout this year. In fact, it is apparent that Americans are essentially eternal optimists; it is rare for them to believe things will not get better for them in the future.

It is not surprising that respondents rate the economy poorly, given that 66% say the economic news they have been hearing recently has been mostly bad. Only 22% say it has been mostly good. At the same time, these numbers are actually more positive than they were in April of this year, when 75% said they had heard mostly bad economic news lately and only 16% had heard mostly good news. However, in 2000, the story was quite different. At that time, 71% said they had heard mostly good economic news, and just 19% had heard mostly bad.

AUGUST 22
INCOME TAX REFUND

Interview Dates: 8/16–19/01
Gallup Poll News Service
Survey #GO 132075

As part of the tax cut that became law earlier this year, the federal government is sending checks for about $300 to $600 to most people who paid taxes this year. Do you think that the new tax cut law will be a good thing for the country, will not make much difference, or will be a bad thing for the country?

Good thing 36%
Not much difference 44
Bad thing 17
No opinion 3

Just your opinion, do you think the tax cut should have been bigger than it was, smaller than it was, or was it about right the way it was passed into law?

Bigger 29%
Smaller 17
About right 47
No opinion 7

Do you approve or disapprove of the way George W. Bush is handling his job as president?

	Approve	Dis-approve	No opinion
2001 Aug 16–19	57%	34%	9%
2001 Aug 10–12	57	35	8
2001 Aug 3–5	55	35	10
2001 Jul 19–22	56	33	11
2001 Jul 10–11	57	35	8

Do you approve or disapprove of the way Congress is handling its job?

	Approve	Dis-approve	No opinion
2001 Aug 16–19	50%	37%	13%
2001 Aug 3–5	47	42	11
2001 Jul 19–22	49	37	14
2001 Jun 11–17	51	34	15
2001 May 10–14	49	34	17

Analysis: A slow economy has experts predicting a smaller than anticipated budget surplus. As a result, some critics have argued that the recently enacted tax cut will force the government to use the Social Security trust fund to pay for many government programs. Some have suggested that the tax cut be repealed or scaled back. President Bush defends it by saying that, despite the tax cut and the slow economy, this year's budget will still result in the second largest surplus in history.

A new Gallup Poll conducted August 16–19 shows that the public does not have major concerns about the tax cut. Only about one in six thinks it will be a bad thing for the country, and a similarly small percentage thinks that, in retrospect, the tax cut should have been smaller than it was. In fact, the percentage who thinks it will be a good thing for the country (36%) is about double the percentage who feels it will be a bad thing (17%). A plurality (44%) believes the tax cut will not make much difference.

The majority of respondents is either content with the size of the tax cut or prefer an even larger one, regardless of calls to scale back or repeal it. Forty-seven percent say the tax cut was "about right," 29% say it should have been bigger than it was, and only 17% agree with critics that it should have been smaller than it was.

President Bush's job approval ratings remain steady despite the recent criticism of the tax cut, which was a key element of his campaign platform and his budget projections, which some Democrats charge are inaccurate and rely on accounting "tricks." Bush's latest approval rating is

57%, unchanged from the prior week, and about the same as it has been throughout July and August. Currently, 34% disapprove of Bush, also similar to his recent scores.

A divided Congress, with Republicans controlling the House and Democrats having just assumed control of the Senate in late May, passed the tax cut earlier this summer. The latest approval rating for Congress is 50%, up slightly from a 47% score earlier this month, while disapproval ratings are at 37%, down from 42% a few weeks ago. Ratings of Congress this year have varied, from a high of 55% in March and April, to a low of 47% this month, but are generally higher than they have been in previous years.

AUGUST 22
ALCOHOLIC BEVERAGES/
UNDERAGE DRINKING

Interview Dates: 7/19–22/01
Gallup Poll News Service
Survey #GO 132074

Do you have occasion to use alcoholic beverages such as liquor, wine, or beer, or are you a total abstainer?

Yes 62%
No, total abstainer .38

Do you, personally, think drinking in moderation, that is, one or two drinks a day, is good for your health, makes no difference, or is bad for your health?

Good for health 22%
Makes no difference 46
Bad for health 27
No opinion 5

Would you favor or oppose a federal law that would lower the drinking age in all states to 18?

Favor 21%
Oppose 77
No opinion 2

Do you think the penalties for underage age drinking should be made more strict, less strict, or remain as they are now?

More strict 60%
Less strict 6
Remain as now 33
No opinion 1

Analysis: Americans favor stronger penalties for underage drinking and are against lowering the drinking age to 18. In a July 19–22 Gallup Poll, a majority (60%) said the penalties for underage drinking should be stricter, 33% say they should remain as they are now, and only 6% think they should be less strict. Additionally, more than seven in ten (77%) say they oppose lowering the drinking age to 18 in all states, while 21% favor such an idea.

The poll also finds that a majority (62%) says they drink alcoholic beverages on occasion, while 38% say they totally abstain from drinking.

AUGUST 24
INDUSTRY RATINGS

Interview Dates: 8/16–19/01
Gallup Poll News Service
Survey #GO 132075

For each of the following business sectors in the United States, please say whether your overall view is very positive, somewhat positive, neutral, somewhat negative, or very negative?

	Very, somewhat positive	Neutral	Somewhat, very negative*
Computer industry . . .67%	20%	10%
Restaurant industry . . .62	28	8
Farming and agriculture 59	24	15
Grocery industry 57	29	13
Accounting 47	40	8
Travel industry 50	35	13
Retail industry 47	34	17

Publishing industry . . .47	32	18
Banking 47	31	20
Real estate industry . . .46	32	20
Automobile industry 45	28	26
Education 50	18	32
Internet industry 44	26	27
Airline industry 37	29	30
Advertising and public relations industry 38	28	32
Television and radio industry 42	22	36
Sports industry 38	28	33
Telephone industry . . .39	24	37
Pharmaceutical industry 39	22	38
Health-care industry 37	19	44
Movie industry 33	23	41
Electric and gas utilities 31	21	47
Legal field 29	24	45
Oil and gas industry 24	21	54

*"No opinion" is omitted.

Analysis: The American public gives the computer and restaurant industries the highest positive ratings among twenty-four industries measured, with farming and agriculture and the grocery industry close behind. At the low end of the scale, with net negative ratings, are the oil and gas industry, the legal field, and electric and gas utilities.

The August 16–19 poll asked: "For each of the following business sectors in the United States, please say whether your overall view of it is very positive, somewhat positive, neutral, somewhat negative, or very negative." Among the twenty-four industries, eighteen receive net positive scores while six receive net negative scores.

Overall, 67% give a positive rating to the computer industry, with just 10% giving it a negative rating, for a net positive score (percent positive minus percent negative) of 57 percentage points. The only other industry to achieve a score above 50 is the restaurant industry, with a net score of 54. The farming and agricultural industry and the grocery industry each receive net positive scores of 44, as close to six in ten rate each industry positively, while only 13% to 15% rate them negatively. Not far behind are the accounting and travel industries, with scores of 39 and 37, respectively.

The next four industries receive scores in the 26 to 30 range, with close to one-half rating them positively and about one in five rating them negatively. They include the retail industry (net score of 30), the publishing industry (29), banking (27), and the real estate industry (26). The next three industries receive similar scores, with just about one-half or a little less giving them a positive rating, and one-quarter or more a negative rating: the automobile industry (19), education (18), and the Internet industry (17).

Six industries receive net positive scores in the poll, but the margin of positive to negative ratings is less than 10 points, and suggests the public is ambivalent about the industry. These include the airline (7), advertising and public relations (6), television and radio (6), sports (5), telephone (2), and pharmaceutical (1) industries.

On the negative side of the ratings—where the ratings are only slightly greater than the positive ratings—are two industries, again indicating a public that is ambivalent. The health-care industry finds a net rating of –7, followed by the movie industry with a net rating of –8. More decidedly negative ratings are given to electric and gas utilities (–16) and the legal field (–16). By far the worst rating goes to the oil and gas industry (–30), the only one to find a majority of Americans giving it a negative rating.

AUGUST 27
CONGRESSMAN CONDIT AND
CHANDRA LEVY

Interview Dates: 8/24–26/01
CNN/*USA Today*/Gallup Poll
Survey #GO 134435

How closely have you been following the news concerning the investigation into the disappearance of Chandra Levy, the twenty-four-year-old Washington intern who disappeared more than three months ago—very closely, somewhat closely, not too closely, or not at all?

	Very, somewhat closely	Not too closely	Not at all; no opinion
2001 Aug 24–26	68%	23%	9%
2001 Aug 3–5	69	20	11
2001 Jul 19–22	62	25	13
2001 Jul 10–11	63	22	15

How likely do you think it is that Gary Condit was directly involved in the disappearance of Chandra Levy—very likely, somewhat likely, not too likely, or not at all likely?

	Very, somewhat likely	Not too, not at all likely	No opinion
2001 Aug 24–26	62%	29%	9%
2001 Aug 3–5	65	27	8
2001 Jul 19–22	64	26	10
2001 Jul 10–11	65	20	15

How likely do you think it is that at any point Gary Condit tried to obstruct the investigation into the disappearance of Chandra Levy—very likely, somewhat likely, not too likely, or not at all likely?

Very likely 45%
Somewhat likely 30
Not too likely 10
Not at all likely 8
No opinion 7

Just your opinion, which of the following better applies to the way you feel about Gary Condit:

He is moral or immoral?

Moral 10%
Immoral 77
Neither (vol.) 3
No opinion 10

He is honest or dishonest?

Honest 10%
Dishonest 79
Neither (vol.) 3
No opinion 8

He is caring or uncaring?

Caring 22%
Uncaring 67
Neither (vol.) 2
No opinion 9

How concerned do you think Gary Condit is about Chandra Levy and her family—very concerned, somewhat concerned, not too concerned, or not concerned at all?

Very concerned 13%
Somewhat concerned 30
Not too concerned .27
Not concerned at all 25
No opinion 5

Did you or did you not happen to see either the interview with Gary Condit that was conducted by Connie Chung on the ABC program "Primetime Live" on Thursday or the interview conducted with Condit on Thursday by a local Sacramento television station?

Did see 35%
Did not see 64
No opinion 1

Did you see parts of the interviews rebroadcast later on the news or other programs, or did you not see any part of the interviews?

Saw "Primetime Live"/Sacramento
  interview 35%
Saw rebroadcast 28
Did not see any part of the interviews 37

Asked of those who saw all or part of the interviews: Do you have a more favorable or less favorable view of Condit as a result of this interview, or did it not affect your opinion either way?

More favorable 2%
Less favorable 51
Did not affect 46
No opinion 1

Also asked of those who saw all or part of the interviews: Did the interview make you more suspicious or less suspicious of Condit's actions concerning the investigation into Chandra Levy's disappearance?

More suspicious 67%
Less suspicious 16
No opinion 17

Also asked of those who saw all or part of the interviews: At several points in the interview, Condit did not directly answer questions about the nature of his relationship with Chandra Levy. Do you think he was justified or unjustified in doing so?

Justified 31%
Unjustified 66
No opinion 3

Also asked of those who saw all or part of the interviews: Do you think Condit did or did not lie during any point in the interview?

Did 71%
Did not 16
No opinion 13

The following questions were asked in California's 18th congressional district:

Do you approve or disapprove of the way Gary Condit is handling his job as your congressman?

Approve 48%
Disapprove 37
No opinion 15

Apart from whether you approve or disapprove of the way Gary Condit is handling his job as your congressman, what do you

think of Condit as a person—do you approve or disapprove of him?

Approve 28%
Disapprove 56
No opinion 16

If Gary Condit were to run for reelection to the House of Representatives from your district, do you think you would vote for him, or not?

Would 29%
Would not 61
No opinion 10

How likely do you think it is that Gary Condit was directly involved in the disappearance of Chandra Levy—very likely, somewhat likely, not too likely, or not at all likely?

Very likely 19%
Somewhat likely 29
Not too likely 18
Not at all likely 26
No opinion 8

How likely do you think it is that at any point Gary Condit tried to obstruct the investigation into the disappearance of Chandra Levy—very likely, somewhat likely, not too likely, or not at all likely?

Very likely 30%
Somewhat likely 29
Not too likely 18
Not at all likely 17
No opinion 6

Are you embarrassed that Gary Condit represents your district in Congress, or not?

Yes 46%
No 53
No opinion 1

How concerned do you think Gary Condit is about Chandra Levy and her family—very concerned, somewhat concerned, not too concerned, or not concerned at all?

Very concerned 25%
Somewhat concerned 33
Not too concerned 19
Not at all concerned 19
No opinion 4

Did you or did you not happen to see either the interview with Gary Condit that was conducted by Connie Chung on the ABC program "Primetime Live" on Thursday or the interview conducted with Condit on Thursday by a local Sacramento television station? And did you see parts of the interviews rebroadcast later on the news or other programs, or did you not see any part of the interviews?

Saw "Primetime Live"/Sacramento
    interview 57%
Saw rebroadcast 15
Did not see any part of the interview 28

Asked of those who saw all or part of the interviews: Do you have a more favorable or less favorable view of Condit as a result of this interview, or did it not affect your opinion either way?

More favorable 3%
Less favorable 46
Did not affect 50
No opinion 1

Also asked of those who saw all or part of the interviews: Did the interview make you more suspicious or less suspicious of Condit's actions concerning the investigation into Chandra Levy's disappearance?

More suspicious 51%
Less suspicious 23
No opinion 26

Also asked of those who saw all or part of the interviews: At several points in the inter-

view, Condit did not directly answer questions about the nature of his relationship with Chandra Levy. Do you think he was justified or unjustified in doing so?

Justified 39%
Unjustified 54
No opinion 7

Also asked of those who saw all or part of the interviews: Do you think Condit did or did not lie during any point in the interview?

Did 58%
Did not 29
No opinion 13

Now thinking about the letter that Gary Condit mailed to all of his constituents, did the letter make you feel more favorably or less favorably toward Condit, or did it have no effect on your view of him?

More favorable 8%
Less favorable 29
No effect 49
No opinion 14

Do you think Condit should or should not apologize to the people who live in your congressional district or to the Levy family?

Apologize to both 63%
Apologize to people in district 8
Apologize to the Levy family 7
Should not apologize (vol.) 13
No opinion 9

Overall, do you feel the news media have acted responsibly or irresponsibly in this situation?

Responsibly 49%
Irresponsibly 43
No opinion 8

Thinking back to the election for Congress in November 2000, did you vote for Gary

Condit, the Democrat, or Steve Wilson, the Republican, or did you not happen to vote for Congress in 2000?

Condit 51%
Wilson 12
Did not vote 31
Other (vol.) 2
No opinion 4

Analysis: After weeks of refusing to speak to the press about his relationship with Chandra Levy, last week U.S. Representative Gary Condit broke his silence in interviews with Connie Chung, a local California television station, and *People* and *Newsweek* magazines. A Gallup Poll (August 25–26) suggests that Condit was unsuccessful in improving his image among the national public, and a separate Gallup Poll in his California district finds substantial opposition to any reelection effort he might make.

According to the national poll, three-quarters of Americans say it is either very likely (45%) or somewhat likely (30%) that Condit tried to obstruct the investigation into Levy's disappearance. In addition, 62% say it is either very likely (31%) or somewhat likely (31%) that Condit was directly involved in her disappearance, figures that are little changed from a Gallup Poll conducted in early August. The public is sharply critical of the California congressman. By overwhelming majorities, they say that Condit is immoral (77%), dishonest (79%), and uncaring (67%).

Although there is little change in the overall percentage of respondents who say that Condit was directly involved in Levy's disappearance, those who saw part of Chung's interview, or the interview conducted by a local Sacramento television station, indicate that the interviews made them think more negatively about the congressman. Only 2% feel more favorably toward Condit after seeing him interviewed, while 51% say they feel less favorably. Similarly, by 67% to 16%, viewers are more, rather than less, suspicious of Condit's actions concerning the investigation, and by 71% to 16%, viewers say he lied at some point during the interview. When asked whether he was justified in refusing to respond to questions about his relationship with Levy, about two-thirds say he was not, by 66% to 31%.

The poll in Condit's congressional district finds the people there generally less negative about their representative than are Americans across the country, but still sufficiently critical to oppose his reelection by greater than a 2-to-1 margin. Overall, Condit's constituents approve of the job he is doing as their representative by 48% to 37%, but disapprove of him "as a person" by the larger margin of 56% to 28%. Residents of the 18th Congressional District in California are somewhat divided over whether they are embarrassed by his actions: 46% say they are and 53% are not. Still, more than seven in ten believe he owes an apology to the people in his district, and to the Levy family. And when asked if they would vote for him if he decided to run for reelection, only 29% say they would while 61% say they would not.

The people in Condit's district are somewhat less skeptical about his behavior than are Americans across the country. When asked how likely it is that Condit was directly involved in Levy's disappearance, 48% of his constituents say it is either very or somewhat likely, substantially smaller than the 62% of the national public expressing that view. Similarly, 59% of Condit's constituents say the congressman tried to obstruct the investigation into Levy's disappearance, compared to 75% of the national public. Also, while only 43% of respondents across the country believe Condit is either very or somewhat concerned about the Levy family, 58% of Condit's constituents hold that opinion of their congressman.

Nevertheless, like the national public, the people in his district also say that seeing his interviews made them feel less rather than more favorably toward the representative by 46% to 3%, with the rest indicating the interviews had no effect on their opinion of him. Earlier, Condit had sent a letter to households in his district, but the effect of that letter also seemed to be more negative than positive—by 29% to 8%—with the rest saying the letter had no effect.

AUGUST 28
FEDERAL BUDGET SURPLUS

Interview Dates: 8/24–26/01
CNN/*USA Today*/Gallup Poll
Survey #GO 134435

As you may know, the federal government currently has a budget surplus, which means the government takes in more money than it spends. Recent reports indicate that the size of the federal budget surplus has decreased by more than $100 billion since April of this year. Please tell me whether you think each of the following is very responsible, somewhat responsible, not very responsible, or not responsible at all for the decrease in the budget surplus:

President Bush?

Very responsible 33%
Somewhat responsible 39
Not very, not responsible at all;
   no opinion 28

The Republicans in Congress?

Very responsible 24%
Somewhat responsible 47
Not very, not responsible at all;
   no opinion 29

The Democrats in Congress?

Very responsible 15%
Somewhat responsible 46
Not very, not responsible at all;
   no opinion 39

Do you think the decrease in the budget surplus is a very serious problem, somewhat serious, not very serious, or not a serious problem at all?

Very serious 34%
Somewhat serious .39
Not very serious 15
Not serious at all 10
No opinion 2

What do you think is more likely to happen to the federal budget by next year—the government will have a budget surplus, or the government will have a budget deficit?

Will have surplus 40%
Will have deficit 54
No opinion 6

Analysis: Much of the discussion in Washington centers on the shrinking budget surplus. Projected to be $281 billion as recently as April, new budget estimates place the surplus at $153 billion, which diverts $9 billion away from Social Security. A new Gallup Poll shows that 34% of Americans think the decrease in the budget surplus is a very serious problem and 39% call it somewhat serious. President Bush is viewed as more responsible for the decrease than are Republicans and Democrats in Congress, although none is seen as "very responsible" by more than one-third of the public. A majority believes that next year's federal budget will show a deficit rather than a surplus.

According to the poll conducted August 24–26, a majority sees Bush, the Republicans in Congress, or the Democrats in Congress as being at least somewhat responsible for the reduced surplus. The public assigns the most responsibility to Bush: 72% think he is at least somewhat responsible, though just 33% believe he is "very responsible." And when asked what they think is likely to happen to the budget by next year, 54% expect a deficit, and 40% predict a surplus.

AUGUST 31
JOB SATISFACTION

Interview Dates: 8/16–19/01
Gallup Poll News Service
Survey #GO 132075

Do you have a strong sense of loyalty to the company or organization you work for, or not?

Yes 83%

No 16
No opinion 1

Does the company you work for have a strong sense of loyalty to you, or not?

Yes 64%
No 32
No opinion 4

Do you think you would be happier in a different job, or not?

Would 33%
Would not 61
No opinion 6

How satisfied or dissatisfied are you with your job—would you say you are completely satisfied, somewhat satisfied, somewhat dissatisfied, or completely dissatisfied with your job?

Completely, somewhat satisfied 85%
Somewhat dissatisfied 11
Completely dissatisfied; no opinion 4

Here are two different ways of looking at your job: some people get a sense of identity from their job; for other people, their job is just what they do for a living. Which of these better describes the way you usually feel about your job?

Sense of identity .54%
Just what you do .44
No opinion 2

All in all, which of the following best describes how you feel about your job—you love it, you like it, you dislike it, or you hate it?

Love it 32%
Like it 59
Dislike it 6
Hate it 2
Neither (vol.) 1

Analysis: With Labor Day set aside to honor the nation's workers, a recent Gallup Poll shows that the vast majority of employed Americans say they are at least somewhat satisfied with their jobs, with more than four in ten "completely" satisfied. In addition, one-third says they love their job, and more than eight in ten say they have a strong sense of loyalty to their employer.

The poll was conducted August 16–19 and finds 41% who are employed either full- or part-time saying they are "completely" satisfied with their jobs while another 44% are "somewhat" satisfied. Just 15% say they are dissatisfied, 11% "somewhat," and 4% "completely."

A separate question in the current poll finds that 32% of workers say they love their job while another 59% say they like it. Just 6% say they dislike it while only 2% say they hate their job.

Some people see their job as just what they do for a living, but others get a sense of identity from their job. The poll finds that this year 54% of Americans say they get a sense of identity from their job. The distinction between these two ways of viewing one's job correlates highly with job satisfaction. Among those who see their job primarily as a way to make a living, just 27% are completely satisfied with their jobs compared to 50% among those who get a sense of identity from their jobs.

The vast majority of workers (83%) says they have a strong sense of loyalty to their company or the organization that employs them. However, only 64% say their company has a strong sense of loyalty to them. These results mean that 63% of all workers express loyalty to their company and feel it is reciprocated. That leaves 18% of workers who express loyalty, but believe it is not reciprocated by their employer, and another 14% who say that loyalty is lacking on both sides. But despite the generally high level of worker satisfaction, one-third of all workers says they would be happier in another job.

**SEPTEMBER 4
PARENTS AND THEIR
CHILDREN'S EDUCATION**

Interview Dates: 8/16–19/01
Gallup Poll News Service
Survey #GO 132075

Overall, how satisfied are you with the quality of education that students receive in Kindergarten through Grade 12 in the United States today—completely satisfied, somewhat satisfied, somewhat dissatisfied, or completely dissatisfied?

Completely satisfied 10%
Somewhat satisfied 38
Somewhat dissatisfied 32
Completely dissatisfied 17
No opinion 3

Thinking about your oldest child in Kindergarten through Grade 12, what grade will he or she be entering this fall?

Kindergarten–Grade 5 ....38%
Grade 6–Grade 8 20
Grade 9–Grade 12 41
No opinion 1

Will your oldest child attend public, private, parochial, or home school this year?

Public school 88%
Private school 5
Parochial school 5
Home school 2

How satisfied are you with the quality of education your oldest child is receiving—completely satisfied, somewhat satisfied, somewhat dissatisfied, or completely dissatisfied?

Completely satisfied 35%
Somewhat satisfied 37
Somewhat dissatisfied 14
Completely dissatisfied 9
Just starting (vol.); no opinion 5

Thinking about your oldest child, when he or she is at school, do you fear for his or her physical safety?

Yes, fear 32%
No, do not 68
No opinion ....*

*Less than 1%

Thinking about the amount of homework your oldest child receives, overall, would you say that child receives too much homework, the right amount, or not enough homework?

Too much 16%
Right amount 57
Not enough 23
No opinion 4

Now, thinking for a moment about social pressures at the school your oldest child attends, how serious a problem are social pressures among students—very serious, somewhat serious, not too serious, or not serious at all?

	Very serious	Somewhat serious	Not too, not at all serious*
Parents of Children K–Grade 12			
Be popular 26%		39%	33%
Achieve specific body image 25		29	45
Wear specific type or brand of clothes 24		27	45
Use drugs 22		26	50
Drink alcohol 22		24	52
Have sexual relations 19		28	48
Smoke cigarettes 16		25	58
Parents of Children Grades 6–12			
Be popular 32		44	23
Wear specific type or brand of clothes 31		28	38
Use drugs 28		33	38
Drink alcohol 28		31	39

Achieve specific body image 27	34	39
Have sexual relations 23	36	38
Smoke cigarettes 19	33	46

*"No opinion" is omitted.

In your oldest child's school, would you say students pressure each other more to perform well academically or not to perform well academically?

To perform well	69%
Not to perform well	21
No opinion	10

In all, how many children do you have that will be attending Kindergarten through Grade 12 this year?

One............................	44%
Two	38
Three	10
Four	5
Five or more	3
No opinion	*

*Less than 1%

Mean 1.9
Median 2.0

Thinking now more broadly about all your school-aged children, do you have any children who will be attending:

A public school?

Yes	93%
No	7

A parochial or church-related school?

Yes	9%
No	91

An independent private school?

Yes	7%
No	93

Home school, meaning not enrolled in a formal school, but taught at home?

Yes	2%
No	98

Analysis: The day after Labor Day traditionally marks the start of a new school year in the United States. A recent Gallup Poll shows that 30% of American households will send children to school this year. The vast majority of students will attend public school: 93% of parents of children in Kindergarten through Grade 12 will send at least one child to public school, while 9% will have a child in parochial school, 7% in an independent private school, and 2% will be home-schooled. The August 16–19 Gallup Poll addressed several issues facing parents of school-age children, each asked in reference to their oldest child, including their child's safety at school, the seriousness of social pressures children face at school, the pressure on academic performance, and the amount of homework they receive.

According to the latest poll, 32% of parents fear for their child's physical safety when the child is at school. Parents with a child in Grade 6 or higher are more likely to say they fear for their child's safety (39%) than are parents whose children are in Grade 5 or lower (22%).

One outcome of the Columbine shooting and related incidents seems to have heightened concern about the social pressures children face at school. When parents are asked about the seriousness of several social pressures their children face at school, no more than one-third rates any item as "very serious." In fact, a majority thinks that the pressure in their child's school to smoke cigarettes, drink alcohol, or use drugs is "not too" or "not at all serious." Topping the list of concerns is the pressure to be popular, which 26% say is a very serious problem and 39% say is somewhat serious. Next on the list are pressures to achieve a specific body image (54% rate as very or somewhat serious) or to wear a specific type or brand of clothes (51%).

Many of these concerns are more applicable to older children—those in middle school and high school—than to younger children. Among parents with a child in Grade 6 through Grade 12, the top concern is still pressure to be popular, followed by wearing a specific brand of clothes, but the pressures to use drugs and drink alcohol are seen as more serious than among parents of younger children.

Some critics say that children receive too much homework in school, especially for students who participate in extracurricular activities or hold part-time jobs outside of school. Parents, however, do not see their children's homework as excessive, as 57% say their children receive the right amount of homework and 23% say they do not receive enough. Just 16% think their children receive too much homework.

Parents of older children are more likely to say their child receives too little homework (30%) than are parents of children in Kindergarten through Grade 5 (13%). Nearly two-thirds of these parents think that their children receive the right amount of homework, while the percentage is 52% among Grade 6 through Grade 12 parents.

In some schools, especially those in urban areas, students speak of pressure to not perform well in school. In other schools, pressure to achieve high grades and get into a good college can be tremendous. Gallup asked parents which type of pressure they thought was more prevalent in the school their oldest child attends. The vast majority (69%) says there is more pressure to perform well academically, while just 21% say the pressure is greater to not perform well. Parents whose oldest child is in Grade 6 through Grade 12 are somewhat more likely than parents of younger children to think the pressure is greater to not perform well by a 24%-to-17% margin.

In general, most parents of school-age children are satisfied with the quality of the education their children receive: 72% are satisfied and just 23% are dissatisfied. Parents whose oldest child is in Kindergarten through Grade 5 are more likely to say they are "completely satisfied" with the quality of education their oldest child is

receiving (43%) than are parents whose oldest child is in Grade 6 through Grade 12 (30%).

SEPTEMBER 5
CONGRESSIONAL AGENDA

Interview Dates: 8/24–26/01
CNN/*USA Today*/Gallup Poll
Survey #GO 134435

Do you think the policies being proposed by the Republican leaders in the U.S. House and Senate would move the country in the right direction or in the wrong direction?

	Right direction	Wrong direction	No opinion
National Adults			
2001 Aug 24–26 . . . . .49%		38%	13%
Registered Voters			
2001 Aug 24–26 49		40	11
2000 Oct 16–18 49		30	21

Do you think the policies being proposed by the Democratic leaders in the U.S. House and Senate would move the country in the right direction or in the wrong direction?

	Right direction	Wrong direction	No opinion
National Adults			
2001 Aug 24–26 . . . . .51%		36%	13%
Registered Voters			
2001 Aug 24–26 49		38	13
2000 Oct 16–18 48		31	21

Do you think the Republican Party or the Democratic Party would do a better job of dealing with each of the following issues and problems?

	Republican Party	Democratic Party	Point advantage
National defense 59%		32%	+27
The federal budget . . .44		45	−1
Energy 43		45	−2

Education 42	47	−5
Social Security 37	52	−15
Health-care policy ...33	55	−22

+ Advantage indicates Republican Party lead
− Advantage indicates Democratic Party lead

Analysis: The 107th Congress is back in session after its August recess. It has a number of items on the agenda, including education reform, prescription drug benefits for older Americans, a patients' bill of rights, campaign finance reform, faith-based initiatives, and next year's budget, among others. Roughly one-half of the public thinks the policies proposed by Congressional Democrats will move the country in the right direction. A similar number thinks this of Republican Congressional policies. However, when asked about specific issues, the public sees a big difference in political ability. Respondents say that the Democrats will do a better job of dealing with health-care policy and Social Security, while the Republicans are better able to handle national defense.

The poll assessed the public's views of which party would do a better job of dealing with each of six issues. Republicans enjoy an advantage on just one measure—national defense—typically a strong Republican issue. The advantage is significant: 27 points, 59% to 32%, the largest of the issues tested. Democrats fare well on health-care policy, currently enjoying a 55%-to-33% edge. The public has regained its confidence in the Democrats' ability to deal with health care.

Congress will devote a lot of time to the thirteen appropriations bills that make up next year's federal budget. The challenge is greater this year, given that the budget surplus is projected to be much smaller than previous estimates. In recent weeks, leaders of both parties have criticized the others' approach to dealing with the federal budget. Americans, though, are divided as to which party would better handle the budget issue, with 45% favoring the Democrats and 44% the Republicans. The public is evenly split on energy, as 45% say the Democrats are better able to deal with the issue while 43% say this of the Republicans.

Gallup Polls conducted throughout this year show education as one of the top priorities for Americans. Both the House and Senate have passed school-reform bills that would require annual testing and would hold schools accountable for their performance. However, Congress must work out differences in the bills before President Bush can sign a measure into law. The Democrats enjoy a very small advantage on education (47% to 42%), but this represents a decline in their education ratings.

SEPTEMBER 6
IMMIGRANT AMNESTY

Interview Dates: 8/24–26/01
CNN/*USA Today*/Gallup Poll
Survey #GO 134435

Do you think the United States should or should not make it easier for illegal immigrants to become citizens of the United States?

Easier 28%
Not easier 67
No opinion 5

Asked of those who answered "easier" or "not easier": Which of the following proposals would you prefer for illegal immigrants currently living in the United States—they should be granted general amnesty, or they should be allowed to stay in the United States only if they have worked and paid taxes for a certain length of time?

Easier, prefer general amnesty 6%
Easier, prefer citizenship for those who have worked and paid taxes 20
Easier, no preference 2
Not easier 67
No opinion 5

Analysis: Mexican President Vicente Fox reportedly surprised his White House hosts at a welcoming ceremony on August 23 by forsaking the usual diplomatic bromides and launching into an intensive lobbying effort on behalf of amnesty for the estimated three million Mexican immigrants now living in the U.S. illegally. Gallup polling about blanket amnesty for illegal immigrants more generally finds the public widely unsympathetic to this proposal, with only 6% supporting it. Twenty percent think that citizenship should be granted selectively to illegal immigrant workers who have been here a specified length of time and paid taxes, but two-thirds think that the U.S. should not do anything to facilitate citizenship for illegal immigrants. The public's opposition to blanket amnesty is not surprising given its long-standing position against expanding immigration to the United States.

SEPTEMBER 7
JOB SATISFACTION

Interview Dates: 8/16–19/01
Gallup Poll News Service
Survey #GO 132075

How satisfied or dissatisfied are you with your job—would you say you are completely satisfied, somewhat satisfied, somewhat dissatisfied, or completely dissatisfied with your job?

Completely satisfied 41%
Somewhat satisfied 44
Somewhat, completely dissatisfied;
  no opinion 15

Now I'll read a list of job characteristics. For each one, please tell me how satisfied or dissatisfied you are with your current job in this regard—are you completely satisfied, somewhat satisfied, somewhat dissatisfied, or completely dissatisfied with:

The physical safety conditions of your workplace?

Completely satisfied 65%
Somewhat satisfied 25
Somewhat, completely dissatisfied 9
No opinion 1

Your relations with coworkers?

Completely satisfied 64%
Somewhat satisfied 28
Somewhat, completely dissatisfied 5
No opinion 3

The flexibility of your hours?

Completely satisfied 57%
Somewhat satisfied 28
Somewhat, completely dissatisfied 14
No opinion 1

The opportunity you have to do what you do best?

Completely satisfied 54%
Somewhat satisfied 32
Somewhat, completely dissatisfied 14
No opinion . . . .*

*Less than 1%

Your job security?

Completely satisfied 54%
Somewhat satisfied 30
Somewhat, completely dissatisfied 15
No opinion 1

The amount of vacation time you receive?

Completely satisfied 52%
Somewhat satisfied 25
Somewhat, completely dissatisfied 18
No opinion 5

The overall contribution your employer makes to society?

Completely satisfied 51%
Somewhat satisfied 32
Somewhat, completely dissatisfied 14
No opinion 3

Your boss or immediate supervisor?

Completely satisfied 51%
Somewhat satisfied 29

Somewhat, completely dissatisfied 14
No opinion 6

The amount of work that is required of you?

Completely satisfied 47%
Somewhat satisfied 35
Somewhat, completely dissatisfied 18
No opinion . . . .*

*Less than 1%

The opportunity you have to learn and grow?

Completely satisfied 47%
Somewhat satisfied 33
Somewhat, completely dissatisfied 19
No opinion 1

The respect your employer has for your opinions?

Completely satisfied 44%
Somewhat satisfied 32
Somewhat, completely dissatisfied 20
No opinion 4

The recognition you receive at work for your work accomplishments?

Completely satisfied 39%
Somewhat satisfied 36
Somewhat, completely dissatisfied 23
No opinion 2

The health insurance benefits your employer offers?

Completely satisfied 36%
Somewhat satisfied 27
Somewhat, completely dissatisfied 26
No opinion 11

Your chances for promotion?

Completely satisfied 32%
Somewhat satisfied 30
Somewhat, completely dissatisfied 25
No opinion 13

The retirement plan your employer offers?

Completely satisfied 31%
Somewhat satisfied 34
Somewhat, completely dissatisfied 24
No opinion 11

The amount of money you earn?

Completely satisfied 24%
Somewhat satisfied 46
Somewhat, completely dissatisfied 30
No opinion . . . .*

*Less than 1%

The amount of on-the-job stress in your job?

Completely satisfied 22%
Somewhat satisfied 40
Somewhat, completely dissatisfied 36
No opinion 2

Analysis: More than eight in ten American workers are satisfied with their current jobs, including 41% who say they are "completely satisfied." When asked to rate their satisfaction with several aspects of their jobs, workers are most satisfied with the physical safety of their workplaces and their relations with coworkers. On-the-job stress and pay are the two aspects with which respondents are least satisfied.

The poll conducted August 16–19 assessed workers' satisfaction with seventeen different aspects of their jobs. More than six in ten workers say they are "completely satisfied" with the physical safety conditions of their workplaces and their relations with coworkers. Slightly fewer are satisfied with the flexibility of their hours. More than one-half expresses a high level of satisfaction with the opportunity they have to do what they do best, their job security, the amount of vacation time they receive, the overall contribution their employers make to society, and their bosses or immediate supervisors.

At the opposite end of the spectrum, less than one-quarter is completely satisfied with the amount of on-the-job-stress in their jobs and the amount of money they earn. Workers also express some displeasure with the benefits they receive from their employers, as only about one-third is completely satisfied with their retirement plans and health insurance benefits.

SEPTEMBER 10
FORD-FIRESTONE CONTROVERSY

Interview Dates: 6/28–7/1/01
Gallup Poll News Service
Survey #GO 133787

How closely have you been following the news about the dispute between Firestone and Ford over who is to blame for the accident rates on Ford Explorers equipped with Firestone tires—very closely, somewhat closely, not too closely, or not at all closely?

Very closely 19%
Somewhat closely .46
Not too closely 23
Not at all closely .12
No opinion . . . .*

*Less than 1%

Which of the following comes closest to your view about who is to blame for the accidents involving Ford Explorers equipped with Firestone tires—the blame lies more with the Ford Explorer, the blame lies equally with the Ford Explorer and Firestone tires, or the blame lies more with the Firestone tires?

More with Ford Explorer 7%
Equally with Ford, Firestone 47
More with Firestone tires 37
No opinion 9

As a consequence of this situation concerning Ford Explorers and Firestone tires, are

you, personally, more concerned about the safety of the tires on your own car or truck, or are you not more concerned?

Yes, more concerned 49%
No, not more concerned 49
No opinion 2

Just your opinion, do you think that the U.S. government should decide whether to impose mandatory recalls on Firestone tires and/or Ford Explorers, or do you think the U.S. government should let Firestone and Ford make their own decisions about recalls of their products?

Let government decide 51%
Let Ford, Firestone decide 43
No opinion 6

Do you have a favorable or unfavorable opinion of the following products:

Firestone tires?

Favorable 23%
Unfavorable 64
Never heard of (vol.) 1
No opinion 12

Ford Explorer sport utility vehicles?

Favorable 36%
Unfavorable 51
Never heard of (vol.) 1
No opinion 12

Do you have a favorable or unfavorable opinion of the following companies:

Bridgestone/Firestone Inc.?

Favorable 31%
Unfavorable 56
Never heard of (vol.) 2
No opinion 11

Ford Motor Company?

Favorable	.57%
Unfavorable	.35
Never heard of (vol.)	.*
No opinion	.8

*Less than 1%

In the dispute between Firestone and Ford over who is more to blame for the accident rates on Ford Explorers equipped with Firestone tires, whose side are you more likely to believe—Firestone's side or Ford's side?

Firestone's side	.23%
Ford's side	.52
No opinion	.25

Analysis: A jury trial involving the Ford Motor Company begins this week in Brownsville, Texas, the first court trial for Ford since the controversy surrounding accidents involving Ford Explorers equipped with Firestone tires began. The American public has been following the controversy on a relatively close basis. In a Gallup Poll conducted in late June, 65% said they were following the controversy at least somewhat closely, putting the story near the top of all news stories tested using this measure this year. But despite the highly negative circumstances involved in the controversy—accidents, deaths, and injuries—there have apparently been at least some benefits. Almost one-half of respondents says they are now more concerned about the safety of the tires on their car or truck as a result of the Explorer/Firestone situation.

Part of the acrimony that has developed between Ford and Firestone has revolved around the issue of recalls: who should initiate them and at what level. The public tilts toward the belief that the federal government itself should decide whether to impose mandatory recalls. Given a choice, 51% say that the government should institute the mandatory recalls while 43% say decisions on recalls should be left up to the two companies themselves.

Additional polling suggests that the overall image of Bridgestone/Firestone may have been more severely damaged—at least temporarily—than the image of the Ford Motor Company has been, perhaps because tires are Firestone's core business, while Ford manufactures many automobiles and trucks other than the Explorer. The poll showed that 57% of Americans had a favorable opinion of the Ford Motor Company, while only 31% had a favorable opinion of Bridgestone/ Firestone.

In terms of assigning responsibility, about one-half says the blame for the accidents involving Ford Explorers equipped with Firestone tires lies equally with the vehicles and the tires. Another 37% say the blame lies more with Firestone tires while 7% say that it lies more with Ford.

SEPTEMBER 12
TERRORIST ATTACKS AS
"ACTS OF WAR"

Interview Date: 9/11/01
CNN/*USA Today*/Gallup Poll
Survey #GO 134673

How worried are you that you or someone in your family will become a victim of a terrorist attack—very worried, somewhat worried, not too worried, or not worried at all?

	Very, somewhat worried	Not too worried	Not worried at all*
2001 Sep 11	.58%	24%	16%
2000 Apr 7–9**	.24	41	34

*"No opinion is omitted.
**Asked of part sample

Do you think today's attacks do or do not represent the beginning of a sustained terrorist campaign against the United States that will continue for the next several weeks?

Do represent	.55%
Do not represent	.29
No opinion	.16

Would you describe today's attacks as an act of war against the United States, or not?

Yes 86%
No 10
No opinion 4

How confident are you in President Bush's ability to handle this situation—very confident, somewhat confident, not very confident, or not confident at all?

Very confident 45%
Somewhat confident 33
Not very confident .11
Not confident at all 7
No opinion 4

As a result of today's attacks, do you think Americans will permanently change the way they live, or not?

Will 49%
Will not 45
No opinion 6

Which comes closest to your view—the U.S. military should conduct military strikes immediately against known terrorist organizations, even if it is unclear who caused today's attacks; the U.S. military should only conduct military strikes against the terrorist organizations responsible for today's attacks, even if it takes months to clearly identify them; or the U.S. military should not conduct military strikes in response to today's attacks?

Should conduct immediate strikes 21%
Should wait to identify those responsible . . .71
Should not conduct strikes 4
No opinion 4

How likely is it that the U.S. government will be able to identify and punish the people responsible for these attacks—very likely, somewhat likely, not very likely, or not at all likely?

Very likely 52%
Somewhat likely 36
Not very likely 6
Not at all likely 3
No opinion 3

Do you think this is or is not the most tragic news event in your lifetime?

Is 87%
Is not 12
No opinion 1

Do you think you will change any aspect of your personal life or activities in order to reduce your chances of being a victim of terrorist attacks, or will you not make any changes in your personal life?

Yes, make changes 36%
No, will not 61
No opinion 3

Do today's events make you less willing to fly on airplanes, or not?

Yes 48%
No 50
No opinion 2

Analysis: According to a new Gallup Poll conducted Tuesday night, today's terrorist attacks, in which hijacked airplanes deliberately crashed into the twin towers of New York City's World Trade Center and into the Pentagon in Arlington, Virginia, are seen by most Americans as an act of war, and as the most tragic news event in their lifetimes. They also are much more worried now than they have been over the past six years that someone in their own family will become a victim of a terrorist attack, and a majority believes that the most recent attacks represent the beginning of a sustained terrorist campaign against the United States that will continue for weeks.

Despite these views, respondents express a high level of confidence that the perpetrators will be identified and punished, and express confidence in President Bush's ability to handle the situation. They also resist any calls for immediate military strikes against known terrorist organizations. Instead, they prefer that the U.S. take the time to clearly identify those who are responsible, even if it takes months to do so, before conducting retaliatory strikes.

The public's immediate reaction about the possible long-term effects of the terrorist attacks is mixed. About one-half thinks that Americans will permanently change the way they live as a consequence of the attacks while the other half disagrees. Just over one-third thinks they will make changes in their lives to reduce their chances of being a victim of a terrorist attack, but six in ten say they will not make any changes. Still, about one-half says that the events on September 11 make them less willing to fly on an airplane.

The poll, completed Tuesday night before President Bush's speech to the nation, shows a remarkable level of consensus among respondents about what the terrorist attacks mean and what the U.S. should do. Overall, 86% view the terrorist attacks as an act of war, while just 10% disagree. Similarly, 87% see the attacks as the most tragic news event in their lifetimes.

When asked what the U.S. should do about the attacks, 71% say the government should conduct military strikes only against the terrorist organizations responsible for the attacks, even if it takes months to clearly identify who they are. Just 21% want quicker action: to conduct military strikes against known terrorist organizations, even if it is unclear who caused the attacks. Just 4% oppose any military retaliation at all.

Americans are worried today about becoming victims of terrorism. The current poll shows 60% are either "very" or "somewhat" worried that they or someone in their family will become a victim. One reason for the increased worry may be that a majority (55%) sees Tuesday's attacks as the beginning of a sustained terrorist campaign "that will continue for several weeks." The rest either disagree with that view (29%) or say they are unsure (16%).

This worry apparently influences how Americans might behave in the future. One-half (49%) predicts that, as a consequence of the terrorist attacks, they will permanently change the way they live while 45% disagree. On a personal level, 36% admit that they will change some aspect of their personal lives or activities to avoid being a victim of terrorism, but 61% say they will not make any changes. Nevertheless, when asked about their fear of flying, 48% of Americans admitted that the terrorist attacks make them less willing to fly on airplanes.

Almost nine in ten (88%) say the government is either very likely (52%) or somewhat likely (36%) to identify and punish the people responsible for the attacks. A large majority is also confident in President Bush's ability to handle the situation. Forty-five percent are very confident, and another 33% are somewhat confident.

SEPTEMBER 14
ECONOMIC CONDITIONS/
PERSONAL FINANCES

Interview Dates: 9/7–10/01
Gallup Poll News Service
Survey #GO 132076

How would you rate economic conditions in this country today—excellent, good, only fair, or poor?

	Excellent, good	Only fair	Poor*
2001 Sep 7–10	32%	49%	19%
2001 Aug 16–19	36	49	14
2001 Jul 19–22	41	47	11
2001 Jun 11–17	42	45	12
2001 May 10–14	40	45	15
2001 Apr 6–8	45	41	14
2001 Mar 5–7	46	43	10
2001 Feb 1–4	51	36	13
2001 Jan 10–14	67	27	6

*"No opinion" is omitted.

Right now, do you think that economic conditions in the country as a whole are getting better or getting worse?

	Getting better	Getting worse	Same (vol.)*
2001 Sep 7–10	19%	70%	9%

2001 Aug 16–19 27	59	11
2001 Jul 19–22 35	53	9
2001 Jun 11–17 29	60	8
2001 May 10–14 25	63	9
2001 Apr 6–8 24	63	9
2001 Mar 5–7 28	61	7
2001 Feb 1–4 23	66	8
2001 Jan 10–14 32	56	8

*"No opinion" is omitted.

Next, we are interested in how people's financial situation may have changed. Would you say that you are financially better off now than you were a year ago, or are you financially worse off now?

	Better off	Worse off	Same (vol.)*
2001 Sep 7–10 . . . . .37%	36%	26%
2001 Aug 16–19 37	41	21
2001 Jul 19–22 39	36	25
2001 Jun 11–17 42	37	20
2001 Apr 6–8 42	36	22
2001 Feb 1–4 46	30	23
2001 Jan 10–14 49	30	21

*"No opinion" is omitted.

Looking ahead, do you expect that at this time next year you will be financially better off than now, or worse off than now?

	Better off	Worse off	Same (vol.)*
2001 Sep 7–10 . . . . . .61%	20%	15%
2001 Aug 16–19 66	18	13
2001 Jul 19–22 64	18	13
2001 Jun 11–17 62	22	11
2001 Apr 6–8 62	18	15
2001 Feb 1–4 61	19	16
2001 Jan 10–14 63	21	13

*"No opinion" is omitted.

Do you think the economy is now in a recession, or not?

	Yes	No	No opinion
2001 Sep 7–10 . . . . . .51%	43%	6%

2001 May 10–14 33	62	5
2001 Apr 6–8 42	52	6
2001 Mar 5–7* 31	64	5
2001 Feb 1–4* 44	49	7

*Based on part sample

Analysis: While most Americans are still trying to absorb the shock of the September 11 attacks, the world's financial markets are both volatile and uneasy. Everyone wonders how the U.S. markets will react after their unprecedented shutdown this week. Monetary authorities in the United States and Europe have announced that liquidity will not be a problem, but no one really knows what to expect or how long it will take to get the markets back to something approaching normal.

On the other hand, we do know how consumer confidence was doing just prior to the events of September 11. And it was not good. New Gallup Poll economic data gathered September 7–10, just before the terrorist attacks, show that 70% of Americans say economic conditions in the country are getting worse while only 19% say they are getting better. This is a complete reversal of consumer sentiment from just a year ago when 60% of consumers said economic conditions were getting better and only 26% said they were getting worse, and is also a deterioration from Gallup's August reading when 59% said things were getting worse.

Gallup's measures of consumer confidence were weakening prior to the tragedy of September 11, and the data suggest that the pillar of strength represented by continued consumer spending, in the otherwise dismal economy, might finally be giving way. It is not clear at this point what the impact of the terrorist attacks will be on the feelings and perceptions of the average American, but it would not necessarily be surprising if the earlier talk of an economic slowdown turns quickly into talk of the first full-fledged U.S. recession in a decade.

Even prior to September 11, one-half (51%) of all Americans said that the U.S. economy was in a recession. This percentage is up from 33% in May. And when asked to rate economic conditions in the country, only about one out of three

(32%) said that the economy is good or excellent. In sharp contrast, three out of four (74%) rated the U.S. economy as good or excellent a year ago.

In this same context, just about the same percentage of consumers (36%) last weekend said they were financially worse off than they were a year ago as said they were financially better off (37%). These perceptions are essentially unchanged from August and July of this year, but stand in sharp contrast to the situation of about a year ago when 55% said they were better off while only 22% said they were worse off.

More important, even as respondents' confidence in the current U.S. economy crumbled earlier this month, consumers' optimism about the future held strong. Six out of ten (61%) expect to be better off at this time next year than they are right now. This is down from 68% about a year ago but still represents an enormous amount of optimism about the future of the U.S. economy.

SEPTEMBER 19
SUPPORT FOR ISRAEL FOLLOWING 9/11

Interview Dates: 9/14–15/01
CNN/*USA Today*/Gallup Poll
Survey #GO 134674

In the Middle East situation, are your sympathies more with the Israelis or more with the Palestinian Arabs?

	Israelis	Pales-tinian Arabs	Both; neither (vol.); no opinion
2001 Sep 14–15	55%	7%	38%
2001 Aug 10–12	41	13	46
2001 Feb 1–4	51	16	33
2000 Oct 13–14*	41	11	48
2000 Jul 6–9	41	14	45
2000 Jan 25–26	43	13	44

*Based on part sample

In the Middle East conflict, do you think the United States should take Israel's side, take the Palestinians' side, or not take either side?

	Israel's side	Pales-tinians' side	Not take either side*
2001 Sep 14–15	27%	1%	63%
2000 Jul 6–9**	16	1	74
2000 Jan 25–26	15	1	72
1998 Dec 4–6	17	2	73
1998 May 8–10	15	2	74

*"No opinion" is omitted.
**Based on part sample

Thinking about the financial aid the United States provides Israel for economic purposes, do you think U.S. economic aid to Israel should be increased, kept the same, or decreased?

Increased 8%
Kept the same 55
Decreased 29
Eliminated (vol.) 1
No opinion 7

Do you think the United States should reduce the amount of economic aid provided to Israel, or stop providing economic aid to Israel altogether?

Reduce 14%
Stop 16
Keep the same (vol.) .55
Increase (vol.) 8
No opinion 7

Thinking about the financial aid the United States provides Israel for military purposes, do you think U.S. military aid to Israel should be increased, kept the same, or decreased?

Increased 16%
Kept the same 47
Decreased 30
Eliminated (vol.) 1
No opinion 6

Do you think the United States should reduce the amount of military aid provided to

Israel, or stop providing military aid to Israel altogether?

Reduce 11%
Stop 20
Keep the same (vol.) 47
Increase (vol.) 16
No opinion 6

Analysis: Palestinian Authority leader Yasser Arafat announced that he would enforce a cease-fire and Israel agreed to suspend military actions, thereby bringing a temporary halt to the fighting in the Middle East. Some believe the break in hostilities is a response to the terrorist attacks on the World Trade Center and the Pentagon on September 11. Prior to Arafat's announcement, but since the terrorist attacks, the latest Gallup Poll showed increased levels of support among Americans for Israel in its conflict with the Palestinian Arabs. A majority (55%) in the September 14–15 poll says their sympathies in the Middle East situation lie more with the Israelis than with the Palestinian Arabs while 7% take the opposite view. Typically, about four in ten expressed greater sympathy for Israel than for the Palestinians, although 51% sided with Israel in a February 2001 poll. Support for the Palestinian Arabs has generally been about twice what it is now.

A majority of Americans continues to favor the U.S. remaining officially neutral in the Middle East conflict, although there has been an increase, when compared to previous polls, in the percentage who advocate that the country favor Israel. The latest poll shows 63% saying the U.S. should not take either side in the conflict, down from 74% in July of last year.

U.S. strong support for Israel over the years is thought to be one of the contributing factors to the anger with America expressed by some citizens of Arab nations. An update on those attitudes this past weekend showed somewhat of an increase in the number who want aid to Israel kept the same while fewer favor decreasing aid. There has been no change in the percentage who want aid increased, however. Specifically, the latest poll shows only about one in three respondents wants the U.S. to decrease economic aid to Israel (14%) or to stop providing Israel with economic aid altogether (16%). A majority (55%) believes that U.S. economic aid to Israel should be kept the same and 8% think it should be increased.

The results are similar when Americans are asked about military aid rather than economic aid. Thirty-one percent says the U.S. should decrease (11%) or stop providing (20%) military aid to Israel. A near majority (47%) says military aid to Israel should be kept the same and 16% want it increased.

SEPTEMBER 24
PRESIDENT BUSH

Interview Dates: 9/21–22/01
CNN/*USA Today*/Gallup Poll
Survey #GO 134675

Do you approve or disapprove of the way George W. Bush is handling his job as president?

	Approve	Dis-approve	No opinion
2001 Sep 21–22	90%	6%	4%
2001 Sep 14–15	86	10	4
2001 Sep 7–10	51	39	10
2001 Aug 24–26	55	36	9
2001 Aug 16–19	57	34	9
2001 Aug 10–12	57	35	8
2001 Aug 3–5	55	35	10

As you may know, President Bush addressed Congress and the nation on Thursday night about the recent terrorist attacks in New York City and Washington, DC. Did you happen to see President Bush's address to Congress and the nation on Thursday night, or not? [Asked of those who did not see Bush's address: Did you see parts of the address rebroadcast later on the news or other programs, or did you not see any part of the address?]

Saw Bush's address 74%
Saw rebroadcasts or excerpts 14
Did not see either 12

From what you have heard or read, would you rate George W. Bush's speech to Congress and the nation on Thursday night as excellent, good, just okay, poor, or terrible?

Excellent 62%
Good 25
Just okay 8
Poor 1
Terrible . . . .*
Did not see (vol.) 3
No opinion 1

*Less than 1%

Do you think President Bush explained the goals of current U.S. military action clearly enough, or not?

Did 78%
Did not 15
No opinion 7

Do you think President Bush has gone too far in terms of a military response to the terrorist attacks, done about right, or not gone far enough in terms of a military response to the terrorist attacks?

Gone too far 4%
About right 75
Not far enough 19
No opinion 2

Do you think President Bush has gone too far in terms of an economic and diplomatic response to the terrorist attacks, done about right, or not gone far enough in terms of an economic and diplomatic response to the terrorist attacks?

Gone too far 4%
About right 79
Not far enough 14
No opinion 3

Do you think the United States should or should not take military action in retaliation for Tuesday's attacks on the World Trade Center and the Pentagon?

	Should	Should not	No opinion
2001 Sep 21–22	.89%	7%	4%
2001 Sep 14–15	.88	8	4

Analysis: President Bush's call to arms in a nationwide address on August 20 has elicited widespread public support for a war against terrorism, as well as the highest presidential job approval rating ever measured by Gallup since it began asking the public for its evaluation of presidents over six decades ago. According to the latest Gallup Poll conducted September 21–22, 90% of Americans approve of the way Bush is handling his job as president, up 4 percentage points from a poll last weekend.

The record-high approval rating for Bush comes in the wake of his address to the nation last week, in which he outlined his approach both to retaliating against the terrorists for attacking the U.S. on September 11 and to mounting a concerted effort to stop global terrorism altogether. Almost three-quarters of all Americans saw the address live, and another 14% saw rebroadcasts or excerpts of the speech. Nine in ten give Bush high marks for the speech, with 62% saying the speech was "excellent" and 25% "good." Another 8% say it was "just okay." Only 1% says it was a "poor" speech. Among those who watched the speech live, 71% say it was excellent and 22% good.

The vast majority also feels that the president did a good job in his speech of explaining the goals of any military action that may occur as a result of the war on terrorism. Among all Americans, 78% say he has explained the goals clearly enough.

Bush's high approval ratings are no doubt in part due to the widespread support Americans give to the president's plan of action. The poll shows that about three in four say that Bush's proposed military response, as well as his proposed diplomatic and economic pressures, are "about right," while among those who disagree, most would opt for more rather than less action. More generally, 89% favor the U.S. taking military action in retaliation for the September 11 attacks, essentially unchanged from responses to the same question asked one week ago.

SEPTEMBER 25
ECONOMIC CONDITIONS/
PERSONAL FINANCES

Interview Dates: 9/21–22/01
CNN/*USA Today*/Gallup Poll
Survey #GO 134675

How would you rate economic conditions in this country today—very good, somewhat good, somewhat poor, or very poor?

	Very, somewhat good	Somewhat, very poor	No opinion
2001 Sep 21–22	57%	42%	1%
2001 Apr 20–22	67	32	1
2001 Feb 9–11	80	19	1
2001 Jan 15–16	82	18	*
2000 Jun 6–7	85	14	1
2000 Mar 10–12	86	13	1

*Less than 1%

Now, thinking about a year from now, do you expect economic conditions in this country will be very good, somewhat good, somewhat poor, or very poor?

	Very, somewhat good	Somewhat, very poor	No opinion
2001 Sep 21–22	77%	20%	3%
2001 Apr 20–24	70	27	3
2001 Feb 9–11	71	27	2
2001 Jan 15–16	68	30	2
2000 Jun 6–7	80	15	5
2000 Mar 10–12	79	17	4

Thinking of your own financial situation just now, do you feel you are in a good position to buy some of the things you would like to have, or is now a rather bad time for you to spend money?

	Good position	Bad time	Both good and bad (vol.); no opinion
2001 Sep 21–22	43%	53%	4%
2001 Apr 6–8	35	61	4

Do you think the economy is now in a recession or not?

	Yes	No	No opinion
2001 Sep 21–22	52%	43%	5%
2001 Sep 7–10	51	43	6
2001 May 10–14	33	62	5
2001 Apr 6–8	42	52	6
2001 Mar 5–7*	31	64	5
2001 Feb 1–4*	44	49	7

*Based on part sample

Thinking about the next twelve months, how likely do you think it is that you will lose your job or be laid off—very likely, fairly likely, not too likely, or not at all likely?

	Very, fairly likely	Not too likely	Not at all likely*
2001 Sep 21–22	13%	25%	62%
2001 Apr 6–8	12	36	52

*"No opinion" is omitted

Just your best guess, would you say the financial prospects of the company or organization you work for have already been hurt by the terrorist attacks, have not yet been hurt but will be, or will not be hurt by the terrorist attacks?

Already been hurt	17%
Not yet hurt, but will be	29
Will not be hurt	52
Has helped (vol.)	1
No opinion	1

Analysis: One of the aspects of American life most immediately affected by the events of

September 11 is the economy. In fact, economic concerns have moved to a point of such potential seriousness that President Bush used his August 22 radio address to make a special effort to rally the country in support of the economy. At the heart of much of this concern is the average American consumer whose spending patterns and behavior will, many economists think, be a pivotal factor in determining the course of the economy in the months ahead.

There is little question that the public perceives at least a short-term negative effect on the economy from the attacks. It is hard to imagine otherwise, given the impact the events have had on the airline and travel industries. On the other hand, Americans remain strongly confident in the longer-term prospects for the U.S. economy as they appear to be highly optimistic that economic conditions will be much improved a year from now.

Conducted September 21–22, the latest Gallup Poll asked respondents about their perceptions of the impact of the terrorist attacks on their companies. Nearly one-half (46%) agrees that their company has been or will be hurt by the terrorist attacks (17% say that their company has already been hurt and another 29% say they expect their company will be hurt).

This negative impact comes on top of an already weak economy. Thus, it is not surprising that when a broad sample is asked directly about the current condition of the economy, only 7% say it is very good. Similarly, 57% say the economy is either very good or somewhat good.

At the same time, while economists may be nearly unanimous in their assumption that the nation is already in a recession, since the attacks there has been almost no increase in the number who agree. About one-half (52%) says we are in a recession. This is essentially unchanged from a poll conducted August 8–9 before the attacks. Further, despite the fact that many say that the attacks and their aftermath have had an effect on their places of business, and despite extensive news coverage of layoffs in the airline industry since the attacks, employee fears of job loss have not increased. Only 13% think they are very likely or fairly likely to be laid off. This is only one point higher (12%) than it was in April.

One of the most closely watched economic issues in the wake of September 11 is whether or not the average American will delay or cancel purchases of goods and services. In the immediate aftermath of the attacks, reports indicated that retail sales were down, that travel was down substantially, and that consumers were delaying large purchases. But weekend poll results show that 43% feel they are in a good position to spend money, up from 35% in April. On a relative basis, this is not outstanding. More than one-half (53%) says that they are not in a good position to spend. Still, the fact that the numbers have become more, rather than less, optimistic compared to April suggests that the September 11 events themselves may not be causing the dramatic curtailing of spending that many anticipated.

The most positive news from the recent poll comes in response to questions about the long-term prospects for the economy. Three out of four (77%) think the economy a year from now will be in very good or somewhat good shape, up from April 2001 and at around 2000 levels.

Similarly, 91% say they are confident that the U.S. economy will be prosperous in the long-term. Long-term confidence in the economy may not produce the short-term benefits many economists are looking for now, but that confidence is essential if the damage done to the economy on September 11 is truly going to be short-term.

OCTOBER 1
TERRORIST ATTACKS

Interview Dates: 9/21–22/01
CNN/*USA Today*/Gallup Poll
Survey #GO 134675

How worried are you that you or someone in your family will become a victim of a terrorist attack—very worried, somewhat worried, not too worried, or not worried at all?

	Very, somewhat worried	Not too worried	Not worried at all*
2001 Sep 21–22	49%	32%	18%
2001 Sep 14–15	51	35	13

2001 Sep 11	58	24	16
2000 Apr 7–9	24	41	34

*"No opinion" is omitted.

Analysis: While personally upset, depressed, and in some cases distracted by the events of September 11 and all their ramifications, the majority of Americans are not highly anxious about the risk of terrorism affecting their own lives. Gallup's most recent survey, conducted September 21–22, finds just 14% feeling very worried that they or a family member will be a victim of a terrorist attack while another 35% are somewhat worried.

Perhaps as a result, few are taking drastic measures such as buying gas masks, but many seem to be taking moderate actions to reduce their exposure to possible terrorism, or to prepare for it. Reluctance to travel by plane seems to lead the list; 43% tell Gallup they are less willing to fly, and 48% are less willing to travel overseas as a result of the events of September 11. Also, 35% are less willing to enter skyscrapers, 30% are less likely to attend events with large crowds, and roughly 30% have already considered or might consider stocking up on extra food and water. Relatively few have purchased or might purchase a gun (22%), a generator (18%), or a gas mask (17%).

OCTOBER 4
MILITARY RETALIATION
AGAINST TERRORISM

Interview Dates: 9/14–15/01, 9/21–22/01
CNN/*USA Today*/Gallup Polls
Surveys #GO 134674, #GO 134675

Do you think that the United States should or should not take military action in retaliation for Tuesday's attacks on the World Trade Center and the Pentagon?

	2001 Sep 21–22	2001 Sep 14–15
Should	...................89%	88%
Should not	7	8
No opinion	4	4

Which comes closer to your view about the actions the United States should take to deal with terrorism—the United States should focus on taking military action to punish the specific terrorist groups involved in last week's attacks, or the United States should mount a long-term war to defeat global terrorist networks?

	2001 Sep 21–22
Punish specific groups	.................38%
Mount long-term war	59
No opinion	3

Do you favor or oppose the United States taking direct military action in Afghanistan?

	2001 Sep 21–22
Favor	...........................82%
Oppose	13
No opinion	5

Do you favor or oppose the United States taking direct military action in Iraq?

	2001 Sep 21–22
Favor	...........................73%
Oppose	20
No opinion	7

Would you support or oppose the United States continuing a campaign against terrorism if you knew that 5,000 U.S. troops would be killed?

	2001 Sep 21–22
Support	...........................76%
Oppose	16
No opinion	8

Would you support or oppose the United States continuing a campaign against terrorism if you knew that 5,000 U.S. civilians would be killed by future terrorist attacks in addition to those already lost in the terrorist attacks?

	2001 Sep 21–22
Support	84%
Oppose	12
No opinion	4

Do you think that the United States should take military action against terrorist organizations in other countries only if the United Nations Security Council authorizes it, or the United States should take military action against terrorist organizations in other countries regardless of whether or not the United Nations Security Council authorizes it?

	2001 Sep 21–22
Action if UN authorizes it	45%
Action whether or not	50
No opinion	5

Would you support or oppose the United States taking military action if you knew each of the following would happen: *

The U.S. military action would continue for a period of several months?

Support	86%
Oppose	11
No opinion	3

U.S. ground troops would be used in an invasion?

Support	80%
Oppose	18
No opinion	2

The military draft would be reinstituted?

Support	77%
Oppose	18
No opinion	5

The U.S. military action would continue for a period of several years?

Support	66%
Oppose	30
No opinion	4

1,000 American troops would be killed?

Support	65%
Oppose	30
No opinion	5

*September 21–22 poll

And would you support or oppose the United States taking military action if you knew each of the following would happen: *

Taxes would be increased?

Support	84%
Oppose	15
No opinion	1

Shortages of oil and gas would occur?

Support	79%
Oppose	18
No opinion	3

Less money to spend on programs such as education and Social Security?

Support	78%
Oppose	18
No opinion	4

A prolonged economic recession would occur?

Support	78%
Oppose	18
No opinion	4

Further terrorist attacks would occur in the United States?

Support	78%
Oppose	19
No opinion	3

*September 14–15 poll

Analysis: Numerous polls conducted since the September 11 terrorist attacks show roughly nine in ten Americans favoring military retaliation. However, the level of support for a military response varies depending on the conditions under which it might occur. While a majority favors retaliation in every situation the polls have asked about, respondents show the least amount of support for military action that would last for several years or involve a significant number of American deaths.

The latest Gallup Poll conducted September 21–22 shows 89% favoring military retaliation for the terrorist attacks in a very general sense. Gallup also has assessed the level of support for military action under five specific circumstances, and finds a range of support from 65% to 86%. The high of 86% support is in reference to military action that would continue for a period of several months. Eighty percent favor military action that would involve the use of U.S. ground troops. Nearly that many (77%) favor military action even if it meant that the military draft would be reinstituted. The lowest level of support is for military action that would last for a period of several years (66%) or would involve the deaths of 1,000 American troops (65%). And about eight in ten favor the U.S. taking direct military action in Afghanistan while 73% favor direct military action in Iraq.

Support for military action is also rather robust to a host of domestic consequences. Roughly eight in ten would support U.S. military action if taxes were increased, shortages of gas and oil would occur, less federal government money would be available for domestic programs such as education and Social Security, a prolonged economic recession would take place, and further terrorist attacks would occur in the U.S.

A slight majority (53%) believes that the U.S. should mount a long-term war to defeat global terrorist networks. About one in three, however, believes that the goal of military action should be limited to punishing the specific terrorist groups involved in the September 11 attacks.

The public is split as to whether the U.S. government should seek United Nations approval prior to taking military action. Half say the U.S. should take action even if the UN does not approve, while 45% would prefer to wait for authorization from the UN Security Council.

OCTOBER 8
WAR ON TERRORISM

Interview Date: 10/7/01
CNN/*USA Today*/Gallup Poll
Survey #GO 134729

As you may know, the United States and Great Britain launched attacks on at least three cities in Afghanistan today in retaliation for the terrorist attacks that occurred in the United States on September 11. Do you approve or disapprove of the United States taking military action in Afghanistan today?

Approve 90%
Disapprove 5
No opinion 5

Do you approve or disapprove of the way President Bush is handling the campaign against terrorism?

Approve 92%
Disapprove 5
No opinion 3

Which of the following comes closest to your view—the United States should have launched military action before now, the United States waited the right amount of time to take military action, or the United States should have waited longer before taking military action?

Should have launched before now 14%
Waited right amount of time 72
Should have waited longer 9
No opinion 5

Looking ahead, would you favor or oppose the United States taking additional direct military action in Afghanistan if:

U.S. ground troops were to be used?

Favor 77%
Oppose 17
No opinion 6

Afghan civilians are killed as a result of the military action?

Favor 65%
Oppose 27
No opinion 8

Do you believe the United States should or should not take military action against other countries that the United States believes are harboring terrorists?

Should 78%
Should not 16
No opinion 6

Now that the United States has taken military action, do you think the fighting in Afghanistan will continue for a few weeks or less, several months, a year or two, or more than two years?

A few weeks or less .10%
Several months 34
A year or two 26
More than two years 22
No opinion 8

How likely is it that there will be further terrorist attacks in the United States over the next several weeks—very likely, somewhat likely, not too likely, or not at all likely?

Very likely 41%
Somewhat likely 42
Not too likely 9
Not at all likely 4
No opinion 4

Analysis: An overwhelming majority of Americans approves of the U.S. launching military attacks in Afghanistan on Sunday, October 7, and of the way President George W. Bush is handling the campaign against terrorism. A special Gallup Poll conducted Sunday night also shows widespread support for taking additional military action in Afghanistan, even if it entails U.S. ground troops and results in Afghan civilians getting killed, and for attacking other countries that the U.S. government believes are harboring terrorists. Americans do not expect, however, that such actions are risk-free. More than eight in ten now believe it is likely that there will be further terrorist attacks in the U.S. over the next several weeks, up from polling conducted two weeks ago. Most also expect that the fighting in Afghanistan will last at least several months, with about one-half expecting the war there to last a year or more.

The poll was conducted between 5:30 and 8:30 P.M. Eastern time on Sunday, within hours after the announcement that the U.S. and Great Britain had launched missile and bombing attacks on at least three cities in Afghanistan. According to the poll, 90% approve of the U.S. taking such military action while just 5% are opposed, and another 5% are unsure. By about the same margin (92% to 5%), Americans also approve of the way Bush is handling the campaign against terrorism.

There is some second-guessing about the timing of the attacks, with 14% saying the action should have been started earlier and 9% saying the U.S. should have waited longer. Still, 72% say the U.S. waited just the right amount of time.

The poll also shows that Americans are ready for more than air strikes against Afghanistan: 77% would favor additional direct military action in that country even if U.S. ground troops are used while just 17% would be opposed. This represents a 10 percentage-point increase over those favoring such action in the two days before the Sunday attacks. If Afghan civilians are killed, support for military action drops by 12 percentage points but still registers at more than a 2-to-1 margin in favor (65% to 27%).

In addition to military action in Afghanistan, Americans are willing to see the U.S. attack other countries that the government believes are harboring terrorists: 78% support it while 16% do not.

Bush administration officials have stressed that the war against terrorism will be a long and complex one, and the public seems to have gotten the message. Just 10% expect the fighting to last only a few weeks or less while 34% say it will last several months. Almost one-half says it will last at least a year, 26% a year or two, and 22% more than two years.

The administration also has warned that the attacks have increased the probability of additional terrorist activity within this country. The FBI on Sunday told law enforcement agencies across the country to be on high alert. There is significant agreement on the part of the public that additional terrorist activities may occur. Overall, 83% say it is likely there will be further terrorist attacks in the U.S. over the next several weeks: 41% say "very" and 42% say "somewhat" likely. This marks a significant increase from a Gallup Poll conducted two weeks ago, when only 22% said "very" likely and 44% "somewhat" likely.

OCTOBER 9
PRESIDENT BUSH

Interview Dates: 10/5–6/01
CNN/*USA Today*/Gallup Poll
Survey #GO 134790

Do you approve or disapprove of the way George W. Bush is handling his job as president?

	Approve	Dis-approve	No opinion
2001 Oct 5–6	87%	10%	3%
2001 Sep 21–22	90	6	4
2001 Sep 14–15	86	10	4
2001 Sep 7–10	51	39	10
2001 Aug 24–26	55	36	9
2001 Aug 16–19	57	34	9
2001 Aug 10–12	57	35	8
2001 Aug 3–5	55	35	10

Do you approve or disapprove strongly or only moderately?

Strongly approve	60%
Moderately approve	27
Moderately disapprove	5
Strongly disapprove	5
No opinion	3

Do you approve or disapprove of the way George W. Bush is handling:

The economy?

	Approve	Dis-approve	No opinion
2001 Oct 5–6	72%	23%	5%
2001 Jul 10–11	54	36	10
2001 May 18–20	51	41	8
2001 Apr 20–22	55	38	7
2001 Mar 9–11	55	32	13
2001 Feb 1–4	53	27	20

Foreign affairs?

	Approve	Dis-approve	No opinion
2001 Oct 5–6	81%	14%	5%
2001 Jul 10–11	54	33	13
2001 May 18–20	55	35	10
2001 Apr 20–22	56	31	13
2001 Mar 9–11	52	27	21
2001 Feb 1–4	46	21	33

Thinking about the following characteristics and qualities, please say whether you think it applies or doesn't apply to George W. Bush?

	Applies
Is sincere in what he says	84%
Can manage the government effectively	79
Is a strong and decisive leader	75
Inspires confidence	75
Cares about the needs of people like you	69
Understands complex issues	69
Generally agrees with you on issues you care about, other than terrorism	60

Analysis: In the wake of the terrorist attacks in the U.S., and even before the latest military actions involving U.S. strikes in Afghanistan, Americans have given their president an extraordinary vote of confidence, resulting in record job approval ratings and high marks on a variety of his personal characteristics.

Just prior to the attacks on September 11, George W. Bush's popularity was waning, with an approval rating of only 51%, down from the

57% he received a month earlier. But three days after the attacks, 86% approved of the job Bush was doing as president, an increase of 35 percentage points and the largest "rally effect" ever recorded by Gallup. A week later, his overall approval reached 90%.

In a Gallup Poll completed on October 6, a day before the launch of American and British retaliatory strikes against Afghanistan, President Bush's overall job approval remained extraordinarily high at 87%. The same poll shows that Bush also receives high approval ratings for his handling of the economy and foreign affairs, 72% and 81%, respectively. Despite the worsening economy, Bush's rating in that area is now 18 points higher than it was in July and his foreign affairs approval rating is 27 points.

The October 6–7 weekend poll asked the public to rate Bush on a series of personal characteristics, and the results show that the current level of support for the president is generalized across a wide variety of these specific measures. On almost every measure included in the poll, the public gives Bush much higher ratings now than they did in previous Gallup Polls. Some of the characteristics were last measured in August, others in July, April, or February, and all but one ("agreement on issues" other than terrorism) show an increase of more than 10 percentage points.

Bush also gets a major boost in his ratings on being a strong and decisive leader and on inspiring confidence, both items up 20 percentage points since the last measurement. The increases are somewhat smaller for "cares about the needs of people like you," and understanding complex issues, up by 12 percentage points each. And on the last item, which was designed to get the public's rating exclusive of terrorism, Bush's rating has risen by just 7 percentage points.

OCTOBER 9
PRESIDENTIAL AND
CONGRESSIONAL PRIORITIES

Interview Dates: 10/5–6/01
CNN/*USA Today*/Gallup Poll
Survey #GO 134790

How important is it to you that the president and Congress deal with each of the following issues in the next year—extremely important, very important, moderately important, or not that important?

	Extremely, very important
Terrorism	95%
Military and defense issues	88
The economy	90
Foreign affairs	86
Education	83
Social Security and Medicare systems	79
Prescription drugs for older Americans	69
A patients' bill of rights	62

Do you think the country would be better off if the Republicans controlled Congress, or if the Democrats controlled Congress?

	Republicans	Democrats	Neither; same (vol.); no opinion
2001 Oct 5–6	38%	37%	25%
2001 Aug 3–5	34	43	23
2001 Apr 20–22	41	43	16
2001 Jan 5–7	39	41	20

Overall, in whom do you have more confidence when it comes to dealing with the economy—the Republicans or the Democrats?

Republicans	45%
Democrats	43
Both (vol.)	4
Neither (vol.)	4
No opinion	4

Overall, in whom do you have more confidence when it comes to dealing with terrorism—the Republicans or the Democrats?

Republicans	56%
Democrats	21

Both (vol.) 8
Neither (vol.) 7
No opinion 8

Analysis: The tasks facing President Bush and Congress are now much different from those they confronted one month ago. The terrorist attacks of September 11 have caused a dramatic shift in the priorities of the American public according to a new Gallup Poll, which shows that 95% think it is "extremely" or "very important" for the president and Congress to deal with terrorism in the next year. The percentage saying that military and defense issues and foreign affairs are important has increased dramatically (by roughly 30 percentage points) when compared to polls taken earlier this year, while the importance attached to most domestic issues other than the economy has declined by about 10 points.

The poll, conducted October 5–6, asked Americans to rate how important it is for the president and Congress to deal with eight different issues. Not surprisingly, in the wake of the attacks on the World Trade Center and Pentagon, respondents overwhelmingly feel that the government should address terrorism. Seven in ten say it is extremely important for the president and Congress to deal with terrorism and 95% think it is at least very important. More than one-half views military and defense issues and foreign affairs as extremely important legislative priorities, putting international issues in three of the top four positions on the list. The only domestic issue that compares in importance is the economy, which 54% rate as extremely important. Other domestic issues are viewed as less important, with education, Social Security, and Medicare rated slightly ahead of prescription drug benefits for older Americans and a patients' bill of rights.

The poll asked Americans, "Overall, in whom do you have more confidence when it comes to dealing with" terrorism and the economy, two of the nation's top priorities. By a significant margin (56% to 21%), respondents say they have more confidence in the Republicans than the Democrats to deal with terrorism. On the economy, the public is divided: 45% have more confidence in the Republicans and 43% express

more confidence in the Democrats. When asked if the country would be better off if the Republicans or Democrats controlled Congress, 38% say the Republicans and 37% say the Democrats, with 25% expressing no preference.

OCTOBER 12
TRUST IN GOVERNMENT

Interview Dates: 10/5–6/01
CNN/*USA Today*/Gallup Poll
Survey #GO 134790

How much of the time do you think you can trust the government in Washington to do what is right—just about always, most of the time, or only some of the time?

	Always, most of the time	Only some of the time	Never (vol.)*
2001 Oct 5–6	60%	38%	1%
2000 Jul 6–9	42	56	2

*"No opinion" is omitted.

Some people think the government is trying to do too many things that should be left to individuals and businesses. Others think the government should do more to solve our country's problems. Which comes closer to your own view?

	Doing too much	Should do more	No opinion
2001 Oct 5–6	41%	50%	9%
2001 Sep 7–10	55	36	9
2000 Sep 11–13	50	37	13
2000 Aug 18–19	54	38	8

Some people think the government should promote traditional values in our society. Others think the government should not favor any particular set of values. Which comes closer to your own view?

	Promote values	Not favor any values	No opinion
2001 Oct 5–6	.59%	39%	3%
2001 Sep 7–10	.53	41	6
2000 Sep 11–13	.54	38	8

Do you agree or disagree with each of the following statements:

I don't think public officials care much what people like me think?

Agree 41%
Disagree 57
No opinion 2

People like me don't have any say about what the government does?

Agree 39%
Disagree 59
No opinion 2

Analysis: One effect of the terrorist attacks of September 11 has been an extraordinary increase in the faith and confidence that Americans have in their federal government. For many years, polling has shown that the public has a distinct wariness of the federal government and the role it should play in the nation's daily life. Now, after September 11, these attitudes have shifted significantly. Six out of ten say they trust their government and half want the government to do more to solve the country's problems. This percentage is the highest it has been in the nine years that Gallup has been asking the question.

There are several explanations for these findings. All of our polling has shown a general rally effect in public attitudes since September 11. Job approval ratings for President Bush jumped up 35 points in the days immediately following the terrorist attacks, and the 90% rating he received on September 21–22 stands as the highest in Gallup Poll history. Satisfaction with the way things are going in the U.S. has gone up, not down, after the attacks, and several indicators of confidence in the U.S. economy also have risen. Support for the way the Bush administration and military are handling the crisis also is at about the 90% level. And so far, we have registered extremely strong support for the military actions now under way in Afghanistan.

Now, in the aftermath of the September 11 attacks, 60% say that they trust the federal government to do what is right either just about always or most of the time. And in recent years, we also have tracked the degree to which Americans think their government should be doing more or doing less in dealing with the country's problems. In a September 7–10 poll, on the eve of the September 11 attacks, 36% said that government should do more. In October that number has risen to 50%, the highest (by 1 percentage point) in the history of this question. Only 41% now say that the government is trying to do too many things that should be left to individuals and businesses.

Another measure reinforces the conclusion that Americans are less cynical about government than they used to be. This conclusion is based on a measure which asked respondents to agree or disagree with the sentiment that public officials "don't care much what people like me think." The percentage who disagree with this sentiment has risen to almost six out of ten, a major shift from the two times this question has been asked. On the other hand, there has been little change in the agreement with the statement that "People like me don't have any say about what the government does." Fifty-nine percent still disagree with that today.

OCTOBER 16
PRESIDENT BUSH/WAR ON TERRORISM

Interview Dates: 10/11–14/01
Gallup Poll News Service
Survey #GO 132077

Do you approve or disapprove of the way George W. Bush is handling his job as president?

	Approve	Disapprove	No opinion
2001 Oct 11–14	.89%	8%	3%
2001 Oct 5–6	.87	10	3

2001 Sep 21–22 90	6	4
2001 Sep 14–15 86	10	4
2001 Sep 7–10 51	39	10
2001 Aug 24–26 55	36	9
2001 Aug 16–19 57	34	9
2001 Aug 10–12 57	35	8
2001 Aug 3–5 55	35	10

Do you approve or disapprove of the way Congress is handling its job?

	Approve	Dis- approve	No opinion
2001 Oct 11–14 . . . .84%	10%	6%
2001 Sep 7–10 42	44	14
2001 Aug 16–19 50	37	13
2001 Aug 3–5 47	42	11

How worried are you that you or someone in your family will become a victim of a terrorist attack—very worried, somewhat worried, not too worried, or not worried at all?

	Very, somewhat worried	Not too worried	Not worried at all*
2001 Oct 11–14 . . . .51%	35%	14%
2001 Oct 5–6 59	27	14
2001 Sep 21–22 49	32	18
2001 Sep 14–15 51	35	13
2001 Sep 11 58	24	16
2000 Apr 7–9 24	41	34

*"No opinion" is omitted.

Do you favor or oppose the United States taking direct military action in Afghanistan?

	Favor	Oppose	No opinion
2001 Oct 11–14 . . . .88%	10%	2%
2001 Oct 5–6 82	14	4
2001 Sep 21–22 82	13	5

Do you approve or disapprove of the United States' decision to take military action in Afghanistan?

Approve 92%

Disapprove 7
No opinion 1

Who do you think is currently winning the war against terrorism—the United States and its allies, neither side, or the terrorists?

United States and its allies 42%
Neither side 44
Terrorists 11
No opinion 3

Analysis: As the United States and its allies target Taliban installations inside Afghanistan with sustained military attacks, the Bush administration continues to receive unprecedented levels of support from the American people. A new Gallup Poll conducted October 11–14 shows that 89% approve of President George W. Bush's overall job performance, and 92% approve of the decision to launch air strikes against Afghanistan in retaliation for the September 11 attacks on the World Trade Center and the Pentagon. President Bush's job approval ratings over the past month remain at near record levels. The current 89% rating is just one point lower than the record 90% measured in Gallup's September 21–22 poll. All of Bush's recent ratings rank among the highest Gallup has ever recorded, particularly remarkable in comparison to Bush's 50%-range job approval ratings in the weeks leading up to September 11.

Defense Secretary Donald Rumsfeld recently commented that U.S. troops "aren't running out of targets . . . Afghanistan is running out of targets." Despite this expression of confidence by one of the war's principals, most are thus far not convinced that the U.S. and its allies are winning the war on terrorism. A slight plurality (44%) believes neither side has an edge while 42% believe the U.S.-led forces are winning. Only 11% believe the terrorists are currently winning the war.

OCTOBER 19
AFGHAN PEOPLE VERSUS
THE TALIBAN

Interview Dates: 10/11–14/01
Gallup Poll News Service
Survey #GO 132077

Please tell me if you have a very favorable, mostly favorable, mostly unfavorable, or very unfavorable opinion of each of the following:

The Arabs?

Very favorable	.9%
Mostly favorable	.45
Mostly unfavorable	.25
Very unfavorable	.12
No opinion	.9

The people of the Islamic faith?

Very favorable	.15%
Mostly favorable	.51
Mostly unfavorable	.16
Very unfavorable	.11
No opinion	.7

The people of Afghanistan?

Very favorable	.9%
Mostly favorable	.43
Mostly unfavorable	.26
Very unfavorable	.14
No opinion	.8

Osama bin Laden?

Very favorable	.1%
Mostly favorable	.*
Mostly unfavorable	.14
Very unfavorable	.83
No opinion	.2

*Less than 1%

The ruling Taliban government in Afghanistan?

Very favorable	.2%
Mostly favorable	.1
Mostly unfavorable	.20
Very unfavorable	.73
No opinion	.4

British Prime Minister Tony Blair?

Very favorable	.49%
Mostly favorable	.33
Mostly unfavorable	.4
Very unfavorable	.3
No opinion	.11

Analysis: The Bush administration has repeatedly stressed that the military campaign under way in Afghanistan is being waged against terrorists and those who harbor terrorists, not against the Afghan people themselves or against those of the Islamic faith. The latest Gallup Poll suggests that the American people are following this line of thought, and are making clear distinctions among the key groups involved in the ongoing campaign against terrorism. A majority holds favorable opinions of Arabs, the people of Afghanistan, and people of the Islamic faith, while at the same time the vast majority views the ruling Taliban government in Afghanistan and Osama bin Laden negatively.

The poll conducted October 11–14 finds 52% with a favorable view of the people of Afghanistan, although only 9% say they are "very favorable." Almost two-thirds also say they have a favorable opinion of people of the Islamic faith. These opinions stand in stark contrast to how respondents view the ruling Taliban government in Afghanistan. Only 3% have a favorable opinion and 93% have an unfavorable opinion, including 73% who say they are "very unfavorable" toward the current ruling body in Afghanistan. The public also has extremely negative views of Osama bin Laden, leader of the al-Qaeda terrorist network. Ninety-seven percent have an unfavorable view of bin Laden, including 83% whose opinion is very unfavorable.

The poll also shows more Americans hold positive views of Arabs today than did so the last time Gallup asked about them. The current poll shows 54% with a favorable opinion of Arabs, 37% with an unfavorable view, and 9% with no opinion.

OCTOBER 22
CRIME

Interview Dates: 10/11–14/01
Gallup Poll News Service
Survey #GO 132077

Is there more crime in your area than there was a year ago, or less?

	More	Less	Same (vol.); no opinion
2001 Oct 11–14	26%	52%	22%
2000 Aug 29–Sep 5	34	46	20

Is there more crime in the United States than there was a year ago, or less?

	More	Less	Same (vol.); no opinion
2001 Oct 11–14	41%	43%	1%
2000 Aug 29–Sep 5	47	41	12

Is there any area near where you live, that is, within a mile, where you would be afraid to walk alone at night?

	Yes	No	No opinion
2001 Oct 11–14	30%	69%	1%
2000 Aug 29–Sep 5	34	66	*

*Less than 1%

How much confidence do you have in the ability of the police to protect you from violent crime—a great deal, quite a lot, not very much, or none at all?

	Great deal	Quite a lot	Not very much; none at all*
2001 Oct 11–14	25%	41%	33%
2000 Aug 29–Sep 5	20	42	37

*"No opinion" is omitted.

How often do you, yourself, worry about the following things—frequently, occasionally, rarely, or never:

Being the victim of terrorism?

Frequently	21%
Occasionally	26
Rarely, never	53
No opinion	*

*Less than 1%

Having your car stolen or broken into?

Frequently	14%
Occasionally	27
Rarely, never	56
No opinion	3

Having a school-aged child of yours physically harmed while attending school?

Frequently	13%
Occasionally	18
Rarely, never	41
No opinion	28

Your home being burglarized when you are not there?

Frequently	12%
Occasionally	28
Rarely, never	59
No opinion	1

Getting mugged?

Frequently	6%
Occasionally	17
Rarely, never	77
No opinion	*

*Less than 1%

Being attacked while driving your car?

Frequently	6%
Occasionally	15
Rarely, never	75
No opinion	4

Your home being burglarized when you are there?

Frequently 6%
Occasionally 16
Rarely, never 78
No opinion . . . .*

*Less than 1%

Being the victim of a hate crime?

Frequently 5%
Occasionally 8
Rarely, never 86
No opinion 1

Getting murdered?

Frequently 4%
Occasionally 9
Rarely, never 87
No opinion . . . .*

*Less than 1%

Being sexually assaulted?

Frequently 4%
Occasionally 15
Rarely, never 81
No opinion . . . .*

*Less than 1%

Being assaulted or killed by a coworker or other employee where you work?

Frequently 2%
Occasionally 5
Rarely, never 80
No opinion 13

Now, thinking about some large cities, both those you have visited and those you have never visited, from what you know and have read, do you consider each of the following cities to be safe to live in or visit, or not?

	Safe
Minneapolis	77%
Seattle	73

Dallas	68
Boston	66
Houston	64
San Francisco	64
Atlanta	62
Philadelphia	60
Chicago	53
Washington, DC	43
New York	41
Detroit	39
Los Angeles	39
Miami	39

Next, I'm going to read some things people do because of their concern over crime. Please tell me which, if any, of these things you, yourself, do or have done?

	Yes
Avoid going to certain places, neighborhoods you might otherwise want to go to	43%
Had special locks installed on your home	32
Keep dog for protection	32
Had burglar alarm installed in your home	23
Bought gun for protection of yourself and your home	21
Taken self-defense course	17
Carry mace or pepper spray	17
Carry gun for defense	11
Carry knife for defense	9

Do you have a gun in your home?

	Yes
2001 Oct 11–14	40%
2000 Aug 29–Sep 5	39
2000 Apr 7–9	42

Analysis: A new Gallup Poll finds that the war on terrorism at home and abroad comes at a time when Americans are feeling safer from crime than they have at any other point in over thirty years. National crime rates have steadily declined over the past decade, and, despite the shock of the September 11 terrorist attacks, the public increasingly recognizes this positive trend.

The October 11–14 survey shows that respondents are more likely to feel safe in their neighborhoods, less likely to worry about being the victim of a serious crime, and more likely to feel that major American cities, including New York and Washington, DC, are safe to live in and visit. Close to one-half of Americans now believes that crime nationwide is declining, the highest level of optimism about crime recorded in over ten years. There also has been a slight increase in confidence in the police to protect people from violent crime.

Despite these positive changes in public perceptions about crime, the fact remains that roughly one-half of respondents are less than optimistic, saying they believe crime rates have risen or stayed the same over the past year, when, in fact, crime has dropped by a record amount.

Dampening the positive ramifications that declining public concern over crime might otherwise have on Americans' way of life, the survey shows that the public is spending more time these days worrying about terrorism than about conventional crime. Close to one-half (47%) frequently or occasionally worries about becoming a terrorist victim, compared to less than half that number who worry about being the victim of conventional violent crimes such as muggings.

Despite the major declines in crime during 2000, responses to a Gallup question that has been asked for a number of years shows that only 43% believe there is less crime in the U.S. today than there was a year ago. A similar number (41%) believes there is more crime today while 10% believe it has remained the same.

Just as Americans are increasingly likely to recognize that crime is less of a problem in their area and the nation than it was in previous years, fewer express fear for their personal safety in their local area, with only, 30% saying they would be afraid to walk alone at night.

Along with declining personal fear, Gallup finds an increase from last year in public confidence in the police to protect people from violent crime. Two-thirds (66%) now express high levels of confidence in the police on this measure, up from 62% last year. And according to the new survey, respondents are more likely to worry about being the victim of terrorism than they are to worry about being murdered, mugged, robbed, carjacked, or any of several other serious crimes, although the difference between worry about terrorism and some of these more conventional crimes is not large. Close to one-half of those interviewed in the October 11–14 survey (47%) say they frequently or occasionally worry about being the victim of terrorism, compared to an average of only 23% who worry this often about conventional crimes.

Top concerns for the public, aside from terrorism, are having their cars stolen or broken into (41% frequently or occasionally worry about this) and having their homes burglarized when they are not there (40%). Close to one-third (31%) worries about a school-aged child of theirs being physically harmed while at school. Violent crimes register far less worry, ranging from 23% who worry about getting mugged, down to 13% who worry about getting murdered. Just 13% also fear being the victim of a hate crime. And only 7% worry about being assaulted or killed in the workplace by another employee.

Looking just at the percentage who "frequently" worry about each crime helps to highlight the terror in terrorism. More than one in five (21%) tells Gallup that they worry frequently about being the victim of terrorism. This is 50% greater than the 14% who worry this much about the second-ranked concern of having a car stolen or broken into. It is up to five times greater than the number who frequently worry about conventional types of violent crime such as getting mugged (6%), murdered (4%), or sexually assaulted (4%).

It should be noted that, taking into account all those injured or killed by the terrorism of September 11, and all those testing positive for anthrax exposure in recent weeks, the number of people who have been terrorist victims is very small compared to those who have been victims of conventional crime. Roughly one in 15,000 are among the victims of terrorism since September 11 compared to the incidence of conventional crime, which is one in five.

Since 1990, Gallup has asked Americans to rate the safety of fourteen large American cities, and, over this period, the number of cities considered "safe" to live in or visit has increased from five to nine. Originally, only Dallas, Seattle, Houston, Boston, and Minneapolis were considered safe by a majority of Americans. But added to their number today are San Francisco, Atlanta, Chicago, and Philadelphia. In addition to New York, more people also continue to see Miami, Los Angeles, Detroit, and Washington, DC, as unsafe than see them as safe. Minneapolis and Seattle have swapped first and second place on Gallup's Safe Cities ranking since 1990, and this year Minneapolis emerged the winner.

OCTOBER 23
EXPOSURE TO ANTHRAX

Interview Dates: 10/19–21/01
CNN/*USA Today*/Gallup Poll
Survey #GO 134866

How worried are you that you or someone in your family will be exposed to anthrax—very worried, somewhat worried, not too worried, or not worried at all?

Very worried 7%
Somewhat worried .27
Not too worried 35
Not worried at all .31
Already exposed (vol.) 0
No opinion . . . .*

*Less than 1%

How likely is it that you or someone in your family will be exposed to anthrax—very likely, somewhat likely, not too likely, or not at all likely?

Very likely 4%
Somewhat likely 16
Not too likely 41
Not at all likely 37
Already exposed (vol.) 1
No opinion . . . .*

*Less than 1%

How confident are you in the ability of the U.S. government to respond effectively to the health threats posed by each of the following—very confident, somewhat confident, not too confident, or not at all confident:

A major outbreak of anthrax?

Very, somewhat confident 77%
Not too, not at all confident 22
No opinion 1

A major outbreak of smallpox?

Very, somewhat confident 66%
Not too, not at all confident 33
No opinion 1

A nuclear attack?

Very, somewhat confident 58%
Not too, not at all confident 40
No opinion 2

Do you think Americans are overreacting, reacting about right, or underreacting to the threat of anthrax? And would you say this overreaction is giving the terrorists what they want, or not?

Overreacting 47%
 Giving terrorists what they want 42
 Not giving terrorists what they want 4
 Unsure 1
Reacting about right 45
Underreacting 5
No opinion 3

Do you think the news media are overreacting, reacting about right, or underreacting to the threat of anthrax? And would you say this overreaction is giving the terrorists what they want, or not?

Overreacting 60%
 Giving terrorists what they want 54
 Not giving terrorists what they want 5
 Unsure 1

Reacting about right 35
Underreacting 4
No opinion 1

As you may know, the U.S. House of Representatives shut down this week because of threats of anthrax. Would you say the U.S. House of Representatives overreacted, or did they react about right? And would you say this overreaction is giving the terrorists what they want, or not?

Overreacted 29%
   Giving terrorists what they want 28
   Not giving terrorists what they want 1
   Unsure . . . . *
Reacting about right 69
Underreacting 2
No opinion 0

*Less than 1%

Do you think the recent incidents involving anthrax do or do not represent the beginning of a sustained campaign against the United States involving anthrax?

Do represent 52%
Do not represent 38
No opinion 10

Just your best guess, do you think members of Osama bin Laden's terrorist network are responsible for all of the recent incidents involving anthrax, some of them, or none of the recent incidents involving anthrax?

All of them 24%
Some of them 60
None 11
No opinion 5

Analysis: A Gallup Poll conducted October 19–21 finds that two-thirds of Americans are not worried about being exposed to anthrax, and that eight out of ten feel it is not likely that they or a family member will be a victim of anthrax. At the same time, about one-half says that the anthrax incidents are the beginning of a sustained terrorist campaign. About one-quarter are now using more caution in handling the mail, and many more are seriously considering it, although only a very small percentage have sought out antibiotics or vaccines. A substantial majority believes the news media are overreacting to the threat, although respondents are divided on whether the public in general is overreacting or reacting about right. Most think the shutdown of the U.S. House of Representatives last week due to threats of anthrax was an appropriate reaction. The poll also shows widespread confidence in the ability of the federal government to respond to the health threats that would be posed by a major outbreak of anthrax or smallpox.

According to the poll, about one-third (34%) is either "very" (7%) or "somewhat" (27%) worried that they, or someone in their family, will be exposed to anthrax. Fewer say it is likely they will be exposed to anthrax than are worried about it. The poll shows that only 4% say it is "very" likely, and another 16% say "somewhat" likely that they or someone in their family will be exposed.

Despite their relatively low level of worry about personal exposure to anthrax, a majority (52%) believes that the recent incidents involving anthrax represent the beginning of a sustained bioterrorism campaign against the U.S. while 38% disagree. And if there is a sustained anthrax attack in the days or weeks ahead, most believe the government will be able to respond effectively. The poll shows that 34% are "very" confident and another 43% "somewhat" confident. Only one in five is either "not too" (17%) or "not at all" (5%) confident. There is less public confidence in the ability of the government to handle the health risks associated with a major outbreak of smallpox or a nuclear attack.

Over the past week, news stories have been dominated by real and suspected cases of anthrax exposure. It has generated a debate over what constitutes appropriate news coverage and warnings on the one hand, and inappropriate stories that create concern and panic on the other. The most recent poll shows that respondents generally think the press has overreacted in its coverage of the anthrax incidents by a 60%-to-35% margin.

However, they are divided on whether the public in general is overreacting to the threat of anthrax. Forty-seven percent say it is and 45% say it is not.

Last week the House of Representatives chose to shut down when mail was discovered in several congressional offices that had traces of anthrax in them. There has been some debate as to whether or not this was the appropriate action. By more than a 2-to-1 margin, Americans support the House leadership decision, saying that the U.S. House of Representatives' reaction was appropriate (69%) rather than an overreaction (29%). Among those who said that the general public, Congress, or the media were overreacting, the vast majority also said that such overreactions are "giving the terrorists what they want."

OCTOBER 24
WAR ON TERRORISM

Interview Dates: 10/19–21/01
CNN/*USA Today*/Gallup Poll
Survey #GO 134866

Do you approve or disapprove of the current military action in Afghanistan?

Approve 88%
Disapprove 10
No opinion 2

If you had to choose, which of the following comes closer to your view—ground troops should be used for limited missions which would send U.S. forces into Afghanistan for only a few days or weeks at a time, or U.S. ground troops should be used to take over areas in Afghanistan for an indefinite period of time?

Use for limited missions 47%
Take over areas 50
No opinion 3

If you had to choose, which of the following would you say is the most important goal of the U.S. military action in Afghanistan— destroying terrorist operations in Afghan-

istan, capturing or killing Osama bin Laden, or removing the Taliban from power in Afghanistan?

Destroying terrorist operations 41%
Capturing or killing bin Laden 25
Removing Taliban from power 29
Other (vol.) 3
No opinion 2

From what you know, do you think the United States is doing too much, the right amount, or too little to provide humanitarian aid to the people of Afghanistan?

Too much 20%
Right amount 64
Too little 12
No opinion 4

There have been reports recently about civilian casualties in Afghanistan as a result of the U.S. military action there. Which comes closer to your view—these civilian casualties are an unavoidable aspect of war, or these civilian casualties could have been avoided if the United States took proper care?

Casualties are unavoidable 85%
Casualties could be avoided 13
No opinion 2

Analysis: The American people continue to express high levels of support for the U.S.-led military action against Afghanistan, and also continue to give President George W. Bush the same high job approval ratings he has earned over the past month. Support for the use of U.S. ground troops in Afghanistan is also high. About one-half of those who support the use of ground troops favors their use to gain and hold Afghan territory rather than the more limited role in which they have been engaged so far.

Nine out of ten Americans interviewed October 19–21 approve of the "current military action in Afghanistan," roughly in line with prospective support levels that existed before the first U.S.-led coalition strikes were launched on

October 7, and similar to support levels in the two weeks since. Support for the use of ground troops in Afghanistan also remains very strong, although slightly below the levels of support for military action generally. This has been the case in most polling conducted since the September 11 attacks. In the latest poll, 80% favor use of ground troops in Afghanistan while 18% are opposed.

News reports suggest that U.S. and allied ground troops so far have been used in very limited, "in and out" missions in Afghanistan. The public is split on the issue of whether these types of actions are most appropriate, or if the U.S. should use its ground forces to take over and hold areas of Afghanistan indefinitely. Of those who support ground troops, about one-half (40%) says that they should be used in more expanded roles while the other half (37%) says that their role should be more limited.

The specific objectives of the current military action in Afghanistan are less clear than they may have been in previous American wars. In recent weeks, however, the administration has moved to emphasize that finding Osama bin Laden is not the only, or even the primary, goal of the actions. Americans appear to have noted this and are significantly more likely to say that either removing the Taliban from power or destroying terrorist operations should be the most important military objective rather than capturing or killing bin Laden. A plurality (41%) says that destroying terrorist operations in Afghanistan is the most important goal.

The war in Afghanistan is unusual in that it has encompassed the delivery of humanitarian aid to the people of a country while that country simultaneously undergoes heavy military bombardment. Earlier this month, Gallup polling found that Americans make a clear distinction between the people of Afghanistan on the one hand and their leaders and terrorists on the other. A majority feels favorably toward the people while feeling decidedly unfavorable toward the Taliban and Osama bin Laden. The evidence from the October 19–21 poll, however, suggests that there is no strong sentiment that more should be done to help the Afghans. About two-thirds say the

U.S. is doing about "the right amount" to provide humanitarian aid to the people of Afghanistan while 20% says it is doing too much. Just 12% say the U.S. is doing too little.

As is inevitably the case in war, there have been reports (some confirmed and some not) of civilian casualties. Most recently, the Taliban government has claimed that U.S. bombs hit a hospital. At this point, 85% say that such casualties may simply be an unavoidable aspect of war while only 13% say more should have been done to avoid them.

OCTOBER 26
BUSINESS AS USUAL FOLLOWING 9/11

Interview Dates: 10/19–21/01
CNN/*USA Today*/Gallup Poll
Survey #GO 134866

Thinking about your daily life since the September 11 attacks, would you say you are going about your business as usual, or not?

Yes 89%
No 11

Now, thinking just about today, how would you describe your mood—has it been very good, somewhat good, neither good nor bad, somewhat bad, or very bad?

Very good 38%
Somewhat good 40
Neither good nor bad 12
Somewhat bad 7
Very bad 2
No opinion 1

How worried are you that you or someone in your family will become a victim of a terrorist attack—very worried, somewhat worried, not too worried, or not worried at all?

	Very, somewhat worried	Not too worried	Not worried at all*
2001 Oct 19–21	. . . . .43%	33%	23%

2001 Oct 11–14	.51	35	14
2001 Oct 5–6	.59	27	14
2001 Sep 21–22	.49	32	18
2001 Sep 14–15	.51	35	13
2001 Sep 11 ^	.58	24	16
2000 Apr 7–9	.24	41	34

*"No opinion" is omitted.

How likely is it that there will be further terrorist attacks in the United States over the next several weeks—very likely, somewhat likely, not too likely, or not at all likely?

	Very, somewhat likely	Not too likely	Not at all likely*
2001 Oct 19–21	.83%	12%	3%
2001 Oct 7	.83	9	4
2001 Sep 21–22	.66	24	8

*"No opinion" is omitted.

How likely is it that there will be further acts of terrorism in the United States over the next several weeks—very likely, somewhat likely, not too likely, or not at all likely?

Very likely	.40%
Somewhat likely	.45
Not too likely	.10
Not at all likely	.3
No opinion	.2

Do you think the efforts by the government to protect Americans since the September 11 attacks have gone too far, been about right, or not gone far enough?

Gone too far	.6%
Been about right	.69
Not gone far enough	.24
No opinion	.1

Would you say the efforts by the government to protect Americans since the September 11 attacks have made the United States safer, or not?

Safer	.77%
Not safer	.20
No opinion	.3

Do you think the government warnings of further terrorist attacks have mostly helped people, or just scared people?

Helped people	.47%
Scared people	.49
No opinion	.4

Next, please tell me if you favor or oppose taking each of the following actions in the United States for at least several years:

Requiring Arabs, including those who have become U.S. citizens, to carry a special ID?

Favor	.49%
Oppose	.49
No opinion	.2

Instituting new security procedures that would require passengers to check in two to three hours before their flight is scheduled to depart?

Favor	.75%
Oppose	.23
No opinion	.2

Limiting airline passengers to carry on only one small item such as a purse or briefcase?

Favor	.80%
Oppose	.18
No opinion	.2

Making it easier for legal authorities to read mail, e-mail, or tap phones without the person's knowledge?

Favor	.37%
Oppose	.60
No opinion	.3

Next, I'm going to read you some things people may do because of their concern about terrorism. For each one, please tell me if it is something you have done, something you are seriously considering, something you are not seriously considering, or something you haven't even thought about:

Using more caution in handling mail?

Done it 23%
Seriously considering 30
Not seriously considering 16
Haven't thought about it 30
No opinion 1

Avoiding airline travel?

Done it 11%
Seriously considering 15
Not seriously considering 20
Haven't thought about it 51
No opinion 3

Consulting a Web site or other source of information about terrorism preparedness?

Done it 10%
Seriously considering 13
Not seriously considering 14
Haven't thought about it 62
No opinion 1

Stockpiling food or water?

Done it 9%
Seriously considering 12
Not seriously considering 20
Haven't thought about it 59
No opinion . . . .*

*Less than 1%

Avoiding public events or crowded areas?

Done it 8%
Seriously considering 11
Not seriously considering 25
Haven't thought about it 54
No opinion 2

Purchasing a weapon?

Done it 8%
Seriously considering 9
Not seriously considering 16
Haven't thought about it 64
No opinion 3

Discussing the treatment of biological or chemical warfare with your doctor?

Done it 3%
Seriously considering 8
Not seriously considering 17
Haven't thought about it 71
No opinion 1

Trying to get a prescription for antibiotics?

Done it 3%
Seriously considering 6
Not seriously considering 20
Haven't thought about it 70
No opinion 1

Trying to get a vaccination for anthrax or smallpox?

Done it 2%
Seriously considering 15
Not seriously considering 21
Haven't thought about it 62
No opinion . . . .*

*Less than 1%

Purchasing a gas mask or other protective clothing?

Done it 2%
Seriously considering 6
Not seriously considering 21
Haven't thought about it 71
No opinion . . . .*

*Less than 1%

Would you say the visible signs of increased security, such as National Guard troops at airports and the Coast Guard boarding ships at major U.S. ports, have made you feel more secure or less secure about potential terrorism, or have they had no effect on you either way?

More secure .... .68%
Less secure 2
No effect; no opinion .... .30

Which of the following comes closer to your view—it is the duty of Americans not to show fear about the threat of terrorism, or there is nothing wrong with showing fear about terrorism?

Duty not to show fear .... .26%
Nothing wrong with showing fear .... .72
No opinion 2

Which of the following comes closer to your view—there is little reason for you, personally, to be afraid of terrorist threats; or there is good reason for you, personally, to be afraid of terrorist threats?

Little reason to be afraid .... .65%
Good reason to be afraid .... .34
No opinion 1

Analysis: Despite lingering fears about terrorism, the vast majority of Americans say they are currently going about their business as usual. The latest Gallup Poll conducted October 19–21 finds 89% saying they are going about their business as usual while 11% are not. When asked to describe their personal mood, little change is evidenced when compared to a January poll, with 78% reporting they are in a good mood now compared to 83% in January. Even so, most admit that it is all right to be afraid. Seventy-two percent think there is nothing wrong with showing fear while just 26% believe it is the "duty of Americans not to show fear about the threat of terrorism." Four out of ten still worry about themselves or family members being a victim of terrorism, although this proportion has declined in recent weeks, and is currently at its lowest point since the Septem-

ber 11 attacks. And most believe that the increased security efforts of the federal government have made the country safer.

The fact that Americans are living their lives as usual is underscored by the fact that very few have personally taken active measures to protect themselves from terrorism. The latest poll asked which of several actions they have taken out of concern for terrorism. The most common action, but one done by only 23% of the public, is to use more caution when handling mail. About one in ten is avoiding airline travel, researching information on terrorism preparedness, or stockpiling food and water. Only 2% have gone to the effort of purchasing a gas mask or other protective clothing, or tried to get a vaccination for anthrax or smallpox. Aside from using caution in handling mail, a majority has not even thought about doing any of these activities.

The latest update shows 43% are at least somewhat worried about themselves or family members becoming the victim of a terrorist attack, including 13% who are very worried. Both percentages are the lowest recorded since the September 11 terrorist attacks on the World Trade Center and Pentagon. For the first time since the attacks, a majority (56%) is not too worried or not worried at all about becoming a victim, although about one in three believes that further terrorist attacks or acts of terrorism are "very likely" over the next several weeks. The percentage saying additional attacks are very likely has fallen 6 points when compared to a poll conducted on the night of October 7, when the U.S. began its bombing campaign in Afghanistan.

Thirty-four percent say they have "good reason" to be personally afraid of terrorist threats while 65% say they have little reason to fear these. Nearly seven in ten think the government's efforts to protect its citizens since the September 11 attacks have "been about right." Only 6% think these have gone too far, but a significant 24% say the efforts have not gone far enough. Similarly, 68% say visible signs of increased security, such as National Guard troops at airports, have made them feel more secure, while only 2% feel less secure and 30% say these signs have had no effect on them.

Most Americans also believe that the government's efforts have made the U.S. safer. All told, 77% believe the nation is safer as a result of these efforts, including 30% who think the country is a lot safer and 47% who think it is only a little safer. One in five believes the nation is not safer following the government's recent steps to protect its citizens.

When considering additional steps the government could take to protect the public over the next several years, respondents are most likely to favor additional security measures at airports. Eighty percent favor limiting airline passengers to a single, small carry-on item such as a purse or briefcase, and 75% favor instituting new security procedures that would require passengers to check in two to three hours prior to their flights' departure. The public is divided as to whether Arabs, including those who have become U.S. citizens, should be required to carry a special ID, a proposal favored by 49% and opposed by 49%. Respondents are least supportive of making it easier for legal authorities to read mail, e-mail, or tap phones without the person's knowledge. Only 37% favor tlis proposal while 60% are opposed.

The nation is divided, though, as to the effects of government warnings of further attacks. Forty-seven percent believe these have "helped people," while a similar proportion (49%) believes these warnings have "just scared people."

OCTOBER 30
HALLOWEEN

Interview Dates: 10/19–21/01
CNN/*USA Today*/Gallup Poll
Survey #GO 134866

Will you or someone in your family be giving out Halloween treats from the door of your home on Halloween this year?

Yes 63%
No 35
No opinion 2

Asked of those who answered "no": Is this due at least partly to concern about terror-

ism, or is it for some other reason not related to terrorism?

Due to concern about terrorism 12%
Not due to terrorism 87
No opinion 1

Do you have any children under the age of fifteen?

Yes 37%
No 63

Will any of your children be going out trick-or-treating door to door on Halloween?

Yes 66%
No 32
No opinion 2

Will you put any restrictions on your children's trick-or-treating this year out of concern for their safety following the September 11 terrorist attacks?

Yes 34%
No 65
No opinion 1

Analysis: A recent Gallup Poll reveals that Americans' Halloween traditions will be little affected by concerns about terrorism this year. According to the October 19–21 survey, more than three in five households will be handing out Halloween treats at their doors, and nearly two-thirds of parents of children under fifteen will send their children out trick-or-treating. These percentages are virtually unchanged compared to previous years and reflect the fact that the vast majority are currently going about their business as usual since September 11. Some concern does manifest itself: one-third of parents of trick-or-treaters say they will restrict their children's activities due to concern about terrorism. A majority, however, do not plan to restrict their children.

Some news reports have suggested that the war on terrorism and the recent incidents involving anthrax would inhibit participation in

Halloween activities this year. However, that does not appear to be the case. Roughly two-thirds of Americans say they will be handing out treats to trick-or-treaters, essentially the same proportion as in previous years. Of those who will not be giving out Halloween treats this year, only 12% (4% of all Americans) say this is due to concern about terrorism and 87% say it is for some other reason.

The percentage of children who will go trick-or-treating is also unchanged when compared to previous years. Sixty-six percent of parents of children under the age of fifteen say their children will be trick-or-treating. An October 1999 poll showed similar numbers. Among parents of trick-or-treaters, about one-third (34%) say they are concerned about their children's safety following the September 11 attacks and will put restrictions on their children's activities, while two-thirds say they will not.

OCTOBER 31
AIRPORT SECURITY

Interview Dates: 10/19–21/01
CNN/*USA Today*/Gallup Poll
Survey #GO 134866

Analysis: The House of Representatives is scheduled to vote this week to determine whether the federal government will take control of airport security in the future. Aside from this debate, a number of specific options for securing the safety of commercial air travel have been floated since the September 11 terrorist hijacking of four passenger planes, and, to varying degrees, the public supports all of them. From armed marshals to longer check-in times, and everything in between, Americans favor a wide range of proposals designed to thwart terrorists from boarding airplanes and gaining command of cockpits.

The most widely supported air safety measure tested in public opinion surveys over the past two months is "making cockpit doors on all passenger airliners stronger and more secure," a proposal initially resisted by some pilots but favored by 96% of the public. Additional measures in-

clude support for placing armed sky marshals on all commercial airliners (90%) and putting pilot control of aircraft ahead of passenger comfort and safety (85%).

Roughly three-quarters or more of the public favor specific proposals that would negatively impact passenger convenience such as requiring passengers to check in two to three hours before a flight (75%) and limiting carry-on luggage to one bag (80%). When asked simply whether they would favor turning over the job of airport security to the federal government, 77% of Americans say yes. And about two-thirds are in favor of arming airline pilots (68%) or other airline personnel (65%). This is clearly more controversial than the sky marshal program that receives close to unanimous public support. and most Americans welcome more visible signs of increased security at airports, with 68% saying the presence of National Guard troops, for instance, makes them feel more secure.

NOVEMBER 5
CRIME

Interview Dates: 10/11–14/01
Gallup Poll News Service
Survey #GO 132077

Which, if any, of these incidents have happened to you or your household within the last twelve months?

	Yes
Money or property stolen from you or another member of your household	11%
A home, car, or property owned by you or other household member vandalized	11
Your house or apartment broken into	3
A car owned by you or other household member stolen	3
You or other household member mugged or physically assaulted	3
Money or property taken from you or other household member by force, with gun, knife, weapon, or physical attack, or by threat of force	1

Net Percentage of Households Experiencing Any Crime   22

	Net Percentage of Households	
Experiencing Violent Crime	4	
Percentage of All Crime *Not*		
Reported to Police	37	

Analysis: Gallup's annual update on Americans and crime shows that 22% of all households experienced some type of crime during the past year, with 15% mentioning one incident and another 7% mentioning two or more incidents. The poll also shows that 37% of all crime was not reported to the police.

The poll, conducted November 11–14, asked respondents if specific crime incidents had happened to them, or to anyone in their household, over the past twelve months. The polls also included questions asking whether each incident mentioned had been reported to the police. The two most frequently mentioned crimes were having money or property stolen (11%) and having one's home, car, or property vandalized (11%). Theft was the least reported crime, with less than one-half of the incidents reported to the police.

Three percent of respondents say each of the following about the past year: their house or apartment was broken into, a car was stolen, or someone in the household was mugged. Separately, 1% report someone in the household being the victim of a robbery. A net total of 4% of all American households experienced one or more violent crimes.

NOVEMBER 6
PRESIDENTIAL ELECTION
CONTROVERSY

Interview Dates: 11/2–4/01
CNN/*USA Today*/Gallup Poll
Survey #GO 134989

If the elections for Congress were being held today, which party's candidate would you vote for in your congressional district—the Democratic Party's candidate, or the Republican Party's candidate? [Asked of those who were undecided: As of today, do you lean more toward the Democratic Party's candidate, or the Republican Party's candidate?]

	Demo-cratic	Repub-lican	Un-decided; other (vol.); no opinion
National Adults			
2001 Nov 2–4	43%	44%	13%
2001 Jun 8–10	50	43	7
Registered Voters			
2001 Nov 2–4	45	45	10
2001 Jun 8–10	49	45	6

How much confidence do you have in the system in which votes are cast and counted in this country—a great deal, quite a lot, some, or very little?

	Great deal; quite a lot	Some	Very little; none (vol.); no opinion
2001 Nov 2–4	41%	32%	27%
2000 Dec 15–17	30	32	38

In general, do you think the system in which votes are cast and counted in this country discriminates against some people, or is fair to all Americans?

	Discri-minates	Is fair to all	No opinion
2001 Nov 2–4	37%	61%	2%
2000 Dec 15–17	44	52	4

Do you think the system in which votes are cast and counted in this country is in need of a complete overhaul, major reforms, minor reforms, or no reforms?

	Complete overhaul; major reforms	Minor reforms	No re-forms; no opinion
2001 Nov 2–4	43%	45%	12%
2000 Dec 15–17	67	27	6

Thinking about the 2000 election for president involving George W. Bush and Al Gore, which comes closest to your view of the way George W.

Bush won the 2000 presidential election—he won fair and square, he won but only on a technicality, or he stole the election?

	Won fair and square	Won on technicality	Stole the election*
2001 Nov 2–4	.50%	32%	15%
2001 Jul 10–11	.48	33	17
2001 Apr 20–22	.50	29	19
2001 Jan 15–16	.45	31	24
2000 Dec 15–17	.48	32	18

*"No opinion" is omitted.

Which of these statements do you think best describes the situation that occurred as a result of the 2000 presidential election last year—it was a constitutional crisis, it was a major problem for the country but was not a crisis, it was a minor problem for the country, or it was not a problem for the country at all?

	Constitutional crisis; major problem	Minor problem	Not a problem*
2001 Nov 2–4	.42%	42%	13%
2000 Dec 10	.63	25	9
2000 Nov 26–27	.60	29	9
2000 Nov 19	.54	32	12
2000 Nov 11–12	.64	25	9

*"No opinion" is omitted.

If Al Gore had been elected president in 2000, do you think he would have done a better job, about the same job, or a worse job than George W. Bush has done in responding to the terrorist attacks?

	Better job	About the same	Worse job*
2001 Nov 2–4	.12%	40%	41%
2001 Oct 5–6	.9	46	40

*"No opinion" is omitted.

If Al Gore had been elected president in 2000, do you think he would have done a better job, about the same job, or a worse job than George W. Bush has done in dealing with the economy?

Better job 26%
About the same 39
Worse job 28
No opinion 7

If Bill Clinton were still president, do you think he would have done a better job, about the same job, or a worse job than George W. Bush has done in responding to the terrorist attacks?

Better job 16%
About the same 34
Worse job 44
No opinion 6

If Bill Clinton were still president, do you think he would have done a better job, about the same job, or a worse job than George W. Bush has done in handling the economy?

Better job 33%
About the same 35
Worse job 29
No opinion 3

Suppose that the presidential election were being held today, and it included George W. Bush as the Republican candidate and Al Gore as the Democratic candidate. Would you vote for George W. Bush, the Republican, or Al Gore, the Democrat? [Asked of those who were undecided: As of today, do you lean more toward George W. Bush, the Republican, or Al Gore, the Democrat?]

	Bush	Gore	Other (vol.); no opinion
National Adults			
2001 Nov 2–4	.61%	35%	4%
2001 Aug 3–5	.48	48	4
Registered Voters			
2001 Nov 2–4	.60	36	4
2001 Aug 3–5	.49	48	3

Analysis: It has been a year since the 2000 presidential election, and the controversy over which candidate, Al Gore or George W. Bush, actually won Florida and hence the election. In the interim, the country has undergone a transforming experience with the terrorist attacks in New York City and Washington, DC. Thus it is not surprising that Americans see the controversy as far less of a problem than they did a year ago. Today, 42% say the events of that time represented either a constitutional crisis or a major problem, while 55% say it was either a minor problem or no problem at all. A year ago, however, the majority leaned the other way, with 64% saying the events constituted a major problem or worse, and only 34% indicating it was a minor problem or less.

These more positive views are also reflected in the public's assessment of the electoral system. The current poll conducted November 2–4 shows that 41% of Americans have "quite a lot" or a "great deal" of confidence in the electoral system (the way votes are cast and counted), while just 26% have "very little" or none. Last year the margins were reversed, with only 30% giving the high rating and 37% the lower rating.

Similarly, this year 43% believe the electoral system needs major reforms or a complete overhaul, while 54% believe minor reforms or no reforms would suffice. In 2000, the majorities were reversed as 67% called for major reforms or more, and just 31% said minor reforms or less were acceptable. These more positive views are also found in the public's assessment of how fair the electoral system is. Overall, 61% believe it is fair to all Americans while 37% say it is not, an improvement over the 52%-to-44% margin of a year ago.

Despite their changed view about the seriousness of the election controversy and the need for change in the electoral system, respondents have not changed their minds about what happened in the election and its aftermath. The poll shows that today 50% say Bush won the presidency fair and square, 32% think he won it on a technicality, and 15% say he stole the election. These numbers are little changed from those found immediately after the Supreme Court decision in December that effectively halted the vote recount and made Bush the winner. At that time,

48% said Bush won fair and square, 32% said he won on a technicality, and 18% said he stole the election.

While much can happen in the next three years, registered voters say that if the presidential election of 2004 were held today, they would re-elect Bush by a major landslide (60% to 36%). Last August the hypothetical race showed a virtual tie, with 49% of registered voters supporting Bush and 48% for Gore. While these numbers should not be interpreted as predicting the outcome of the next presidential election, they are indicative of how the political landscape is fundamentally changed.

A major factor in the shift toward Bush has been the public's view of his response to the terrorist attacks. Public approval for the president's handling of the war has been at or above 90% for the last several weeks, and his general job approval score has been almost as high. In addition, by 41% to 12%, Americans say that, compared with Bush, Gore would have done a worse job rather than a better job in dealing with terrorism. Another 40% say that Gore would have done as well as Bush.

On the economy, Americans remain evenly divided over which of the two men would have done a better job. While 39% say Gore would have done about the same as Bush, 28% say Gore would have done worse and 26% say better.

The poll also shows that the public is evenly divided on which party's congressional candidates they are most likely to support in the election next year. If the election were held today, 45% of registered voters would support the Republicans, 45% would support the Democrats, and 10% are unsure. In June 2000 the Democrats had a slight advantage of 49% to 45%.

NOVEMBER 7
TERRORIST ATTACKS

Interview Dates: 11/2–4/01
CNN/*USA Today*/Gallup Poll
Survey #GO 134989

How worried are you that you or someone in your family will become a victim of a terror-

ist attack—very worried, somewhat worried, not too worried, or not worried at all?

	Very, somewhat worried	Not too worried	Not worried at all*
2001 Nov 2–4	40%	28%	31%
2001 Oct 19–21	43	33	23
2001 Oct 11–14	51	35	14
2001 Oct 5–6	59	27	14
2001 Sep 21–22	49	32	18
2001 Sep 14–15	51	35	13
2001 Sep 11**	58	24	16

*"No opinion" is omitted.
**Based on one-night poll

How worried are you that you or someone in your family will become a victim of terrorism—very worried, somewhat worried, not too worried, or not worried at all?

Very worried 11%
Somewhat worried 28
Not too worried 34
Not worried at all 26
No opinion 1

How likely is it that there will be further acts of terrorism in the United States over the next several weeks—very likely, somewhat likely, not too likely, or not at all likely?

	Very, somewhat likely	Not too likely	Not at all likely*
2001 Nov 2–4	74%	16%	6%
2001 Oct 19–21	85	10	3

*"No opinion" is omitted.

How likely is it that there will be further acts of terrorism in your community over the next several weeks—very likely, somewhat likely, not too likely, or not at all likely?

Very likely 3%
Somewhat likely 20
Not too likely 41

Not at all likely 32
No opinion 4

Do you think the government warnings of further terrorist attacks have mostly helped people, or just scared people?

	Helped people	Scared people	No opinion
2001 Nov 2–4	55%	40%	5%
2001 Oct 19–21	47	49	4

If the government believes a terrorist attack may occur somewhere in the United States but cannot release any of the details, which do you think is better for the government to do—issue a nationwide alert without any details, or not issue any alert at all?

Issue alert without details 71%
Not issue an alert 26
No opinion 3

Analysis: Nearly two months after the September 11 terrorist attacks, Americans are still adjusting to life during the war on terrorism. The latest Gallup Poll shows that 40% are at least somewhat worried about becoming the victim of a terrorist attack. This is, however, the lowest level of concern measured by Gallup since the September 11 attacks.

Despite the drop in overall concern about personally being victimized by terrorism, nearly three-quarters believe that future terrorist attacks on American soil are at least somewhat likely in the next several weeks, although this number, too, has shown some decline in recent weeks. Respondents generally believe that government warnings of possible terrorist attacks are more beneficial than harmful, and would rather the government issue a vague warning rather than no warning at all.

According to the poll conducted November 2–4, 40% of the public are at least somewhat worried about being victimized by a terrorist attack, including 10% who are very worried. Both of these numbers are at their lowest point since the September 11 attacks. Currently, 31% say they are "not at all worried" about being a victim, nearly twice as many as on the night of the attack (16%). Polling from September 11 to mid-October showed roughly half the public saying they were at least somewhat worried about being victimized. The level of concern peaked at 59% in an October 5–6 Gallup survey, but by mid-October had dropped to 43%.

Public concern about the possibility of further terrorist attacks is also declining, although a majority still believes that more attacks are possible. The percentage who say that further acts of terrorism in the U.S. are at least somewhat likely has dropped to 75% from an 85% reading in an October 19–21 poll. Currently, 24% think future attacks are very likely, as did 40% in the previous survey.

When asked about the likelihood of acts of terrorism occurring in their communities, the public shows a great deal less concern. Just 23% say it is at least somewhat likely, including 3% who say it is very likely.

Americans' views about the impact of government terrorism alerts have shifted. A majority (55%) now believes that government warnings about further attacks help people rather than scare them (40%). Two weeks ago the public was less positive about the alerts, with 47% saying they help people and 49% saying they scare people. This latest reading on the issue comes a week after a second warning from federal officials of a possible terrorist attack. Some have criticized the federal government for the vagueness of its warning, which did not provide any specific details about possible targets. Nevertheless, the public believes it is better for the government to issue an alert without any details (71%) than not to issue any alert at all (26%).

NOVEMBER 8
PRESIDENT BUSH/EXPOSURE
TO ANTHRAX

Interview Dates: 11/2–4/01
CNN/*USA Today*/Gallup Poll
Survey #GO 134989

Do you approve or disapprove of the way George W. Bush is handling the response to the recent incidents involving anthrax?

Approve 75%
Disapprove 17
No opinion 8

Now, thinking about the members of the Bush administration, including his Cabinet secretaries and top advisers but not Bush himself, do you approve or disapprove of the way the Bush administration is handling the response to the recent incidents involving anthrax?

Approve 76%
Disapprove 19
No opinion 5

How likely is it that you or someone in your family will be exposed to anthrax—very likely, somewhat likely, not too likely, or not at all likely?

	2001 Nov 2–4	2001 Oct 19–21
Very likely	5%	4%
Somewhat likely	24	16
Not too likely	45	41
Not at all likely	24	37
Already exposed (vol.)	*	1
No opinion	2	1

*Less than 1%

How worried are you that you or someone in your family will be exposed to anthrax—very worried, somewhat worried, not too worried, or not worried at all?

	2001 Nov 2–4	2001 Oct 19–21
Very worried	10%	7%
Somewhat worried	24	27
Not too worried	37	35
Not worried at all	28	31
Already exposed (vol.)	0	0
No opinion	1	*

*Less than 1%

How worried are you that you or someone in your family will be exposed to anthrax through the mail—very worried, somewhat worried, not too worried, or not worried at all?

Very worried 9%
Somewhat worried .... .26
Not too worried .... .42
Not worried at all .... .23
Already exposed (vol.) 0
No opinion .... *

*Less than 1%

How confident are you in the ability of the U.S. government to respond effectively to the health threats posed by a major outbreak of anthrax—very confident, somewhat confident, not too confident, or not at all confident?

	2001 Nov 2–4	2001 Oct 19–21
Very confident	28%	34%
Somewhat confident	52	43
Not too confident	14	17
Not at all confident	5	5
No opinion	1	1

How confident are you in the ability of the U.S. government to prevent additional people from being exposed to anthrax—very confident, somewhat confident, not too confident, or not at all confident?

Very confident .... .14%
Somewhat confident .... .50
Not too confident .... .24
Not at all confident .... .10
No opinion 2

Analysis: Americans' frame of mind about the nation's anthrax problem is fairly upbeat, with the majority expressing at least qualified confidence in the government's ability to handle it. Similarly, most are confident in their own families' safety from anthrax, saying they have little to no risk of exposure to it.

According to a Gallup Poll conducted November 2–4, a majority is at least somewhat confident that the government is prepared to deal effectively with the health threats that could be posed by a major outbreak of anthrax: 80% are either very or somewhat confident. Only 19% express low levels of confidence. However, the percentage who are "very confident" in the government's ability to handle anthrax is now just 28%, down from 34% in mid-October. An additional 52% today are "somewhat" confident.

Respondents are somewhat less confident in the government's ability to prevent further anthrax exposures, as only 64% say they are very or somewhat confident about this. Nevertheless, the vast majority (76%) approves of the way the Bush administration is handling the anthrax incidents.

While no new cases of anthrax exposure or infection have been reported in the last week, the latest poll found a slight increase compared to mid-October in the number who consider it likely that they or a family member will be exposed to the potentially deadly disease. Twenty-nine percent now say this is very or somewhat likely, up from 20% in an October 19–21 survey. More than two-thirds (69%) think it is unlikely that they will be exposed. Despite the increase in Americans' perception that they may be at risk of exposure to anthrax, their worry about it has remained exactly the same since October. Just one-third is very or somewhat worried about themselves or a family member being exposed to anthrax, while two-thirds are generally not worried. The stability in this measure could be due to the fact that most of the anthrax cases thus far have proved treatable with antibiotics, thus allaying initial public fears.

NOVEMBER 12
WAR ON TERRORISM

Interview Dates: 11/2–4/01
CNN/*USA Today*/Gallup Poll
Survey #GO 134989

Do you approve or disapprove of the current U.S. military action in Afghanistan?

	2001 Nov 2–4	2001 Oct 19–21
Approve	.86%	88%
Disapprove	11	10
No opinion	3	2

Do you approve or disapprove strongly or only moderately?

Strongly approve 71%
Moderately approve .15
Moderately disapprove 5
Strongly disapprove .6
No opinion 3

Do you favor or oppose the United States sending large numbers of ground troops into combat in Afghanistan?

Favor 66%
Oppose 28
No opinion 6

Do you feel that you have a clear idea of what this war is all about, that is, what we are fighting for?

Yes 89%
No 10
No opinion 1

How satisfied are you with the amount of progress made by the U.S. military in the war in Afghanistan—very satisfied, somewhat satisfied, not too satisfied, or not at all satisfied?

Very satisfied 27%
Somewhat satisfied 52
Not too satisfied 11
Not at all satisfied 7
No opinion 3

In your opinion, do you think the current U.S. military action in Afghanistan has been successful, unsuccessful, or is it too soon to tell?

Successful 17%
Unsuccessful 6

Too soon to tell 76
No opinion 1

In dealing with the problem of terrorism, which do you think the United States government should do—use only diplomatic and economic pressure, or use military forces in combat along with diplomatic and economic pressure?

Use diplomatic, economic only 6%
Use military forces in combat too 89
Other (vol.) 1
No opinion 4

How long would you be willing to use combat forces to deal with the problem of terrorism—less than one year, one to two years, three to five years, or more than five years if it takes that long?

Less than one year 8%
One to two years 15
Three to five years .10
More than five years 63
No opinion 4

Continuing to think about how the U.S. government should deal with terrorism, which would you prefer—to continue with the use of combat forces regardless of how many U.S. military service people are killed, or to stop using combat forces if the number of U.S. military service people who are killed becomes too high?

Continue regardless 53%
Stop if number killed is too high 41
No opinion 6

How many U.S. military service people do you think would be too high a number killed and would cause you to stop supporting the use of military forces—one hundred, one thousand, five thousand, ten thousand, or some higher number?

100 . . . . .24%
1,000 27

5,000 15
10,000 12
Some higher number 13
No opinion 9

Thinking specifically about Afghanistan, how long would you be willing to continue using military action in Afghanistan without either capturing Osama bin Laden or removing the Taliban from power—six months or less, one year, two to three years, more than three years, or do you think the U.S. military action should stop now?

Six months or less 11%
One year 21
Two to three years 23
More than three years 34
Should stop now 6
No opinion 5

Analysis: The military action in Afghanistan is now entering its second month, and the latest Gallup Poll shows that most Americans appear strongly committed to winning the war on terrorism, regardless of the time and consequences involved. Strong majorities say they are willing to send large numbers of ground troops into Afghanistan and to engage in combat for several years. Almost one-half says the U.S. should continue fighting regardless of how many American military personnel are killed. And nearly nine in ten have a clear idea of what this war is all about, the highest reading Gallup has measured for any war dating back to World War II.

Several questions in the most recent poll conducted November 2–4 indicate that at this early stage the public is willing to go to great lengths to win the war on terrorism. For example, 66% favor "sending large numbers of ground troops into combat in Afghanistan" while just 28% are opposed. They also are willing to use military combat forces for an extended period. Seventy-eight percent favor using military forces in combat for at least one year, and 56% would favor using forces for more than five years if it takes that long.

A majority would be willing to continue fighting in Afghanistan for extended periods, even if the U.S. fails to make visible signs of progress such as capturing Osama bin Laden or removing the ruling Taliban government from power. Additionally, 47% say the U.S. should continue to use combat forces regardless of how many military service people are killed while 36% say the fighting should stop if the number killed is too high.

Gallup asked those who say the U.S. should stop fighting "if the number of U.S. military service people who are killed becomes too high" to specify how many deaths they thought would be too many. Twenty-four percent said 100 deaths, 27% said 1,000, 15% said 5,000, 12% said 10,000, and 13% gave "some higher number." This translates into 19% saying the fighting should stop if 100 to 1,000 American military service personnel are killed, and 9% saying that fighting should stop if 5,000 to 10,000 American military service personnel are killed; 5% think the fighting should continue if more than 10,000 are killed. The actual reaction to a large number of American deaths in the fighting will depend to a significant degree on the circumstances involved and the overall progress of the war effort. These answers suggest that while respondents are willing to support military action even though there may be serious consequences, there would be some point at which a considerable portion of the public would want to call a halt to it and seek another way to reach the country's objectives.

NOVEMBER 13
TERRORIST ATTACKS AND
AIRLINE TRAVEL

Interview Dates: 11/2–4/01
CNN/*USA Today*/Gallup Poll
Survey #GO 134989

Do you think you will change any aspect of your personal life or activities in order to reduce your chances of being a victim of terrorist attacks or will you not make any changes in your personal life?

Will 36%
Will not 61
No opinion 3

Do today's events make you less willing to fly on airplanes, or not?

Yes 48%
No 50
No opinion 2

Before the September 11 terrorist attacks, were you considering flying somewhere for the Thanksgiving or Christmas holidays, or not?

Yes 26%
No 74

As a result of the September 11 terrorist attacks, are you less likely to fly on major commercial airlines for the coming holidays, or not?

Yes 38%
No 62

Analysis: It remains to be seen whether the November 1 crash of an American Airlines passenger jet in New York City was related to terrorism or the result of mechanical failures, but recent polling shows that it happened at a time when Americans' fear of more terrorist attacks was subsiding. Whatever the cause, the perceived safety of air travel may hang in the balance, as fear of air travel was one of the top public responses to the events of September 11, and close to one-half admitted to being less likely to fly as a result.

Gallup polling after the September 11 attacks found close to one-half of the public (48%) saying they were less likely to fly on airplanes. More recently, Gallup found that, among Americans who had previously intended to travel by air during the Thanksgiving or Christmas seasons, 38% were now less likely to fly. And about one-third told Gallup that the attacks would affect their daily lives more generally, saying that they would change their personal lives or activities in order to reduce their chances of being a victim of terrorist attacks.

NOVEMBER 16
WAR ON TERRORISM

Interview Dates: 11/8–11/01
Gallup Poll News Service
Survey #GO 132078

Do you approve or disapprove of the way the following people are handling the war on terrorism since September 11:

George W. Bush?

Approve 89%
Disapprove 8
No opinion 3

Secretary of State Colin Powell?

Approve 87%
Disapprove 6
No opinion 7

Defense Secretary Donald Rumsfeld?

Approve 80%
Disapprove 8
No opinion 12

Attorney General John Ashcroft?

Approve 77%
Disapprove 10
No opinion 13

Congress?

Approve 77%
Disapprove 16
No opinion 7

The U.S. Postal Service?

Approve 77%
Disapprove 19
No opinion 4

Dick Cheney?

Approve 75%
Disapprove 11
No opinion 14

The Centers for Disease Control, or CDC?

Approve 71%
Disapprove 20
No opinion 9

Homeland Security Director Tom Ridge?

Approve 60%
Disapprove 14
No opinion 26

The news media?

Approve 43%
Disapprove 54
No opinion 3

Analysis: The latest Gallup Poll shows that the vast majority of Americans approve of the way top administration officials and the major governmental institutions are handling the war on terrorism, but that a majority disapproves of the news media's performance.

The November 8–11 poll found 89% approving of the way President George W. Bush is handling the war, and 87% approving of Secretary of State Colin Powell's performance. Eighty percent approve of Defense Secretary Donald Rumsfeld's performance, while 77% each approve of the performance of Attorney General John Ashcroft, Congress, and the U.S. Postal Service. Vice President Dick Cheney's approval rating is at 75%, compared with 71% for the Centers for Disease Control (CDC) and 60% for Homeland Security Director Tom Ridge. The lower approval rating for Ridge is partly due to the fact that about one-quarter of the public has not heard of him. Only 14% say they disapprove. By comparison, just 43% approve of the way the news media have been handling the war, and 54% disapprove.

NOVEMBER 19
MOST IMPORTANT PROBLEM

Interview Dates: 11/8–11/01
Gallup Poll News Service
Survey #GO 132078

What do you think is the most important problem facing this country today?

Economic Problems	**24%**
Economy in general	16
Unemployment; jobs	6
High cost of living; inflation	1
Recession	1
Taxes	1
Wage issues	*
Trade relations, deficit	*
Gap between rich and poor	*
Federal budget deficit; federal debt	–
Fuel; oil prices	–
Other specific economic	–
Noneconomic Problems	**79%**
Terrorism	37
Fear of war; feelings of fear in this country	13
National security	9
Ethics; moral, religious, family decline; dishonesty; lack of integrity	4
Education	3
Immigration; illegal aliens	3
Dissatisfaction with government, Congress, politicians, candidates; poor leadership; corruption	3
Poverty; hunger; homelessness	2
International issues, problems	2
Poor health care, hospitals; high cost of health care	25
Unifying the country	2
Foreign aid; focus overseas	1
The media	1
Crime; violence	1
Drugs	1
Environment; pollution	1
Race relations; racism	1
Judicial system; courts; laws	1
Lack of money	1
Lack of energy sources; the energy crisis	*
Children's behavior; way they are raised	*
Medicare, Social Security issues	*
Care for the elderly	*

Guns, gun control	*	
Abortion	*	
Lack of respect for each other	*	
Lack of military defense	*	
Overpopulation	*	
Losing personal freedoms because of war	–	
Welfare	–	
School shootings; school violence	–	
AIDS	–	
Child abuse	–	
Advancement of computers; technology	–	
Other noneconomic	3	
No opinion	4	

*Total adds to more than 100% due to multiple replies.

Analysis: The American psyche was jolted on September 11 in a way never seen before. Terrorism, thought until then to be the province of those living in the Middle East or Northern Ireland, became a stark reality at home and changed the priorities of many Americans.

In the latest Gallup Poll, conducted the weekend of November 8–11, 37% of those surveyed named terrorism as the "most important problem facing the country," another 13% responded with fear of war or "feelings of fear," and 9% mentioned national security. This represents only a slight change from a Gallup Poll in mid-October when 46% cited terrorism as the "most important problem," 10% mentioned fear, and 8% mentioned national security.

NOVEMBER 20
HOLIDAY SPENDING/
PERSONAL FINANCES

Interview Dates: 11/8–11/01
Gallup Poll News Service
Survey #GO 132078

How would you rate economic conditions in your local community today—excellent, good, only fair, or poor?

	2001 Nov 8–11	2001 Oct 11–14
Excellent	6%	8%
Good	44	51
Only fair	37	32
Poor	13	9

Right now, do you think that economic conditions in your local community as a whole are getting better or getting worse?

	2001 Nov 8–11	2001 Oct 11–14
Getting better	40%	41%
Getting worse	42	40
Same (vol.); no opinion	18	19

How would you rate your financial situation today—as excellent, good, only fair, or poor?

	2001 Nov 8–11	2001 Oct 11–14
Excellent	8%	9%
Good	46	46
Only fair	34	32
Poor	12	13

Right now, do you think that your financial situation as a whole is getting better or getting worse?

	2001 Nov 8–11	2001 Oct 11–14
Getting better	45%	50%
Getting worse	33	30
Same (vol.); no opinion	22	20

Thinking of your own financial situation just now, how good of a position are you in to buy some of the things you would like to have—a very good position, somewhat good, neither good nor bad, somewhat bad, or a very bad position?

	2001 Nov 8–11	2001 Oct 11–14
Very good position	12%	14%
Somewhat good position	37	37

Neither good nor bad 23	24
Somewhat bad position 17	13
Very bad position 10	11
No opinion 1	1

Analysis: As we approach the prime Christmas shopping days of 2001, there is some good economic news to go along with the bad news that has dominated the media since September 11. Gasoline prices and interest rates are down, and the stock market is up to preattack levels. Nonetheless, new Gallup economic data suggest that Americans may be less inclined to spend money this holiday season than last.

Prior to September 11, consumer confidence was plunging. Following the terrorist attacks, consumer perceptions of the economy benefited from a significant "rally effect." Over the past two months, however, the economic rally effect has dissipated. The net result is that consumer perceptions of the national economy are now back to the same low level they had reached just before the attacks. Even more important, it appears that employees' perceptions of the health of their companies have also declined between October and November. And, although consumers perceive their local economies to be better than the national economy, these perceptions have also declined over the past month. Finally, consumers seem most optimistic about their own personal financial situations. Still, even these perceptions seem consistent with a recession.

All of this is probably not good news for the Christmas shopping season. The implications for the breadth, depth, and length of the U.S. recession are less clear. The kind of recession we will have depends in large part on whether consumer perceptions are going to stay at their current weak levels or get even weaker during the months ahead. This is particularly true at the local level, where employees' perceptions of their companies, and consumers' perceptions of their local economies, may be lagging behind those of the national level.

New Gallup Poll economic data from November 8–11 show 50% of consumers rating conditions in their local economy as good (44%) or excellent (6%). This is down from the October 11–14 poll that showed 59% rating conditions in their local economy as good (51%) or excellent (8%). November Gallup Poll economic data also show 42% of Americans saying economic conditions in their community are getting worse, while 40% say they are getting better. This is just about the same as in October, when 40% said economic conditions in their community were getting worse and 40% said better.

In November, one out of four (25%) expects that the number of workers employed by their companies will go down a lot or a little over the next six months. This percentage is up from October 11–14, when one out of five (20%) expected the number of workers at their companies to go down a lot or a little. Similarly, in November, about one out of four (24%) expects their companies' revenues to go down a lot or a little. This was virtually the same in October, when 22% of private sector employees said that they expected the revenues of the company where they work to go down a lot or a little. Finally, only about one out of ten (11%) expects the price of their companies' products and services will go down a lot or a little over the next six months. Nine percent expressed that view in October.

In addition, the new poll shows 54% of consumers rating their own financial situation as good (46%) or excellent (8%), essentially unchanged from October. However, it also shows that 45% say their financial situation as a whole is getting better, while only 33% say it is getting worse. This is less optimistic than in October, when 50% of Americans said their financial situation as a whole was getting better while only 30% said it was getting worse.

In sum, employees seem somewhat less optimistic about the health of their companies than they did a month ago. Consumers also seem slightly less optimistic about their local economies and even their personal financial situations than they did last month. Combined with their perceptions of a weak national economy, it would not be surprising if many consumers spend conservatively this holiday season, even if they have more money in their pockets than they expected.

NOVEMBER 21
WEIGHT AND BODY IMAGE

Interview Dates: 11/8–11/01
Gallup Poll News Service
Survey #GO 132078

Would you like to lose weight, stay at your present weight, or put on weight?

	Lose weight	Put on weight	Stay at present weight*
National Adults	59%	7%	34%
Men	49	12	39
Women	68	2	30

*No opinion is omitted.

At this time, are you seriously trying to lose weight?

	Yes	No*
National Adults	25%	75%
Men	17	82
Women	32	68

*"No opinion" is omitted.

Analysis: Many Americans sitting down to a feast on a traditional Thanksgiving meal are likely to feel conflicted about the calories on their plates. Close to one-half (44%) tells Gallup they are overweight, a solid majority (59%) say they would like to lose weight, and 66% indicate they weigh more than their preferred weight. For better or worse, only 25% are actively trying to lose weight today, a figure that has changed little since the 1950s.

Despite the high degree of concern about weight, only 25% of all respondents are currently taking steps to lose weight, and of those 43% describe themselves as overweight.

NOVEMBER 27
ENERGY CONSERVATION

Interview Dates: 11/8–11/01
Gallup Poll News Service
Survey #GO 132078

Here are some things that can be done to deal with the energy situation. For each one, please say whether you generally favor or oppose it:

Investments in new sources of energy such as solar, wind, and fuel cells?

Favor 91%
Oppose 8
No opinion 1

Investing in new power-generating plants?

Favor 81%
Oppose 13
No opinion 6

Mandating more energy-efficient cars?

Favor 77%
Oppose 20
No opinion 3

Opening up the Alaskan Arctic National Wildlife Refuge for oil exploration?

Favor 44%
Oppose 51
No opinion 5

Increasing the use of nuclear power as a major source of power?

Favor 42%
Oppose 52
No opinion 6

Analysis: America's energy concerns of the past year have been overshadowed by the events of September 11 and the attacks on Afghanistan. However, the memories of electricity shortages and $2-per-gallon gasoline apparently remain strong for many. A new Gallup Poll shows widespread support for investment in the nation's energy infrastructure, including the construction of new power generation plants and development of alternative energy sources, such as wind and solar power.

During the spring of 2001, electricity grids around the nation struggled to meet demand. While some analysts blame utility deregulation for the supply problems, many Americans saw a need for new power plants. A May 7–9 Gallup Poll found that 83% favored investing in new power generation plants, and the most recent poll, conducted November 8–11, found no appreciable change. However, the public's desire to increase the electricity supply by the use of nuclear power has slipped over the last six months. In the latest poll, 42% support increased use of nuclear power. This may well be linked to the events of September 11, which pointed out the potential vulnerability of nuclear power facilities to terrorist attacks.

Additionally, the poll shows continued near-universal support for development of alternative energy sources, including solar, wind, and fuel cell technology. Nine out of ten (91%) expressed their favor for investments in alternative power sources. But now that prices at the pump have declined in many cities, 77% expressed support for mandated energy-efficient automobiles.

The September 11 attacks highlighted America's potential vulnerability incurred by dependence on foreign sources of oil. Still, there has been only a slight increase in support for one of President Bush's top energy priorities: opening the Arctic National Wildlife Refuge in Alaska for oil exploration. Supporters argue that the possible oil reserves in the refuge could help reduce America's dependence on imported oil for many years, while critics claim that the environmental impact does not justify the perceived benefits. By a slight majority, the public continues to oppose opening ANWR to oil exploration. However, that opposition has been falling slightly, and now stands at a mere 51% majority.

NOVEMBER 28
PHYSICAL AND MENTAL HEALTH

Interview Dates: 11/8–11/01
Gallup Poll News Service
Survey #GO 132078

We have some questions about your personal health that are designed to give us a better understanding of the health problems faced by the American public. First, how would you describe your own physical health at this time—excellent, good, only fair, or poor?

Excellent 29%
Good 49
Only fair 17
Poor 5

Now, thinking about your physical health, for how many days during the past month was your physical health not good?

None 52%
Less than one day . . . .*
One 7
Two 9
Three 4
Four 3
Five to ten 11
Eleven or more 12
No opinion 2

*Less than 1%

Mean 4.0
Median 0

During the past month, for about how many days did poor physical health keep you from doing your usual activities, such as self-care, work, or recreation?

	Experienced poor health*	All adults
None	43%	73%
Less than one day	**	**
One	10	5
Two	8	4
Three	7	3
Four	3	2
Five to ten	14	6
Eleven or more	14	7
No opinion	**	**

*Based on those who experiences day(s) of poor physical health
**Less than 1%

Mean 5.0   2.3
Median 1   0

Thinking about your own health, which, if any, of the following applies to you:

You have a long-term medical condition, illness, or disease?

Yes 28%
No 72

You have been sick with a short-term illness sometime in the past thirty days?

Yes 24%
No 76

You have a physical disability that limits your activity?

Yes 21%
No 79

How would you describe your own mental health or emotional well-being at this time— would you say it is excellent, good, only fair, or poor?

Excellent 43%
Good 42
Only fair 12
Poor 3

Now, thinking about your mental health or emotional well-being, for how many days during the past month was either of these not good?

None 62%
Less than one day . . . .*
One 5
Two 8
Three 4
Four 2
Five to ten 9
Eleven or more 8
No opinion 2

*Less than 1%

Mean   2.7
Median 0

During the past month, for about how many days did poor mental health or emotional well-being keep you from doing your usual activities, such as self-care, work, or recreation?

	Experienced poor health*	All adults
None	.58%	85%
Less than one day	**	**
One	.7	3
Two	.5	2
Three	.4	1
Four	.2	1
Five to ten	.11	4
Eleven or more	.12	4
No opinion	.1	**

*Based on those who experienced day(s) of poor mental health
**Less than 1%

Mean   3.7   1.3
Median 0   0

Analysis: Most Americans rate both their physical and mental health as excellent or good, while very few people rate either condition as poor. Still, more give high ratings to their mental than to their physical health. A recent Gallup Poll focusing on Americans' health also shows that a substantial majority says they have lost no days in the past month due to health problems, although a small percentage have.

According to the poll conducted November 8–11, 78% rate their physical health as either excellent (29%) or good (49%). An additional 17% say their physical health is only fair, while just 5% say it is poor. A somewhat larger percentage (85%) gives high marks to their mental health, with 43% saying it is excellent and 42% good. Another 12% say their mental health is only fair and just 3% say poor.

The average American lost 2.3 days of activity in the last month due to poor physical health, and the average number of days lost because of poor mental health was 1.3. These averages can be somewhat misleading, however, since they are caused by a small number of people who miss large numbers of days of activity. Overall, 73% suffered no days of lost activity last month due to physical health problems, and 85% say that about mental health problems. On the other hand, 13% have lost five or more days of activity due to physical health problems, and 8% have lost five or more days due to mental health problems.

A relatively high number of Americans have either a physical disability that limits their activities (21%) or a long-term medical condition (28%). Another 24% have been sick with a short-term illness in the past thirty days.

NOVEMBER 29
WAR ON TERRORISM

Interview Dates: 11/26–27/01
CNN/*USA Today*/Gallup Poll
Survey #GO 135096

Which of the following comes closest to your view about the actions the United States should take to deal with terrorism—the United States should mount a long-term war to defeat global terrorist networks, the United States should take military action only to punish specific terrorist groups responsible for the attacks on the World Trade Center, or the United States should not take military action but should rely only on economic and diplomatic efforts to deal with terrorism?

	2001 Nov 26–27	2001 Oct 5–6
Mounting long-term war	62%	49%
Punish specific terrorists	31	43
Should not take military action	5	6
No opinion	2	2

Do you approve or disapprove of the current U.S. military action in Afghanistan?

	2001 Nov 26–27	2001 Nov 2–4
Approve	92%	86%
Disapprove	6	11
No opinion	2	3

Do you approve or disapprove of the presence of U.S. ground troops in Afghanistan?

Approve	91%
Disapprove	7
No opinion	2

How satisfied are you with the amount of progress made by the U.S. military in the war in Afghanistan—very satisfied, somewhat satisfied, not too satisfied, or not at all satisfied?

	2001 Nov 26–27	2001 Nov 2–4
Very satisfied	58%	27%
Somewhat satisfied	35	52
Not too satisfied	4	11
Not at all satisfied	2	7
No opinion	1	3

Analysis: Americans remain highly supportive of the military action in Afghanistan and are also overwhelmingly supportive of the use of U.S. ground troops in the war. Compared to a month ago, Americans have become more satisfied with the progress of the war, and have become more likely to support the idea of a long-term war against global terrorism that goes beyond just finding those responsible for the September 11 attacks.

In early October, just before the military action in Afghanistan began, 49% of respondents said they favored a long-term war against global terrorism, while 43% favored limiting military efforts to finding those responsible for the September 11 attacks. Now, in the latest Gallup Poll conducted November 26–27, 62% favor a long-term war while only 31% say that the war effort should focus just on those responsible for the attacks.

An early November Gallup Poll showed mixed levels of satisfaction with the "progress made by the U.S. military in the war." But that sentiment has changed dramatically since recent reports of the retreat of the Taliban from key Afghan cities and regions. Just 27% were "very satisfied" with the progress of the war in early November, while in the current poll, 58% are very satisfied.

Almost from the day the terrorist attacks occurred, the public has been resolute in its support for military action against those responsible. In the latest poll, approval has increased to 92%.

NOVEMBER 30
EXPOSURE TO ANTHRAX

Interview Dates: 11/26–27/01
CNN/*USA Today*/Gallup Poll
Survey #GO 135096

How worried are you that you or someone in your family will be exposed to anthrax—very worried, somewhat worried, not too worried, or not worried at all?

	2001 Nov 26–27	2001 Nov 2–4
Very worried	7%	10%
Somewhat worried	26	24
Not too worried	34	37
Not worried at all	33	28
No opinion	*	1

*Less than 1%

How confident are you in the ability of the U.S. government to prevent additional people from being exposed to anthrax—very confident, somewhat confident, not too confident, or not at all confident?

	2001 Nov 26–27	2001 Nov 2–4
Very confident	13%	14%
Somewhat confident	49	50
Not too confident	28	24
Not at all confident; no opinion	10	12

Who do you think is responsible for most, if not all, of the recent cases involving

anthrax—U.S. citizens, or people who are not U.S. citizens?

U.S. citizens	40%
People who are not citizens	48
No opinion	12

How likely is it that the U.S. government will be able to identify and punish the people responsible for the recent cases involving anthrax and bring them to justice—very likely, somewhat likely, not too likely, or not at all likely?

Very likely	21%
Somewhat likely	45
Not too likely	28
Not at all likely	6
No opinion	*

*Less than 1%

Analysis: In recent days, news coverage of anthrax has resurfaced following the death of a Connecticut woman from inhaling anthrax and reports about a letter mailed to Senator Patrick Leahy that contained the bacteria. However, the public's concern about being exposed to anthrax has shown little change in recent weeks. The latest Gallup Poll, conducted November 26–27, shows just 7% of Americans are "very worried" and 26% are "somewhat worried" that they will be exposed to anthrax. The level of concern is unchanged from polls conducted in October and early November, when 34% were worried about being exposed.

The poll shows that a majority (62%) is confident in the government's ability to prevent additional people from being exposed to anthrax, but only 13% are "very confident." Thirty-eight percent are "not too" or "not at all confident." Again, these figures are little changed from earlier this month, when 64% were confident, including 14% who were very confident.

The public also expresses qualified confidence in the government's ability to apprehend those who have been involved in spreading the anthrax bacteria in the U.S. More than two-thirds say it is likely that the government will be able to identify and punish those responsible for the recent cases involving anthrax, but only 21% say this is "very likely" to happen.

So far, legal authorities have not determined who is behind the anthrax cases. Speculation continues as to whether the mailings were part of a foreign-based terrorist plan or the work of domestic terrorists unconnected with other countries. Americans are divided on the matter, with 40% believing the culprits are U.S. citizens and 48% thinking they are not.

DECEMBER 3
CHRISTMAS SPENDING

Interview Dates: 11/26–27/01
CNN/*USA Today*/Gallup Poll
Survey #GO 135096

Roughly how much money do you think you personally will spend on Christmas gifts this year?

	2001	2000
Overall	$794	$797
By Gender		
Male	$850	$876
Female	$745	$726
By Age		
18 to 29 Years	$689	$687
30 to 49 Years	$901	$854
50 to 64 Years	$821	$890
65 Years and Over	$623	$710
By Age and Gender		
Males under 50 Years	$851	$876
Males 50 Years and Over	$855	$892
Females under 50 Years	$820	$719
Females 50 Years and Over	$625	$745
By Region		
East	$929	$846
Midwest	$692	$826
South	$835	$804
West	$704	$706

Analysis: Americans expect to spend about the same amount for Christmas this year as last year, according to a recent Gallup Poll. The average

projected spending for this year is $794, down just $3 from 2000. But economic considerations apparently exert a significant influence on the public's spending plans for this year. The longer people think the current recession will last, the less money they expect to spend for Christmas.

The poll conducted November 26–27 shows that almost one-third (32%) expects to spend $1,000 or more for Christmas this year, 30% between $500 and $1,000, and another 30% plan to spend less than $500. The average of $794 is down just slightly from last year's average of $797.

DECEMBER 4
WAR ON TERRORISM/
OSAMA BIN LADEN

Interview Dates: 11/26–27/01
CNN/*USA Today*/Gallup Poll
Survey #GO 135096

How likely is it that the United States will be able to capture or kill Osama bin Laden—very likely, somewhat likely, not too likely, or not at all likely?

Very likely	34%
Somewhat likely	44
Not too likely	15
Not at all likely	6
No opinion	1

Which comes closer to your view—the United States' accomplishments in Afghanistan will be a success even if Osama bin Laden is not captured, or the United States' accomplishments in Afghanistan will not be a success until Osama bin Laden is captured?

Success	41%
Not a success	55
Both; neither (vol.)	2
No opinion	2

In your opinion, which of the following would be better for the United States—if

Osama bin Laden is killed, or if Osama bin Laden is captured alive?

Killed 54%
Captured alive 43
No opinion 3

Suppose Osama bin Laden is captured alive by the United States. Which of the following would be better for the United States to do to him—execute him immediately, or put him on trial in either a civilian or a military court?

Execute him immediately 35%
Put him on trial 62
No opinion 3

Suppose Osama bin Laden is captured alive and put on trial. Which of the following would you prefer—that he be put on trial publicly by an international court with judges from different countries; put on trial by a secret military tribunal by the United States; put on trial publicly in a regular civilian court in the United States; or would it make no difference to you?

International court .41%
Secret military tribunal 29
Regular civilian court 17
No difference 11
No opinion 2

Based on what you have heard or read, how do you feel about Osama bin Laden's role in the September 11 terrorist attacks—you have no doubt whatsoever that he is guilty, you think he is guilty but have some doubts, or you do think he is not guilty?

No doubt that he is guilty 80%
Think he is guilty, have doubts 19
Not guilty; no opinion 1

Analysis: Now that the Taliban government has been removed from power in Afghanistan, the focus of the continuing war on terrorism has shifted to the search for Osama bin Laden, the prime suspect in the September 11 terrorist attacks. According to the latest Gallup Poll, a majority of Americans say the U.S. accomplishments in Afghanistan will not be a success until bin Laden is captured. About one in three believes it is very likely that the U.S. will be able to capture or kill bin Laden. Additionally, a majority of the public feels it would be better for the U.S. if bin Laden were killed rather than captured alive, but, if he were captured alive, believes it would be better to put him on trial than to execute him immediately.

In recent weeks, U.S.-led military action in Afghanistan has caused the Taliban government to surrender its control of several major cities, including the capital of Kabul. While this is a key development in the war on terrorism, a majority views the capture of Osama bin Laden as crucial to the success of the military operations. According to the most recent Gallup Poll conducted November 26–27, 55% say that the U.S. accomplishments in Afghanistan will not be a success until bin Laden is captured, while 41% say the accomplishments represent a success even if bin Laden is not captured.

U.S. officials believe bin Laden is still in Afghanistan and are searching the southern and eastern parts of the country in an attempt to find the leader of the al-Qaeda terrorist network. The poll shows that respondents are generally optimistic that bin Laden will be caught. Thirty-four percent say it is "very likely" that the U.S. will be able to capture or kill bin Laden, and 44% say it is "somewhat likely." Only 21% feel that bin Laden's capture is not very likely.

By a 54%-to-43% margin, the public believes it would be better for the U.S. if bin Laden were to be killed rather than captured alive. However, if bin Laden is captured, respondents say it would be better for the U.S. to put him on trial (62%) than to execute him immediately (35%).

Recently, the U.S. government announced that it could opt to try suspected terrorists in military tribunals, which would be conducted in secret by military judges and would not allow for appeals of the verdict. While several polls have shown strong public support for military tribunals in the abstract, when given a choice, Americans prefer that bin Laden be tried in an international court. Among three options for trying bin Laden, 41% prefer he be tried in an international court, 29% prefer a secret military tribunal, and 17% prefer a regular civilian court, while 11% say it makes no difference to them.

It is safe to say that the public has strong expectations on the outcome of a bin Laden trial. When asked to assess his responsibility for the September 11 terrorist attacks, 80% have no doubt whatsoever that he is guilty. Nineteen percent think he is guilty but say they have some doubts, and just 1% has no opinion or thinks that bin Laden is not guilty.

DECEMBER 5
HONESTY AND ETHICAL STANDARDS

Interview Dates: 11/26–27/01
CNN/*USA Today*/Gallup Poll
Survey #GO 135096

Please tell me how you would rate the honesty and ethical standards of people in these different fields—very high, high, average, low, or very low?

	Very high, high
Firefighters	90%
Nurses	84
Members of U.S. military	81
Policemen	68
Druggists, pharmacists	68
Medical doctors	66
Clergy	64
Engineers	60
College teachers	58
Dentists	56
Accountants	41
Bankers	34
Journalists	29
Congressmen	25
Business executives	25
Senators	25
Auto mechanics	22
Stockbrokers	19
Lawyers	18
Labor union leaders	17
Insurance salesmen	13
Advertising practitioners	11
Car salesmen	8

Analysis: In the wake of the September 11 terrorist attacks in the United States, firefighters and other rescue personnel have been widely praised for their heroics as they risked their lives to save others caught in the devastation of the attacks. The annual Gallup Poll ranking of the honesty and ethics of professions reflects this respect, as firefighters rank first among people of different professions for their honesty and integrity, with 90% rating them "high" or "very high" on these characteristics.

Close behind in the ratings are nurses and members of the military, with more than eight in ten giving them high ratings on their honesty and ethics. The police, pharmacists, medical doctors and the clergy are bunched together in fourth place, with about two-thirds giving each group a high rating. More than one-half also gives high ratings to engineers, college teachers, and dentists. At the lowest end of the scale are car salesmen, the only group given a low or very low rating on honesty and ethics by a majority of respondents. Other groups receiving low ratings are lawyers, insurance salesmen, and labor union leaders.

The annual Gallup Poll rating of professions was conducted on November 26–27. This is the first year when the public was asked to rate firefighters and members of the military, and only the third year nurses were rated. Nurses came in first the past two years, given high ratings by 73% and 79%, respectively.

Of the twenty-three groups rated in the poll, thirteen receive high or very high ratings from less than one-half of the public. However, for twelve of these thirteen groups, most of the ratings that are not "high" are nevertheless "average" so that all but one group are rated "average" or better by a majority of the public. Fifty-two percent rate car salesmen either "low" (39%) or "very low" (13%) on honesty and ethics, the largest number by far for any group. Four groups receive low or very low ratings from about three in ten: lawyers (31%), insurance salesmen (30%), labor union leaders (30%), and advertising practitioners (27%).

DECEMBER 7
PEARL HARBOR VERSUS 9/11 ATTACKS

Interview Dates: 11/26–27/01
CNN/*USA Today*/Gallup Poll
Survey #GO 135096

A hundred years from now, which event do you think historians will say had a greater impact on the United States—the attack on Pearl Harbor on December 7, 1941, or the terrorist attacks on the World Trade Center and the Pentagon on September 11, 2001?

Pear Harbor 25%
September 11 terrorist attacks 72
No opinion 3

Analysis: Today marks the 60th anniversary of the Japanese bombing of Pearl Harbor. President George W. Bush will not be at Pearl Harbor to commemorate the occasion but instead will remember the historic event aboard an aircraft carrier at the U.S. Naval Base in Norfolk, Virginia.

The anniversary comes at a time when many Americans are comparing the events in 1941 to the September 11 terrorist attacks in New York and Washington, the first time that America has been attacked by foreign powers on its own soil since World War II. One might expect that Americans now sixty-five and older—many of whom have memories of both Pearl Harbor and the war that followed—would be most likely to give historical preference to Pearl Harbor. They do, but only to a degree. Seventy-seven percent of young Americans, ages 18 to 29, say that a hundred years from now historians will claim the September 11 attacks will have had a greater impact on the U.S. A somewhat smaller, but still substantial, 62% of those sixty-five and older agree.

DECEMBER 10
TERRORIST ATTACKS

Interview Dates: 11/26–27/01
CNN/*USA Today*/Gallup Poll
Survey #GO 135096

How worried are you that you or someone in your family will become a victim of terrorism—very worried, somewhat worried, not too worried, or not worried at all?

	Very, somewhat worried	Not too worried	Not worried at all*
2001 Nov 26–27	35%	34%	30%
2001 Nov 2–4	39	34	26
2001 Oct 19–21	43	33	23
2001 Oct 11–14	51	35	14
2001 Oct 5–6	59	27	14
2001 Sep 21–22	49	32	18
2001 Sep 14–15	51	35	13
2001 Sep 11	58	24	16

*"No opinion" is omitted.

How confident are you that each of the following will happen—extremely confident, very confident, moderately confident, not very confident, or not confident at all?

	Total confi-dent	Total not confi-dent*
The American way of life will be preserved	63%	7%
The U.S. economy will be prosperous in the long term	56	9
The U.S. will be able to prevent major acts of terrorism from occurring in the U.S. in the future	29	23
Every global terrorist organization will be defeated	21	46

*"No opinion" is omitted.

Analysis: For better or worse, the U.S. public seems to be adapting to the new terrorist reality confronting the country. According to a Gallup

Poll conducted November 26–27, Americans continue to see terrorism as a substantial threat to the nation and consider it unlikely that all terrorists around the globe can be defeated. These attitudes have not changed since mid-September. Nevertheless, respondents' anxiety about terrorism possibly striking their own lives has diminished greatly over the same period.

Americans' fear of terrorism affecting their own lives started to wane in the first few weeks after the September 11 attacks but surged in early October immediately after the first of the recent spate of anthrax cases was reported on October 4. Since then, this fear has been dropping steadily and is now nearly as low as it was in a Gallup Poll three years ago. Just 8% today say they are "very worried" about terrorism affecting themselves or a family member, down from 23% on September 11. A total of 35% are now either very or somewhat worried about this risk, and close to two-thirds (64%) are "not too" or "not at all" worried.

The new poll indicates that this decline in fear is not tied to a corresponding increase in public confidence about homeland security. In fact, the survey shows there has been virtually no change since September in the percentage of Americans who feel confident that the U.S. is capable of preventing another major act of terrorism on domestic soil. Only 29% express high confidence in this today, including 7% who are "extremely" confident and 22% who are "very" confident. Another 48% are just "moderately" confident, while 23% are "not very" or "not at all" confident.

Confidence about the chances of defeating all terrorist organizations around the globe has declined slightly since September. Only 21% currently say they are extremely or very confident about defeating all terrorists. Another 32% are moderately confident and 46% are not very or not at all confident.

Americans' characteristic optimism seems intact when they are asked to look at the big picture or further into the future. A majority (56%) feels either "extremely" or "very" confident that the U.S. economy will be prosperous in the long term, and an even larger number (63%) are highly confident that "the American way of life will be preserved."

DECEMBER 11
WAR ON TERRORISM

Interview Dates: 12/6–9/01
Gallup Poll News Service
Survey #GO 132079

Do you approve or disapprove of the current U.S. military action in Afghanistan?

	Approve	Dis-approve	No opinion
2001 Dec 6–9	.88%	9%	3%
2001 Nov 26–27	.92	6	2
2001 Nov 2–4	.86	11	3
2001 Oct 19–21	.88	10	2

Who do you think is currently winning the war against terrorism—the United States and its allies, neither side, or the terrorists?

	United States and allies	Terrorists	Neither side; no opinion
2001 Dec 6–9	.64%	5%	31%
2001 Nov 8–11	.53	11	36
2001 Oct 11–14	.42	11	47

Analysis: Today marks the three-month anniversary of the terrorist attacks on the World Trade Center and the Pentagon. A new Gallup Poll reveals an increasingly optimistic American public: almost two-thirds now say that the U.S. is winning the war on terrorism. Respondents remain strongly committed to the military action in Afghanistan, and over one-half feels that the war will be over in several months. At the same time, there is evidence from the new poll that the dominance of terrorism and the war is receding in the minds of Americans. A considerably lower percentage of the public now mentions terrorism and the war as the nation's number one problem, compared to previous months.

Despite repeated reminders from the Bush administration that the war on terrorism is far from over, our most recent poll shows that the public has become increasingly likely to guess that it may end soon. Over one-half now says that the war in Afghanistan will be over within several months or less. About four out of ten say the fighting will last at least a year. This marks a significantly more optimistic position than was taken by the public in polling conducted just as the military action got under way.

Support for the war in Afghanistan remains at about the 90% level. This high level of support has been remarkably unchanged over the last three months. Even before military action began, Gallup polling showed that about nine out of ten supported the concept of going to war to find those responsible for the attacks. That level of support did not change once the war began, and has not changed in the weeks since.

DECEMBER 12
ECONOMIC CONDITIONS

Interview Dates: 12/6–9/01
Gallup Poll News Service
Survey #GO 132079

How would you rate economic conditions in this country today—excellent, good, only fair, or poor?

	Excellent; good	Only fair	Poor*
2001 Dec 6–9	31%	53%	16%
2001 Nov 8–11	31	50	19
2001 Oct 11–14	38	48	13
2001 Sep 14–15	46	44	9
2001 Sep 7–10	32	49	19

*"No opinion" is omitted.

Right now, do you think that economic conditions in the country as a whole are getting better or getting worse?

	Getting better	Getting worse	Same (vol); no opinion
2001 Dec 6–9	44%	48%	8%
2001 Nov 8–11	30	59	11
2001 Oct 11–14	33	55	12
2001 Sep 14–15	28	60	12
2001 Sep 7–10	19	70	12

How do you think economic conditions will be in this country six months from now—excellent, good, only fair, or poor?

	Excellent, good	Only fair	Poor*
2001 Dec 6–9	49%	39%	10%
2001 Nov 8–11	44	41	12
2001 Oct 11–14	48	38	11

*"No opinion" is omitted.

Over the next six months, do you think that each of the following will go up a lot, go up a little, remain the same, go down a little, or go down a lot:

The stock market?

Go up a lot, a little	51%
Remain the same	21
Go down a little, a lot	23
No opinion	5

Economic growth?

Go up a lot, a little	49%
Remain the same	25
Go down a little, a lot	23
No opinion	3

Unemployment?

Go up a lot, a little	48%
Remain the same	17
Go down a little, a lot	34
No opinion	1

Inflation?

Go up a lot, a little	48%
Remain the same	33
Go down a little, a lot	17
No opinion	2

Interest rates?

Go up a lot, a little	37%
Remain the same	34

Go down a little, a lot 28
No opinion 1

Analysis: The latest monthly Gallup Poll on public sentiment toward current economic conditions shows little change from last month, although optimism about the future has risen since November. Overall, 31% rate the current economy as excellent or good, and 16% as poor, little changed from last month. At the same time, however, 44% say the economy is getting better, up considerably from the 30% who said that last month.

In the immediate aftermath of the September 11 attacks, Gallup measured a surge in economic ratings, which appeared to be part of the general "rally effect" enjoyed by several governmental officials and agencies. In October, however, the rating of the economy dropped back somewhat but still above the preattack levels. Then, in November, the rating fell to about the same level as it was in the September 7–10 poll. This month, 44% say the economy is getting better while 48% say worse, which is considerably more hopeful than last month, when 59% said it was getting worse and just 30% said better. In fact, this month's "future" rating is the best since December of last year, when the trend was headed the opposite way.

In the wake of the terrorist attacks, this measure changed direction and, except for last month's minor glitch, has been moving in a positive direction. In the September 7–10 poll, 70% said the economy was getting worse and only 19% said better. A week later, after the attacks, that worse-to-better ratio improved to a 60%-to-8% level, and the next month it improved even more, to 55% to 33%. November's rating showed a slight regression, 59% to 30%, but this month's rating shows the most positive change in at least two years.

Expectations about the economy's future appear to be quite positive. About one-half (49%) thinks that economic conditions a year from now will be excellent or good, while just 10% say poor. These figures are much higher than the 31%-to-16% ratings of the current economy. Also, 51% believe the stock market will go up

over the next six months while just 23% expect it to decline. This sentiment is even more positive than last month's when respondents expected the stock market to rise over the next six months by a margin of 42% to 30%.

Another positive change from November is the public's expectations about economic growth. This month, by a margin of 49% to 23%, Americans say that economic growth will increase rather than decrease over the next six months. This margin is better than last month's of 39% to 32%.

DECEMBER 13
WAR ON TERRORISM

Interview Dates: 12/6–9/01
Gallup Poll News Service
Survey #GO 132079

Do you approve or disapprove of the way the following people are handling the war on terrorism since September 11:

George W. Bush?

	2001 Dec 6–9	2001 Nov 8–11
Approve	87%	89%
Disapprove	10	8
No opinion	3	3

Defense Secretary Donald Rumsfeld?

	2001 Dec 6–9	2001 Nov 8–11
Approve	82%	80%
Disapprove	9	8
No opinion	9	12

Attorney General John Ashcroft?

	2001 Dec 6–9	2001 Nov 8–11
Approve	76%	77%
Disapprove	14	10
No opinion	10	13

Homeland Security Director Tom Ridge?

	2001 Dec 6–9	2001 Nov 8–11
Approve	67%	60%
Disapprove	12	14
No opinion	21	26

The news media?

	2001 Dec 6–9	2001 Nov 8–11
Approve	59%	43%
Disapprove	38	54
No opinion	3	3

Analysis: One result of the terrorist attacks of September 11 has been the American public's rally behind its government officials. In the days following the attacks, approval ratings for President Bush and Congress reached record highs, and general trust in government achieved levels not seen since the 1960s. Three months following the attack, that overwhelming support is still evident. The latest Gallup Poll shows very high approval of various government leaders' handling of the war on terrorism, virtually unchanged from last month. This is even the case for Attorney General John Ashcroft, who has been criticized by some for advocating military tribunals and for other actions he has taken.

The poll conducted December 6–9 shows that 87% approve of the way President Bush is handling the war on terrorism, very similar to his overall job approval rating of 86%. Bush's rating is little changed from a month ago, when 89% approved of the way he was handling the war. The public also rates Secretary of Defense Donald Rumsfeld highly, giving him an 82% approval for his handling of the war effort. In November, 80% approved of Rumsfeld. Homeland Security Director Tom Ridge's performance is rated favorably by 67%, up 7 points from last month. This is due mainly to the fact that more Americans today have an opinion about the job Ridge has done, although 21% say they have no opinion of Ridge. And despite some controversial actions,

Americans rate Attorney General John Ashcroft's handling of the war on terrorism very positively. Seventy-six percent say they approve and only 14% disapprove, similar to last month when 77% approved and 10% disapproved.

In the November 8–11 Gallup Poll, only the news media received a negative evaluation from the public for their handling of the war on terrorism. At that time, 43% approved while 54% disapproved. The latest poll shows the public's assessment of the media has greatly improved since then, as now 59% approve and 38% disapprove.

DECEMBER 17
MOOD OF AMERICA POST 9/11

Interview Dates: 12/6–9/01
Gallup Poll News Service
Survey #GO 132079

In general, are you satisfied or dissatisfied with the way things are going in your own personal life?

Satisfied	84%
Dissatisfied	15
No opinion	1

Now thinking just about today, how would you describe your mood—has it been very good, somewhat good, neither good nor bad, somewhat bad, or very bad?

Very good	45%
Somewhat good	38
Neither good nor bad	8
Somewhat bad,	7
Very bad	2
No opinion	*

*Less than 1%

Generally speaking, do you have enough time to do what you want to do these days, or not?

Yes 50%
No 49
No opinion 1

In general, how often do you experience stress in your daily life—never, rarely, sometimes, or frequently?

Never 2%
Rarely 18
Sometimes 38
Frequently 42

Usually, how many hours of sleep do you get at night?

Two hours or less . . . .*
Three hours 1
Four hours 4
Five hours 10
Six hours 27
Seven hours 28
Eight hours 23
Nine hours 3
Ten hours or more 1
No answer 1

*Less than 1%

Mean   6.70
Median 7.00

Analysis: Despite the tragic events of September 11 and the unmistakable effect they had on Americans in the days immediately following, a Gallup Poll conducted December 6–9 suggests that Americans' emotional state is now similar to what it was at the start of 2001.

For the first several weeks after September 11, national surveys documented that the attacks had a major emotional impact on Americans. Fear for personal safety was high; most Americans described themselves as "depressed;" and a majority felt tense, sad, and had difficulty concentrating. In the past month, however, it appears that most Americans feel their lives are getting back to normal.

Today, more than four in five respondents tell Gallup they are satisfied with their personal lives, including a majority who report feeling "very satisfied." When asked to reflect on "just today," close to one-half describe their personal mood as "very good" and another 38% as "somewhat good," while just 9% report being in a bad mood. Other questions suggest that Americans' levels of stress and the amount of sleep they get are at normal levels. However, for many this means a fairly high frequency of stress and not enough sleep. Only one-half feels they have enough time to do the things they want in life, and about four in ten "frequently" experience stress in their daily lives.

DECEMBER 18
WAR ON TERRORISM/
OSAMA BIN LADEN

Interview Dates: 12/14–16/01
CNN/*USA Today*/Gallup Poll
Survey #GO 135256

If Osama bin Laden is captured or killed and his terrorist network in Afghanistan is destroyed, should the United States end its current military action and bring most U.S. military forces home, or actively use U.S. military forces in other countries that harbor terrorists?

End current military action 30%
Actively use military forces 67
No opinion 3

Which comes closer to your view about what capturing or killing Osama bin Laden means for the United States—it will mean the United States has accomplished its goals in the war on terrorism, or it will be just one step in a long campaign against terrorism worldwide?

Accomplished goals 5%
One step in long campaign 93
No opinion 2

How likely is it that the United States will be able to capture or kill Osama bin Laden—very likely, somewhat likely, not too likely, or not at all likely?

	2001 Dec 14–16	2001 Nov 26–27
Very likely	43%	34%
Somewhat likely	33	44
Not too likely	16	15
Not at all likely	6	6
No opinion	2	1

How likely is it that there will be further acts of terrorism in the United States over the next several weeks—very likely, somewhat likely, not too likely, or not at all likely?

	Very, somewhat likely	Not too likely	Not at all likely*
2001 Dec 14–16	62%	27%	8%
2001 Nov 2–4	74	16	6
2001 Oct 19–21	85	10	3
2001 Oct 7	83	9	4
2001 Sep 21–22	66	24	8

*"No opinion" is omitted.

How satisfied are you with the amount of progress made by the U.S. military in the war in Afghanistan—very satisfied, somewhat satisfied, not too satisfied, or not at all satisfied?

	Very, somewhat satisfied	Not too satisfied	Not at all satisfied*
2001 Dec 14–16	92%	5%	2%
2001 Nov 26–27	93	4	2
2001 Nov 2–4	79	11	7

*"No opinion" is omitted.

If the United States goes to war in Iraq, do you think it will be as successful as the efforts in Afghanistan have been, or not?

Yes	66%
No	26
No opinion	8

Analysis: More than nine in ten Americans express satisfaction with the amount of progress made by the U.S. military in the war in Afghanistan, and almost eight in ten think it is likely the troops there will be able to capture or kill Osama bin Laden. Despite these optimistic feelings, the public does not see the war ending any time soon, as more than nine in ten say the neutralization of bin Laden would be just one step in a long campaign against terrorism. In addition, if and when bin Laden is killed or captured and his terrorist network destroyed, two-thirds would support continued U.S. military operations in other countries that are harboring terrorists, while just 30% would want to bring the troops home.

These findings come from the latest Gallup Poll conducted December 14–16, which also shows that respondents appear somewhat less pessimistic this month than they did last month about the possible occurrence of more terrorist attacks. Only 17% say it is "very" likely that there will be further acts of terrorism, and another 45% say "somewhat" likely, down from 24% and 50%, respectively, from early November.

The poll shows that Americans are willing to support the war in the long haul and are quite confident of success. More than three-quarters say it is likely that the U.S. military will be able to capture or kill bin Laden, with 43% saying "very" likely, up from 34% who shared this view three weeks ago. Also, by a 66%-to-26% margin, respondents believe that if the war were extended to Iraq, the U.S. would be just as successful there as it has been in Afghanistan.

The willingness of the public to stay in the war for the long haul is reflected in the increased satisfaction with the way the war is going. The poll shows that 69% are currently very satisfied with the amount of progress made by the U.S. military in Afghanistan. Three weeks ago, a similar measure showed 58% very satisfied, while in early November just 27% were very satisfied.

DECEMBER 19
OSAMA BIN LADEN

Interview Dates: 12/14–16/01
CNN/*USA Today*/Gallup Poll
Survey #GO 135256

Based on what you have heard or read about the videotape of Osama bin Laden, which of the following comes closer to your view—it proves beyond a reasonable doubt that he helped to plan the September 11 terrorist attacks, or it proves that he was happy that the September 11 terrorist attacks occurred but did not prove that he helped to plan them?

Planned attacks 73%
Happy with attacks 17
No opinion 10

Suppose Osama bin Laden is captured alive and put on trial. Do you think he should be tried by an international court, or by U.S. authorities?

International court .37%
U.S. authorities 59
No opinion 4

Suppose Osama bin Laden is captured alive and put on trial by the United States. Would you rather see that happen in a regular court of law in which evidence would be presented in a public trial, or a military tribunal in which U.S. officers would examine evidence in secret hearings?

Regular court 41%
Military tribunal 54
No opinion 5

If suspected terrorists are captured and put on trial, do you think they should be tried by an international court, or by U.S. authorities?

International court .41%
U.S. authorities 56
No opinion 3

If suspected terrorists are captured and put on trial by the United States, would you rather see that happen in a regular court of law in which evidence would be presented in a public trial, or a military tribunal in which U.S. officers would examine evidence in secret hearings?

Regular court 42%
Military tribunal 53
No opinion 5

Suppose Osama bin Laden is captured alive, put on trial, and found guilty. Do you think he should be sentenced to death, or should he be sentenced to spend the rest of his life in prison with no chance of parole?

Death 69%
Life, no parole 28
No opinion 3

Some U.S. allies say they will not turn over suspected terrorists for trial in the United States unless the United States agrees to not seek the death penalty for them. What should President Bush do in this situation—should he agree to the terms to not seek the death penalty for those suspected terrorists so that they can be put on trial by the United States; or should he refuse to accept these terms, in which case those suspected terrorists would be tried in an international court that would not seek the death penalty?

Agree to terms 36%
Refuse to accept terms 52
No difference (vol.) .3
No opinion 9

Analysis: The hunt for suspected terrorist mastermind Osama bin Laden continues in Afghanistan, and U.S. officials admit that finding him will be difficult. So far, it is unclear what legal steps the U.S. would take with bin Laden if he is captured alive, including the type of trial he would face and the possible sentence for him if found guilty. The latest Gallup Poll assesses Americans' attitudes about these issues. It finds that they prefer that bin Laden be tried by the U.S. rather than by an international court, that he be tried in a military tribunal rather than a regular court of law, and that he be given the death penalty if convicted.

Respondents have little doubt that bin Laden is responsible for the September 11 terrorist attacks. However, the videotape released last week by the Bush administration showing bin Laden discussing the September 11 attacks did not convince all Americans of his guilt. When asked to evaluate the tape in the latest poll conducted December 14–16, 73% say the tape proves bin Laden helped plan the attacks. Roughly one in six says the tape proves he was pleased with the outcome of the attacks but does not show he helped plan them, and 10% have no opinion.

Given the overwhelming belief that bin Laden is guilty, it is not surprising that Americans prefer swift and severe justice for him. When offered a choice, 54% say bin Laden should be tried in "a military tribunal in which U.S. officers would examine evidence in secret hearings," while 41% say he should be tried in "a regular court of law in which evidence would be presented in a public trial." Roughly six in ten believe bin Laden should be tried by U.S. authorities, while 37% think an international court should try him. Nearly seven in ten believe bin Laden should be sentenced to death if he is found guilty, while 28% believe he should be imprisoned for life with no chance of parole. This percentage is somewhat higher than the usual support for the death penalty when given a choice between it and an alternative of life in prison with no possibility of parole.

The prospects for a death penalty sentence are complicated by the fact that several European nations have said they would not hand over bin Laden or other suspects in their custody to the U.S. if they could face the death penalty on conviction. These European nations would allow the U.S. to try bin Laden or other terrorists only if they received a guarantee that the terrorists would not be sentenced to death. In the latest poll, 52% say the U.S. should refuse to agree to these terms, in which case an international court (that would not give a sentence of death) would try terrorists. Thirty-six percent say the U.S. should agree to the terms so that terrorists can be tried in this country.

The poll results also show that Americans' attitudes about possible legal action against ter-

rorists more generally are very similar to those they express about bin Laden. A majority (56%) would want U.S. authorities to try terrorists rather than having them tried in an international court (41%). Additionally, respondents show a preference to try terrorists in a military tribunal (53%) as opposed to a regular court of law (42%).

DECEMBER 20
ECONOMIC CONDITIONS

Interview Dates: 12/14–16/01
CNN/*USA Today*/Gallup Poll
Survey #GO 135256

As you may know, the federal government has announced that the country is currently in a recession and has been since March of this year. How would you rate economic conditions in this country today—very good, somewhat good, somewhat poor, or very poor?

	Very, somewhat good	Somewhat poor	Very poor*
2001 Dec 14–16	50%	37%	12%
2001 Sep 21–22	57	34	8
2001 Apr 20–22	67	25	7
2001 Feb 9–11	80	16	3
2001 Jan 15–16	82	14	4

*"No opinion" is omitted.

Now, thinking about a year from now, do you expect economic conditions in this country will be very good, somewhat good, somewhat poor, or very poor?

	Very, somewhat good	Somewhat poor	Very poor*
2001 Dec 14–16	76%	14%	7%
2001 Sep 21–22	77	15	5
2001 Apr 20–24	70	18	9
2001 Feb 9–11	71	21	6
2001 Jan 15–16	68	22	8

*"No opinion" is omitted.

In general, do you prefer the Republicans' or the Democrats' approach to deal with the country's current economic problems?

Republicans 44%
Democrats 35
Both (vol.) 4
Neither (vol.) 5
No opinion 12

Please tell me whether you think each of the following deserves a great deal of blame, some blame, not much blame, or no blame at all for the country's current economic recession?

	Great deal, some blame
The Clinton administration	62%
Congress	75
The current Bush administration	44

How much of the country's current economic problems are a result of the September 11 terrorist attacks—a great deal, a moderate amount, not much, or none at all?

Great deal 36%
Moderate amount 43
Not much 16
None at all 4
No opinion 1

Which of the following comes closer to your view of the U.S. economy—the federal government should take immediate action to improve the country's current economic problems, or the country's current economic problems are part of the natural business cycle and immediate government action is not necessary?

Take immediate action 47%
Immediate action not needed 49
No opinion 4

How much do you think Congress and the president can improve the economy by their actions—a great deal, a fair amount, not much, or not at all?

Great deal 34%
Fair amount 50
Not much 13
Not at all 2
No opinion 1

Analysis: As Washington leaders wrangle over the specifics of the economic stimulus bill currently stalled in Congress, a new Gallup Poll suggests that Americans may be wondering what all the fuss is about. Only one-half of the nation's adults believes that immediate government action is necessary to improve the country's economic woes; the other half sees these problems as part of the natural business cycle and says that immediate government action is not needed. Furthermore, only 34% believe Congress and the president can greatly improve the economy by their actions according to a Gallup poll conducted December 14–16.

The economic recovery package, initiated by President Bush after the September 11 terrorist attacks, is supposed to infuse the economy with a fresh wave of consumer spending and deliver financial relief to unemployed workers, many of whom lost their jobs in the current recession. However, it appears most Americans believe the economy is already on course for improvement. With characteristic optimism, three-quarters say that the U.S. economy will be in either very good shape or somewhat good shape a year from now, more than the 50% who currently think the economy is good.

The current legislative battle between President Bush and Democratic leaders in Congress over the stimulus bill may be the toughest political fight of Bush's presidency. Both sides are digging in on behalf of their economic approach, and both claim to represent the will of Americans. Although neither side wins the support of a majority, the new survey indicates that the Republicans have the political edge. When asked whose approach they prefer in dealing with the country's current economic problems, 44% choose the Republicans, compared with 35% who choose the Democrats. About one in five says it does not make a difference or has no opinion on the matter.

Overall, the public has not tagged any group or event with responsibility for the current recession, but the Bush administration ranks as the least responsible among those measured. Only 7% say the present administration deserves a great deal of blame for the recession, compared to 15% who blame Congress, 24% the Clinton administration, and 36% the September 11 terrorist attacks. When factoring in those who assign "some" blame to each factor, the Bush team is the only one that is blamed by less than a majority.

DECEMBER 21
RELIGION AFTER 9/11

Interview Dates: 12/14–16/01
CNN/USA Today/Gallup Poll
Survey #GO 135256

How important would you say religion is in your own life—very important, fairly important, or not very important?

	Very impor- tant	Fairly impor- tant	Not very impor- tant*
2001 Dec 14–16	.60%	26%	13%
2001 Sep 21–22	.64	24	12
2001 May 10–14	.57	28	15
2001 Feb 19–21	.55	30	15

*"No opinion" is omitted.

At the present time, do you think religion as a whole is increasing its influence on American life or losing its influence?

	Increasing influ- ence	Losing influ- ence	Same (vol.); no opinion
2001 Dec 14–16	.71%	24%	5%
2001 Feb 19–21	.39	55	6

Do you happen to be a member of a church or synagogue?

	Yes	No
2001 Dec 14–16	.66%	34%
2001 Feb 19–21	.65	35

Did you, yourself, happen to attend church or synagogue in the last seven days, or not?

	Yes	No
2001 Dec 14–16	.41%	59%
2001 Nov 8–11	.42	58
2001 Sep 21–22	.47	53
2001 May 10–14	.41	59
2001 Feb 19–21	.41	59

How often do you attend church or synagogue—at least once a week, almost every week, about once a month, seldom, or never?

	Once a week; almost every week	Once a month	Seldom; never*
2001 Dec 14–16	.45%	15%	40%
2001 Jun 11–17	.41	12	47
2001 Feb 19–21	.42	15	42

*"No opinion" is omitted.

Would you describe yourself as "born-again" or evangelical?

	Yes	No	No opinion
2001 Dec 14–16	.42%	49%	9%
2001 Feb 19–21	.45	49	6

Do you believe that religion can answer all or most of today's problems, or that religion is largely old-fashioned and out of date?

	Can answer	Old fashioned	No opinion
2001 Dec 14–16	.61%	21%	18%
2001 Feb 19–21	.63	22	15

Analysis: There are no indications in regular Gallup Poll measures of a significant change in religious behavior since September 11. The poll questions ask people directly about their religiosity—without any direct reference to September 11—and are probably the best measures of any real or enduring impact that the events may have had.

Church attendance is one of the putative changes in religion that has received the most discussion. There was a great deal of anecdotal evidence that the pews in churches, synagogues, and other houses of worship were filled to capacity in the week or two immediately after the terrorist attacks. But the answers to the classic Gallup question, "Did you, yourself, happen to attend church or synagogue in the last seven days, or not?" show no lasting change.

Over the last decade the responses to this question have averaged at about 40%, with the usual fluctuation that occurs from survey to survey. The last time the question was asked before September 11 was in May, when 41% of Americans replied that they had gone to church or synagogue within the last seven days. Right after the attacks, in the September 21–22 survey, the percentage moved up slightly to 47%, but in two subsequent surveys, in early November and this past weekend, December 14–16, the percentages have been 42% and 41%, respectively. In other words, church attendance as measured by this question has settled right back down to where it was.

A different question asks the public to estimate how often they attend church or synagogue, and the 45% who say "once a week or almost every week" is little changed from what we have found in recent years. The self-reported importance of religion is no different now than before September 11. Sixty percent in the December 14–16 poll said that religion was very important to them in their daily life. That is down slightly from the 64% who said religion was very important immediately after September 11. Additionally, survey polls find a continuation of a slight decrease in the number who say that religion can answer all or most of life's problems. Sixty-one percent now say that religion can answer life's problems.

Interestingly, there has been a wholesale change in perceptions of the impact of religion "out there" across America. For many years,

Gallup has asked, "At the present time, do you think religion as a whole is increasing its influence on American life, or losing its influence?" The percentage of Americans saying "increasing" in response to that question has now skyrocketed to 71%, the highest in Gallup Poll history. To put that in perspective, only 39% said yes in February of this year.

DECEMBER 26
COLLEGE FOOTBALL

Interview Dates: 12/14–16/01
CNN/*USA Today*/Gallup Poll
Survey #GO 135256

Are you a fan of college football, or not?

Yes, a fan	39%
Somewhat of a fan (vol.)	8
No, not a fan	53

Asked of those who are a fan of college football: Which of the following teams do you think should play the University of Miami for the college football national championship this year—the University of Nebraska, the University of Colorado, or the University of Oregon?

Nebraska	35%
Colorado	34
Oregon	21
No opinion	10

Also asked of those who are a fan of college football: Which of the following comes closest to your view of how the national championship should be determined in major college football—drop the current Bowl Championship Series, keep the Bowl Championship Series but change the way standings are computed, keep the current Bowl Championship Series as it currently is, or move to a playoff tournament?

Drop current BCS	3%
Change standings computation	15

Keep BCS as is 21
Move to playoff tournament 54
No opinion 7

Analysis: The question of whether college football's national champion should be decided by polls or a playoff has been raging for many years, and this year's debate about the Bowl Championship Series (BCS) is no exception. A new Gallup Poll finds that 54% of college football fans would prefer to scrap the BCS in favor of a playoff tournament, while just 21% prefer the current system. An additional 15% say the BCS should be kept but with a change in the way the standings are computed, and 3% say the BCS should be dropped altogether.

The BCS, instituted in 1998, was designed to guarantee that the top two teams in college football meet in a final championship game to determine the sport's national champion. To do so, a complicated formula, including a team's overall record, strength of schedule, and poll rankings, is used. This year the formula produced a matchup between the top-ranked University of Miami Hurricanes and the University of Nebraska Cornhuskers. Nebraska was only rated fourth in both major opinion polls despite finishing second in the BCS standings. Nebraska's appearance in the championship game is especially controversial since the Cornhuskers lost to currently third-ranked Colorado by a score of 62 to 36 in late November. It is clear that the majority of college football fans would like to see some team other than Nebraska in the championship game against Miami. When asked to choose among Nebraska, Colorado, and Oregon, only 35% choose Nebraska, while 34% pick Colorado and 21% select Oregon.

DECEMBER 27
MOST ADMIRED PERSON

Interview Dates: 12/14–16/01
CNN/*USA Today*/Gallup Poll
Survey #GO 135256

What man whom you have heard or read about, living today in any part of the world, do you admire the most? And who is your second choice?

The following are listed in order of frequency of mention, with first and second choices combined.

George W. Bush
Colin Powell
Rudolph Giuliani
Pope John Paul II
Billy Graham
Bill Clinton
Tony Blair
Michael Jordan
Jimmy Carter
Nelson Mandela

What woman whom you have heard or read about, living today in any part of the world, do you admire the most? And who is your second choice?

The following are listed in order of frequency of mention, with first and second choices combined.

Laura Bush
Hillary Rodham Clinton
Oprah Winfrey
Barbara Bush
Condoleezza Rice
Margaret Thatcher
Madeleine Albright
Elizabeth Dole
Julia Roberts
Madonna

Analysis: Gallup's annual "most admired man and woman" poll finds President George W. Bush and First Lady Laura Bush topping the list. Americans have typically rated presidents and First Ladies as the most admirable, so 2001 does not represent a dramatic change from previous years. However, George W. Bush received more mentions than has any other man in the fifty-plus years Gallup has asked this question. Secretary of State Colin Powell places second behind Bush, followed by New York City Mayor Rudolph Giuliani, and Pope John Paul II. The Reverend Billy Graham made the list again this year, the forty-fourth time he has done so, far more often than any other man. Also named by respondents are Ronald Reagan, Secretary of Defense Donald Rumsfeld, UN Secretary General Kofi Annan, and Mormon leader Gordon Hinckley.

Americans mention Laura Bush as the most admired woman in 2001, although by not nearly the same margin as her husband in the most ad-mired man category. New York Senator and former First Lady Hillary Rodham Clinton placed second, ending her eight-year run as the most admired woman. Talk show host Oprah Winfrey is third, followed by the president's mother and former First Lady, Barbara Bush. National Security Adviser Condoleezza Rice and former British Prime Minister Margaret Thatcher tie for fourth place. Ranked below the top ten are broadcast journalists Barbara Walters and Christiane Amanpour and poet Maya Angelou.

INDEX

A

Aaron, Hank
  as greatest baseball player of all time, 83
Abortion
  as most important problem, 59, 121, 256
  satisfied with nation's policies regarding, 29
Academy Awards
  aware of the five nominated movies for Best
    Picture [list], 72
  like Crystal, Goldberg, Letterman, or Martin as
    host this year, 72
  like to see win Oscar for best picture [list], 73
  movies you have seen or plan to see this year
    [list], 72–73
  plan to watch this year's, 72
  See also Movies and movie stars
Accountants
  rate honesty and ethical standards of, 265
Accounting
  overall view of, 200
Acid rain
  worry about, 90
Actress
  recommend as career for young woman, 109
Advertising and public relations industry
  overall view of, 201
Advertising practitioners
rate honesty and ethical standards of, 265
Afghanistan
  as America's greatest enemy today, 84
  how long should military action continue with-
    out capturing bin Laden or removing
    Taliban from power, 253
  opinion of the people of, 233
  opinion of the Taliban government in, 233
  United States doing too much to provide
    humanitarian aid to the people of, 239
  See also Terrorist attacks; War on terrorism
Agassi, Andre
  as greatest athlete in world of sports today, 142
AIDS (acquired immune deficiency syndrome)
  as most important problem, 59, 121, 256
Airline industry
  overall view of, 201

Airline stewardess
  recommend as career for young woman, 109
Airline strikes
  Bush should use his emergency powers to
    prevent strikes, 85
  strike would be major inconvenience to you, 85
  would favor airline workers or airlines if there
    is a strike, 85
Airline travel
  before attacks of 9/11 were you considering
    flying somewhere for the holidays, 254
  events of 9/11 make it less likely you will fly
    somewhere for the holidays, 254
  events of 9/11 make you less willing to fly,
    254
  have done or considered avoiding since
    terrorist attacks, 242
Air pollution
  worry about, 90
Airport security
  Gallup analysis of, 245
Alaskan Arctic National Wildlife Refuge
  favor opening up for oil exploration, 68, 100,
    118–19, 258
Albright, Madeleine
  as most admired person, 278
Alcoholic beverages
  drinking moderately is good for your health,
    200
  favor federal law to lower drinking age to 18 in
    all states, 200
  have occasion to use, 200
  penalties for underage drinking should be
    made more strict, 200
American people
  American consumers are to blame for
    country's energy problems, 131
  can retain their lifestyle and the current energy
    problems can be solved, 131
  consider yourself a feminist, 152
  describe your mood today, 270
  do you have enough time to do what you want
    to these days, 270–71
  fears of [list], 70
  gap between rich and poor, as most important
    problem, 58, 121, 255
  how many hours of sleep do you get a night,
    271
  how much do the American people do to
    protect the environment, 100
  how often you experience stress in your daily
    life, 271
  important immigrants learn to speak English,
    89

American people (*continued*)
    important to learn another language other than English, 88–89
    personally speak language other than English well enough to hold a conversation, 89
    prefer to have job outside the home, 152
    racial minorities have equal job opportunities, 152
    racial minorities have equal job opportunities with whites (by race), 147
    satisfied with job (by race), 147
    satisfied with the way things are going in your personal life, 270
    satisfied with way things going in your local community, 26
    satisfied with way things going in your state, 26
    satisfied with your community as place to live (by race), 146
    satisfied with your current housing (by race), 146
    satisfied with your education (by race), 146
    satisfied with your family life (by race), 146
    satisfied with your financial situation (by race), 146
    satisfied with your opportunities to succeed in life (by race), 147
    satisfied with your personal health (by race), 146–47
    satisfied with your safety from physical harm or violence (by race), 147
    which foreign language do you speak (asked of foreign-speaking people), 89
    women have equal job opportunities with men, 152
Anaheim Angels
    as favorite major league baseball team, 82
Anthrax
    Americans overreacting to the threat of, 237
    approval rating, way Bush administration is handling response to incidents involving, 250
    approval rating, way Bush is handling response to incidents involving, 250
    confident in ability of U.S. government to prevent additional people from being exposed to, 251, 262
    confident in ability of U.S. government to respond to major outbreak of, 237, 251
    have done or considered trying to get a vaccination for, 242
    likely U.S. government will be able to identify and punish people responsible for, 262
    likely you or someone in your family will be exposed to it, 237, 250

    members of Bin Laden's terrorist network are responsible for recent incidents, 238
    news media are overreacting to the threat of, 237–38
    recent incidents represent a sustained campaign against the United States, 238
    who is responsible for recent cases of, U.S. citizens or others, 262
    worried you or someone in your family will be exposed to it, 237, 250, 262
    worried you or someone in your family will be exposed to it through the mail, 251
Arabs
    opinion of, 233
Arizona Diamondbacks
    as favorite major league baseball team, 82
Armed Forces. *See* Veterans
Armstrong, Lance
    as greatest athlete in world of sports today, 142
Arts
    immigrants are making the arts better or worse, 171
Ashcroft, John
    approval rating, way he is handling the war on terrorism, 254, 269
    opinion of, 16
    should Senate confirm as Attorney General, 16
    support for, if he opposed abortion, 16
    support for, if he opposed affirmative action, 16
    support for, if he opposed appointment of federal judge because of his record on sentencing criminals, 16
    support for, if he opposed appointment of federal judge because of race, 16
    support for, if he voted against gay rights bills, 16
Asians
    satisfied with treatment of in our society, 158–59
Astrology
    believe in, 137
Atlanta
    as city safe to live in or visit, 235
Atlanta Braves
    as favorite major league baseball team, 81
Attorney
    recommend as career for young woman, 109
Australia
    opinion of, 35, 43, 84
Auto mechanics
    rate honesty and ethical standards of, 265
Automobile industry
    overall view of, 201
Auto racing
    fan of, 81

B

Baltimore Orioles
  as favorite major league baseball team, 81
Baltimore Ravens
  team you would like to see win this year's
    Super Bowl, 25
  which team will win Super Bowl, Ravens or
    Giants, 25
Bankers
  rate honesty and ethical standards of, 265
Banking
  overall view of, 201
Banks
  confidence in, 149
  confidence in (by political party), 149
Baseball, professional
  addition of wild-card playoff team in each
    league has been change for the better, 83
  designated hitter rule has been change for the
    better, 82
  fact that Yankees won series three years
    straight increased interest in big-league
    baseball, 82
  fact that Yankees won series three years
    straight lessened interest in big-league
    baseball, 82
  fan of, 80
  favorite major league baseball team, 81–82
    [list]
  greatest baseball player of all time [list], 83
  increases in average salary paid to players has
    been change for the better, 82
  increases in number of teams has been change
    for the better, 82
  interleague play has been change for the better,
    83
  most like to get a ticket to World Series, 24
  owners of teams should be allowed to put cap
    on players' salaries, 82
  playoffs in each league determining who goes
    to World Series has been change for the
    better, 82
  See also World Series
Basketball, college
  fan of, 81
  most like to get a ticket to the men's finals, 24
Basketball, professional
  fan of, 81
  most like to get a ticket to NBA finals, 25
Beautician
  recommend as career for young woman, 109
Biden, Joe
  as Democratic choice for presidential nominee
    in 2004, 192

as Democratic choice for presidential nominee
  in 2004 if Al Gore doesn't run, 192
Bin Laden, Osama
  better for the United States if he is killed or if
    he is captured alive, 263–64
  have no doubts about his role in the September
    11 terrorist attacks, 264
  how long should military action continue
    without capturing him, 253
  if captured, tried, and found guilty, he should
    be sentenced to death or given life, no
    parole, 273
  if captured, United States should execute him
    immediately, 264
  if captured and put on trial, should be tried by
    international court, secret military tribunal,
    or civilian court, 264
  if captured and put on trial, should be tried by
    international court or by U.S. authorities,
    273
  if captured and put on trial, should be tried by
    regular court or military tribunal, 273
  if captured or killed, United States will have
    accomplished its goals, 271
  likely United States will be able to capture or
    kill him, 263, 272
  members of his terrorist network are
    responsible for recent incidents involving
    anthrax, 238
  opinion of, 233
  United States will be a success in Afghanistan
    even if he is not captured, 263
  videotape of him proves he planned the terror
    ist attacks, 273
Blacks, asked of
  approval rating, way Bush is handling his job
    as president, 145
  approval rating, way Congress is handling its
    job, 145
  approval rating, way Supreme Court is
    handling its job, 145
  how often do you feel discriminated against,
    147
  racial minorities have equal job opportunities
    with whites, 147, 152
  satisfied with position of blacks in the nation,
    29
  satisfied with treatment of in our society, 158
  satisfied with your community as place to live,
    146
  satisfied with your current housing, 146
  satisfied with your education, 146
  satisfied with your family life, 146
  satisfied with your financial situation, 146

approval rating, handling the war on terrorism, 226, 254, 269

approval rating, way he is handling incident of midair collision with Chinese plane, 92

approval rating, way he is handling taxes, 110

approve his decision not to adhere to the Kyoto treaty, 102, 181

approve of him personally, 7, 36, 168

Cabinet-level nominees, rate his choices for, 7, 19

Cabinet-level nominees, too liberal or conservative, 7

can he fulfill the proper role of the United States in world affairs, 20

can he handle an international crisis, 20

can he manage the government effectively, 36

can he prevent major scandals in his administration, 20

can he set a good moral example, 20

can he use military force wisely, 20

can he work effectively with Congress, 20

can manage the government effectively, 228

cares about needs of people like you, 37, 228

cares about the needs of people like you, 168

confident in his ability to carry out his duties as president, 48

confident in his ability to handle situation caused by terrorist attacks, 216

did he win fair and square, 20–21

explained the goals of current U.S. military action clearly enough, 221

favor his energy plan, 156

favor his tax cut proposals, 23, 38, 48–49

good job improving nation's energy policies, 68, 102

good job keeping America prosperous, 68, 102

good job protecting the environment, 68, 102

good job representing America to the world, 139, 180

has gone too far in his economic and diplomatic response to the terrorist attacks, 221

has personality and leadership qualities of a president, 139

as honest and trustworthy, 36, 168

how many weeks vacation should a president take each year, 185

how much can he improve the economy, 275

how much credit for the tax cut checks do you give him, 195

if tax cut enacted, he will have fulfilled his campaign promise, 124

if tax cut enacted, it will be major accomplishment for him, 124

important that following issues are dealt with in the next year [list], 229

important that following issues are dealt with next year [list], 141

important that he deals with patients' bill of rights next year, 141, 144

inauguration of as celebration by all Americans, 18

inauguration speech, expectations for, 18–19

income tax cut would cause a federal budget deficit, 39

income tax cut would make recession more likely, 39

income tax cut would take money from Social Security, 39

inspires confidence, 37, 228

interested in hearing a live speech by, 79

is a strong and decisive leader, 228

is he a uniter or divider, 20

is in touch with daily problems of Americans, 169

is responsible for decrease in budget surplus, 206

is sincere in what he says, 228

is tough enough for the job, 168

is working hard enough to be effective president, 106

leaders of other countries have respect for him, 56, 139, 180–81

leading the country in right direction, 48

main reason you oppose his energy plan [list], 156

more influence in direction the nation takes, Bush or Democrats in Congress, 37

more influence in direction the nation takes, Bush or Republicans in Congress, 37

more qualified to be president, Bush or Cheney, 135

as most admired person, 278

opinion of, 19–20, 139

as person you admire, 37

policies more conservative than you thought, 106

priorities of his programs [list], 8–9

priority of tax cuts, 49

rate his speech on the terrorist attacks, 221

reaction to State of the Union Speech, 48

respect him, regardless of his political views, 169

saw his address to Congress and the nation about the recent terrorist attacks, 220

shares your values, 36, 168–69

should agree not to seek death penalty for terrorists turned over by our allies, 273

Bush, George (*continued*)
  should pardon Clinton, 12
  should use his emergency powers to prevent strikes by airline workers, 85
  stance on issues or leadership skills most important to decide whether he is doing a good job, 169
  as a strong and decisive leader, 36, 168
  supporter of, 7
  support for proposals outlined in State of the Union speech, 48
  thirty days vacation at his ranch in Texas is too much time away from the White House, 185
  as of today, do you lean toward Bush or Gore for president in 2004, 193
  top priority of his programs (by ideology) [list], 9
  as tough enough for job, 36
  understands complex issues, 37, 228
  United States should take military action in retaliation for terrorist attacks on 9/11, 221
  very interested in hearing a live speech by (by politics), 80
  who really won the election, Bush or Gore, 20
  will Bush or Cheney make the important decisions, 7
  will Bush or others make the important decisions, 20, 106
  will go too far delegating authority, 7
  will govern in a compassionate way, 20
  will pass his proposed cuts, 23
  won fair and square or stole the election, 167–68, 246–47
  See also Presidential election dispute
Bush, Laura
  as most admired person, 278
Bush administration
  able to make proposed changes to Social Security, 24
  approval rating, handling response to incidents involving anthrax, 250
  balanced budget, dealing with, as priority for, 38
  big business has too much influence over decisions made by, 106, 169
  consider first six months to be a success or failure, 187
  education as priority for, 38
  energy problems, dealing with, as priority for, 38
  environmental protection policies will be strengthened over next four years, 102
  favor proposal to put portion of Social Security taxes into stocks and bonds, 24

is to blame for country's energy problems, 130
  military security for country as priority for, 38
  a prosperous America as priority for, 38
  tax cuts as priority for, 38, 49, 119
  top priorities of [list], 38–39
  will be able to do the following [list], 105, 106
  will it enact certain policies [list], 22
Bush daughters
  behavior has been worse than most college students their age, 140
  media have acted responsibly in this situation, 140
  media should have reported about citations issued to them by police, 140
Business
  recommend as career for young woman, 109
Business and industry
  big business has too much influence over decisions of Bush administration, 169
  confidence in big business, 149
  confidence in big business (by political party), 149
  overall view of business sectors [list], 200–201
Business executives
  rate honesty and ethical standards of, 265

C

Cabinet nominations
  justified for senator to oppose nomination only because of policy disagreements, 17
  rate Bush's choices for, 7, 19
  too liberal or conservative, 7
  See also specific nominees
Cage, Nicholas
  as favorite star of all time, 76
  make special effort to see, 76
Campaign finance reform
  approval rating, way Bush is handling, 167
  closely followed debate over, 71
  favor new laws limiting amount individuals or group can contribute to national political parties, 71
  important to deal with this issue next year, 141
  as priority for Bush administration, 9
  satisfied with nation's campaign finance laws, 30
  whose approach preferred, Bush or McCain, 70–71
  will make our government work much better, 71
Canada
  opinion of, 35, 43, 84
Cancer
  as most important problem, 121

Cincinnati Reds
  as favorite major league baseball team, 81
Clairvoyance
  believe in, 137
Clemente, Roberto
  as greatest baseball player of all time, 83
Clergy
  rate honesty and ethical standards of, 265
Cleveland Indians
  as favorite major league baseball team, 81
Clinton, Bill
  actions in last week in office worse than other
    presidents', 41
  agree with criticism of his actions during his
    last week in office, 41
  approval rating, 11, 14, 31
  approval rating, as person, 11
  approve of his presidential pardons, 31
  closely followed news about his presidential
    pardons, 31
  glad he's leaving or will miss him, 12, 40–41
  as greatest U.S. president, 44
  as honest and trustworthy, 11
  interested in hearing a live speech by, 79
  as most admired person, 278
  as most outstanding president in history, 11
  remembered for accomplishments or scandal, 12
  should Bush pardon him, 12
  supporter of, 11
  very interested in hearing a live speech by (by
    politics), 80
  when he leaves office, he should remain in
    public life, 12
  would have done better job in dealing with the
    economy if he were still president, 247
  would have done better job in response to
    terrorist attacks if he were still president,
    247
  See also Presidential pardons by Bill Clinton
Clinton, Hillary Rodham
  approval rating, 1
  as Democratic choice for presidential nominee
    in 2004, 192
  as Democratic choice for presidential nominee
    in 2004 if Al Gore doesn't run, 192
  interested in hearing a live speech by, 79–80
  as most admired person, 278
  opinion of, 1, 31
  very interested in hearing a live speech by (by
    politics), 80
Clinton administration
  is to blame for country's energy problems, 130
Cloning
  of animals should be allowed, 136

of humans should be allowed, 136
Clooney, George
  as favorite star of all time, 77
  make special effort to see, 76
Closed in a small place
  fear of, 70
Cobb, Ty
  as greatest baseball player of all time, 83
Colombia
  opinion of, 44, 84
Colorado Rockies
  as favorite major league baseball team, 81
Computer industry
  advancement of, as most important problem,
    59, 121, 256
  Microsoft domination of software markets
    positive for, 157
  overall view of, 200
  recommend as career for young woman, 109
  See also Microsoft Corporation
Condit, Gary
  approval rating, way he is handling his job as
    congressman (asked of his California
    constituents), 203
  approve of him as a person (asked of his
    California constituents), 203
  as caring or uncaring, 202
  did he lie at any point during these interviews,
    203
  did he lie at any point during these interviews
    (asked of his California constituents), 204
  did his letter to you make you feel more or less
    favorably toward him (asked of his
    California constituents), 204
  embarrassed he represents your district (asked
    of his California constituents), 203
  he should take a lie detector test about
    disappearance of Chandra Levy, 165
  he was justified in not answering questions
    about his relationship with Chandra Levy,
    203
  he was justified in not answering questions
    about his relationship with Chandra Levy
    (asked of his California constituents), 204
  as honest or dishonest, 202
  how concerned is he about Chandra Levy and
    her family, 202
  how concerned is he about Chandra Levy and
    her family (asked of his California
    constituents), 203–4
  interviews made you more or less suspicious of
    his actions during the investigation, 203
  likely he tried to obstruct the investigation into
    disappearance of Chandra Levy, 202

likely he tried to obstruct the investigation into disappearance of Chandra Levy (asked of his California constituents), 203

likely he was directly involved in disappearance of Chandra Levy, 165, 188, 202

likely he was directly involved in disappearance of Chandra Levy (asked of his California constituents), 203

as moral or immoral, 202

more or less favorable view of him as result of these interviews, 202–3

more or less favorable view of him as result of these interviews (asked of his California constituents), 204

news media have acted responsibly in this situation (asked of his California constituents), 204

saw his Connie Chung and/or Sacramento station interview, 202

saw his Connie Chung and/or Sacramento station interview, live or rebroadcast, 202

saw his Connie Chung and/or Sacramento station interview, live or rebroadcast (asked of his California constituents), 203

should apologize to people in your district or to the Levy family (asked of his California constituents), 204

should resign from Congress immediately, 188

voted for Condit or Steve Wilson for Congress in 2000 (asked of his California constituents), 205

would vote for him if he runs for reelection (asked of his California constituents), 203

See also Levy, Chandra

Congress

approval rating, handling the war on terrorism, 254

approval rating, way it is handling its job, 13, 186, 199, 232

approval rating, way it is handling its job (by race), 145

confidence in, 3, 149

confidence in (by political party), 149

consider first six months to be a success or failure, 187

dissatisfaction with, as most important problem, 121

House overreacted to threats of anthrax by closing down, 238

how much can they improve the economy, 275

if elections held today, would vote for Democratic or Republican candidate, 141–42

important that following issues are dealt with in the next year [list], 229

important that following issues are dealt with next year [list], 141

important they deal with patients' bill of rights next year, 144

is to blame for country's energy problems, 130–31

likely to deal with major issues facing nation today, 141

more influence in direction the nation takes, Bush or Congress, 37

See also Republicans in Congress; Democrats in Congress

Congressmen

rate honesty and ethical standards of, 265

Connery, Sean

as favorite star of all time, 76

make special effort to see, 76

Consumers

Microsoft domination of software markets positive for, 157

Contamination of soil and water

by radioactivity from nuclear facilities, worry about, 90

by toxic waste, worry about, 90

Cooper, Gary

as favorite star of all time, 77

Corporations, major

satisfied with size and influence of, 28

Corruption

as most important problem, 121

Costner, Kevin

as favorite star of all time, 76

make special effort to see, 76

Cost of living

as most important problem, 58, 121, 255

Creationism

believe more in theory of evolution or creationism, 53

Charles Darwin's theory of evolution supported by evidence, 53

human beings have developed by a God-guided process, 53

informed about theory of creationism, 52–53

informed about theory of evolution, 52

Credit cards

amount you pay on your credit cards each month, 114

how many credit cards do you have, 113–14

worry about not being able to make minimum payments on, 113

Crime

amount of confidence in the police to protect you from violent crime, 234

Crime (*continued*)

area within a mile of where you live where you
would be afraid to walk alone at night, 234

cities you consider safe to live in or visit [list],
235

do you have a gun in your home, 235

frequently worry about being assaulted or
killed by coworker, 235

frequently worry about being attacked while
driving your car, 234

frequently worry about being sexually
assaulted, 235

frequently worry about being victim of a hate
crime, 235

frequently worry about being victim of
terrorism, 234

frequently worry about getting mugged, 234

frequently worry about getting murdered, 235

frequently worry about having your car broken
into or stolen, 234

frequently worry about having your child
physically harmed while at school, 234

frequently worry about your home being
burglarized when you are not there, 234

frequently worry about your home being
burglarized when you are there,
234–35

immigrants are making crime situation better
or worse, 171

more or less crime in the United States than a
year ago, 234

more or less crime in your area than a year
ago, 234

as most important problem, 58, 121, 255

percentage of all crime not reported to police,
245

percentage of households experiencing any
crime, 245

percentage of households experiencing violent
crime, 245

against pregnant women, criminal should face
additional charges for harming fetus, 108

against pregnant women, criminal should face
additional charges for harming unborn
child, 108

satisfied with policies to reduce or control
crime, 29

which, if any, of these incidents have happened
to you or your household in past twelve
months [list], 245

which of these things you do because of
concern over crime [list], 235

will Bush administration reduce, 22

worry about this problem, 59, 66

Crosby, Bing
as favorite star of all time, 77

Crouching Tiger, Hidden Dragon
have seen or plan to see, 73
like to see win Oscar for best picture, 73

Crowds
fear of, 70

Crowe, Russell
as favorite star of all time, 77

Cruise, Tom
as favorite star of all time, 76
make special effort to see, 76

Cuba
as America's greatest enemy today, 84
opinion of, 44, 84

D

Dallas
as city safe to live in or visit, 235

Dark
fear of, 70

Daschle, Tom
as Democratic choice for presidential nominee
in 2004, 192
as Democratic choice for presidential nominee
in 2004 if Al Gore doesn't run, 192

Davis, Bette
as favorite star of all time, 77

Dean, Dizzy
as greatest baseball player of all time, 83

Death penalty
favor death penalty for murder, 50–51
favor moratorium on, in states with death
penalty, 94
should be moratorium on, until determined if it
is being administered accurately and fairly,
94
should penalty be death or life imprisonment, 51
what should be the penalty for murder, 51
why do you favor death penalty for murder, 51
See also McVeigh, Timothy

Declaration of Independence
think signers of would be pleased by way
United States has turned out, 155

Defense, national
important that Congress and Bush deal with
issues about in the next year, 229
Republican or Democratic Party would do
better job dealing with, 210
strength of today, 34

Democratic Party
or Republican Party would do better job
dealing with these issues [list], 210–11

Democrats, asked of
if Al Gore doesn't run, who would be your
second choice for Democratic presidential
nominee in 2004 [list], 192
which candidates would you most likely
support for Democratic presidential
nominee in 2004 [list], 192
Democrats in Congress
approval rating, way they are handling their
job, 141, 187
are responsible for decrease in budget surplus,
206
confidence in Bush or Democratic leaders
about issue of patients' bill of rights, 144
confidence more in Republicans or Democrats
in dealing with terrorism, 229–30
country better off if controlled by Democrats
or Republicans, 187
country better off if controlled by Republicans
or Democrats, 229
country better off if controlled by vs.
Republicans, 7–8
how much credit for the tax cut checks do you
give to them, 195
more influence in direction the nation takes,
Bush or Democrats in Congress, 37, 141
policies proposed by would move country in
right direction, 210
De Niro, Robert
as favorite star of all time, 76
make special effort to see, 76
Dentists
rate honesty and ethical standards of, 265
Depp, Johnny
make special effort to see, 76
Detroit
as city safe to live in or visit, 235
Detroit Tigers
as favorite major league baseball team, 81
Dietitian
recommend as career for young woman, 109
DiMaggio, Joe
as greatest baseball player of all time, 83
Disease
as most important problem, 121
Divorce
as morally acceptable, 127
Doctors, medical
fear of going to, 70
rate honesty and ethical standards of, 265
Dogs
dog or cat make better pet, 55
do you or member of household own a dog or
dogs, 55

fear of, 70
how many dogs do you own, 55
Dole, Elizabeth
as most admired person, 278
Douglas, Michael
as favorite star of all time, 77
make special effort to see, 76
Dow Jones Industrial Average
below 10,000 mark, as significant economic
milestone, 65
See also Stock market; Economic conditions
Drugs, illegal
as most important problem, 58, 121, 255
as priority for Bush administration, 8, 9
worry about this problem, 59, 66
Drugs, prescription, for older Americans
approval rating, way Bush is handling, 166
important to deal with this issue in the next
year, 141, 229

E
Eastwood, Clint
as favorite star of all time, 76
make special effort to see, 76
Economic conditions
approval rating, way economy is handled by
Bush, 55, 166, 228
confidence more in Republicans or Democrats
to deal with the economy, 229
confident the economy currently strong, 49
Dow Jones below 10,000 mark, as significant
economic milestone, 65
economic news mostly good or bad, 93, 198
economy now in a recession, 58, 93, 120, 218,
222
getting better or worse, 14, 32, 93, 120, 144,
183, 197, 217–18, 268
government should take immediate action to
improve, 275
how long before economy starts to get better,
93
how much can Congress and the president
improve the economy, 275
how much of current economic problems due
to September 11 terrorist attacks, 275
immigrants are making the economy in general
better or worse, 171
important that Congress and Bush deal with
issues about in the next year, 229
likelihood of recession in the next year, 32–33,
58
Microsoft domination of software markets
positive for, 157

one person you e-mail most often at home or at work [list], 178
use e-mail at home, 175
use e-mail at work, 175
what percentage of e-mail each week is "spam," 176
See also Internet
Employers
should have access to genetic information, 162
Energy policies
Americans can retain their lifestyle and the current energy problems can be solved, 131
approval rating, way Bush is handling, 166–67
Bush administration is to blame for country's energy problems, 130
Bush's plan will make major difference to you and your family, 187
Clinton administration is to blame for country's energy problems, 130
closely followed news about Bush's energy plan, 156
Congress is to blame for country's energy problems, 130–31
conservation issues, important to deal with this issue next year, 141
consumers are to blame for country's energy problems, 131
country is in state of crisis because of price of gasoline, 130
country is in state of crisis because of price of natural gas or home heating oil, 130
country is in state of crisis because of shortages of electricity, 130
energy sources, as most important problem, 59
environmental laws and regulations are to blame for country's energy problems, 131
favor Bush's energy plan, 156
favor construction of nuclear energy plant in your area, 68
favor drilling for natural gas on federal lands, 118
favor federal government partnership with auto industry working toward energy-efficient cars, 118
favor increased use of nuclear power as major source of power, 118, 258
favor investing in more electrical transmission lines, 118
favor investing in more energy-efficient cars, 258
favor investing in more solar, wind, and fuel cells, 258
favor investing in new power-generating plants, 118, 258

favor investments in new sources of energy, such as solar, wind, and fuel cells, 118
favor mandating more energy-efficient appliances, 118
favor mandating more energy-efficient buildings, 118
favor mandating more energy-efficient cars, 118
favor opening up Alaskan Arctic Wildlife Refuge for oil exploration, 118–19, 258
foreign countries that produce oil are to blame for country's energy problems, 131
good job by Bush in improving, 68, 102
how serious is energy situation in the United States, 68, 114, 156
importance of dealing with in the next year, 27
lack of energy sources as most important problem, 121, 255
likelihood of critical energy shortage during next five years, 68
main reason you oppose Bush's energy plan [list], 156
oil and gas production, important to deal with this issue next year, 141
price increases caused financial hardship, 47, 115
Republican or Democratic Party would do better job dealing with, 210
satisfied with state of nation's policies, 27, 29
set legal limits on amount which consumers can use, 68
should protection of environment be given priority over development of energy supplies, 67
solve energy problems by more production of energy supplies or by conservation of existing energy supplies, 68
United States should emphasize production of more oil, gas, and coal supplies, 118
U.S. electric companies are to blame for country's energy problems, 131
U.S. oil companies are to blame for country's energy problems, 131
worry about availability and affordability of energy, 59, 66
Engineering
recommend as career for young woman, 109
Engineers
rate honesty and ethical standards of, 265
Environment
actions we should take concerning the environment, 100
active participant in environmental movement, 99

opinion of, 186
Gere, Richard
  as favorite star of all time, 77
  make special effort to see, 76
Germany
  opinion of, 35, 43, 84
Gibson, Mel
  as favorite star of all time, 76
  make special effort to see, 76
Giuliani, Rudolph
  as most admired person, 278
Gladiator
  have seen or plan to see, 73
  like to see win Oscar for best picture, 73
Global warming ("greenhouse effect")
  how well do you understand the issue of global
    warming, 90
  most scientists agree global warming is
    occurring, 90
  seriousness of global warming is exaggerated,
    90
  view of when the effects of global warming
    will happen, 90
  will pose serious threat to you in your lifetime,
    90
  worry about, 90
Goldberg, Whoopi
  make special effort to see, 76
Golf, professional
  fan of, 41, 81
  See also Woods, Tiger
Gordon, Jeff
  as greatest athlete in world of sports today, 142
Gore, Al
  as Democratic choice for presidential nominee
    in 2004, 192
  if elected, would have done better job in
    dealing with the economy, 247
  if elected, would have done better job in
    response to terrorist attacks, 247
  interested in hearing a live speech by, 80
  as of today, do you lean toward Bush or Gore
    for president in 2004, 193
  very interested in hearing a live speech by (by
    politics), 80
  who really won the election, Bush or Gore, 20
Government, federal
  agree people like me don't have any say about
    what government does, 231
  agree public officials don't care much about
    what people think, 231
  approval rating, (by race), 145
  dissatisfaction with, as most important
    problem, 58, 121

doing too many things that should be left to
    individuals and businesses, 230
  how much does it do to protect the
    environment, 100
  immigrants are making government better or
    worse, 171
  satisfied with size and power of, 28
  satisfied with system of government and how
    well it works, 28
  should promote values, 231
  should spend money to build nuclear defense
    system, 181
  trust in, to always do what is right, 230
  trust in, to handle domestic problems, 56
  trust in, to handle international problems, 56
Government career
  recommend as career for young woman, 109
Graham, Billy
  as most admired person, 278
Grant, Cary
  as favorite star of all time, 76
Great Britain
  opinion of, 35, 43, 84
"Greenhouse effect." See Global warming
  ("greenhouse effect")
Griffey, Ken, Jr.
  as greatest baseball player of all time, 83
Grocery industry
  overall view of, 200
Guns and gun control
  do you have a gun in your home, 235
  importance of availability and ease of obtaining
    guns in school shootings and violence, 87
  importance of portrayal of use of guns in
    entertainment and music in school
    shootings and violence, 87
  s most important problem, 59, 121, 256
  satisfied with quality of laws or policies on, 29

H

Habitat for wildlife
  worry about loss of, 90
Halloween
  have children under age of fifteen, 244
  will any of your children be trick-or-treating
    door to door on, 244
  will give out treats from door of your home on,
    244
  will not give out treats from door of your home
    on because of terrorism, 244
  will you put restrictions on your children's
    trick-or-treating out of safety concerns due
    to the September 11 attacks, 244

Hanks, Tom
    as favorite star of all time, 76
    make special effort to see, 76
Hastert, Dennis
    opinion of, 186
Health, personal
    describe your own mental or emotional health
        at this time, 260
    describe your own physical health at this time,
        259
    how many days during past month did poor
        mental or emotional health keep you from
        your usual activities, 260
    how many days during past month did poor
        physical health keep you from your usual
        activities, 259
    how many days during past month was your
        mental or emotional health not good, 260
    how many days during past month was your
        physical health not good, 259
    you have been sick with short-term illness in
        past thirty days, 260
    you have long-term medical condition, illness,
        or disease, 260
    you have physical disability that limits your
        activity, 260
Health-care industry
    overall view of, 201
Health-care system
    Bush administration will improve, 22, 105, 106
    high cost of care, as most important problem,
        121
    hospitals, as most important problem, 121
    as most important problem, 58, 255
    poor care, as most important problem, 121
    as priority for Bush administration, 8, 9
    Republican or Democratic Party would do
        better job dealing with, 211
    satisfied with availability of affordable health
        care, 30
    satisfied with quality of, 29
    worry about availability and affordability of,
        59, 66
    worry about not being able to pay medical
        costs, 113
Heights
    fear of, 70
Hepburn, Katharine
    as favorite star of all time, 77
Heston, Charlton
    as favorite star of all time, 76
Heterosexuals
    find portrayal of sexual activity in movies
        offensive, 126

Hispanics
    satisfied with treatment of in our society, 158
Hispanics, asked of
    approval rating, way Bush is handling his job
        as president, 145
    approval rating, way Congress is handling its
        job, 145
    approval rating, way Supreme Court is
        handling its job, 145
    how often do you feel discriminated against,
        147
    racial minorities have equal job opportunities
        with whites, 147, 152
    satisfied with your community as place to live,
        146
    satisfied with your current housing, 146
    satisfied with your education, 146
    satisfied with your family life, 146
    satisfied with your financial situation, 146
    satisfied with your opportunities to succeed in
        life, 147
    satisfied with your personal health, 146–47
    satisfied with your safety from physical harm
        or violence, 147
    what percentage of U.S. population is
        Hispanic, 135
HMOs (health maintenance organizations)
    confidence in, 149
    confidence in (by political party), 149
Hockey, professional
    most like to get a ticket to Stanley Cup finals,
        25
Hoffman, Dustin
    make special effort to see, 76
Home economics
    recommend as career for young woman, 109
Homelessness
    as most important problem, 58, 255
    satisfied with nation's effort to deal with, 29
    worry about this problem, 59, 67
Homemaker
    recommend as career for young woman, 109
Homosexuals and homosexuality
    favor law allowing legally formed civil unions
        of homosexual couples, 134
    find portrayal in movies of homosexual
        activity offensive, 126
    is something a person is born with, 134
    relations between consenting adults should be
        legal, 133
    satisfied with acceptance of in the nation, 29
    should be clergy, 133
    should be considered an acceptable alternative
        life style, 133

should be doctors, 133
should be elementary school teachers, 133
should be high-school teachers, 133
should be hired as salespersons, 133
should be members of Armed Forces, 133
should be members of president's cabinet, 133
should have equal rights in terms of job
    opportunities, 133
Honesty
    approval rating, honesty and ethical standards
      of people in these fields [list], 265
    decline in, as most important problem, 255
Hopkins, Anthony
    as favorite star of all time, 77
    make special effort to see, 76
Hospitals
    as most important problem, 121, 255
Hotels and motels
    should set aside areas for, or ban, smoking in,
      182
Houston
    as city safe to live in or visit, 235
Houston Astros
    as favorite major league baseball team, 82
Hubbell, Carl
    as greatest baseball player of all time, 83
Human cloning. *See* Cloning
Hunger
    as most important problem, 58, 255
    worry about this problem, 59, 67

I

Ice hockey, professional
    fan of, 81
Immigrants
    illegal, as most important problem, 121
    importance of immigrants learning to speak
      English, 89
    making crime situation better or worse, 171
    making food, music, and the arts better or
      worse, 171
    making job opportunities better or worse, 171
    making overall quality of life in the country
      better or worse, 170
    making politics and government better or
      worse, 171
    making quality of public schools better or
      worse, 171
    making social and moral values better or
      worse, 172
    making taxes better or worse, 171
    making the economy in general better or
      worse, 171

prefer illegal immigrants be given general
    amnesty, 211
satisfied with treatment of in our society, 158
should blend in with American culture or
    maintain their own, 170
United States should make it easier for illegal
    immigrants to become citizens, 211
were any of your grandparents born in the
    United States or another country, 162
were either of your parents born in the United
    States or another country, 161
were you born in the United States or another
    country, 161
which foreign language do you speak (asked of
    foreign-speaking people), 89
Immigration
    as good thing for country today, 170
    as good thing for United States in the past, 170
    illegal, worry about this problem, 59, 67
    as most important problem, 59, 121
    satisfied with level of into country today, 29
    should be kept at present level, 170
India
    opinion of, 44, 84
Inflation
    as most important problem, 58, 121, 255
    will go up a lot over the next six months, 268
Insurance companies
    should have access to genetic information, 162
Insurance salesmen
    rate honesty and ethical standards of, 265
Integrity
    decline in, as most important problem, 121,
      255
Interest rates
    will go up a lot over the next six months,
      268–69
International issues
    as most important problem, 59, 121, 255
Internet
    activities you do most online, 175
    best describe your use of Instant Messages, or
      IMs, 178
    comfortable giving credit card number over, 150
    comfortable giving date of birth over, 150
    comfortable giving home phone number over,
      151
    comfortable giving Social Security number
      over, 150
    comfortable giving street address over, 150
    comfortable giving work phone number over,
      151
    concerned about companies using your records
      for marketing purposes, 150

likely you will lose your job in next twelve
 months, 103–4
likely you would find a job just as good as one
 you now have, 104
as most important problem, 58, 121, 255
prefer to have job outside home, 152
satisfied with amount of money you earn, 213
satisfied with amount of on-the-job stress, 213
satisfied with amount of vacation time you
 receive, 212
satisfied with amount of work is required of
 you, 213
satisfied with flexibility of your hours, 212
satisfied with opportunity you have to do what
 you do best, 212
satisfied with opportunity you have to learn
 and grow, 213
satisfied with overall contribution your
 employer makes to society, 212
satisfied with physical safety conditions of
 your workplace, 212
satisfied with recognition you receive for your
 accomplishments, 213
satisfied with respect your employer has for
 your opinions, 213
satisfied with your boss or supervisor, 212–13
satisfied with your chances for promotion, 213
satisfied with your health insurance benefits,
 213
satisfied with your job, 207, 212
satisfied with your job security, 212
satisfied with your relations with coworkers, 212
satisfied with your retirement plan, 213
women have equal job opportunities with men,
 152
you would be happier in a different job, 207
John Paul II
 as most admired person, 278
Johnson, Walter
 as greatest baseball player of all time, 83
Jones, Tommy Lee
 make special effort to see, 76
Jordan, Michael
 as greatest athlete in world of sports today, 142
 as most admired person, 278
Journalism
 recommend as career for young woman, 109
Journalists
 rate honesty and ethical standards of, 265
Judicial system
 as most important problem, 59, 121, 255
Justice Department
 closely followed its lawsuit against Microsoft,
 157

should drop case against Microsoft, 157
See also Microsoft Corporation

K
Kansas City Royals
 as favorite major league baseball team, 81
Kennedy, John F.
 assassination of, one man was responsible for, 95
 as greatest U.S. president, 44, 45
Kerry, John
 as Democratic choice for presidential nominee
 in 2004, 192
 as Democratic choice for presidential nominee
 in 2004 if Al Gore doesn't run, 192
Kilmer, Val
 make special effort to see, 76
Kyoto treaty
 approve Bush's decision not to adhere to the
 treaty, 102

L
Labor, organized
 confidence in, 149
 confidence in (by political party), 149
 leaders of, rate honesty and ethical standards
 of, 265
Lawyer
 recommend as career for young woman, 109
Lawyers
 rate honesty and ethical standards of, 265
Leadership
 dissatisfaction with, as most important
 problem, 121
Legal field
 overall view of, 201
Leno, Jay
 interested in hearing a live speech by, 80
 very interested in hearing a live speech by (by
 politics), 80
Levy, Chandra
 case involving her disappearance will be
 solved, 165, 188
 closely followed news about her
 disappearance, 164, 188, 201–2
 less likely to vote for own congressman if
 involved in matter like this, 165
 likely Gary Condit was directly involved in her
 disappearance, 188, 202
 news media have acted responsibly in this
 situation, 165, 188
 would advise own daughter to take internship
 in Washington, DC, 165
See also Condit, Gary

Librarian
    recommend as career for young woman, 109
Libya
    as America's greatest enemy today, 84
    opinion of, 44, 84
Lieberman, Joe
    as Democratic choice for presidential nominee
        in 2004, 192
    as Democratic choice for presidential nominee
        in 2004 if Al Gore doesn't run, 192
Lincoln, Abraham
    as greatest U.S. president, 44, 45
    would he or Washington be best president
        today, 45
Los Angeles
    as city safe to live in or visit, 235
Los Angeles Dodgers
    as favorite major league baseball team, 81

M

"Mad cow" disease
    concerned about it becoming problem in the
        United States, 74
    how much have you heard about it, 74
Madonna
    as most admired person, 278
Major League Baseball
    See Baseball, professional; World Series
Mandela, Nelson
    as most admired person, 278
Mantle, Mickey
    as greatest baseball player of all time, 83
Marital status
    which describes your marital status, 26
Marriage and morality
    divorce is morally acceptable, 127
    ideal number of children to have, 127
    it is morally acceptable for unmarried man and
        woman to live together, 127
    it is morally wrong for married person to have
        sex with someone other than their marriage
        partner, 159
    it is morally wrong to have a baby if couple is
        not married, 127
    it is morally wrong to have sexual relations
        before marriage, 127, 159
    sex is morally acceptable between an
        unmarried man and woman, 127
Mathewson, Christy
    as greatest baseball player of all time, 83
Mays, Willie
    as greatest baseball player of all time, 83

McCain, John
    approach to campaign finance reform preferred
        to Bush's, 70–71
McGwire, Mark
    as greatest athlete in world of sports today, 142
    as greatest baseball player of all time, 83
McVeigh, Timothy
    closely watched news about scheduled
        execution of, 116
    convinced he was guilty before files
        discovered, and still are, 132
    execution should be shown on television, 110
    FBI knowingly withheld evidence in his case,
        132
    FBI should hold a new trial for him, 138
    has not revealed names of everyone who
        helped him in the Oklahoma City bombing,
        138
    his execution will act as a deterrent to future
        acts of violence and murder, 117
    his execution will help the families cope with
        the tragedy and reach closure, 117
    his execution will increase your support of the
        death penalty, 117
    his execution will make him a martyr to some
        Americans, 117
    how interested are you in watching news cov-
        erage of his execution on May 16th, 116–17
    should delay execution to review FBI files, 132
    support death penalty, McVeigh should be
        executed, 110, 132, 138
    would watch execution on television, 110
    would watch execution on television if your
        family member had been a victim in
        Oklahoma City bombing, 110
Media
    acted responsibly in situation about citations
        issued to Bush daughters, 140
    approval rating, way they are handling the war
        on terrorism, 255, 270
    are overreacting to the threat of anthrax, 237–38
    have acted responsibly in reporting about the
        Chandra Levy disappearance, 165, 188
    as most important problem, 59, 121, 255
    should have reported about citations issued to
        Bush daughters by police, 140
Medical field
    recommend as career for young woman, 109
Medical system
    confidence in, 149
    confidence in (by political party), 149
Medicare
    important Congress and Bush deal with issues
        about in the next year, 229

as most important problem, 59, 121, 255
as priority for Bush administration, 8, 9
satisfied with system, 29
will Bush administration ensure long-term
    strength of, 22
Men
    approval rating, way Bush is handling his job
        as president, 145
    approval rating, way Congress is handling its
        job, 145
    approval rating, way Supreme Court is
        handling its job, 145
    characteristics more true of men or women
        [list], 45–46
    fears of [list], 70
    prefer to work for man or woman, 10
    satisfied with your community as place to live,
        146
    satisfied with your current housing, 146
    satisfied with your education, 146
    satisfied with your family life, 146
    satisfied with your financial situation, 146
    satisfied with your opportunities to succeed in
        life, 147
    satisfied with your personal health, 146–47
    satisfied with your safety from physical harm
        or violence, 147
    were any of your grandparents born in the
        United States or another country, 162
Mexico
    opinion of, 35, 43, 84
Miami
    as city safe to live in or visit, 235
Mice
    fear of, 70
Microsoft Corporation
    domination of software markets by as positive
        for computer industry, 157
    domination of software markets by as positive
        for consumers, 157
    domination of software markets by as positive
        for economy, 157
    followed news about Justice Department
        lawsuit against, 157
    government should drop case against, 157
    opinion of, 157
Middle East situation
    as America's greatest enemy today, 84
    Israel and the Arab nations will settle their
        differences and live in peace, 34–35, 194
    peaceful solution to Palestinian-Israeli
        situation as foreign policy goal, 34
    United States should take an active role to find
        a diplomatic solution to violence in, 194

United States should take Israel's or
    Palestinian Arabs' side in conflict, 35
your sympathies more with Israelis or
    Palestinian Arabs, 34
Military, U.S.
    confidence in, 3, 149
    confidence in (by political party), 149
    important Congress and Bush deal with issues
        about in the next year, 229
    lack of defense, as most important problem,
        59, 121, 256
    maintaining superior military power worldwide
        as important goal for U.S., 57
    military security as priority for
        Bush administration, 22, 38
    as priority for Bush administration, 8, 9
    rate honesty and ethical standards of, 265
    satisfied with military strength and
        preparedness, 29
    should immediately conduct strikes against
        known terrorist organizations, 216
Milwaukee Brewers
    as favorite major league baseball team, 82
Minneapolis
    as city safe to live in or visit, 235
Minnesota Twins
    as favorite major league baseball team, 81
Minorities
    as priority for Bush administration, 8, 9
    racial minorities have equal job opportunities
        with whites, 147, 152
    satisfied with position of blacks and other
        racial minorities in the nation, 29
    will Bush administration improve conditions
        for, 22
Missile defense
    important to deal with this issue next year, 141
Mitchum, Robert
    as favorite star of all time, 77
Modeling
    recommend as career for young woman, 109
Money
    lack of, as most important problem, 121, 255
    See also Christmas shopping
Monroe, Marilyn
    as favorite star of all time, 77
Montreal Expos
    as favorite major league baseball team, 82
Moral values
    Bush administration will improve, 22, 105, 106
    decline in, as most important problem, 121
    immigrants are making moral values better or
        worse, 172
    as most important problem, 255

O

Oakland Athletics
    as favorite major league baseball team, 81
Oil and gas industry
    overall view of, 201
Oil companies
    are to blame for country's energy problems, 131
O'Neal, Shaquille
    as greatest athlete in world of sports today, 142
Open spaces
    worry about loss of, 90
Overpopulation
    as most important problem, 59, 121, 256
Ozone layer damage
    worry about, 89–90

P

Pacino, Al
    as favorite star of all time, 76
    make special effort to see, 76
Paige, Satchel
    as greatest baseball player of all time, 83
Palestinian Arabs
    peaceful solution to Palestinian-Israeli situation as foreign policy goal, 34
    sympathies with Israelis or Palestinian Arabs, 219
    United States should take Israel's or Palestinian Arabs' side in conflict, 35, 219
    will Israel and the Arab nations live in peace, 34–35
    your sympathies more with Israelis or Palestinian Arabs, 34
Palestinian Authority
    as America's greatest enemy today, 84
    opinion of, 44, 84
Paranormal phenomena. *See* Psychic and paranormal phenomena
Parents, asked of
    amount of homework your oldest child receives, 208
    do you fear for safety of oldest child while at school, 208
    do you have any children who will be attending home school, 209
    do you have any children who will be attending independent private school, 209
    do you have any children who will be attend-ing parochial or church-related school, 209
    do you have any children who will be attending public school, 209

grade your oldest child will enter this fall, 208
how many children of yours will be attending Kindergarten through Grade 12 this year, 209
if one parent stays home to raise the children, should it be husband or wife, 111
if one parent works full time, should it be husband or wife, 111
at oldest child's school students pressure each other to perform well or not, 209
oldest child will attend public, private, parochial, or home school, 208
satisfied with quality of education received in Kindergarten through Grade 12, 208
satisfied with quality of education your oldest child is receiving, 208
should work full time, 111
social pressures are serious problem among students in Grades 6–12 [list], 208–9
social pressures are serious problem among students in K-Grade 12 [list], 208
Patients' bill of rights
    approval rating, way Bush is handling, 166
    closely followed news about, 160
    confidence in Bush or Democratic leaders about this issue, 144
    favor Congress passing this bill, 160
    how much you know about differences between Republican and Democratic approaches to, 160
    important Congress and Bush deal with issues about in the next year, 229
    important to deal with this issue next year, 141, 144
    more likely to trust Republican or Democratic approach to, 160
    what does that mean to you [list], 160
    will make major difference to you and your family, 187
Pearl Harbor vs. 9/11 attacks
    a hundred years from now, which event will historians say had a greater impact on the United States, 266
Pentagon, attack on
    See Terrorist attacks
Persian Gulf War
    favor sending American troops back to remove Saddam Hussein from office, 47
    situation was worth going to war over, 47
Pharmaceutical industry
    overall view of, 201
Pharmacists
    rate honesty and ethical standards of, 265
Philadelphia
    as city safe to live in or visit, 235

Philadelphia Phillies
as favorite major league baseball team, 81
Philbin, Regis
interested in hearing a live speech by, 80
very interested in hearing a live speech by (by
politics), 80
Philippines
opinion of, 35, 44, 84
Pitt, Brad
make special effort to see, 76
Pittsburgh Pirates
as favorite major league baseball team, 81
Poitier, Sidney
as favorite star of all time, 76
make special effort to see, 76
Police
confidence in, 149
confidence in (by political party), 149
rate honesty and ethical standards of, 265
Political divisions
Bush administration will heal, 22, 105, 106
Politicians
dissatisfaction with, as most important
problem, 121
Politics
immigrants are making politics and
government better or worse, 171
Pollution
of drinking water
worry about, 90
as most important problem, 59, 121, 255
of ocean and beach, worry about, 90
pay $100 more each year to reduce air
pollution, 68–69
pay $500 more each year to reduce air
pollution, 69
of rivers, lakes, and reservoirs
worry about, 90
See also Environment
Poor people
Bush administration will improve conditions
for, 22
gap between rich and poor, as most important
problem, 58, 121, 255
as priority for Bush administration, 8, 9
Postal Service
approval rating, handling the war on terrorism,
254
Poverty
as most important problem, 58, 121, 255
satisfied with nation's effort to deal with, 29
Powell, Colin
approval rating, way he is handling the war on
terrorism, 254

interested in hearing a live speech by, 79
as most admired person, 278
very interested in hearing a live speech by (by
politics), 80
Presidency
best president today, Washington or Lincoln,
45
better for country if president comes from
same political party that controls Congress,
128–29
Bush administration will increase respect for,
105, 106
confidence in, 3, 149
confidence in (by political party), 149
greatest presidents [list], 44
greatest presidents [list] asked of Democrats,
44–45
greatest presidents [list] asked of Republicans,
45
will Bush administration increase respect for,
22
Presidential election dispute
accept Bush as legitimate president, 168
Bush won fair and square or stole the election,
167–68, 246–47
Clinton would have done better job in dealing
with the economy, 247
Clinton would have done better job in response
to terrorist attacks, 247
election last year was a constitutional crisis,
247
Gore would have done better job, if elected, in
dealing with the economy, 247
Gore would have done better job, if elected, in
response to terrorist attacks, 247
how much confidence in system of vote
casting and counting in this country, 246
if election held today, would vote for Bush or
Gore, 247
system of vote casting and counting in this
country discriminates against some people,
246
system of vote casting and counting in this
country is in need of a complete overhaul,
246
which party's candidate would you vote for in
your congressional district today, 246
who really won, Bush or Gore, 20
Presidential pardons by Bill Clinton
approve of pardon of Marc Rich, 63
are his actions relating to the pardons illegal
and/or unethical, 63
are the pardons he granted important issue to
the nation, 63

closely followed news about, 31
hearings should continue into pardon of Marc
Rich, 63–64
Prosperity in America
as priority for Bush administration, 8, 9
Psychic and paranormal phenomena
believe extraterrestrial beings have visited
Earth at some time in the past, 137
believe ghosts, or spirits of dead people can
come back, 137
believe houses can be haunted, 137
believe in astrology, 137
believe in "channeling," 137
believe in clairvoyance, 137
believe in ESP or extrasensory perception, 136
believe in psychic or spiritual healing, 136
believe in reincarnation, 137
believe in telepathy, 137
believe in witches, 137
believe people can communicate mentally with
someone who has died, 137
believe people on Earth are sometimes
possessed by the devil, 137
Public schools
confidence in, 149
confidence in (by political party), 149
immigrants are making quality of public
schools better or worse, 171
See also Religion in public schools; School
shootings and violence
Public speaking
fear of, 70
Publishing industry
overall view of, 201
Putin, Vladimir
as ally of the United States, 143

Q

Quality of life
immigrants are making overall quality of life
in the country better or worse, 170

R

Race relations
Bush administration will improve, 105, 106
as most important problem, 59, 121, 255
as priority for Bush administration, 9
satisfied with state of, 29
satisfied with treatment of Asians in our
society, 158–59
satisfied with treatment of blacks in our
society, 158

satisfied with treatment of Hispanics in our
society, 158
satisfied with treatment of immigrants in our
society, 158
satisfied with treatment of women in our
society, 158
will Bush administration improve, 22
worry about this problem, 59, 67
Racism
find portrayal of negative racial stereotypes in
movies offensive, 125–26
as most important problem, 255
Radioactivity
worry about contamination of soil and water
by, 90
Reagan, Ronald
as greatest U.S. president, 44, 45
Real estate industry
overall view of, 201
Recession
economy now in recession, 58, 93, 120, 218, 222
likelihood of recession in the next year, 32–33, 58
as most important problem, 58, 121, 255
will Bush's tax cut make recession more likely,
39
Redford, Robert
as favorite star of all time, 76
make special effort to see, 76
Reeves, Keano
make special effort to see, 76
Reincarnation
believe in, 137
Religion
are you a member of church or synagogue, 98,
276
believe it can answer all or most of today's
problems, 276
Bible is actual word of God to be taken
literally, 98
can answer all or most of today's problems, 98
confidence in, 149
confidence in (by political party), 149
decline in, as most important problem, 255
describe self as "born-again" or evangelical,
98, 276
did you attend church or synagogue in last
seven days, 98, 276
how important is it in your own life, 276
how often do you attend church or synagogue,
98, 276
importance of in your own life, 97
is increasing its influence on American life, 98,
276
satisfied with influence of, 28

Religion in public schools
    allow daily prayer in the classroom, 50
    allow students to say prayers during graduation
        program, 50
    amount of, present in schools today, 50
    favor facilities available for use by student
        religious groups, 50
Republican Party
    agree it has become too conservative under
        Bush, 128
    or Democratic Party would do better job
        dealing with these issues [list], 210–11
Republicans in Congress
    approval rating, way they are handling their
        job, 141, 186
    are responsible for decrease in budget surplus,
        206
    confidence more in Republicans or Democrats
        in dealing with terrorism, 229–30
    country better off if controlled by Republicans
        or Democrats, 7–8, 9, 187, 229
    how much credit for the tax cut checks do you
        give to, 195
    more influence in direction the nation takes,
        Bush or Republicans in Congress, 37, 141
    policies proposed by would move country in
        right direction, 210
Respect for each other
    as most important problem, 59, 121, 256
Restaurant industry
    overall view of, 200
Restaurants
    should set aside areas for, or ban, smoking in,
        182
Retail industry
    overall view of, 200
Retirement
    401(k), retirement savings plans, personal
        savings rates, 123
    annuities, insurance, personal savings rates,
        123
    annuities, insurance will be major source for
        money, 123
    inheritance, personal savings rates, 123
    inheritance will be major source for money,
        123
    part-time work, personal savings rates, 123
    part-time work will be major source for
        money, 123
    rent, royalties, personal savings rates, 123
    rent, royalties will be major source for money,
        123
    retirement accounts will be major sources for
        money, 122–23

saving enough for retirement, 122
    savings accounts or CDs, personal savings
        rates, 123
    savings accounts or CDs will be major source
        for money, 123
    Social Security, personal savings rates, 123
    Social Security will be major source for
        money, 123
    stocks, mutual funds, personal savings rates,
        123
    stocks, mutual funds will be major source for
        money, 123
    work-sponsored pension plan, personal savings
        rates, 123
    work-sponsored pension plan will be major
        source for money, 123
    See also Social Security
Revolutionary War
    from what country did America gain its
        independence following, 155
Rice, Condoleezza
    as most admired person, 278
Ridge, Tom
    approval rating, way he is handling the war on
        terrorism, 255, 270
Ripken, Cal, Jr.
    as greatest athlete in world of sports today, 142
    as greatest baseball player of all time, 83
Roberts, Julia
    as favorite star of all time, 76
    make special effort to see, 76
    as most admired person, 278
Robinson, Jackie
    as greatest baseball player of all time, 83
Rock, Chris
    as favorite star of all time, 77
    make special effort to see, 76
Roosevelt, Franklin
    as greatest U.S. president, 44, 45
Roosevelt, Theodore
    as greatest U.S. president, 44
Rose, Pete
    as greatest baseball player of all time, 83
Rumsfeld, Donald
    approval rating, way he is handling the war on
        terrorism, 254, 269
Russia
    as America's greatest enemy today, 84
    opinion of, 44, 84
Ruth, Babe
    as greatest baseball player of all time, 83
Ryan, Meg
    as favorite star of all time, 76
    make special effort to see, 76

Ryan, Nolan
  as greatest baseball player of all time, 83

S

Saddam Hussein
  favor sending American troops back to remove
    him from office, 47
Sales
  recommend as career for young woman, 109
Sales clerk (department store)
  recommend as career for young woman, 109
San Diego Padres
  as favorite major league baseball team, 82
San Francisco
  as city safe to live in or visit, 235
San Francisco Giants
  as favorite major league baseball team, 81
Satisfaction index. *See* American people; United
  States (America)
Saudi Arabia
  as America's greatest enemy today, 84
  opinion of, 44, 84
School shootings and violence
  fear for safety of oldest child at school (asked
    of parents), 78
  government can take effective action to prevent
    these shootings (asked of parents), 78
  importance of availability and ease of
    obtaining guns, 87
  importance of bullying and teasing of students
    at school, 87
  importance of coverage by the media, 87
  importance of families moving around and not
    having roots, 87
  importance of home life and relationship with
    parents, 87
  importance of portrayal of violence and use of
    guns in entertainment and music, 87
  importance of size of high schools today in
    terms of number of students, 87
  importance of way schools discipline students, 87
  likely to happen in your community (asked of
    parents), 78
  as most important problem, 59, 121, 256
  most important thing that could prevent another
    incidence of school shootings [list], 87–88
  news media have acted responsibly in this
    situation, 88
  school-aged children expressed worry or
    concern about feeling unsafe at school
    (asked of parents), 78
  something seriously wrong in the country, or
    isolated incidents (asked of parents), 78

Schwarzenegger, Arnold
  as favorite star of all time, 76
  make special effort to see, 76
Seagal, Steven
  as favorite star of all time, 76
  make special effort to see, 76
Seattle
  as city safe to live in or visit, 235
Seattle Mariners
  as favorite major league baseball team, 81
Secondhand smoke
  harmful to adults, 182
  should set aside areas or ban smoking in hotels
    and motels, 182
  should set aside areas or ban smoking in
    restaurants, 182
  should set aside areas or ban smoking in work
    places, 182
Secretary
  recommend as career for young woman, 109
Security, national
  favor airline passengers check in three hours
    before flight time, 241
  favor limiting airline passengers to carry on
    only one small item, 241
  favor making it easier for authorities to read
    e-mail, or tap phones without person's
    knowledge, 241
  favor that Arabs, even U.S. citizens, carry a
    special ID, 241
  as most important problem, 59, 121, 255
Self-employment
  recommend as career for young woman, 109
Selleck, Tom
  as favorite star of all time, 77
  make special effort to see, 76
Senators
  rate honesty and ethical standards of, 265
Senior citizens
  care of, as most important problem, 59
  prescription drugs for, approval rating, way
    Bush is handling, 166
  prescription drugs for, important to deal with
    this issue next year, 141
  as priority for Bush administration, 8, 9
September 11 attacks
  See Terrorist attacks; Terrorist attacks, civilian
    response to; War on terrorism
Shopping habits
  are you type of person who more enjoys
    spending or saving money, 189
  how often do you go shop at malls, department
    stores, or other shopping areas, 189
  how often do you shop by catalog, 189

changes in made you consider canceling/ postponing a big purchase, vacation, or other expenditure, 65

changes in made you less confident about a comfortable retirement, 64–65

changes in made you less confident about the nation's economy, 64

changes in made you less confident about your personal financial situation, 65

changes in made you less confident of your job situation, 65

changes in made you less likely to invest in, 64

concerned about direction it takes in the next year, 64

describe yourself as bull or bear, 65

did fall in Dow Jones Industrial Average affect your financial position, 64

Dow Jones below 10,000 mark, as significant economic milestone, 65

good idea to invest in, 15

have money invested in, 66, 196

have your investments made money over the past year, 196

person you most trust for information or advice about, 196

still support tax cut after drop in market, 65–66

will go up a lot over the next six months, 268

Streep, Meryl
as favorite star of all time, 77
make special effort to see, 76

Streisand, Barbra
as favorite star of all time, 77
make special effort to see, 76

Super Bowl
are you a sports fan, 24
sports event you would most like a ticket to, 24
team you would like to see win this year's Super Bowl, 25

Supreme Court, U.S.
approval rating, way it is handling its job, 13
approval rating, way it is handling its job (by race), 145
confidence in, 3, 149
confidence in (by political party), 149
"Survivor" television show
happened to have watched, 62
how truthful are several reality-based programs, 62
would vote off whom next, 62

Swayze, Patrick
as favorite star of all time, 77
make special effort to see, 76

T

Taiwan
opinion of, 44, 84

Taliban government in Afghanistan
how long should military action continue without capturing bin Laden or removing Taliban from power, 253
opinion of, 233

Tampa Bay Devil Rays
as favorite major league baseball team, 82

Taxes
approval rating, way Bush is handling, 166
approval rating, way Bush is handling taxes, 110
immigrants are making taxes better or worse, 171
as most important problem, 58, 121, 255

Taxes, income (federal)
adjust plan in favor of lower-income taxpayers, 60
amount you have to pay as too high, 96
amount you will pay this year as fair, 96
approve of House plan to cut income taxes, 60
Bush administration will cut taxes, 22, 105, 106, 110
Bush's tax cut will cause a federal budget deficit, 39
Bush's tax cut will make recession more likely, 39
Bush's tax cut will take money from Social Security, 39
Bush will pass his proposed cuts, 23, 38
favor $100 billion tax cut effective immediately (asked of representatives), 120
favor Bush's income tax cuts, 23, 38, 109
favor giving larger tax cuts to lower- and middle-income taxpayers (asked of representatives), 120
favor lowering total amount of tax cuts, 60
favor reducing the amount of payroll taxes for Social Security and Medicare (asked of representatives), 120
favor substantial tax cut in this year's budget, 124
favor tax cut going to lower-income taxpayers, 60
government has enough money for important programs and paying down federal debt, as well as tax cuts, 60
government should cut taxes if it means putting off some important programs, 39
have you, or will you, use a computer program to prepare your taxes, 96
how do you feel about doing your income taxes, 96

make you less willing to fly on airplanes, 216

as most tragic news event in your lifetime, 216

since the attacks, are you going about your business as usual, 240

U.S. military should immediately conduct military strikes against known terrorist organizations, 216

vs. Pearl Harbor, a hundred years from now, which event will historians say had a greater impact on the United States, 266

who is currently winning the war against terrorism, 232

worried you or someone in your family will become victim of, 215, 223–24, 232, 240–41, 248–49, 266

See also War on terrorism

Terrorist attacks, civilian response to

have done or considered avoiding airline travel, 242

have done or considered avoiding public events or crowded areas, 242

have done or considered consulting Web site or other source for information about preparedness, 242

have done or considered discussing treatment of biological or chemical warfare with your doctor, 242

have done or considered purchasing a gas mask or protective clothing, 242

have done or considered purchasing a weapon, 242

have done or considered stockpiling food or water, 242

have done or considered trying to get a prescription for antibiotics, 242

have done or considered trying to get a vaccination for anthrax or smallpox, 242

have done or considered using more caution when handling mail, 242

it is the duty of Americans not to show fear, 243

little reason for you personally to be afraid of terrorist threats, 243

visible signs of increased security make you feel more secure, 242–43

Terrorists

Bush should agree not to seek death penalty for terrorists turned over by our allies, 273

if captured and put on trial, should be tried by international court or by U.S. authorities, 273

if captured and put on trial, should be tried by regular court or military tribunal, 273

Texas Rangers

as favorite major league baseball team, 81

Thatcher, Margaret

as most admired person, 278

Thunder and lightning

fear of, 70

Toronto Blue Jays

as favorite major league baseball team, 82

Tracy, Spencer

as favorite star of all time, 77

Trade deficit

as most important problem, 58, 121, 255

Traffic

have seen or plan to see, 73

like to see win Oscar for best picture, 73

Travel industry

overall view of, 200

Travolta, John

as favorite star of all time, 76

make special effort to see, 76

Tropical rain forests

worry about the loss of, 90

Truman, Harry

as greatest U.S. president, 44

U

Unemployment

as most important problem, 58, 121, 255

will go up a lot over the next six months, 268

worry about this problem, 59, 67

United Nations

doing good job in solving problems, 74

role of in world affairs today, 57, 74

United States (America)

Bush administration will improve respect for America abroad, 105, 106

Bush administration will keep America prosperous, 105, 106

foreign aid spending by, 56

good job by Bush keeping America prosperous, 68, 102

most important problem facing country today [list], 58–59, 121

rated in the eyes of the world, 56

role of in solving international problems, 56

satisfied with certain aspects of life in America [list], 28–30

satisfied with opportunities to get ahead in, by working hard, 28

satisfied with overall quality of life in, 28

satisfied with position of in the world today, 56

satisfied with role it plays in world affairs, 29

satisfied with way things are going in the U.S. at this time, 25, 122

if United States goes to war in Iraq, it will be
as successful as the efforts in Afghanistan,
272
likely further terrorist attacks in United States
over next several weeks, 227, 272
most important goal of U.S. military action in
Afghanistan, 239
number of U.S. forces would be too high a
number killed, 252–53
satisfied with amount of progress made by
U.S. military in this war, 252, 261, 272
support continuing campaign against terrorism
if 5,000 U.S. citizens would be killed,
224–25
support continuing campaign against terrorism
if 5,000 U.S. troops would be killed, 224
support taking military action if 1,000
American troops would be killed, 225
support taking military action if a prolonged
economic recession would occur, 225
support taking military action if further
terrorist attacks would occur in the United
States, 225
support taking military action if ground troops
would be used in an invasion, 225
support taking military action if it would
continue for several months, 225
support taking military action if it would
continue for several years, 225
support taking military action if military draft
reinstituted, 225
support taking military action if shortages of
gas and oil would occur, 225
support taking military action if taxes would be
increased, 225
support taking military action if there's less
money to spend on programs such as
education and Social Security, 225
United States should have launched military
action before now, 226
United States should mount a long-term war to
defeat terrorist networks, 261
United States should punish specific groups or
mount long-term war, 224
United States should take military action
against other countries that harbor
terrorists, 227
United States should take military action
against terrorist organizations in other
countries only if UN authorizes it, 225
United States should take military action in
retaliation, 224
who is currently winning the war against
terrorism, 267

See also Bin Laden, Osama
Washington, DC
as city safe to live in or visit, 235
Washington, Denzel
as favorite star of all time, 76
make special effort to see, 76
Washington, George
as greatest U.S. president, 44, 45
would he or Lincoln be best president today,
45
Wayne, John
as favorite star of all time, 76
make special effort to see, 76
Weight and body image
are trying to lose weight, 258
would like to lose weight, 258
Welfare
as most important problem, 59, 121, 256
Western Europe
United States should strengthen our ties with,
139
Wife
recommend as career for young woman, 109
Wildlife
worry about loss of habitat of, 90
Williams, Robin
make special effort to see, 76
Williams, Ted
as greatest baseball player of all time, 83
Williams, Venus
as greatest athlete in world of sports today, 142
Willis, Bruce
as favorite star of all time, 76
make special effort to see, 76
Wilson, Steve
voted for Condit or Wilson for Congress in
2000 (asked of Condit's California
constituents), 205
Winfrey, Oprah
interested in hearing a live speech by, 79
as most admired person, 278
very interested in hearing a live speech by (by
politics), 80
Witches
believe in, 137
Women
approval rating, way Bush is handling his job
as president, 145
approval rating, way Congress is handling its
job, 145
approval rating, way Supreme Court is
handling its job, 145
careers you would recommend for a young
woman [list], 109

Women (*continued*)

characteristics more true of men or women [list], 45–46

consider yourself a feminist, 152

country governed better if more women were in political office, 4

crimes against pregnant women, criminal should face charges for harming fetus, 108

crimes against pregnant women, criminal should face charges for harming unborn child, 108

fears of [list], 70

prefer to work for man or woman, 10

satisfied with position of in the nation, 29

satisfied with treatment of in our society, 158

satisfied with your community as place to live, 146

satisfied with your current housing, 146

satisfied with your education, 146

satisfied with your family life, 146

satisfied with your financial situation, 146

satisfied with your opportunities to succeed in life, 147

satisfied with your personal health, 146–47

satisfied with your safety from physical harm or violence, 147

would vote for woman for president, 4

Woods, Tiger

fan of professional golf, 41

as greatest athlete in world of sports today, 142

more likely to watch tournament on television if he is playing, 42

Nicklaus or, as better golfer, 143

opinion of, 142

Workplaces

should set aside areas for, or ban, smoking in, 182

World Series

fact that Yankees won World Series three years straight increased your interest in big-league baseball, 82

fact that Yankees won World Series three years straight lessened your interest in big-league baseball, 82

playoffs in each league determining who goes to World Series have been changed for the better, 82

sports event you would most like a ticket to, 24

See also Baseball, professional

World Trade Center, attack on

See Terrorist attacks

Wrestling, professional

fan of, 81

ISBN 0-8420-5001-9

9 780842 050012